# FEMINIST
# INTERPRETATIONS
# OF
# HANNAH ARENDT

## RE-READING THE CANON

NANCY TUANA, GENERAL EDITOR

This series consists of edited collections of essays, some original and some previously published, offering feminist reinterpretations of the writings of major figures in the Western philosophical tradition. Devoted to the work of a single philosopher, each volume contains essays covering the full range of the philosopher's thought and representing the diversity of approaches now being used by feminist critics.

Already published:

Nancy Tuana, ed., *Feminist Interpretations of Plato* (1994)

Margaret A. Simons, ed., *Feminist Interpretations of Simone de Beauvoir* (1995)

# FEMINIST INTERPRETATIONS OF HANNAH ARENDT

EDITED BY BONNIE HONIG

THE PENNSYLVANIA STATE UNIVERSITY PRESS
UNIVERSITY PARK, PENNSYLVANIA

Library of Congress Cataloging-in-Publication Data

Feminist interpretations of Hannah Arendt / edited by Bonnie Honig.
         p.         cm.—(Re-reading the canon)
    Includes bibliographical references and index.
    ISBN 0-271-01446-6 (alk. paper)
    ISBN 0-271-01447-4 (pbk.)
    1. Arendt, Hannah—Contributions in political science.
2. Feminist theory.   I. Honig, Bonnie.   II. Series.
JC251.A74F46   1995
320.5'092—dc20                                        94-40823
                                                          CIP

It is the policy of The Pennsylvania State University Press to use acid-free paper for the first printing of all clothbound books. Publications on uncoated stock satisfy the minimum requirements of American National Standard for Information Sciences— Permanence of Paper for Printed Library Materials, ANSI Z39.48–1992.

*For Noah*

# Contents

# Acknowledgments

I thank first and foremost the contributors to this volume, from whom I have learned much in the past year about Arendt, feminism, and the pleasures of collegiality and joint projects. I am grateful to the Center for Advanced Study in the Behavioral Sciences and to the National Science Foundation grant #SES-9022102 for providing the year of academic leave and the staff support that enabled me to work on this project from start to finish. Additional financial support for this project was provided by Harvard University's Clark Fund. Thanks also to Routledge Press for permission to reprint "Toward an Agonistic Feminism: Hannah Arendt and the Politics of Identity," in revised and expanded form. At Penn State Press, it has been a pleasure to work with Sandy Thatcher, Cherene Holland, and Steve Kress. I am especially indebted to Patchen Markell for his very competent preparation of the final manuscript, to Linda Zerilli for keeping me in touch with my vision of the project, and to Michael Whinston for seeing me through it.

# Preface

## Nancy Tuana

Take into your hands any history of philosophy text. You will find compiled therein the "classics" of modern philosophy. Since these texts are often designed for use in undergraduate classes, the editor is likely to offer an introduction in which the reader is informed that these selections represent the perennial questions of philosophy. The student is to assume that she or he is about to explore the timeless wisdom of the greatest minds of Western philosophy. No one calls attention to the fact that the philosophers are all men.

Though women are omitted from the canons of philosophy, these texts inscribe the nature of woman. Sometimes the philosopher speaks directly about woman, delineating her proper role, her abilities and inabilities, her desires. Other times the message is indirect—a passing remark hinting at woman's emotionality, irrationality, unreliability.

This process of definition occurs in far more subtle ways when the central concepts of philosophy—reason and justice, those characteristics that are taken to define us as human—are associated with traits historically identified with masculinity. If the "man" of reason must learn to control or overcome traits identified as feminine—the body, the emotions, the passions—then the realm of rationality will be one reserved primarily for men,[1] with grudging entrance to those few women who are capable of transcending their femininity.

Feminist philosophers have begun to look critically at the canonized texts of philosophy and have concluded that the discourses of philosophy are not gender-neutral. Philosophical narratives do not offer a universal perspective, but rather privilege some experiences and beliefs over others. These experiences and beliefs permeate all philosophical theories whether they be aesthetic or epistemological, moral or metaphysical. Yet this fact has often been neglected by those studying the traditions of philosophy. Given the history of canon formation in Western philosophy, the perspective most likely to be privileged is that of upper-class, white males. Thus, to be fully aware of the impact of gender biases, it is imperative that we re-read the canon with attention to the ways in which philosophers' assumptions concerning gender are embedded within their theories.

This new series, *Re-Reading the Canon,* is designed to foster this process of reevaluation. Each volume will offer feminist analyses of the theories of a selected philosopher. Since feminist philosophy is not monolithic in method or content, the essays are also selected to illustrate the variety of perspectives within feminist criticism and highlight some of the controversies within feminist scholarship.

In this series, feminist lenses will be focused on the canonical texts of Western philosophy, both those authors who have been part of the traditional canon, as well as those philosophers whose writings have more recently gained attention within the philosophical community. A glance at the list of volumes in the series will reveal an immediate gender bias of the canon: Arendt, Aristotle, de Beauvoir, Derrida, Descartes, Foucault, Hegel, Hume, Kant, Locke, Marx, Mill, Nietzsche, Plato, Rousseau, Wittgenstein, Wollstonecraft. There are all too few women included, and those few who do appear have been added only recently. In creating this series, it is not my intention to reify the current canon of philosophical thought. What is and is not included within the canon during a particular historical period is a result of many factors. Although no canonization of texts will include all philosophers, no canonization of texts that exclude all but a few women can offer an accurate representation of the history of the discipline as women have been philosophers since the ancient period.[2]

I share with many feminist philosophers and other philosophers writing from the margins of philosophy the concern that the current canonization of philosophy be transformed. Although I do not accept the position that the current canon has been formed exclusively by power relations, I do believe that this canon represents only a selective history of the tradition. I share the view of Michael Bérubé that "canons are at once the location, the index, and the record of the struggle for cultural representation; like any other hegemonic formation, they must be continually reproduced anew and are continually contested."[3]

The process of canon transformation will require the recovery of "lost" texts and a careful examination of the reasons such voices have been silenced. Along with the process of uncovering women's philosophical history, we must also begin to analyze the impact of gender ideologies upon the process of canonization. This process of recovery and examination must occur in conjunction with careful attention to the concept of a canon of authorized texts. Are we to dispense with the notion of a tradition of excellence embodied in a canon of authorized texts? Or, rather than abandon the whole idea of a canon, do we instead encourage a reconstruction of a canon of those texts that inform a common culture?

This series is designed to contribute to this process of canon transformation by offering a re-reading of the current philosophical canon. Such a re-reading shifts our attention to the ways in which woman and the role of the feminine is constructed within the texts of philosophy. A question we must keep in front of us during this process of re-reading is whether a philosopher's socially inherited prejudices concerning woman's nature and role are independent of her or his larger philosophical framework. In asking this question attention must be paid to the ways in which the definitions of central philosophical concepts implicitly include or exclude gendered traits.

This type of reading strategy is not limited to the canon, but can be applied to all texts. It is my desire that this series reveal the importance of this type of critical reading. Paying attention to the workings of gender within the texts of philosophy will make visible the complexities of the inscription of gender ideologies.

## Notes

1. More properly, it is a realm reserved for a group of privileged males, since the texts also inscribe race and class biases that thereby omit certain males from participation.

2. Mary Ellen Waithe's multivolume series, *A History of Women Philosophers* (Boston: M. Nijhoff, 1987), attests to this presence of women.

3. Michael Bérubé, *Marginal Forces/Cultural Centers: Tolson, Pynchon, and the Politics of the Canon* (Ithaca: Cornell University Press, 1992), 4–5.

# 1

## Introduction:
## The Arendt Question in Feminism

### Bonnie Honig

Appearing in 1995, this volume marks the twentieth anniversary of
Hannah Arendt's death. In that time much has happened to warrant a
reconsideration of her work. In political and feminist theory, the past
two decades have witnessed a powerful surge of interest in topics to
which Arendt repeatedly returned.[1] Identity, ethnicity, race and racism,
nationalism, imperialism, and postcolonialism have all undergone major
theoretical reconsideration. Often, however, this new theoretical work
has developed in relation to feminism, a topic that interested Arendt
hardly at all. Arendt was impatient with feminism, dismissing it as
merely another (mass) movement or ideology. She believed strongly that
feminism's concerns with gender identity, sexuality, and the body were
politically inappropriate. She worried that these issues might overwhelm

the public sphere and she herself approached them through indirection and allusion.

But the feminisms of 1995 are quite different from those that Arendt so hastily dismissed.[2] Shaped by new multicultural and postcolonial contexts, recent work in feminist theory tends to focus on *plural* asymmetries of power, on how sex-gender identities are riven by race, class, and other differences, and on how differences of race, class, nationality, ethnicity, and sexuality are often feminized or sexualized.[3] Whatever Arendt might have thought about these developments, they enable a set of feminist engagements with Arendt's work that are quite different from those of their predecessors.

In the 1970s and early 1980s, feminists turned to Arendt as a woman thinker with the expectation that she would have something uniquely gynocentric to offer them. (And, indeed, some still do.) Many commentators came away disappointed. Arendt's heroic, agonistic account of political action and her public/private distinction led some feminists to charge her with masculinism. In Adrienne Rich's oft-quoted words, Arendt's *The Human Condition* is a "lofty and crippled book" that "embodies the tragedy of a female mind nourished on male ideology."[4] Others, like Nancy Hartsock, found a nascent feminism in Arendt's work and praised her particularly for identifying political action with natality and for replacing the male or patriarchal view of power as the ability to achieve certain outcomes with a more feminine, cooperative, and practice-oriented vision of power as action in concert.[5] These otherwise opposing judgments share two assumptions: that Arendt's primary or essential identity is her sex-gender and that, because she is a woman, she may be expected to have developed a gynocentric political theory.

Recent developments in feminist theory and gender studies challenge these dichotomizing approaches. Rather than treat male and female or masculine and feminine as categories that organize uniform and already gendered artifacts, new theorists of gender argue that the categories themselves help to produce and reinforce the very uniformities they claim merely to describe. These developments have prompted a reconsideration of Arendt that includes a critical reevaluation of earlier feminist judgments of her work. From feminist perspectives that interrogate, politicize, and historicize—rather than simply redeploy—categories like "woman," "identity," or "experience," Arendt's hostility to feminism and her critical stance toward identitarian and essentialist definitions of "woman" begin to look more like an advantage than a liability.[6] For those critical of identity-based politics (in this volume, Dietz, Kaplan, Honig, Zerilli, Cocks, Disch, Orlie), Arendt offers an important reassurance and challenge: she theorizes a democratic politics built not on already existing identities or shared experiences but on contingent sites of principled coalescence and shared practices of citizenship.

The move to interrogate concepts such as "woman," "identity" and "experience" has produced a shift in Arendt studies. The earlier feminists' exclusive focus on the "Woman Question in Arendt" has given way to a more explicit concern with the "Arendt Question in Feminism." The "Woman Question" focuses our attention on a thinker's treatment of women: Where are the women in the theory located? What are their roles and responsibilities and what value is accorded to their unique qualities, spheres, activities, or standpoint? This perspective assumes a uniformity among women and their "experience" and it sets a standard that Arendt can only pass or fail. Posing the "Arendt Question in Feminism," by contrast, gets us past that assumption and the judgmentalism it tends to foster. Once we stop focusing exclusively on whether Arendt was properly attentive to women and their "experience," we can ask what resources, if any, Arendt has to offer a feminist theory and politics whose constituency is diverse and often fractious. This is the question to which the contributors to this volume were invited to respond: What possible relevance could Arendt have for feminist theory today?

The "Arendt Question in Feminism" pushes feminists into an engagement with Arendt that is not merely a reinterrogation of her work but a dynamic and mutual encounter. While those who posed the "Woman Question in Arendt" thought Arendt's public/private distinction was obviously and hopelessly masculinist, feminists who pose the "Arendt Question in Feminism" are prodded to reconsider their own commitment to dismantle that distinction. The question is no longer simply, How does feminist theory change the way we think about Arendt? but also always, How does reading Arendt change the way we think about feminist theory?

I borrow the useful distinction between the "Woman Question in Arendt" and the "Arendt Question in Feminism" from Sandra Harding, who first framed it with reference to feminism's relation to science.[7] But the distinction has its limits. It wrongly implies that the "Woman Question in Arendt" can simply be transcended or replaced by the

"Arendt Question in Feminism" when, on the contrary, the move from the former question to the latter requires and presupposes a resignification of the "Woman Question." Occasioned by the conviction that "Woman" is no longer a site of unproblematic identification nor a self-evident point of departure for a feminist theory or politics, the resignified "Woman Question" puts "Woman" into question. It moves us to focus not merely on the place of *actual women* in a theory but on the theory's symbolic *construction* of woman as a stable figure marked by certain roles, predispositions, perspectives, and experiences.[8] From this vantage point, Arendt's famous reluctance to identify herself as a woman and to address women's issues looks less like a personal problem of male-identification and more like a political stand that resists the reach of a symbolic order that seeks to define, categorize, and stabilize her in terms of one essential, unriven, and always already known identity.

The "Arendt Question in Feminism" and the "Woman Question in Arendt" need not exclude one another. Many of the essays in this volume are informed by both. Indeed, those who pose the "Arendt Question in Feminism" soon find that the "Woman Question" in Arendt begins to open up in new ways. Again and again, the volume's contributors find that Arendt's account is too rich, nuanced, and varied for simple, gendered dichotomizations to apply. In "Feminist Receptions of Hannah Arendt" (Chapter 2) Mary G. Dietz finds that Arendt's feminist critics and admirers alike misread her work because they approach her through the lens of a gender binary that she herself sought to transcend. Dietz looks at "what happens when a feminist politics driven by an analytically gendered and normatively weighted binary conceptual framework meets a surveyor's map like *The Human Condition*, with its proliferating (mostly) nonbinary concepts." Focused on the public/ private distinction that is centrally important to them rather than on the tripartite distinction among labor, work, and action that was most vital to Arendt, Arendt's feminist readers fail to notice "the provocative gender subtext" of *The Human Condition*. "The two concepts that Arendt does relentlessly gender are not 'private' and 'public' but *animal laborans* [feminine] and *homo faber* [masculine]," Dietz argues. Action is existentially superior to both. Dietz endorses Arendt's "action concept of politics" because it invites "a rebirth in the feminist understanding of politics as 'a kind of theatre where freedom could appear' beyond the phallocentric:gynocentric divide." But, Dietz cautions, feminists should avoid Arendt's error of centering politics too closely upon speech and freedom to the detriment of justice, which Arendtian politics is unfortunately "unable to accommodate."

Insofar as Dietz explores the spaces of Arendtian politics, action, agency, and freedom in ways that shape and respond to the concerns of her own brand of feminism, her essay is typical of all those that follow it. The next three essays, by Hanna Fenichel Pitkin, Seyla Benhabib, and Morris B. Kaplan, explore the same questions, taking as their point of departure Arendt's early analysis of salon society and her later theorizations of the social. Pitkin's essay sets the scene by tracing the complex set of textual and biographical transformations whereby Arendt's early concerns about the conformism of "society" become fastened on the now powerfully monstrous and normalizing "social" of *The Human Condition*. The puzzle Pitkin seeks to deepen and solve is why Arendt, "a thinker whose main effort was to teach us our powers," came to undermine her "best teaching" by theorizing the social as the source of our disempowerment in modernity. How might we recover the empowering impulse of Arendt's political theory and rescue her and ourselves from her image of the social, which Pitkin compares to the all-conquering Blob of 1950s science-fiction films?

Pitkin's essay starts us on the road back to agency by denaturalizing the social and tracing its complex and varied genealogy in Arendt's life and thought, from the concept "society" in Arendt's *Rahel Varnhagen* and the New York essays collected in *The Jew as Pariah* to its later emergence as "the social" in *The Human Condition*. Pitkin also calls on us to attend to "the unconscious symbolism of the Blob image, because it is so clearly, and so complexly gender-related." In ordinary usage as well as in Arendt's own account, the social is clearly linked to women's work; that is, to labor, which (as Dietz also points out) Arendt genders feminine, and to housekeeping. Moreover, from a psychoanalytic perspective, "the Blob is a fantasy of regression, of losing one's separate self and being once more dissolved in—swallowed up by—an engulfing mother." But the problems figured by the Blob are not fantasies, they are real, "from world starvation and nuclear war to the real possibility of rendering the earth uninhabitable." If we are to engage them productively, we must move away from the image of the engulfing mother—the Blobbish social—for it paralyzes our agency and petrifies our powers.

In contrast with Pitkin, Seyla Benhabib welcomes the gendered character of Arendt's treatment of the social, in her early work on the salon. Working with *Rahel Varnhagen*, Benhabib rescues Arendt for

feminism by juxtaposing the feminized space of the salon to the masculinized space of the agon that is so central to *The Human Condition*.
This allows Benhabib "to decenter Arendt's political thought" and to
"displace her fascination with the polis to make room for her more
modernist and women-friendly reflections on the salons." Benhabib
values the salons not only because they are women-friendly but also
because they secure the modern ideals of sociability, friendship, equality,
and humanity. She figures the salons as precursors of the kinds of modern
civic and associational spaces of concerted action that, in her view, are
implied by Arendt's call for a revitalized public life that "does not mean
the strengthening of the state."

Benhabib's argument is challenged in two subsequent essays, implicitly
in Morris Kaplan's essay (Chapter 5), which gives a rather different
reading of Arendt's treatment of the salon, and explicitly in my own
(Chapter 6), which rejects feminist genderings of agonism as the provenance of male action and endorses an Arendtian agonism for feminism.
(Mary Dietz's essay analyzes some of the issues at stake in the debate
between Benhabib's associationism and my own agonistic feminism.)
Kaplan finds support for a contemporary democratic politics of sexuality
in Arendt's commitment to equal citizenship and in her belief that
"political freedom depends upon a capacity to establish private households." Most valuable, however, is Arendt's relentless historicization of
the Jewish question, an analysis that Kaplan extends (by way of Arendt's
reading of Proust) to trace critically the nineteenth-century racialization
and naturalization of homosexuality and Jewishness as identities rather
than as contingent, historical sets of practices. "By marking as inherent
qualities the effects of shared historical circumstance, racialized identities
served to naturalize and internalize the subordination of marginal groups,
subjecting them to continuing social control as distinct, transparent,
and permanent minorities." The fascination with these minorities in the
context of the salon in this period did not mitigate this political problem.
Rendered exotics one day, the newly racialized groups of Jews and
homosexuals were liable to be marked as targets for extermination the
next. Kaplan concludes that Arendt's insights on these fronts—albeit
limited by her failure to attend to the historical imbrication of the
process of racialization with gender and sexuality—call for a democratic
politics of sexuality that knows that "the politics of naturalized identities
is at odds with democratic commitments to plurality and contestation."

My own essay proceeds from this same conclusion. Arendt's attentiveness to the historical processes whereby Jewishness became a naturalized identity is not matched by a similarly critical analysis of the naturalization of sex-gender identities. The body, for Arendt, is a site and source of mute inaction, cyclical nature, or senseless violence that ought to be confined to the private realm. Like Hanna Pitkin, I ask why this theorist of empowerment and agency comes to such disempowering conclusions. Why does Arendt grant so much power to the body rather than see it as the (resistible if sedimented) product "of the actions, behaviors, norms, and institutional structures of individuals, societies, and political cultures?" I conclude that Arendt's own performative account of political action warrants a radicalization of her view that would "push us to de-essentialize and denaturalize the body, perhaps pluralize it, maybe even see *it* as a performative production, a possible site of action in Arendt's sense."

These arguments about the body apply also to identity, which Arendt also insisted was a private not a political fact. By way of a reading of Arendt's exchange with Gershom Scholem about the terms of Jewish identity (occasioned by her controversial *Eichmann in Jerusalem*), I endorse Arendt's concerns about the homogenizing effects of an identity-based politics. But I depart from her in arguing that since political action is always imbricated in identitarian issues and assumptions, it is more effective to engage and interrupt established identities agonistically than to insist in a separatist way, as Arendt does, on their fixity or privacy. I conclude that the power of Arendt's (now radicalized) agonistic and performative politics can be harnessed by a feminism that "presupposes not an already known and unifying identity of 'woman' but agonistic, differentiated, multiple nonidentified beings that are always becoming, always calling out for augmentation and amendment."

Linda Zerilli (Chapter 7) sees more ambiguity than I do in Arendt's theorization of the body and in that ambiguity, she argues, lies Arendt's promise for feminism. Also, contra Mary Dietz, Zerilli claims that Arendt's importance to feminism lies precisely in her failure or refusal to "symbolize the laboring and generative body in clear, unchanging and all-too-familiar gendered terms (although it sometimes participates in such symbolization)." Rather than seek the gendered subtext of Arendt's account, Zerilli (reading Arendt with and against Julia Kristeva) points out that Arendt's "prose stages and amplifies the terror of embodiment and of the asymbolic *chora* for readers of both sexes." Arendt's response to that terror is not unambiguous. "Although it appears that, for Arendt, the desiring, semiotic, and private body is at odds with the bounded, symbolic space of the public world, she also shows that the law that maintains this opposition (and keeps the difference between the sexes) was sustained in the city-state through violence and the repudiation of life itself." For Zerilli, the Arendtian body is not just a site of violence but also a site of vitality and pleasure; it is not just a locus of sameness but also a semiotic drive force that animates the plural subject of action and "resists the formalization of meaning and conformity Arendt deplores." Oddly enough, these observations lead Zerilli to a conclusion that recalls Mary Dietz's: "Arendt's account of the subject of action shows that identity always exceeds the symbolic terms that name it, including 'male' and 'female.'" Nonetheless an important difference remains: In Dietz's account, Arendtian action transcends the terms of sexual difference; in Zerilli's it can only exceed them.

The themes of embodiment, sex-gender, power, and violence all recur in the next three essays, which take as their points of departure regime-related topics to which Arendt repeatedly returned: revolution and founding, nationalism, constitutional amendment, democratic practice, and civil disobedience. None of these authors sees in Arendt's other texts the ambivalence about the body that Zerilli traces in *The Human Condition*. Focusing on Arendt's reading of the French Revolution in *On Revolution*, Joan Landes (Chapter 8) notes Arendt's preference for the failed Girondiste alternative to the Jacobins but argues that, in her search for "the 'lost treasure' of modern revolution," Arendt "overlooks *another* failed revolution in France, one that promised a new beginning for women as political actors." Recovering the stories of militant women, such as Pauline Léon, Théroigne de Méricourt, and Olympe de Gouges, Landes shows how their actions both exemplify an Arendtian commitment to "empowered and self-governing action" and challenge the binary oppositions that Arendt's treatment of revolution produces and upon which it depends. Again and again, Arendt's distinctions "between freedom and [bodily] necessity, spontaneity and determinism, political rights and human rights, freedom and equality and public and private" are disrupted by those embodied political actors whose calls for bread "prompted the establishment of a constitutional monarchy." Worried that Arendt's failure "to recognize women's plurality" and their diverse revolutionary activities effectively endorses "the revolutionary government's assignment of women to the home," Landes nonetheless concludes on a quintessentially Arendtian note: the hope that her recovery of this other lost revolutionary treasure may augment and amend the terms of Arendt's founding theorization of politics, while inspiring and empowering future women activists.

In her analysis of Arendt's study of nationalism, part 1 of *The Origins of Totalitarianism*, Joan Cocks (Chapter 9) also prods Arendt to come to terms with the embodied dimensions of political agency. Putting Arendt into a sustained engagement with Frantz Fanon and Rosa Luxemburg, Cocks canvasses their different views on the source and place of violence in politics. "Is Arendt right or wrong to find Fanon politically irresponsible for advocating violence as part of national liberation?" For Cocks, the question calls attention not only to Fanon's commitments but to those of Arendt, whose criticisms of Fanon "are animated by a primary antagonism to the presence of the body in politics rather than by a primary antagonism to the political infliction of bodily pain." Fanon, by contrast, is "unprejudiced against the body and consequently is not compelled to pry the realm of the body and the realm of speech and action apart. Thus he can see violence as a feature simultaneously of visceral and political experience."

In Cocks's view, all three of these thinkers have something important to teach contemporary feminisms. Together they press upon us the need to move from celebrations of difference, diversity, and multiculturalism to hard-edged engagements with current ethno-nationalist movements. Luxemburg also provides a much-needed antidote to the current neglect of "the question of material class distinction," while Arendt is helpful in her insistence that the national question is a "riddle with no solution." If Arendt does not take up Luxemburg's formula of a "unity of political identity and ethnic difference" that is because she is "alert to the difference between what it is possible to do in words to transcend the dilemmas of nationalism and what it is possible to *do*." It is a difference to which, Cocks suggests, we too should be alert. But Cocks gives Fanon the last word, endorsing his refusal "to condemn violence in a flat, blanket way," and calling upon feminists to broaden the scope of their analyses of the body to match his: "the same importance feminism attributes to bodily sensation, sexual desire, and the concrete pains and pleasures of intimate life, also must be attributed to the bodily component of resentment, indignation, and rage, and hence to the visceral pressures to violence against a social order that is felt to be unjust."

Fanon's lesson for Arendt and for feminism? "Under certain circumstances, the absence of the impulse to violence must be counted as a puzzle, not a virtue."

The place of the body and of violence in politics are also the central themes of Anne Norton's essay (Chapter 10). Focusing on Arendt's *Origins of Totalitarianism* in combination with her 1950s and 1960s essays on desegregation in Little Rock, civil disobedience, and democratic political action, Norton argues that Arendt racializes her distinctions among power and violence, speech and the body, identifying the disinterested and peaceful political activism she admired with the white student movement while associating black activism with violence and self-interest. In Arendt's account, Norton charges, "Black students represent interest, not intellect. They are moved by material rather than ideal concerns, bound not to an abstract conception of justice, but to the interests of a particular community. They are moved by need, and so, according to Arendt's strict dichotomies, they operate in the realm of necessity, not in the realm of freedom and will."

These oppositions govern Arendt's perspective on the place of African Americans in American history as well. Norton wonders at Arendt's characterization of the United States as a "Europe-determined world," arguing that "only a determined sequestering of historical events, a studied indifference to cultural provenance, can conceal the African origins of American practices and the American people." And she criticizes Arendt's reading of abolition politics, which denies "historical agency, cultural work, and constitutional will" to African Americans and occludes the "events and practices that might suggest that African Americans claimed America, that they had made that territory, that history, that complex of ideas their own through labor and work." The result—the effective exclusion of African Americans from the founding and maintenance of the American political and cultural regime—is ironic given Arendt's goal, which is to call for an "explicit constitutional amendment" to invite "the Negro people of America" into the nation. For Norton, however, Arendt's invitation is itself problematic because it presupposes the absence of an already established African American presence in the regime. Moreover, insofar as it rests on the claim that "African Americans are 'the only ones' for whom the promise of America 'was not true,'" Arendt's invitation also works to absolve the American regime "from responsibility for a more extensive complex of inequalities" that shaped the fates and agencies of women, Jews, Asians, and others.

Like Landes, Norton criticizes Arendt's account of a revolution for its exclusion of a valuably contributive set of agencies that helped constitute and maintain the regimes or movements she admired. Norton worries, too, about the lasting disempowering effects of that exclusion. Arguing that these problems arise from Arendt's "denials of the presence of the body in politics, or the presence of politics in the body," Norton echoes Cock's and Landes's calls for the raced, gendered, classed, sexed and enraged body to be engaged as a site of political-historical construction and contestation.

Arendt's essay on Little Rock (coupled with her "Crisis in Education" in *Between Past and Future*) also provides Jean Bethke Elshtain (Chapter 11) with her point of departure. But Elshtain's critique of Arendt moves to a different register, preparing the way for the volume's final three essays, which look to Arendt for inspiration in theorizing the conditions and strategies of feminist politics in late modern democracies. Like Landes, Cocks, and Norton, Elshtain deploys stories of political action that put pressure on Arendt's "categorical distinctions between private and public, politics and everything else." Noting Arendt's ban on political children, Elshtain insists that in the worlds of Little Rock, Birmingham, and contemporary pro-life protests, worlds rocked by the activism of political children, Arendt's "distinctions between the social and the political" blur.

The question of political children implies another question, that of political mothers. Should children be protected from politics, urged into activism, or permitted to take the lead? In answering these questions, Elshtain argues, we must attend not to "the *fact* of politicization . . . but, rather, to the banner under which this 'going public' takes place. In whose name? Under what auspices? In what cause? To what ends?" Arendt's ban on political children grew out of her own experience of Nazi Germany's use of children as "instruments of a policy aimed at destroying the independence of all associations." There is a world of difference between that and "Mother Jones's brigade, desegregation children, and anti-abortion children who fight with and for particular, plural communities of belief and memory—familial, religious, local associational—beliefs held with their union, their church, their families." Thus, Elshtain supports the activism of political children on Arendtian grounds, arguing that "they strengthen rather than evacuate associational possibilities of a plural nature." But she notes an "irony" worthy of further exploration: In the desegregation and pro-life cases, the associational character of these movements may be merely instrumental and therefore self-defeating, as both call upon the state "to implement passionately held convictions that segregation and abortion are wrong, undermining the moral community."

The volume's final three essays further unsettle Arendt's distinctions between public and private, social and political, as they look to Arendt's theory and example for strategies of political action, judgment, and perspective that might support and empower concerted feminist political agencies. All address the issue of identity in politics in connection with other issues of concern to Arendt and to feminists. Lisa Disch (Chapter 12) reads Arendt's Lessing Address (in *Men in Dark Times*) as an example of a disputational practice of "vigilant partisanship" that would serve feminists well. The Lessing Prize "was quite blatantly an attempt to initiate a reconciliation between Germans and German Jews by reaffirming the *Aufklärung* as their shared history." Arendt refuses the reconciliation, positioning herself and Lessing as *critics* of enlightened humanism, arguing against the abstract values of (Kantian) humanism and in favor of the concrete goods of friendship (here Disch implicitly opposes the modernist reading of Arendt offered earlier by Benhabib). "Effectively taking up the humanism that is offered her as the unquestioned ground of the occasion and turning it back on her hosts as the question of 'humanity in dark times,'" Arendt anticipates the strategies of those contemporary feminists who refute "gender as a common standpoint, redeploying it to pose the question of how women are differently implicated in oppressive social relations, and rejecting women's experience as the shared ground of the movement." Also anticipatory are Arendt's refusal to allow her position as a Jewish refugee to be erased by the award and her refusal to accept it simply as a Jew. ("To speak as a Jew in the changed political circumstances of 1959 'would seem like a pose' that succumbs to 'the spirit of Hitlerism' in its own way.") But, in the end, Arendt was not entirely successful. When her speech was later cited at a session of the Bundestag, she was referred to as a "Jewish emigrant," not a refugee. And her mentor, Karl Jaspers, continued to press her to return to the very intellectual tradition that, in Arendt's account, was both implicated in and destroyed by "the brutal realities of German nationalism."

The limited effectiveness of Arendt's careful acceptance of the Lessing Prize suggests that Susan Bickford (Chapter 13) is right to seek a supplement for Arendt's speech-centered political theory. From Gloria

Anzaldúa, Bickford suggests, we might learn to appreciate the complex importance of listening in addition to that of speaking and acting. Bickford approaches this issue by way of what she calls "the paradox of public appearance," which involves "our urge to appear in the world as a particular, mobile [unique self] and the fact that such appearance requires the attention of peers who will judge for themselves." The paradox is important because "appearance is the only ground of human reality." The paradox is complicated because the craving for appearance cannot be satisfied by "either the singularity of identity or the unity of political community, for such conceptions cannot do justice to the complex selves that we are." These complex selves are the necessary conditions of Arendt's practice of representative thinking as well as of the *mestiza* creativity that, in Anzaldúa's account, is the generative source of an "emancipatory capacity to shift perspectives." Both of these practices help us to move beyond established social identities to form a "public self with a new consciousness, a new view, a new opinion."

The need to move beyond established social identities is the starting point of this volume's concluding essay, by Melissa Orlie. Focusing primarily (but not exclusively) on *The Human Condition* and reading Arendt with and against Michel Foucault, Orlie accounts for that need in ethical and political terms, arguing that "when we are indifferent to our conduct's continuation and expansion of [asymmetrical] social rules, we not only exclude others. We also intensify the social necessities that circumscribe our own action." In so doing we limit our own freedom. But there is no escaping this. As Arendt knew, "necessity and compulsion persist wherever human life is sustained." Trespasses are inevitable. They "arise as we live our locations; they are effects of our bodies' ways of being in the world. Sometimes we retrace old wounds, at other times we trespass anew." The unavoidable and shifting character of trespass is confirmed, Orlie argues, "as I move through the streets of a city where my race bestows protection, my gender is perceived as vulnerability, and my sexuality is viewed as provocation."

Returning us to the themes of the social with which the volume began, Orlie argues that Arendt releases us from responsibility for "what we are—how and what we have been made to be by history, institutions, and patterns of social rule preceding us," so "that we may become responsible for *who* we are—for how we carry and pass on the social effects configuring what we appear to be." Arendt's theorization of promising and forgiveness as forms of political action plays an important role here. In Orlie's account, forgiveness is a necessary component of Arendtian action not only because promises are sometimes broken but also because they are often kept. Whatever else they do, the actions in concert that promising helps to forge necessarily involve us in trespasses that we, as feminists, must interrupt for the sake of the "more promising futures afforded when we seek political forgiveness and transfigure trespasses in the hope of redirecting their future effects." On this forward-looking and responsible note, the volume turns to end with Patchen Markell's annotated bibliography of feminist engagements with Hannah Arendt.

As these brief summaries indicate, the contributors' focus on the "Arendt Question in Feminism" leads them to engage a diverse set of sources and topics, rethinking the body, sexuality, identity, desire, difference, and the necessary conditions of politics itself. Where the 1970s and early 1980s feminist engagements with Arendt tended to focus almost exclusively on *The Human Condition*, probably the most distinction-laden of her works, the feminists in this volume find inspiration in a broader, more differentiated selection of her writings: her early biographical work, *Rahel Varnhagen: The Life of a Jewish Woman* (1974); her remarkable *The Origins of Totalitarianism* (1951); her essays on specifically Jewish issues and Zionism in *The Jew as Pariah* (1978); her account of modern revolutions and the practice of political founding and maintenance in *On Revolution* (1963), *Crises of the Republic* (1972), *Between Past and Future* (1968), and "Reflections on Little Rock" (1959); her essays in admiration of exemplary figures in *Men in Dark Times* (1968); and her late reflections on human agency and the mental faculties in *The Life of the Mind* (1978). This diversity of sources is matched by a diversity of methods and approaches: historicist, hermeneutic, deconstructive, poststructuralist, humanist, materialist, and psychoanalytic, all informed by recent developments in gender theory cultural feminism, and gay and lesbian studies.

The result is a startling plurality of findings and judgments, a diverse array of feminist theories and practices, and a Hannah Arendt who, while not herself a feminist, emerges as a vital and reinvigorating thinker for feminists to engage. In this volume, Arendt is not only a theorist of political action but also a historian of anti-Semitism, salon society, imperialism, and the development of the modern nation-state, a public and engaged intellectual, an astute if sometimes outrageous political commentator, and a trenchant critic of identitarianism in politics. Most of the volume's authors claim a debt to Arendt, finding something in her thought on which a feminism can profitably build or from which it can learn; others are more critical. Such difference is appropriate for a volume of feminist interpretation. Feminism is not a *single* methodology or ideology. It is itself a site of contestation over the meaning, practice, and politics of sex-gender and sexuality.

This plurality of perspectives is also particularly appropriate for a volume on Hannah Arendt. The contributions to this volume exemplify the difference and plurality that are the sine qua non of Arendtian politics. On Arendt's account, plurality secures the separation and relation that are necessary protections against the dogmatism and uniformity that arise in mass society and spell the end of a properly democratic politics. I believe that, Arendt's dismissal of feminism notwithstanding, she herself might have seen promise in this diversity: it suggests a feminism that is (to borrow her binaries) political not ideological; a site of concerted action, not a plain of homogeneous behavior.

Much remains to be done. Arendt believed that the mark of a good founding and a healthy new regime was their openness to later augmentation and amendment. As these introductory remarks indicate, I see this volume not just as a re-reading of canonical treatments of Arendt (though it is that, too) but also as an augmentation of earlier *feminist* engagements with her work. I hope that it will move others to further the project of re-reading Hannah Arendt and her interpreters in ways that deepen and provoke feminist theory and practice.

## Notes

1. I forego any treatment of Arendt's biography in this introduction because, in Chapter 3, Hanna Fenichel Pitkin provides a good discussion of some of the details of Arendt's life in relation to her work. Those interested in a fuller account should consult Elisabeth Young-Bruehl, *Hannah Arendt: For Love of the World* (New Haven: Yale University Press, 1982).

2. In highlighting the differences between earlier and more recent feminisms, I do not mean to suggest that Arendt was right to be so dismissive of earlier moments of feminist political theory, practice, and female political agency. Her prejudices on these fronts are discussed briefly in Chapter 6 and at greater length in Chapter 8, in this volume.

3. Those who emphasize the differences within the category "women" include Kathy Ferguson, *The Man Question: Visions of Subjectivity in Feminist Theory* (Berkeley and Los Angeles: University of California Press, 1993); and Cherrié Moraga and Gloria Anzaldúa, eds., *The Bridge Called My Back: Writings by Radical Women of Color* (New York: Kitchen Table, Women of Color Press, 1983). Those who focus more on the feminization and sexualization of the other include Judith Butler, *Bodies That Matter: On the Discursive Limits of*

"*Sex*" (New York: Routledge, 1993); Linda Zerilli, *Signifying Woman: Culture and Chaos in Rousseau, Burke, and Mill* (Ithaca: Cornell University Press, 1994); and Morris B. Kaplan, "Refiguring the Jewish Question: Arendt, Proust, and the Politics of Sexuality," Chapter 5 in this volume.

4. Adrienne Rich, *On Lies, Secrets and Silence: Selected Prose 1966–1978* (New York: Norton, 1979), 211–12.

5. Nancy Hartsock, *Money, Sex, and Power: Toward a Feminist Historical Materialism* (New York: Longman, 1983). Mary G. Dietz's essay in this volume (Chapter 2) gives a detailed picture and critique of these and other feminist receptions of Arendt.

6. On the construction and the role of "woman," "identity," and, specifically, "experience" in feminist political theory and practice, see Catharine A. MacKinnon, "Feminism, Marxism, Method and the State: Toward a Feminist Jurisprudence," in *Feminism and Methodology: Social Science Issues,* ed. Sandra Harding (Bloomington: Indiana University Press, 1987), 135–56; and Nancy Hartsock, "The Feminist Standpoint: Developing the Ground for a Specifically Feminist Historical Materialism," in Harding, ed., *Feminism and Methodology,* 157–80; Teresa de Lauretis, "Semiotics and Experience," in *Alice Doesn't: Feminism, Semiotics, Cinema,* (Bloomington: Indiana University Press, 1984), 158–86; and Joan W. Scott, "Experience," in *Feminists Theorize the Political,* ed. Judith Butler and Joan W. Scott (New York: Routledge, 1992), 22–40.

7. *The Science Question in Feminism* (Ithaca: Cornell University Press, 1986), 9. I first learned to appreciate the usefulness of Harding's distinction from Kirstie McClure, "The Issue of Foundations: Scientized Politics, Politicized Science, and Feminist Critical Practice," in Butler and Scott, eds., *Feminists Theorize the Political,* 341–78.

8. On the need to resignify the "Woman Question," see Linda Zerilli, *Signifying Woman,* chaps. 1 and 5.

# 2

# Feminist Receptions of Hannah Arendt

## Mary G. Dietz

Hannah Arendt was not invited to the Dinner Party, but Judy Chicago did count her as one of the nine hundred and ninety-nine "women of importance" in herstory. In many respects, Arendt was unprecedented: "a major political philosopher of our time, a woman greatly respected in the intellectual establishment";[1] "the central political thinker of this century whose work has reminded us . . . of the loss of public space";[2] "one of the most powerful figures" in the tradition of civic republicanism;[3] "the political theorist who wrote most powerfully on [the theme of public and private] in our time, and who tried hardest to renew our access to politics as . . . a 'public happiness.' "[4] For those who keep track

I thank Bonnie Honig for her insightful commentary on earlier drafts of this essay.

of such things, Arendt was also exceptional: the first woman to give the Christian Gauss seminars at Princeton University (1953); the first woman appointed to the rank of full professor at Princeton University (1959), one of only a few female academicians to receive honorary degrees at a dozen American universities, one of the very few to be awarded the prestigious Lessing Prize of the Free City of Hamburg (Germany, 1959), the Emerson-Thoreau Medal of the American Academy (1969), and the Sigmund Freud Prize of the Deutsche Akademie für Sprache und Dichtung (1967).[5] Arendt's friend Mary McCarthy thought her a goddess—a "chthonic goddess, or a fiery one, rather than the airy kind . . . enacting a drama of mind."[6] At her funeral in 1975, Arendt's friend Hans Jonas said, "She has set a style of inquiry and debate which will ensure that no cheap formula for the human predicament will pass muster, so long as her example is remembered."[7]

Yet the woman who is arguably the most influential theorist of action, participatory politics, and the public realm in the twentieth century appears to have had no discernible influence upon the second-wave feminist movement in either North America or Europe, in either its theory or its public, political practice. In part, no doubt, the gulf between feminism and Arendt—at least in the United States—was occasioned by the pragmatic rather than theoretical character of the American feminist movement itself, and probably by Arendt's own personal reluctance to "venture into the public realm."[8] An academic political theorist who located her origins not in the Left, but in "the tradition of German philosophy,"[9] Arendt was an unlikely source of inspiration for the activists of American feminism, in any of their ideological varieties. Even in its theoretical vein, however, feminism was unlikely to find in Arendt a line compatible with the idea that "the personal is political." As Anne Phillips notes, "When Hannah Arendt defines politics in terms of the pursuit of public happiness or the taste for public freedom, she is employing a terminology almost opposite to that adopted within the contemporary women's movement."[10]

Certainly the gulf between feminism and Arendt was enforced by her unwavering inclination to distance herself from Women's Liberation in general. As Elizabeth Young-Bruehl notes, Arendt "became uneasy whenever she saw the 'woman problem' generate either a political movement separated from others or a concentration on psychological problems."[11] Like Rosa Luxemburg, whom she greatly admired "for who she was and what she did," and Simone de Beauvoir, whom she brusquely dismissed as "not very bright,"[12] Arendt was unsympathetic to a politics that divorced "women's issues" from a broader range of emancipatory concerns.[13] Like the two other most famous female political theorists of the twentieth century, Arendt was by no means free of conventional, patriarchal attitudes. She was "suspicious of women who 'gave orders,' skeptical about whether women should be political leaders and steadfastly opposed to the social dimensions of Women's Liberation."[14]

Nonetheless, feminism has smiled more benevolently upon Luxemburg's and Beauvoir's antifeminist traces than it has upon Arendt's. In practical terms at least, and especially in the United States, Rosa Luxemburg's influence has in any case always been negligible. Too heroic a Sparticist, too little a womanist, and muted by time, Luxemburg left a legacy that is informed less by her politics than by her brutal death in 1919 at the hands of creatures she would have called "another zoological species."[15] Beauvoir's is, of course, a different and more definitive story. Her opposition to the women's movement (which relaxed considerably in the 1970s) was fully eclipsed as a matter of comment by *The Second Sex* (1949), the totemic postwar manifesto that gave birth and impetus to the cause of female liberation, and earned Beauvoir the dubious but unparalleled title "first-generation Mother."[16] Arendt is yet another matter. A German-Jewish refugee from fascist Europe to the United States, her life story has aspects of bravery to rival Luxemburg's[17] and, later, works of singular meaning and importance that easily equal any of Beauvoir's. But, as Maria Markus notes, during her lifetime Arendt was "almost totally ignored" by feminists.[18] After her death, however, and as her work began "its uncertain, always adventurous course through history" (*MDT* 71), things took a different turn. The influential poet Adrienne Rich declared *The Human Condition* "a lofty and crippled book."[19] Not long after, Mary O'Brien, the indomitable midwife-turned-theorist, leveled a scorching attack upon "such female male supremacists as Hannah Arendt," in her widely read book *The Politics of Reproduction.*[20]

Even in less virulent and more lofty theoretical reaches, the feminist reception of Hannah Arendt has been on the whole an open polemical and hyperbolic affair that has probably generated more heat than light on her work. The polemics, as we shall see, are partly symptomatic of some tensions within feminist theorizing itself, and thus they reveal as much about certain analytical presuppositions in contemporary academic feminism as they do about Arendt.[21] Nevertheless, it is also true that

Arendt's ideas seem to invite among feminists an intensity of response that few other women thinkers—and surely none of her stature—have received.

In what follows, my instincts are both critical and programmatic. First, I want to explore one particular arena of feminist commentary that aligns some of Arendt's most unforgiving critics[22] against some of her most enthusiastic defenders.[23] I shall show that, regardless of their specific views, the commentaries in this arena are driven by a shared feminism of "difference" that "genders Hannah Arendt." That is, they reproduce gender as the primary category of their critiques of both Arendtian theory and of Arendt the theorist. Ironically, under the weight of this powerful analytical category, these commentaries miss what I take to be the true "gender subtext" of Arendt's theory; and they miss the way in which Arendt's action concept of politics displaces the binary of gender as well. My second and more programmatic aim is to suggest that in Arendt's most systematic political text, *The Human Condition*, we can uncover a conceptual strategy that rejects gender in favor of a politics of "unique distinctiveness" and action as self-revelation in speech. In elaborating upon this Arendtian strategy, I will consider a variety of recent feminist commentaries that are either concerned with bringing Arendt to feminism as a political movement, or with bringing feminism as an "identity politics" to Arendt in ways that do not necessarily endorse the presuppositions of difference feminism.[24] By and large, these commentaries are critically attuned to the problem of action, and to the conditions that might constitute a genuinely Arendtian politics. Whether this augurs well or ill for feminism is, of course, itself an interpretive question, and what follows from it remains to be seen.

# The Gendering of Hannah Arendt

The activity of textual interpretation and the reception of any author always take place against the background of particular but invariably complex historical, ideological, and practical realities. Not only does much hinge upon the texts that are available to or selected by interpreters, but also upon the discursive context within which the practice of interpretation transpires. Although a full accounting of the background against which the feminist reception of Arendt initially unfolds is impossible here, we should note that from the start it is shaped by one specific text and a specific discursive context.

In the years immediately following Arendt's death most secondary studies of her work focused primarily, if not exclusively, upon the text that appeared in Europe under the title *Vita Activa* and in the United States as *The Human Condition* (1958). Given the scope and power of almost all of Arendt's writings, it was not altogether predictable that the text she wanted to call *Amor Mundi* (love of the world) would become her most widely read and interpreted work.[25] From a contemporary political perspective, *The Origins of Totalitarianism* (1951) is more vivid and compelling; Young-Bruehl is right to say that "no one who wishes to study totalitarianism can ignore it."[26] *Eichmann in Jerusalem* (1963) is stunning and courageous; *Rahel Varnhagen* (1974) maneuvers deftly at the intersection of biography, gender, class, and ethnicity. *On Revolution* (1963) is the work Justice William O. Douglas foresaw as a "classic treatise"; and *Between Past and Future* (1963–68) is the text that Arendt thought was the best of her books.[27] Yet it is in *The Human Condition* that the panorama upon which the conceptual schematic of Arendt's thinking unrolls more vividly and completely than anywhere else. To borrow Mary McCarthy's metaphor, *The Human Condition* is the "vast surveyor's map of concepts and insights"[28] in which the main elements of Arendt's rich and complex valuation of the conditions of human existence are explicitly and systematically put forward for the first and last time. So in this sense, *The Human Condition* is also a map to the hidden treasure of Arendt's own thinking, as well as a guide to all of the rest of her work.

The concepts that constitute Arendt's map appear in ones, twos, and threes; sometimes they multiply into fours and sixes. One term constitutes this text-map itself: the *vita activa*. Three others—conditions, activities, and spaces—constitute its outer boundaries. A complex of related concepts—some binaries, others not—emerges inside: earth, world, private, public, social, household, polis, society, worldliness, worldlessness, labor, work, action, natality, mortality, plurality, *animal laborans*, *homo faber*, process, life, necessity, means-end, instrumentality, fabrication, action, speech, freedom.[29] Arendt's concepts assume spatial, geometric relations to each other; they are variously parallel, transverse, orthogonal, and homologous, but always circumscribed, delimited, and specified. Arendt wants to refocus our attention on certain distinctions that have transformed over time and also become blurred. Hence the concepts in *The Human Condition* take on various temporal relationships that she poses as "reversals." For example, in the classical age the human capacity for action enjoys existential priority over the capacity for work; in early modernity, work triumphs over action; in late modernity, labor and life are victorious over action and work. Increasingly, "social" invades the public world, *animal laborans* overwhelms *homo faber*, and freedom falls prey to necessity. Arendt's concepts are fluid; they mix and match, intermingle, separate, change position, appear, disappear and reappear along a narrative course that is itself a tale of cyclicalities, lineations, reversals, dead stops, and boundless possibilities. What this adds up to is an exceedingly dense and complex, always provocative, and often frustrating text that has focused the scholarly attention to Arendt for the past fifteen years. Feminist scholarship is no exception.

The background for the reception of Arendt is also set by what might be called the dominant discursive context of feminist theorizing in the United States in the late 1970s and early 1980s. Against the increasingly dreary landscape of the androgyny debates, Marxist feminist arguments over capitalist patriarchy and socialist feminism, and radical Beauvoirian proclamations about childbearing and childrearing as "the heart of woman's oppression,"[30] a new perspective on "the woman question" emerged. We now have a series of terms that identify it: "feminist standpoint theory";[31] "standpoint epistemology";[32] "cultural feminism";[33] "gynocentric feminism,"[34] or "difference theory."[35] The difference feminists, who cast rather romantic figures against the grain of oppression studies, were determined to reassert the concept of woman as the starting point for academic feminism. They were also skillful purveyors of rhetoric who often relied on attractive phrases and striking images to advance the "celebration of female difference."[36] Accordingly, difference feminism advanced insights drawn from psychology, epistemology, and moral philosophy and undertook to counterpose certain so-called female attributes or values (such as motherhood, connectedness, caring, reciprocity, and other-directedness) against certain so-called male attributes or values (such as violence, domination, competitiveness, power, and self-centeredness). As Nancy Fraser argues, difference feminism holds that "in some respects, women really [are] different from men, and . . . the differences [are] to women's credit."[37]

At least two analytical presuppositions are embedded in the discursive context of difference feminism. First, the binary of gender is simply reproduced and treated unproblematically. Female:Male or Women:

Men, to paraphrase Parveen Adams and Jeff Minson, "simply mark the always already given gender in the category of humanity."[38] This static polarity is taken as a structural premise and simply read off history, society, discourse, language, a text—whatever the target of analysis happens to be. Second, the binary carries with it a heavily weighted normative dimension that formulates the female (or "women") positively and the male (or "men") negatively. Thus the conditions for emancipation are constructed out of the struggle between these differently weighted gender identities, and women's liberation is resolutely connected to the victory of the female side of the gendered opposition. The female side carries with it a host of secondary conceptual terms (naturally posed against their male opposition): life (death), nature (culture), reproduction (production), birth (death), the body (mind), the household (polis), the maternal (paternal) and finally, perhaps the most decisive duality in feminist political theory: private (public).

Next I shall consider what happens when a feminist interpretation driven by an analytically gendered and normatively weighted binary conceptual framework meets a vast surveyor's map like *The Human Condition*, with its proliferating (mostly) nonbinary concepts. We should not forget that the deployers of the binary framework are themselves women who bring a feminist celebration of female difference to their work. Thus what is at stake in the initial interpretive feminist context of Arendt studies is both the gendering of *The Human Condition* and the gendering of Hannah Arendt. The question at issue in difference feminism is (and can only be) this: Is Arendt a woman who thinks like a woman, or a woman who thinks like a man? The verdict, as we shall see, ultimately depends upon the way in which the gender binary is read off of Arendt's major theoretical text.

## Phallocentric Arendt

Adrienne Rich and Mary O'Brien set the initial tone for the feminist reception of Arendt, and both of them, in effect, declare that Arendt is a woman who thinks like a man. Rich and O'Brien also bring decisive interests to bear upon *The Human Condition*. In keeping with the strategy of difference feminism, they posit a feminist emancipatory politics of "women's work" (Rich) or "reproductive consciousness" (O'Brien) over and against a male politics of the public or political realm, which the engulfing meta-narrative of Western "male-stream thought" or "male ideology" supports.[39] From this vantage point, *The Human Condition* is, to say the least, a deeply flawed book, and not only because Arendt barely alludes to the condition of women in the human condition and thereby shows contempt for the efforts of women in labor.[40] The problem also involves Arendt's celebration of "the common world of men,"[41] especially in the form of "Paterfamilias on his way to the freedom of the political realm."[42] In this glorification of the public [man] over the private [woman], Rich sees "the tragedy of a female mind nourished on male ideologies,"[43] and O'Brien reads "a woman who accepts the normality and even the necessity of male supremacy."[44]

Since there is much at issue for both Arendtian political theory and also for feminist politics in these views, it is worth considering how Rich and O'Brien arrive at their reading of *The Human Condition* as a masculinist text and Arendt as a male ideologue. As difference feminists, both bring to *The Human Condition* a perspective that is substantively geared toward gaining access to the true nature or meaning of women as human beings.[45] Methodologically, they follow a strategy that places Arendt's text under the logic of a binary interpretive schema that posits a static gender polarity as its core analytical category. From this "difference" starting point follow at least three interpretive moves that have some significant consequences for the conceptual integrity of *The Human Condition* as a political theory. First, Arendt's text must be approached from an analytical prospect fixed upon being, nature, and subjectivity, and not upon "doing," "activities," and interaction, which is where Arendt herself begins.[46] Thus, O'Brien characterizes Arendt's discussion of the *vita activa* in terms of "the two natures of man."[47] Second, O'Brien poses the problem of human nature as a binary male:female opposition that effectively erases Arendt's commitment to a tripartite notion of activities (labor:work:action) with its corresponding "basic conditions" (life:worldliness:plurality) (*HC* 7–8), and substitutes the category nature:society. So activities become subjectivities, and a triplet becomes a doublet. As a result of these two moves, O'Brien can argue that Arendt supports an "action metaphysics" that simply recapitulates Aristotle's justification of male (society) over female (na-ture), and "polis life" (man's second nature) over "bodily need and species continuity" (man's first nature).[48] Following hard upon the logical must of the gender binary, O'Brien's third move seizes the

Arendtian spatial category that best accommodates the logic she imposes, and that is the category public:private. Thus the one obvious pairing in Arendt's conceptual map is hypermagnified in O'Brien's analysis, while all other conceptual configurations are blurred, if not altogether erased, even as O'Brien criticizes the "artificiality" and "literal thoughtlessness" of Arendt's own analytical categories.[49] Under the category "private/female" O'Brien reloads her terms "first nature/body/species life"; under "public/male" she reloads "second nature/uniqueness/politics." Keeping in mind Arendt's privileging of the public realm of politics, O'Brien now suggests that "Arendt stands in a long line of social and political thinkers who, in failing to analyse the significance of reproductive consciousness, are able to find all kinds of ontological, metaphysical and ultimately ideological justification of male supremacy."[50]

As a result of these three moves, O'Brien reads the hierarchy that Arendt establishes in the *vita activa* not as the existential superiority of action (plurality) over labor (life) and work (worldliness), but as the superiority of one ontological realm (Male Public) over another (Female Private).[51] In O'Brien's hands, Arendt's *vita activa* is transmuted from an *Existenz* category that reveals three differentially illuminated human activities within the human condition into an ontological category that assigns two differentially weighted gender subjectivities (women:MEN) to human nature, and two differentially weighted realms (private:PUBLIC) to human life. Moreover, Arendt's action concept of politics is rendered as "patriarchy and the doctrine of potency, the creations of a brotherhood of fathers acting collectively to implement their definitions of manhood in social and ideological forms."[52] O'Brien does not have to go far to conclude, then, that the "ideology of male supremacy"[53] infects *The Human Condition* and that Arendt herself is a "female male-supremacist."[54] Rich follows suit and denounces "the power of male ideology to possess such a female mind, to disconnect it as it were from the female body which encloses it and which it encloses."[55]

What follows from these adamantly dismissive views is, in essence, a series of feminist contestations over the gender of the mind that thinks in Hannah Arendt's female body. As the text most representative of that mind, *The Human Condition* remains the source of feminist inquiry into the genderic allegiances of Arendtian thinking, and (following O'Brien) the Greek polis becomes a popular excavation site for evidence of Arendt's phallocentrism.[56] Nowhere, perhaps, are the phallocentric possibilities of Arendt's polis envy more vividly rendered than in Hanna Pitkin's depiction of the Arendtian public sphere as a bunch of "posturing little boys clamoring for attention . . . and wanting to be reassured that they are brave, valuable, even real."[57] Although "Arendt was female," Pitkin avers, "there is a lot of *machismo* in her vision . . . the men she describes strive endlessly to be superhuman."[58]

Along these same lines, Wendy Brown, in her *Manhood and Politics*, praises Pitkin's "marvelous account" and forwards a critique of Arendtian politics that bears numerous similarities to O'Brien's (61). Like O'Brien, Brown imposes a binary category that erases Arendt's tripartite construction (*animal laborans:homo faber*:action) and maps a gender dichotomy with masculinist preferences upon Arendt's text. In the machismo of Arendtian politics, Brown argues, we find the celebrated image of the Greek polis and its "strutting young men in restless pursuit of honor" (148) who "stomped the ground that fed them [and] suppressed and violated their connectedness with others and with nature" (27). This machismo is enshrined in what Brown takes to be the dichotomy Arendt constructs between *animal laborans* (life, body, necessity, and "woman") and action (politics, freedom, and "manhood"). By locating freedom in the realm of politics, Arendt fulfills the phallocentric desire for release from the realm within which "Woman" has been traditionally configured: bodily maintenance, necessity, and life (180). Thus Brown arrives at O'Brien's conclusion, although from a different direction.[59] Arendt's public realm reasserts an "unapologetic attachment to a politics of manly deeds liberated from concern with life and the lives of others" (29) and Arendt herself exhibits an "extraordinary level of horror at 'the natural.'"[60] Like Rich, Brown notices "something perilously close to pathology" in Arendt's attempt to situate action in a "free space" outside the (female) body. What Arendt cannot admit, Brown says, is that "the body is the locus or vehicle of action, hence of freedom" (196).

## Gynocentric Arendt

For other feminists, the female body as a locus of freedom is precisely what Arendt's thinking mind embraces, and a gynocentric project is something that *The Human Condition* supports.[61] Thus Terry Winant finds Arendt useful for a philosophy that "takes the side of woman and sticks to it,"[62] and Nancy Hartsock concludes that "Arendt remains an interesting and important example whose work indicates some of the beneficial theoretical effects women's experience of both connection and individuation may have. . . . She has, despite her adherence to the Homeric model, reinterpreted it in ways much more congruent with women's than men's experience."[63] If the feminists who read a phallo-centric Arendt magnify the Greek polis of posturing boys, then these commentators redefine Arendtian concepts as gynocentric images that contest Pitkin's bracing metaphor[64] and, in the words of Jean Bethke Elshtain, "stir recognition of our own vulnerable beginnings and our necessary dependency on others, on (m)other."[65] Within this context, nothing takes on more importance for Elshtain and the (m)others than the Arendtian concept of *natality*, which along with "life," "mortality," "worldliness," "plurality," and the "earth," Arendt deems a "condition of human existence" (*HC* 11). In Arendt's phenomenology, natality contrasts to mortality, and marks the human capacity for "beginning something anew" or "acting," not ending.[66]

Hartsock, Winant, Elshtain, and Ruddick appropriate natality or birth in various ways, but all of them find in this category a gynocentric Arendt whose feminist theory (a) is unique to political theorists as women and to "women's experience" with motherhood;[67] (b) invites us to counter the massive denial of " 'the female,' " and restore "commemo-ration and awe" for "the birth of new human beings";[68] (c) provides a context for "a maternal history of human flesh" that celebrates "a birthgiving woman's labor" and "the child who has been born";[69] and/or (d) brings to a feminist "standpoint" insights concerning "a multiplicity of 'mother tongues' " and "cultural and discursive birthplaces."[70] In arriving at this gynocentric Arendt, all of these views link political natality primarily to the domain of *animal laborans* (i.e., to the biological process of the [female] human body, or to activities involved with "vital necessities" like caring and tending for vulnerable human life). This is an inventive move that certainly rescues Arendt from the clutches of hateful machismo, and it goes a long way to correct O'Brien's and Brown's insistence upon the violence inherent in Arendtian power politics. (For her part, Elshtain goes a rather exceedingly long way, casting Arendt as a kind of redemptive figure and finding in Arendtian politics a "pacific image that evokes love, not war."[71] Given Arendt's view of love as "the most powerful of all *antipolitical* human forces," this is a little difficult to sustain) (*HC* 242; my emphasis).

Whatever their advances, however, these gynocentric interpretations proceed from conceptual assumptions that are no less problematic than those that drive the phallocentric readings of Arendt. Most problematically, perhaps, they resolutely erase the very distinctions between labor: action and political:metaphysical upon which Arendt insists. Nowhere is this erasure conceptually more evident and mistaken than in Hartsock's appropriation of an Arendtian concept of power "grounded at the epistemological level of reproduction."[72] To ground Arendtian politics in reproduction and thereby make *animal laborans* (e.g., biology, metabolism, birth, birthgiving, parturition) the source of power is to blur labor:action (power) so thoroughly as to make its uniquely Arendtian aspect unrecognizable. Moreover, although the gynocentric difference feminists have a better grasp of Arendt's action concept of politics than do Rich, O'Brien, and Brown,[73] we should notice that, in the end, they release the very same analytically gendered and normatively weighted binary against *The Human Condition* as do those who charge Arendt with phallocentrism. The only difference lies in that, with the aid of the reconstituted concept of natality, they gender Arendt along the feminine side of the binary rather than the masculine side. The key to this gendering lies in accepting natality as the central category of politics (as Arendt does) and then configuring it literally as women's experience in giving birth and mothering, or figuratively as a feminist concept derived from women's "life activity" (as Arendt does not). As a result of this natalization, Arendt can be coded as a woman who thinks like a woman in a female body, rather than a woman who thinks like a man.

In what I have characterized as the difference feminist struggle between phallocentric and gynocentric accounts of the Arendtian public realm, we might also notice two looming images of Arendt herself, ironically not unlike the images she thinks came to characterize the myth of Rosa Luxemburg. On the one hand, there looms the "propaganda image" of the patriarchal male supremacist; on the other, there looms the "sentimentalized image" of the good-woman-as-mother (*MDT* 36). As Arendt says of Luxemburg so we might say of Arendt: "Her new admirers have no more in common with her than her detractors" (*MDT* 38). This is because Arendt's admirers and detractors both bring to "the vast surveyor's map" nothing more than projections of a problematic interpretive schema that is wedded to a static binary of gender. In so doing, they render little justice to *The Human Condition* and perhaps even less to Arendt herself. We need to turn elsewhere than to difference feminism, then, for more promising and emancipatory receptions of Arendt's political thought.

## Displacing the Gender Binary

Even those feminists who do not share the analytical presuppositions of difference feminism often find it necessary to acknowledge that Arendt's distinction public:private is "historically invidious,"[74] "astounding" in its "denial of the 'women's issue,'"[75] or at least inappropriately viewed as a "preferred state of affairs."[76] In effect, the public:private distinction is often taken as evidence that Arendt is far less compelling as a theorist of gender than she is, in Bonnie Honig's words, "as a theorist of a politics that is potentially activist."[77] But Arendt's conceptual map is contested terrain. Some (nondifference) feminists see the Arendtian public:private as a key to problems of exclusion and to the historical condition of women in particular.[78] Thus Joanne Cutting-Gray argues that "as early as 1933 Arendt saw that the private sphere to which most women are relegated devalues their potential because it valorizes the life process."[79]

I shall return to some of these feminist interpretations momentarily. But as a first response to these projects, I suggest that, the "Woman Issue" notwithstanding, *The Human Condition* carries a far more provocative gender subtext than most feminists have noticed to date.[80] In this provocative (and perhaps unintended) subtext, Arendt not only thematizes gender as a dominant category of modernity; she also displaces it through an action concept of politics. In order to appreciate how Arendt does this, we need to move away from the category public:private and repair instead to the tripartite category labor:work:action (i.e., to the triplet that difference feminists reduce to the doublet PUBLIC/freedom/politics/male:PRIVATE/necessity/labor/female). By recovering the Arendtian triplet, we will discover that the two concepts that Arendt does relentlessly gender as feminine and masculine are not "private" and "public," but *animal laborans* and *homo faber.* Once we understand this, we can also see how the third concept, action, is existentially superior as the embodiment of freedom to both the biological cyclicalities of "earth's servant," *animal laborans,* and the means-end fabrication of "earth's lord and master," *homo faber.*[81]

Arendt's gendering of the *vita activa* takes form in what Hanna Pitkin calls "a pair of inappropriate attitudes or states of mind, both connected with the social: the attitudes of expedient utility [*homo faber*] and of 'process' thinking [*animal laborans*]."[82] If we look to the subtext of Arendt's text, we might notice that the social realm is not only "a historically emergent societal space specific to modernity"[83] but also a symbolic order within which the two attitudes of mind that Pitkin identifies are repeatedly inscribed and represented as feminine and masculine signifiers (or as what Arendt in other contexts calls *feminini generis* and *masculini generis*).[84] Thus, the crisis of modernity—which Arendt brilliantly casts as the struggle between worldless technological automatism and the world of work (*HC* 126–35)—is also a matrix of social attitudes relentlessly driven by the binary of gender. From this Arendtian perspective we might think of the difference feminists as thoroughly in the grip of modernity's favorite symbolic category.

As the subtext of Arendt's text proceeds, the gender binary *animal laborans:homo faber* appears as a complex and multifaceted relationship in at least three aspects.[85] From the first aspect, the relationship is (mutually) beneficial. Thus, "nature and the earth constitute the condition of human *life*" (*HC* 134); but at the same time, "*homo faber* [comes] to the help of the *animal laborans*" by making "the effort of its sustenance and the pain of giving birth, easier and less painful than it has ever been" (*HC* 121). From a second aspect, the relationship is (mutually) oppositional. *Animal laborans* threatens to "consume," "devour," and subjugate *homo faber* by sucking him into "an enormously intensified life process" (*HC* 132). When this happens, "the ideals of *homo faber*" are "sacrificed to abundance, the ideal of *animal laborans*" (*HC* 126). At the same time, with the "huge arsenal" of implements and tools that he uses to "erect the world," *homo faber* tears materials "out of the womb of the earth," and does unspeakable violence to *animal laborans* (*HC* 155). Thus, "the work process takes matter out of nature's hands without giving it back to her in the swift course of the natural metabolism of the living body."[86] With these two aspects in mind, I want to suggest that Arendt is engaged in a double project. By affiliating *animal laborans* with the female and *homo faber* with the male, she sets up a conceptual structure that simultaneously embodies and unmasks the pervasive gender norms of modernity.

In the temporal story that Arendt tells of the *vita activa*, the reproductive-birthing-consuming fertility of the female *animal laborans* eventually triumphs in the modern world over the productive-violating-fabricating artifice of the male *homo faber*. But it would be a mistake to find here the celebration of female difference. For whatever the reversals within this opposition, the gender-symbolic *animal laborans:homo faber* is in its totality for Arendt a "restricted frame of reference" (*HC* 308–9). Taken together, neither "the driving necessity of biological life and labor nor the utilitarian instrumentalism of fabrication and usage" (*HC* 174) foster the condition where freedom appears as the actualization of speech and action in a space of appearances in the world. Indeed, both *animal laborans* and *homo faber* do much to defeat such a space of appearances, and thus they threaten freedom itself. From a third aspect, then, the *animal laborans* and *homo faber* are, despite their opposition, in alliance against an alien power. What Pitkin calls "the twin dangers of process and expediency"—the automatism of labor and the instrumentalism of work—conspire in the modern world to obliterate the human capacity for action.[87]

If in the temporal dimension of Arendt's *vita activa, animal laborans* appears to have triumphed in modernity over *homo faber* and action, then in its existential dimension, which concerns "the basic conditions under which life on earth has been given to man," action is victorious over both labor and work (*HC* 7). Action requires *animal laborans* and *homo faber;* for in order to act, human beings must first satisfy the demands of life and achieve stability, not only to protect "man from nature" but also to "build the world of the human artifice" within which action can take place (*HC* 137, 230). Yet action also triumphs existentially over labor and work because its corresponding condition of plurality and its coequal element of speech actualize in human life the acting together in concert of unique and distinctive persons who are speakers of words and doers of deeds. This solidarity born of unique distinctness, spontaneity, and new beginnings (natality) Arendt also calls politics. In Arendt's theory, then, the action concept of politics sets off an existential experience that is profoundly different from either the singular collectivity of *animal laborans'* repetitive labor or the collective singularity of *homo faber's* instrumental work.[88]

If we keep in mind *The Human Condition's* gender subtext, then for feminism Arendt's recovery of action is significant on at least two levels. On the level of theory, action is a category that can release feminism from the generic-generic force of the familiar bifurcation that divides all human capacities relevant to agency into masculine:feminine (*animal laborans:homo faber).* In its gender subtext, Arendtian theory distances freedom from the static language *(langue)* of gender identity, and locates it instead in acts of personal speech-revelation *(parole)* that resolutely resist the control of predetermined, descriptive, bifurcated signifiers. Once released from the tenacity of such signifiers, feminist theory in its action-coordinating mode is free to reimagine an account of agency that is, among other things, not committed to a gendered telos of the human condition. In keeping with Arendt's emphasis upon freedom as the "who-ness of acting" and not the "what-ness of Being," feminism might theorize human persons as sui generis (HC 205), and thereby liberate subjectivity (feminist theory's current bête noire) from the damaging and unnecessarily repressive scrutiny of the binary of gender. On a practical-normative level, Arendtian action is a category that revivifies feminism as a politics committed to the spontaneity and unpredictability of persons acting together in concert as speakers of words and doers of deeds. By refusing to collapse the labor of *animal laborans* (as woman) into the politics of action, the Arendtian subtext renounces the restrictive language and the nostalgic celebration of "women's traditional capacities" (or the female body) in order to open capacities, as speech-acts, to their full emancipatory potential. Like other social movements in modernity, feminism has had its difficulties distinguishing politics as an action concept from the power of the patriarchal state or (to recall O'Brien) as "paterfamilias" in the public realm. But in the displacement of the gender binary, Arendt not only leaves the celebration of woman *(animal laborans)* out of politics; she also releases politics from the stultifying grasp of *homo faber,* and the negative formulations "masculinity," "patriarchy," and "paterfamilias." As a result, Arendtian theory invites a rebirth in the feminist understanding of politics as "a kind of theatre where freedom could appear," beyond the phallocentric:gynocentric divide (BPF 154).

## The (De)Gendering of Arendtian Politics

From the vantage point of the radical gender subtext and the action concept of politics that I have identified in *The Human Condition,* we might now assess how a new wave of feminist readings have appropriated Arendt's thought for feminist projects. These readings are not interested in gendering the mind and body of Hannah Arendt; nor do they summon the spirits of machismo and maternity to Arendt's corpus. Rather, they seek to bring Arendtian theory to bear upon a conceptual problem that bedevils much contemporary theoretical feminism, and upon which the meaning of a "feminist politics" itself hinges: the identity of the female as *woman*. Since many recent feminist interpretations appropriate Arendt in order to address the gender-identity question, I shall sketch first how academic feminism writ large has brought "the politics of identity" to the political movement called feminism. Then I shall consider how feminists have brought the politics of identity to Arendt.

In academic feminism writ large, the politics of identity is not a unified domain of inquiry but rather a multifaceted enterprise that has unfolded in three discrete (if not dialectical) moments, as the cunning of gender and the concept of woman work their way through feminist inquiry. In the first moment, the problem of identity is formulated in a fashion that resurrects the epistemological assumptions of *difference* feminism for expressly political purposes. Thus it grounds feminist action-coordination in "women's life activity" or a privileged epistemological "feminist standpoint."[89] Feminist politics is linked to the distinctive character of women as a group, and to the undifferentiated subjectivity of (certain) persons as women. In the second moment, the politics of identity takes shape in feminist appeals to *diversity*, with an aim toward hybridizing and complicating "women" in terms of an identity complex of race, class, ethnicity, culture, sexual identity and/or sexuality, and so forth, that may be open to "choosing."[90] In effect, diversity feminism posits "woman" as a "relational term" and a "positional perspective" from which a feminist politics can emerge."[91] In its third moment, the feminist politics of identity theorizes its own negation by designating "women" an "undesignatable field of differences, one that cannot be totalized or summarized by a descriptive identity category."[92] Thus *deconstructive* feminism disrupts all of the univocal and stable social categories that difference and diversity feminisms embrace and instead poses the term "women" as a "site where unanticipated meanings might come to bear."[93]

Just as the initial receptions of Arendt developed against the dominant discursive context of difference feminism, so many recent commentaries map upon Arendt's thinking one or another of the moments I have just sketched in the feminist discourse of identity. From a difference position that reaffirms gender as the "self-conscious development of [women's]

own latent tradition";[94] or "women's power" and "material life activity";[95] or "a community of speaking women,"[96] Arendtian politics is
celebrated as a context within which distinctive persons are reaffirmed
as "women." In this vein, Patricia Yaeger recovers Arendt's figuration of
the polis and imagines "a nexus of women 'combining and covenanting,'
'acting and speaking together.' "[97] Ann Lane suggests that Arendt's
concept of politics is uniquely suited to "the meaning of women's hidden
tradition . . . of doing rather than making."[98] Thus Arendtian politics
provides a "regenerative potential"[99] within which (the unitary subjectivity) "women" can achieve liberation.[100]

From a diversity position that complicates gender with other social-
descriptive categories, Arendtian politics is sometimes redeemed as
(sympathetic to) the idea of a "multiplicity of publics" or "subaltern
counterpublics" that promote "intercultural communication."[101] In this
context, Arendtian plurality absorbs gender into a hybrid of cultural
identities "woven of many different strands."[102] Hence, the Arendtian
public becomes "publics" wherein the "what-ness of Being" is, in all of
its multiculturality, discursively revealed. In another guise, diversity
feminism folds the politics of identity into biographical questions of
Arendt's own Jewish-female-ness, read through the critical categories of
"pariah" and "parvenu" that inform her analyses of anti-Semitism,
totalitarianism (1978), and Zionism (1973), as well as her studies of
Rahel Varnhagen (1974) and her essay on Rosa Luxemburg (1968).
Taken as a whole, this complex of elements allows diversity feminists to
move beyond *The Human Condition* and seize the pariah category as a
useful device for complicating various contexts of difference,[103] exclusion,[104] and marginalization[105] in ways that either elide, assimilate, or
hybridize gender into an identity complex.

Whether they complicate gender or simply reaffirm it, diversity and
difference feminists all take possession of Arendt in order to mobilize
descriptive characteristics—or the "what-ness" of group identity—in the
interests of a liberatory feminist politics. But in this gendering of
Arendtian politics, they also reconfigure Arendt's action concept of
politics beyond recognition. Specifically, these feminist readings blur
the very distinction between a "what" and a "who" upon which Arendtian politics rests. In doing so, they miss the emancipatory point: for, as
we have seen, Arendt locates freedom in the "who-ness of acting"
(speech), not the "what-ness of Being." Arendtian action, understood
as the displacement of the binary of gender (*animal laborans:homo faber*),

decisively forfeits the "description of qualities [one] shares with others," in favor of the existential display of "unique distinctness" in the company of peers, which is the locus of freedom itself (HC 179, 181). Thus Arendt argues that once one becomes a "what" in an action-context, a person's "specific uniqueness escapes us" and freedom disappears.[106] If we take this point seriously, and in relation to the gender subtext of *The Human Condition*, then it seems that an emancipatory Arendtian feminism must reject both the reaffirming strategy of difference feminism that posits the generic-generic "woman," and the complicating strategy of diversity feminism that posits a hybridized subjectivity ("everyone is *mestizo*") as gender-race-class-ethnicity-sexuality under the rubric of social or cultural positionalities.[107] For insofar as both of the latter feminisms reduce action to the reclamation of a particular descriptive social or cultural category/categories, and freedom to identity "standpoints" or a complex of "positions," they fundamentally misconstrue the raison d'être of Arendtian politics.[108] Thus the feminist freedom that these feminisms promote in the name of Arendt is not, in view of Arendt's action concept of politics, freedom at all.

There is a third alternative, however. Hence in response to difference and diversity feminisms, Joanne Cutting-Gray and Bonnie Honig bring a deconstructive conceptual sensibility to Arendt's action concept that comes closer, I think, to the spirit of an Arendtian feminist politics. Implicitly at least, both Cutting-Gray and Honig pose Arendtian action as the displacement of gender (and unitary subjectivity), and recommend to feminism a politics that dismantles the "inhibiting polarities" of gender[109] and contests "(performatively and agonistically) the prevailing construction of sex and gender into binary and binding categories of identity."[110] By degendering Arendtian politics, deconstructive feminism rescues Arendt's action concept from difference in a way that does not commit it to diversity. Thus Cutting-Gray notes that "identities like 'Jew' or 'Woman' are historically constituted" and should not be closed to dialectical resistance.[111] Similarly, Honig calls for resistance to "the violent closures" imposed by "some Jewish and feminist politics of identity," and she unleashes Arendt's theory of action against any concept of "a political community that constitutes itself on the basis of a prior, shared and stable identity" and threatens to "close the spaces of politics."[112]

In effect, deconstructive feminism aims to restore the Arendtian whoness of acting over the what-ness of Being. Hence it recommends a politics of "alterity,"[113] or an "agonistic politics of performativity,"[114] and urges feminism to disrupt an identity politics of generis in favor of the sui generis. Along these lines, Honig rereads Arendtian space(s) agonistically, as both external and internal "sites of critical leverage" within which (communities) and (self) rupture, fragment, and proliferate.[115] In Honig's challenge to proliferate, the sturdy "what-ness of Being" is repeatedly confounded by what Arendt calls the "startling unexpectedness" of the disclosure of "who." At the same time, the who's univocal identity is strategically opened to an unpredictable flux of multiple significations and unanticipated meanings (HC 178). Somewhat similarly, in the name of "a genuine feminist politics of alterity," Cutting-Gray recommends a "plurality to the female political subject" that embraces "unique difference" and the irreducible particularity of "otherness."[116] By emphasizing uniqueness, particularity, and contingency rather than sameness, generality, and fixity, Cutting-Gray argues, Arendtian politics prepares feminist politics "for the dissolution of the female as any set identity."[117] Consequently, both Honig and Cutting-Gray appropriate Arendt in order to disrupt the solid positionalities of "identity" with an evanescent politics of irreducible "identities" (Honig) and radically pluralized otherness (Cutting-Gray). In deconstructive feminism, the meaning of Arendt's action concept of politics as the overcoming of gender (or any and all complexes of "what-ness") is effectively preserved, and feminist identity politics is released to the full Arendtian flux of "[r]esistibility, openness, creativity and incompleteness."[118]

# Existentially Speaking

The strength of deconstructive feminism rests in its appropriation of Arendt's action concept for purposes of freeing identity (and the term "women") from restrictive categories that reduce acting to being and "efface difference for the sake of an equality of sameness."[119] Once it is opened to the equivalent of a play of "resignifications,"[120] Arendtian politics becomes a powerful theoretical starting place for the articulation of an action-coordinating feminism that maintains the category "women" as the critical focus of its politics, *but does not assert it as the political identity of its agents.*[121] For in its recovery of Arendtian action, deconstructive feminism dismantles the fixity of identity-in-kind in favor of "identities"; thereby it makes it impossible for "women" to serve as the unexamined posit of an action-coordinating feminist politics.[122]

In its Arendtian deconstruction of the stability of "what-ness" into the instability and fragmentation of disclosing "who-ness," feminism's third identity moment introduces a new set of complexities into feminist politics. For given the "coeval and coequal" relationship that Arendt's action concept of politics forges with an action concept of speech (HC 189), deconstructive feminism's disclosure of the "who-ness" of Arendtian politics is also, and unavoidably, an encounter with how "who-ness" gets disclosed—or with what it means collectively to speak—in the Arendtian public realm. Thus in Honig's deconstructive feminism, we find not only an agonistic Arendtian politics, but also a dramatic picture of political speech as agon in the Arendtian space—as a verbal game of struggle, dispute, competition, and contest wherein, perhaps, the very terms of political discourse explode and fragment even as they are uttered. Now, if we have gained anything from the linguistic turn of the twentieth century, we have learned that the link between a theory of language (or speech) and a theory of politics is not trivial. So the agonistic account that Honig offers of Arendtian speech-acts directly raises for feminists the question of what constitutes truly emancipatory speech, or expressive collective interaction, in the public space of politics. In responding to this question, Seyla Benhabib has explicitly challenged Honig's formulation with an alternative conception of what constitutes the Arendtian public space. Thereby she opens the possibility of yet another feminist struggle over the Arendtian public realm.

As part of a larger project that is directed to the ethical content of an action politics and "models of public space," Benhabib poses a (Habermasian) communicative concept of "associational public space" as an alternative to the (Nietzschean) disruptive concept of "agonistic public space" that Honig purportedly supports.[123] Although Benhabib traces both of these models in Arendt, she deems the agonistic one "at odds with the sociological reality of modernity."[124] But Arendt's associational model, which seems to have a close affiliation with what Benhabib calls Habermas's "discourse model," is an appropriate starting point "for the feminist transformation of public life."[125] Benhabib understands the associational model in terms of "common action coordinated through speech and persuasion," that takes place in any space that is "the object and location of an 'action in concert.'"[126] In such spaces she imagines speech not as agonistic verbal performativity, but rather as "a conversation of justification" that unfolds in accordance with a norm of "egalitarian reciprocity."[127] In casting Arendtian politics under the spell of Habermas, Benhabib encourages a feminist politics wherein speech "acts" in the interest of proliferating *issues* in a public space, rather than proliferating identities. Unlike Honig, whose Nietzschean agon focuses upon the performative "multiplicity" of the public and the self as a spectacular "event,"[128] Benhabib imagines the Arendtian space as a context of procedural debate, where "the voice of persuasion and conviction" is governed by "the reflexive questioning of issues by all those affected by their foreseeable consequences."[129]

While Honig commandeers Arendtian speech in the service of agonistic disruption and the "who-ness of acting," Benhabib notarizes it for purposes of sustaining the "spontaneity, imagination, participation and empowerment" that is the mark of "what our 'res publica' is all about."[130] As a result, Benhabib's associationalism asserts something for feminism that Honig's agonism diminishes: the power of Arendt's concept of freedom as the politics of citizens speaking and acting in concert in the space of appearances.[131] In this associationalism, feminist theory might be able to find a way out of its current fixation on subjectivity and social recognition (wherein freedom is frequently formulated as the opening of spaces for the celebration of previously repressed group identities), and into a theoretical purchase that thematizes plurality over subjectivity, and politics as collective action and deliberation over politics as group recovery and celebration. Yet at the same time, Benhabib's associationalism presupposes something that Honig's agonism deconstructs: the coherence of the gender identity of feminist performers in the public realm. Thus, even though she calls for a "feminized" practical discourse that challenges "unexamined normative dualisms as between justice and the good life, norms and values . . . from the standpoint of their gender context,"[132] Benhabib posits an "elective affinity" between discourse ethics and "social movements like the women's movement" that derives from "a postconventional and egalitarian morality."[133] By assigning to the women's movement a normative position of superiority, Benhabib does not displace gender so much as reinforce it.[134] In this sense, then, Benhabib is correct to see Honig's agonistic model as at odds "with the sociological reality of modernity." For it is precisely modernity's favorite "reality"—gender—that Honig subverts in her deconstructive appropriation of Arendtian politics, and Benhabib does not.

The details of the exchange between Honig and Benhabib notwithstanding, in the exchange itself we might note the return of a dichotomy
to the feminist receptions of Hannah Arendt. Only in its more recent
incarnation, the dichotomy does not pose Arendtian politics in terms of
a phallocentric:gynocentric attitude, but rather as a Nietzschean:Ha-
bermasian orientation toward the politics of Arendtian speech. (Thus
the identity of an *Arendtian* Arendtian politics of speech in the public
realm—an Arendtian politics as sui generis—remains for the moment
an open interpretive question). Although it may be premature to spot a
new feminist binary lurking in the agonistic:associational formulation of
Arendtian public speech and space, the reading of the category off the
Arendtian corpus confirms that Arendt's political theory continues to be
a locale upon which academic feminism plays out its dominant discursive
struggles, whatever those struggles may be. Even more important, however, we might see in the associative:agonistic struggle the continuing
contemporary fascination with what Hanna Pitkin (not entirely face-
tiously) calls "that endless palaver in the [Arendtian] *agora*"[135]—a
fascination with the way in which public speech takes place.

Indeed, what looms large on the current stage of feminist political
theory are debates over models of discourse (as a symbolic system or a
social practice) and disagreements about the dynamic that constitutes
the emancipatory quality (or qualities) of political speech. Is it consensus
or resistance? Procedure or aesthetics? Communication, negotiation,
argumentation, agonism, persuasion, debate, disruption, deliberation,
theatricality, storytelling or dialogue? Insofar as the Arendtian action
concept of politics places speech at its center, and Arendtian speech is
hermeneutically open-ended, it brings these discourse dilemmas in all of
their ambiguity not only to the question of what constitutes a feminist
politics, but also to the discursive activity of feminist theorizing itself.

Yet in the end, as Pitkin reminds us, "my fellow citizens are less an
audience before whom I try to present a memorable image of self, than
fellow actors in collective self-definition, determining along with me not
our image but who we shall be, for what we shall stand."[136] With this
observation, Pitkin ultimately takes Arendtian politics to task not for
machismo, but for failing to encompass adequately the "for what shall
we stand" question: the question of what politics and public discourse
are *about*, rather than the question of how they "appear." In her critique
of Arendt, Pitkin reminds us that speech-acts and the presentation of
the self (whether as agonal or associative) do not exhaust the activity of

politics. Nor should they exhaust the feminist activity of theorizing about politics. Politics is not only the action context of speaking, which Arendt decisively redeems as freedom. Politics is also the action-context of doing, the strategic practice of pursuing ends and determining means that Pitkin redeems in the question of *justice*, or "what is to be done?"

If strategic action does indeed reside in the question of justice, then justice is something that Arendtian politics—whose focus on freedom resolutely downplays the "what-ness of doing" in favor of the "who-ness of speaking"—is unable to accommodate. But the focus on what is to be done, and doing it, is a political imperative nonetheless. Feminists would do well to maintain this focus, even as we continue to struggle within the Arendtian flux.

## Notes

1. Adrienne Rich, *On Lies, Secrets and Silence: Selected Prose 1966–1978* (New York: Norton, 1979), 211.

2. Seyla Benhabib, "Feminist Theory and Hannah Arendt's Concept of Public Space," *History of the Human Sciences* 6 (1993): 74.

3. Anne Phillips, *Engendering Democracy* (University Park: Pennsylvania State University Press, 1991), 46.

4. Hanna Fenichel Pitkin, "Justice: On Relating Private and Public," *Political Theory* 9 (1981): 327.

5. Elisabeth Young-Bruehl, *Hannah Arendt: For Love of the World* (New Haven: Yale University Press, 1982), 272, 392.

6. Mary McCarthy, "Saying Good-by to Hannah," *New York Review of Books* (22 January 1976): 5.

7. Hans Jonas, "Hannah Arendt 1906–1975," *Social Research* 43 (1976): 3–5.

8. Hannah Arendt, *Men in Dark Times* (New York: Harcourt Brace and World, 1968), 72; hereafter cited as *MDT*.

9. Hannah Arendt, *The Jew as Pariah: Jewish Identity and Politics in the Modern Age*, ed. Ron Feldman (New York: Grove, 1978), 246.

10. Phillips, *Engendering Democracy*, 113; also Benhabib, "Feminist Theory," 98.

11. Young-Bruehl, *Hannah Arendt*, 273.

12. Arendt gave some advice to her friend William Phillips on the occasion of his *Partisan Review* interview with Beauvoir, or "the Prettiest Existentialist" as Janet Flanner called her. Responding to Phillips's complaint about Beauvoir's "endless nonsense," Arendt advised, "Instead of arguing with her [William], you should flirt with her." Carol Brightman, *Writing Dangerously: Mary McCarthy and Her World* (New York: Clarkson Potter, 1992), 330.

13. Arendt, *MDT* 56; Brightman, *Writing Dangerously*, 330.

14. Young-Bruehl, *Hannah Arendt*, 238. In her essay on Rosa Luxemburg, Arendt appreciatively remarks that Luxemburg had a "distaste for the women's emancipation movement, to which all other women of her generation and political convictions were irresistibly drawn" (*MDT* 44). In the face of "suffragette equality," she continues, Luxemburg "might have been tempted to reply, *Vive la petite différence*" (44). Young-Bruehl suggests that this

"maxim," along with an urge to be independent, constituted Arendt's "motherly advice" to young women as well (238). Yet whatever *la petite différence* signified in terms of a woman's intimate relations with a man, Arendt obviously recoiled when it was congealed into the social identifier "woman," in order to represent someone as "exceptional" within her kind. The complex social history of the Jews of Germany provided Arendt with this particular frame of reference (272). So strong were Arendt's views on this matter that she initially threatened to refuse the invitation to become a full professor at Princeton "because the university stressed the 'first woman' aspect in their report to the *New York Times*" (272). And she responded by placing herself within a category that denied the exception in favor of the "kind": *feminini generis* (272).

15. This is a phrase Arendt uses in discussing Luxemburg in a related context in *Between Past and Future: Eight Exercises in Political Thought* (New York: Viking, 1969), 55.

16. Dorothy Kaufmann, "Simone de Beauvoir: Questions of Difference and Generation," *Yale French Studies* 72 (1986): 131; also Mary Dietz, "Debating Simone de Beauvoir," *Signs: Journal of Women in Culture and Society* 18 (1992): 74–88.

17. For an account of Arendt's refugee flight to France, and her subsequent detention and escape from an internment camp at Gurs, whose remaining inmates later died in Nazi concentration camps, see Young-Bruehl, *Hannah Arendt*, 152–66, and Arendt, *The Jew as Pariah*, 57–60.

18. Maria Markus, "The 'Anti-Feminism' of Hannah Arendt," *Thesis Eleven* 17 (1987): 76.

19. Rich, *On Lies, Secrets and Silence*, 212.

20. Mary O'Brien, *The Politics of Reproduction* (Boston: Routledge and Kegan Paul, 1981), 9.

21. Other evaluations of feminist approaches to Arendt include Ann M. Lane, "The Feminism of Hannah Arendt," *democracy: a journal of political renewal and radical change* 3 (1983): 101–17; Markus, "The 'Anti-Feminism' of Hannah Arendt," and Mary Dietz, "Hannah Arendt and Feminist Politics," in *Feminist Interpretations and Political Theory*, ed. Mary Shanley and Carole Pateman (Cambridge: Polity, 1991). For a more extensive review of the literature, see Benhabib, "Feminist Theory."

22. Rich, *On Lies, Secrets and Silence*; O'Brien, *The Politics of Reproduction*; Wendy Brown, *Manhood and Politics* (Totowa, N.J.: Rowman and Littlefield, 1988).

23. Nancy Hartsock, *Money, Sex, and Power: Toward a Feminist Historical Materialism* (Boston: Northeastern University Press, 1985); Jean Bethke Elshtain, *Meditations on Modern Political Thought: Masculine/Feminine Themes from Luther to Arendt* (New York: Praeger, 1986); Terry Winant, "The Feminist Standpoint: A Matter of Language," *Hypatia* 2 (1987): 123–48; Sara Ruddick, *Maternal Thinking: Toward a Politics of Peace* (New York: Ballantine Books, 1989).

24. Pitkin, "Justice"; Lane, "Feminism"; Nancy Fraser, "Rethinking the Public Sphere: A Contribution to the Critique of Actually Existing Democracy," in *Habermas and the Public Sphere*, ed. Craig Calhoun (Cambridge: MIT Press, 1993); Bonnie Honig, "Toward an Agonistic Feminism: Hannah Arendt and the Politics of Identity," in *Feminists Theorize the Political*, ed. Judith Butler and Joan W. Scott (New York: Routledge, 1992); Joanne Cutting-Gray, "Hannah Arendt, Feminism, and the Politics of Alterity: 'What Will We Lose if We Win'?" *Hypatia* 8 (1993): 35–54; Seyla Benhabib, *Situating the Self: Gender, Community, and Postmodernism in Contemporary Ethics* (New York: Routledge, 1992); and Benhabib, "Feminist Theory."

25. Young-Bruehl, *Hannah Arendt*, 244.

26. Ibid., 472.

27. Ibid., 473.

28. McCarthy, "Saying Good-by to Hannah," 8.

29. As Young-Bruehl notes, Arendt wrote numerous topical essays in which she employed the "complex schematism" articulated in *The Human Condition*, but "she seldom paused to recapitulate its main elements," and this "paved the way for many misunderstandings" (*Hannah Arendt*, 318). The proliferation of conceptual distinctions and categories that Arendt put forth in her initial schematism also paved the way for misunderstandings of *The Human Condition* itself, as we shall see. For a very different account of *The Human Condition* as a conceptual configuration of layers of mutually reinforcing "binaries," see Honig, "Toward an Agonistic Feminism," 223.

30. Shulamith Firestone, *The Dialectic of Sex: The Case for Feminist Revolution* (New York: Bantam Books, 1970), 72.

31. Mary Hawkesworth, "Knowers, Knowing, Known: Feminist Theory and Claims of Truth," *Signs: Journal of Women in Culture and Society* 14 (1989): 536.

32. Sandra Harding, "The Instability of the Analytical Categories of Feminist Theory," *Signs: Journal of Women in Culture and Society* 11 (1985): 292.

33. Linda Alcoff, "Cultural Feminism Versus Post-Structuralism: The Identity Crisis in Feminist Theory," *Signs: Journal of Women in Culture and Society* 13 (1988): 408.

34. Iris Marion Young, *Justice and the Politics of Difference* (Princeton: Princeton University Press, 1990).

35. Nancy Fraser, Introduction to *Revaluing French Feminism: Critical Essays on Difference, Agency and Culture*, ed. Nancy Fraser and Sandra Lee Bartky (Bloomington: Indiana University Press, 1992), 6.

36. Linda M. G. Zerilli, "Rememoration or War? French Feminist Narrative and the Politics of Self-Representation," *differences: A Journal of Feminist Cultural Studies* 5 (1991): 1.

37. Fraser, Introduction to *Revaluing French Feminism*, 6.

38. Parveen Adams and Jeff Minson, "The 'Subject' of Feminism," in *The Woman in Question*, ed. Parveen Adams and Elizabeth Cowie (Cambridge: MIT Press, 1990), 83.

39. Rich, *On Lies, Secrets and Silence*, 205–7; O'Brien, *The Politics of Reproduction*, 93, 101. Rich, a lesbian feminist poet and essayist, was active in the antiwar movement and became one of the most influential cultural feminist thinkers of the 1970s. O'Brien comes to political theory with, as she puts it, "the sensibilities of a woman and a midwife" (11). But she also arrives trailing remnants of a socialist feminist perspective analytically indebted to Marx, methodologically attuned to (formal) dialectics, and academically directed toward the study of social and political thought. O'Brien's perspective is primarily theoretical and critical, and her framework links a Marxist analysis of labor as emancipatory activity to a difference feminism of women's labor as reproduction—literally, to labor as birth. Thus she contends that "birth is a subject and object of an integrative feminist philosophy" (92). For a sympathetic account of O'Brien that is equally critical of Arendt, see Virginia Held, "Birth and Death," in *Feminism and Political Theory*, ed. Cass Sunstein (Chicago: University of Chicago Press, 1990).

40. Rich, *On Lies, Secrets and Silence*, 206, 212; O'Brien, *The Politics of Reproduction*, 100. As I shall argue shortly, *The Human Condition* contains a gender subtext, but that does not necessarily suppose that it also contains an adequate theorization of how women have fared within the reversals of the *vita activa*. Thus O'Brien and Rich are correct to notice the androcentrism of Arendt's analysis; that is, how Arendt relegates the struggles of women "to footnotes" (Rich 1979, 204). For a related critique, see my "Hannah Arendt and Feminist Politics."

41. Rich, *On Lies, Secrets and Silence*, 208.

42. O'Brien, *The Politics of Reproduction*, 101.

43. Rich, *On Lies, Secrets and Silence*, 212.

44. O'Brien, *The Politics of Reproduction*, 100.

45. Since O'Brien offers the more explicit and systematic critique of Arendt, I focus my attention in what follows primarily upon her argument in *The Politics of Reproduction*. Given O'Brien's emphasis upon feminist political praxis and reproduction as a "process," it may seem that my characterization of her strategy as an "ontological politics" misrepresents her feminist philosophy. Indeed, she argues that it is Arendt's phenomenological analysis of the *vita activa* that bears insuperable "ontological burdens" to which her own theory is presumably invulnerable. Nevertheless, despite her objection to the "genderic apartheid" of such categories as public:private, and her call for "the abolition of the phoney wall between public and private, first nature and second nature, continuity and discontinuity" (115), O'Brien grounds her notion of a feminist political praxis in a "feminist principle" that is animated by "woman's reproductive consciousness" and "reproductive labor" (59). The latter, she says, "is a synthesizing and mediating act" that "confirms women's unity with nature experientially and guarantees that the child is hers" (59). Unlike women, men are "naturally alienated from their children" (58) and possess a "splintered and discontinuous" rather than "continuous and integrative" reproductive consciousness (59). Thus on a metaphysical and ontological level, O'Brien recapitulates through the category "reproduction" the very gendered oppositions she apparently wants to demolish in praxis.

46. Hannah Arendt, *The Human Condition* (Chicago: University of Chicago Press, 1958), 7; hereafter cited as *HC*.

47. O'Brien, *The Politics of Reproduction*, 100. To appreciate what a disastrous initial move this is for O'Brien's analysis, we might recall the explicit disclaimer with which Arendt begins her conceptual analysis: "To avoid misunderstanding: the human condition is not the same as human nature, and the sum total of human activities and capabilities which correspond to the human condition does not constitute anything like human nature" (*HC* 9–10). Starting from the perspective of an *Existenz* philosophy that theorizes "doing" not "being," Arendt dismisses the question of human nature or essence as something "only a god could know and define . . . and the first prerequisite would be that he be able to speak about a 'who' as though it were a 'what'" (10). O'Brien misses this crucial point because her analysis is captured by a singular conceptual category and a philosophical strategy that grants priority to the idea of being over doing, subjectivity over interaction, and "what" over "who." This is the category of *woman*. As a result, she erroneously assumes that the concepts that Arendt designates as labor:work:action are sociological categories of humans as male:female beings, rather than concepts that designate potential human capacities, or mentalities embodied in human capacities, as Arendt intends.

48. O'Brien, *The Politics of Reproduction*, 100, 121.

49. Ibid., 110. In order to understand what O'Brien loses by erasing the Arendtian configuration of labor:work:action in favor of the conceptual (gendered) dualism public:private, we should remember that Arendt assigns a "public" realm to both *homo faber* (work) and to action (politics) (*HC* 160). Arendt also identifies an "actual historical development that brought labor out of hiding and into the public realm" (87). Thus, public and private (and social) cut across labor, work, and action in a variety of ways. Because she misses this, O'Brien cannot appreciate Arendt's critique of the predominance of the public realm of the "exchange market" in modernity. Nor can O'Brien grasp Arendt's action concept of politics as a counter to the very sphere her own "politics of reproduction" is meant to challenge: the sphere of (economic, capitalist) production.

50. O'Brien, *The Politics of Reproduction*, 101.

51. For her part, Rich does not appear to have a secure understanding of the way in which *vita activa* operates in Arendt's theory. Commenting upon Arendt's failure to consider women's condition, she writes, "The withholding of women from participation in the *vita*

*activa*, the 'common world,' and the connection of this with reproductivity, is something from which [Arendt] does not so much turn her eyes as stare straight through unseeing" (212). From an Arendtian perspective this claim is incoherent, because the *vita activa* is neither a category of "participation" nor a "realm" that some humans are allowed and others denied. Rich may be confusing *vita activa* with Arendt's notion of "action" (politics). For Arendt, however, labor:work:action are within the *vita activa* (*HC* 7–11).

52. O'Brien, *The Politics of Reproduction*, 103–4. O'Brien also argues that from this perspective of politics, Arendt indirectly sanctions the continuing violence of "paterfamilias," who must maintain the "separation of public and private" (103). Given Arendt's anti-instrumentalist conception of politics as action, and her condemnation of violence as antipolitical, this is perhaps O'Brien's most astonishing (and wrongheaded) claim.

53. O'Brien, *The Politics of Reproduction*, 110.

54. Ibid., 9.

55. Rich, *On Lies, Secrets and Silence*, 212.

56. Regardless of their sympathies, almost all feminist interpreters seize upon the Greek polis image that Arendt employs of the public realm. I suspect that this is partly because of the provocative quality of the image itself, but also because feminist interest in Arendt's work develops alongside a significant amount of feminist scholarship on the representation of women in ancient political thought, the social history of women in classical Greece and goddess worship in ancient cultures. As for Arendt's own views, it is important to remember that she is not concerned "with the historical causes for the rise of the Greek city-state," but rather with how the polis (as a metaphor for politics) functions as a "remedy" for the "frailty" of human action (*HC* 196). This claim was not enough to inoculate the Arendtian public realm concept against charges of irrelevance, nostalgia, or romanticism in the general literature, or masculinism in feminist commentary.

57. Pitkin, "Justice," 338.

58. Ibid., 338. Pitkin's influential essay is a common reference point for many feminist interpretations of Arendt (e.g., Hartsock, *Money, Sex, and Power*; Markus, "The 'Anti-Feminism' of Hannah Arendt"; Karen Hansen, "Feminist Conceptions of Public and Private: A Critical Analysis," *Berkeley Journal of Sociology* 32 (1987): 105–28; Brown, *Manhood and Politics*; Jennifer Ring, "The Pariah as Hero: Hannah Arendt's Political Actor," *Political Theory* 19 (1991): 433–52; Honig, "Toward an Agonistic Feminism"; Benhabib, "Feminist Theory." A considerable portion of these commentaries (Hartsock, Brown, Benhabib, Ring) is directed toward negotiating the metaphor of the posturing boys, with a view toward securing a fix on Arendt. In a sense, then, Pitkin's essay provides a second scene upon which the (often) hyperbolic gendering of Arendt is played out. Matters are further complicated by the fact that Pitkin renders her formulation of Arendtian machismo in a deliberately provocative way that sets up an Arendtian macho politics of superhuman male immortals initially (338–39), only to reject this reading of Arendtian politics as "empty posturing" later (341). Some commentators recognize the conceptual implications of Pitkin's rhetorical shift (Hartsock, Benhabib); others apparently do not (Brown).

59. That is, Brown rejects "a prefigured conception of masculinity" grounded in some biological "maleness" (14), and she distances herself from feminist projects tied to "revaluing reproductive work" and "childrearing" (205). Thus she conceptualizes gender as a textual and symbolic construct open to interpretive critique, rather than as a mode of consciousness or a "process" linked to reproduction, as O'Brien does. Nonetheless, her feminist project is grounded in an interpretive binary of gender that consistently formulates "life" and "body" positively and "manhood" and "politics" negatively. Hence, for Brown, the *vita activa* represents Arendt's "fear of being consumed by the life process, by natural necessity and the body" (31). Brown reads this as an unfortunate vestige of Arendt's being "a female intellectual

prior to the days of the 'second-wave' women's movement"—by which I take her to mean that second-wave feminism reunited woman, life, and body in an appropriate and meaningful way (31). So perhaps she celebrates a kind of female difference after all.

60. Ibid., 28. It is worth noting that Brown, like O'Brien, tends to (mis)read the *vita activa* through the category of human nature, and the fundamental activities of labor, work and action as sociological entities that identify people in terms of class, occupation, or gender (24–27). So, even as she correctly interprets Arendt as arguing that speech and action in the public realm "embody defiance of the incorrigible fact of [human] mortality," Brown mistakenly concludes that Arendt deems people who have historically been denied access to the public realm as "animal laborans," "idiotic," and "deprived" (24). This mistake is so pervasive in the feminist critiques of Arendt that it bears repeating that the concepts labor:work:action do not function as empirical, historical, or sociological generalizations in her theory, much less as validations of some historical status quo. They are existential categories intended to reveal what it means to be human and in the presence of other human beings on earth and in the world. It is from this existential imperative to "think what we are doing" that Arendt theorizes the world alienation of nearly all individuals as *animal laborans* in the modern age. (See Dietz, "Hannah Arendt and Feminist Politics," 234; also Pitkin, "Justice," 342; and Sandra Hinchman, "In Heidegger's Shadow: Hannah Arendt's Phenomenological Humanism," *Review of Politics* 46 (1984): 183–211.

61. Hartsock, *Money, Sex, and Power;* Elshtain, *Meditations on Modern Political Thought;* Ruddick, *Maternal Thinking;* Winant, "The Feminist Standpoint."

62. Winant, "The Feminist Standpoint," 146.

63. Hartsock, *Money, Sex, and Power,* 253–54.

64. Ibid., 211.

65. Elshtain, *Meditations on Modern Political Thought,* 110.

66. HC 9. Although natality is "intimately connected" to all three human activities of labor:work:action, it bears its closest connection, Arendt argues, not with labor or work, but with action (politics) in its aspects of spontaneity, unpredictability, and irreversibility, which neither the automatic processes of *animal laborans* nor the means-end lineations of *homo faber* allow. For Arendt, then, natality is "the central category of *political,* as distinguished from metaphysical, thought" (9; my emphasis). Natality exhibits itself as freedom in the realm of action and speech, not in the realm of biological life, metabolism and growth (7). Insofar as the gynocentric-difference feminists reassign natality to the (female) body and motherhood, they mistake Arendt's meaning. For a somewhat different perspective on Arendtian natality that is nevertheless sympathetic to Elshtain and Ruddick, see Kathleen Jones, *Compassionate Authority: Democracy and the Representation of Women* (New York: Routledge, 1993), 173–85. For a nongynocentric perspective that is closer to Arendt's meaning, see Patricia Yaeger, *Honey-Mad Women: Emancipatory Strategies in Women's Writing* (New York: Columbia University Press, 1988), 94–96.

67. Hartsock, *Money, Sex, and Power,* 224–26, 237.

68. Elshtain, *Meditations on Modern Political Thought,* 110.

69. Ruddick, *Maternal Thinking,* 209–11.

70. Winant, "The Feminist Standpoint," 127.

71. Elshtain, *Meditations on Modern Political Thought,* 110.

72. Hartsock, *Money, Sex, and Power,* 259.

73. This is especially true of Hartsock, who offers a number of interpretive corrections to formulations like O'Brien and Brown's. For example, in contrast to Brown who argues that Arendt reenacts Plato's pathology toward the body (*Manhood and Politics,* 25), Hartsock correctly insists that Arendt "rejects Plato's argument that the body is merely a shadow of the soul" in favor of a "Homeric" view of the primacy of the body and "embodied action" (*Money,*

*Sex, and Power*, 213). Relatedly, against O'Brien, Hartsock recognizes that what Arendt views with horror "is not nature itself but the failure to differentiate oneself from the world of nature" (214). Finally, and in an *Existenz* spirit that both Brown and O'Brien fail to appreciate, Hartsock casts the polis not as a form of machismo, but as "a guarantee against the futility of individual life" (217) that Arendt finds in the automatic processes and artificial cyclicalities that distinguish modern world alienation.

74. Honig, "Toward an Agonistic Feminism," 222.

75. Benhabib, *Situating the Self*, 115.

76. Nancy Fraser, *Unruly Practices: Power, Discourse and Gender in Contemporary Social Theory* (Minneapolis: University of Minnesota Press, 1989), 160.

77. Honig, "Toward an Agonistic Feminism," 215.

78. Markus, "The 'Anti-Feminism' of Hannah Arendt," 82; also Lane, "The Feminism of Hannah Arendt"; Hansen, "Feminist Conceptions"; Cutting-Gray, "Hannah Arendt"; Benhabib, "Feminist Theory."

79. Cutting-Gray, "Hannah Arendt," 50 n. 1.

80. Here I am deliberately distinguishing between, as Susan Okin puts it, an analytical focus "on either the absence or the assumed subordination of women in a political theory," and a focus on "the gendered structure" of a society, a culture, a theory, or a text. Okin, "Reason and Feeling in Thinking about Justice," in *Feminism and Political Theory*, ed. Sunstein, 15. In turning to the second focus, I find *The Human Condition* far more positively illuminating for feminist purposes than it is on the first. I have already noted such a subtext in Arendt's action concept of labor, which I take as a symbolic representation of *women's* practices and activities (Dietz, "Hannah Arendt and Feminist Politics"). Now, however, I wish to amplify this subtext in a way that introduces *homo faber* and action into the gendering of the *vita activa*.

81. On this score, I disagree with Joan Landes, who contends that "although [Arendt] is nowhere concerned either with women or with the gendered construction of subjectivity . . . [she] addresses the performative dimension of human action and human speech" in a way that is useful for feminists. Landes, "Jürgen Habermas, *The Structural Transformation of the Public Sphere*: A Feminist Inquiry." *Praxis International* 12 (1992): 114–15. To the contrary, I shall argue that Arendt's "performative" concept of action/speech is useful for feminists precisely because it is, at once, posed against and displaces the gendered subjectivity of *animal laborans* and *homo faber*.

82. Pitkin, "Justice," 340; also Arendt, *HC*, 82.

83. Fraser, *Unruly Practices*, 160.

84. Arendt, *Men in Dark Times*, 45; Young-Bruehl, *Hannah Arendt*, 272.

85. The gender binary of *animal laborans:homo faber* is complex in another way as well. Both are good examples of Arendtian concepts that, no matter how externally differentiated, are internally loaded with numerous (and sometimes contradictory) dimensions of meaning. It is little wonder, for example, that Arendt's feminist critics have had difficulty sustaining a coherent account of labor, for this term as *animal laborans* carries (at least) the following connotations: nature, animality, (human) biology, (human) body, fertility, birth, reproduction, childbirth, cyclicality, seasons, basic life-needs (food, clothing, shelter), certain kinds of toil, repetition, "everyday" tasks (eating, cleaning, mending, tending, washing, cooking, resting, etc.), housework, the domestic sphere, abundance, the blessing of life as a whole, the female; but also life:death, pain:pleasure, necessity, routinized processes, consumption, (economic) demand, "automatism," automation, technological determinism, the society of jobholders, and the nullity that is advanced capitalism in late modernity. Given Arendt's otherwise discerning sense for conceptual distinctions, it is odd that she could reduce so many irreducible aspects of human experience into one specifically gendered category—unless that is precisely what she wants us to think about.

86. *HC* 100. Arendt suggests that both *animal laborans* and *homo faber* exercise violence toward each other (labor "consumes" man-made things; work "violates" nature, etc.) and both are destructive (labor from the standpoint of the world, work from the viewpoint of nature) (100). But nowhere does Arendt more vividly encompass the violent character of the labor:work relationship than when she represents *homo faber* as the male supremacist whose ideology of instrumental fabrication carries with it "both violence and violation" over the life process of the female body of *animal laborans* (139). In this vivid encounter between nature and artificer, labor and work, Arendt captures in *homo faber*'s mentality the fear "of being consumed by the life process, by natural necessity and the body"—the fear that Wendy Brown mistakenly assigns to Arendt herself (*Manhood and Politics*, 31 n. 29). Here as well, Arendt recognizes precisely what Mary O'Brien claims she overlooks: that "violence is needed to overcome the imperiousness of biological necessity" (*Politics of Reproduction*, 103).

87. Pitkin, "Justice," 341.

88. Within the *vita activa*, action carries with it no singular or unitary Latin equivalent such as *animal laborans* is to labor and *homo faber* is to work. This is because Arendt designates action not as an "identity" (animal, man) but as a context of collective performativity that reveals identities in plurality.

89. Hartsock, *Money, Sex, and Power*, 226.

90. Alcoff, "Cultural Feminism Versus Post-Structuralism," 432.

91. Ibid., 434. Not all diversity feminists adopt Linda Alcoff's distinctive spin on gender, race, class, and ethnic identity as "choices" or "positions" from which woman can constitute herself. But her argument has had considerable influence on those feminist theorists and philosophers who are inclined to focalize identity in terms of what Alcoff calls "immediately recognizable oppressed groups" such as "Jewish people," "black men," "women of all races," etc. (432). Such individuals, Alcoff argues, "can practice identity politics by choosing their identity as a member of one or more groups as their political point of departure" (432). Acting out such "choices" constitutes what Alcoff calls "positionality." For a related perspective on the politics of "social group differences," see Young, *Justice and the Politics of Difference*.

92. Judith Butler, "Contingent Foundations: Feminism and the Question of 'Postmodernism,' " *Praxis International* 11 (1991): 160.

93. Ibid.

94. Lane, "The Feminism of Hannah Arendt," 115.

95. Hartsock, *Money, Sex, and Power*, 253, 261.

96. Yaeger, *Honey-Mad Women*, 277.

97. Ibid., 276.

98. Lane, "The Feminism of Hannah Arendt," 115.

99. Ibid.

100. When Lane refers to "the self-conscious development of [feminists'] own latent tradition," she seems to mean women's moral distance from the construction of "the modern capitalist and technological state" (115). Although Lane rejects any sort of essentialist view of women's traditional activities, she comes rather close in this notion to confusing exclusion with a collectively superior morality, grounded in the identity of "women." Furthermore, by automatically reading "women" out of the capitalist picture, Lane preempts the need to approach gender, morality, and politics in advanced capitalist societies from an analytical perspective that is highly attuned to the particularities and complexities of discrete historical and social contexts (all of which include women, in various ways).

101. Fraser, "Rethinking the Public Sphere," 126.

102. Ibid., 127.

103. Markus, "The 'Anti-Feminism' of Hannah Arendt."

104. Ring, "The Pariah as Hero"; Lane, "The Feminism of Hannah Arendt."

105. Norma Moruzzi, "Re-Placing the Margin: (Non)Representations of Colonialism in Hannah Arendt's *The Origins of Totalitarianism*," *Tulsa Studies in Women's Literature* 10 (1991): 109–20.

106. *HC* 181. I emphasize the "action context" because I do not mean to suggest that Arendt undervalues the "what-ness of Being" over the "who-ness of acting" in all possible contexts. The relationship she establishes between these two things is complex. On at least two occasions, Arendt herself had recourse to expressions of "Being": when she called herself *feminini generis* (see note 14); and when she observed in her address on the occasion of accepting the Lessing Prize, "I cannot gloss over the fact that for many years I considered the only adequate reply to the question, Who are you? to be: a Jew. That answer alone took into account the reality of persecution" (*MDT* 17).

What do these appeals to gender and ethnicity mean, especially in light of Arendt's critique of the "what-ness" that obliterates the unique distinctiveness of the agent? Perhaps a clue lies in the Lessing address, where she clarifies that in the extreme situation of Nazism it was imperative to acknowledge "not a special kind of human being . . . [nor] a reality burdened . . . by history . . . but a political fact through which my being a member of this group outweighed all other questions of personal identity" (18). Thus in the totalitarian context of the Third Reich, identifying oneself as a Jew is an act of purposeful will, a response to the political fact of "a hostile world" (18). Arendt also suggests that in a different world, where the space of appearances flourishes, and action and plurality are actualized, "such an attitude would seem like a pose" (18). In this latter world, expressing oneself in terms of a solidified group identity impedes rather than enhances the solidarity that springs from the "disclosure of 'who,' " or personal identity (*HC* 179). Thus, Arendt wants to free the personal from the group in the action context of speech-politics; but in dark times, when political speech is silenced, she insists upon the individual's responsibility to confront political reality, embrace the language of Being (or group identity), and speak.

107. Fraser, "Rethinking the Public Sphere," 141 n. 27.

108. I do not mean to suggest that the difference and diversity feminists completely erase the significance of the "who-ness of acting" or the revelation of personal identity through speech in Arendtian politics. Hartsock, for example, appreciates that "for Arendt, human plurality results in the 'paradoxical plurality of unique beings' " (*Money, Sex, and Power*, 215). Fraser acknowledges "the salience of discourse" in the "construction" of "cultural identities" ("Rethinking the Public Sphere," 141); Ring recognizes that "display of individuality" is integral to Arendtian action ("The Parish as Hero," 445); and Markus notes Arendt's concern for " *'Who' we are*" ("The 'Anti-Feminism' of Hannah Arendt," 78). Nevertheless, none of these accounts confronts the problematic relationship that Arendt herself establishes between the "what-ness of Being" and the "who-ness of acting." Thus "women's life activity" (Hartsock), "cultural identities" (Fraser), or the "pariah" as a "group identity" (Ring, Marcus), rest rather uncomfortably alongside Arendt's action concept that rejects a politics of (descriptive, social, passive) identity in favor of a politics of "the unique and distinct identity of the agent" as disclosed in (performative, political, active) speech and deed (*HC* 180). Markus even obfuscates Arendtian natality when she takes it to define " *'what'* we are in a society" ("The 'Anti-Feminism' of Hannah Arendt," 78); for Arendt clearly associates natality with action, "the one miracle-working faculty of man" that is aligned with "originality and unprecedentness," not with predictable social categorizations (*HC* 246–47).

109. Cutting-Gray, "Hannah Arendt," 49.

110. Honig, "Toward an Agonistic Feminism," 216.

111. Cutting-Gray, "Hannah Arendt," 49.

112. Honig, "Toward an Agonistic Feminism," 231, 227.

113. Cutting-Gray, "Hannah Arendt," 36. There is a problem of conceptualization in

Cutting-Gray's appropriation of "alterity" as "distinctness," however, and it makes hers a less fully deconstructive feminism than Honig's (50 n. 2). Arendt notes that alterity or "otherness" is possessed by everything that "is"—it *transcends* "every particular quality" (*HC* 176). As such, alterity distinguishes the human as species-being, but not as a unique person who is "alive." Only "distinctness," which humans reveal in and through expression and communication, secures each one of us as sui generis (176–81). By collapsing distinctness into alterity (otherness), Cutting-Gray forfeits the very concept she needs for a more radical (and genuinely Arendtian) insistence upon the irreducible multiplicity of our distinct "identities." As a result, when she targets "all who have shared in the historical condition of otherness" as one of the aspects of "a genuine feminist politics of alterity," Cutting-Gray sounds more like a diversity than a deconstructive feminist ("Hannah Arendt," 49).

114. Honig, "Toward an Agonistic Feminism," 225.

115. Ibid., 231.

116. Cutting-Gray, "Hannah Arendt," 49.

117. Ibid. Similarly, Honig notes that Arendt would have been wary of "any proclamation of homogeneity in 'women's experience' or in 'women's ways of knowing' " or in any feminist politics that "relies on a category of woman that aspires to or implies a universality that belies . . . significant differences and pluralities within—and even resistances to—the bounds of the category itself" ("Toward an Agonistic Feminism," 227).

118. Honig, "Toward an Agonistic Feminism," 217; also Cutting-Gray, "Hannah Arendt," 48–50.

119. Honig, "Toward an Agonistic Feminism," 231; also Dietz, "Hannah Arendt and Feminist Politics," 244–45.

120. Butler, "Contingent Foundations," 161.

121. I am not arguing that recourse to the term "woman" has no part in the speech-action of a feminist politics, only that it must be rejected as an "identity" posit that is prior and "politically paramount" (Alcoff, "Cultural Feminism Versus Post-Structuralism," 432). It seems not only inevitable but also necessary that in the domain of speech-action (politics) feminists will have to deploy descriptive identity categories. First, these categories are integral to the critical activity of unmasking existing conditions, institutions, relations of power, policies, and ideologies that systematically exclude, or overtly oppress persons by explicitly or implicitly imposing group identities that are formulated negatively. Second, descriptive terms are a part of the strategy and rhetoric of speech-action (politics) itself. Depending upon the action context, self-revelatory speech that makes an appeal to a particular group identity may be a more effective tactic than speech that eschews such utterances as an absolute rule. Nevertheless, purposeful appeals to "what-ness" ("as an Anglo, middle-class, heterosexual woman, I . . . ;" "we Chicanas . . . ;" "all gay African-Americans . . .") are speech-acts that an Arendtian deploys warily at best, in recognition of the havoc they wreak upon spontaneity and the damage they inflict upon the unique distinctiveness, or the "who-ness," of the speaker.

122. What I mean to imply in this reference to "identities" is a paradox of deconstructive feminism: even as it seeks to disrupt "identity," it stays fixated upon it. Honig (upon whom my discussion of deconstructive feminism will now focus) demolishes "identity" as a congealed term of political discourse; but it remains a conceptual a priori in her political critique, insofar as, ruptured and proliferated, it comes back around in the form of "identities" ("Toward an Agonistic Feminism," 231–32). Whether Honig is simply appropriating Arendt's action concept as a critical tool against difference and diversity-identity feminisms, or whether she thinks that the proliferation of identity/identities is and must be what politics is all about, is not entirely clear. Her concluding remarks appear both to separate and align "matters of identity" and "politics," thus leaving uncertain what she takes to constitute the action content of politics as performative (232). This may be a subset of a larger problem, since the

actual "action content" of Arendtian politics is, as we shall see, a long-standing matter of debate (see Pitkin, "Justice").

123. Benhabib, *Situating the Self*, and "Feminist Theory." Honig clearly aligns Arendt more on the "Nietzschean" than the "Habermasian" side, although she recognizes Arendt's distance from Nietzsche as well ("Toward an Agonistic Feminism," 232). In any case, it is not obvious to me that Honig shares Benhabib's notion of public space as "a sphere that comes into existence whenever and wherever all affected by general social and political norms of action engage in a practical discourse" (105). Insofar as she posits Arendtian "space" not only in/as political communities, but also as "sites of critical leverage" "within the frame of . . . 'identities' themselves" (231), Honig treats "space" as also a site of *internal* disruption wherein the agent subverts his or her own "identity" performatively. On this account, then, speech is presumably the act whereby the agent discloses this internal disruption-resistance publicly. Hence while Honig makes speech problematic both inside the agent and in the act, Benhabib makes it problematic only as the agent in the act (i.e., in the agent's already given engagement in collective, practical discourse). Two rather different theories of language/speech/agency/self seem to be driving Honig's and Benhabib's Arendtian sensibilities, and I think that in some ways both of them distort aspects of Arendt's thought. But pursuing this matter is beyond the scope of the present essay.

124. Benhabib, "Feminist Theory," 110.

125. Benhabib, *Situating the Self*, 95; "Feminist Theory," 110.

126. Benhabib, "Feminist Theory," 102.

127. Benhabib, *Situating the Self*, 89.

128. Honig, "Toward an Agonistic Feminism," 220, 234 n. 40.

129. Benhabib, *Situating the Self*, 95.

130. Ibid.

131. Benhabib is not the only commentator to find in Arendt's public-realm theory a source for a critical and emancipatory account of what constitutes a specifically feminist politics. Other studies use particular Arendtian concepts to analyze gender or women in historical publics and public spheres—Joan Landes, *Women and the Public Sphere in the Age of the French Revolution* (Ithaca: Cornell University Press, 1988); Mary P. Ryan, *Women in Public: Between Banners and Ballots, 1825–1880* (Baltimore: Johns Hopkins University Press, 1990); Fraser, "Rethinking the Public Sphere"—or to clarify the nature of republicanism and "engendering democracy" (Phillips, *Engendering Democracy*), feminist citizenship (Mary Dietz, "Context is All: Feminism and Theories of Citizenship," *Daedalus* 116 [1987]: 1–24), and the problem of authority (Jones, *Compassionate Authority*).

132. Benhabib, *Situating the Self*, 113.

133. Ibid., 110.

134. Apparently, gender is a sociological reality that Benhabib is willing to question in the name of feminist politics, but it is not something that her discourse model actively displaces or thoroughly subverts. By congealing feminism as a politics into the category "women's movement," and linking the latter with a normative ideal indebted to Carol Gilligan, Benhabib simply reaffirms the validity of gender difference on the level of social movements. Thus her "ethics of dialogue" is an odd notion: on the practical-normative level, it allows for challenges to conventional gendered arrangements, but at the level of social theory, it designates a form of human interaction ("the women's movement") in terms of a gendered ideal.

135. Pitkin, "Justice," 336.

136. Ibid., 346.

# 3

# Conformism, Housekeeping, and the Attack of the Blob: The Origins of Hannah Arendt's Concept of the Social

*Hanna Fenichel Pitkin*

Hannah Arendt was arguably the greatest political theorist of the mid-twentieth century. Her greatness centered on the constellation of three interrelated concepts that she treated as almost synonymous: action, politics, and freedom. Though we all use these words, she thought, we do not really understand their meaning because we have lost the experiences to which they correspond. She regarded these experiences as the most valuable that human beings could have—called them our "lost treasure"—and tried to restore the full significance of these words so that we might recover the experiences as well.

By these complex, interrelated terms Arendt meant, first of all, the human capacity for creativity, spontaneity, doing the unexpected, launching something unprecedented and valuable. Second, because we tend to associate creativity and initiative with science, technology, and the material world, she stressed nonmaterial culture, what she called the "web of relationships": all the institutions, norms, standards, customs, practices, rituals, and ideas that make up a human culture. Culture doesn't just grow like a tree; people make it, enact it. Yet we are mostly not aware of the degree to which the patterns by which we live are our own doing; we do not want to know the actual extent of our responsibility. Of course no one of us can do much to change the web, but since it consists in what we all do, we all together can surely change it. Therefore, lastly, Arendt stressed our collective powers and responsibilities, and focused on politics and public life. Real freedom, she held, means jointly bringing our human capacity for initiative to bear on what's wrong in our present arrangements.

Those were her most valuable teachings, and they have rightly gotten the most attention from commentators. This essay will say no more about them. It concerns not what Arendt considered valuable and lost to us, but what she considered harmful and very much with us, what gets in the way of recovering her lost treasure. Each of the three elements in that treasure has its negative counterpart. To freedom corresponds necessity; to action, behavior; and the negative counterpart to politics is society or "the social." It is primarily the social that keeps us from our lost freedom, and that is the topic of this essay.

## The Concept of the Social in *The Human Condition*

Best to begin in medias res, with the fully developed concept of the social in Arendt's most systematic and best-known work of political theory, *The Human Condition*.[1] What is most striking about it is that Arendt not only hypostasizes the adjective "social" into a noun even though there is a perfectly good noun, "society," available, and even though she plays no comparable games with "politics" and "political"; she also personifies, perhaps even demonizes the social. Clearly, in *The Human Condition* Arendt thinks that we moderns are in a bad fix, but if one asks whose fault that is, the answer seems to be, the social.

It is worth cataloging some of the verbs Arendt employs with the nouns "society" and "social," to discover the extent of the menacing activities of this "curiously independent Moloch," as Dagmar Barnouw calls it.[2] In *The Human Condition* society or the social is variously said to "absorb," "embrace," "devour" people or other entities; to "emerge," "rise," "grow," and "let loose" growth; to "enter," "intrude" upon, and "conquer" realms or spheres; to "constitute" and "control," "pervert" and "transform"; to "impose" rules on people, "demand" certain conduct from them; to "exclude" or "refuse to admit" other conduct, or people; to "try to cheat" people and to act under a "guise." It's like a science-fiction story: an evil monster, a Blob, entirely external to and separate from us, has appeared as if from outer space, intent on taking us over, gobbling up our freedom and our politics.

The menacing liveliness of the social contributes greatly to the book's central structural paradox: having traced at length the inexorable advance of this monster, Arendt concludes in a way that can only strike a reader as blithe, that "needless to say" we have lost none of our human "capacities." In particular, in her last paragraph she invokes our capacity for critical thought, calling the reader back to the "very simple" proposal made in the prologue, that we must "think what we are doing" (HC 324, 5). What *we* are doing? But *we* are not doing anything; our troubles are the work of the social. Coming from a thinker whose main effort was to teach us our powers—that we are the cause of our troubles and should stop doing as we do—the science-fiction vision of the social as Blob is truly astonishing. When and how did Arendt come to think about society in a manner diametrically opposed to, and undermining, her best teaching?

One looks in vain for a definition of "the social" in *The Human Condition;* Arendt never defines her terms. She acknowledges that the concept of society is very old, our English word deriving from the Latin *societas,* which she says meant "an alliance . . . for a specific purpose," such as "to rule others or to commit a crime." Nevertheless, the social as Arendt understands it is modern. "The emergence of the social realm . . . is a relatively new phenomenon," no older than "the modern age."[3]

The focus is society in this—the modern—sense. The nearest thing to a definition is an aside shortly before the chapter called "The Rise of the Social," a passing allusion to "the rise of society, *that is,* the rise of the 'household' (*oikia*) or of economic activities to the public realm" (HC 33; my emphasis; see also 38, 43, 56). Arendt contends that the ancient Greeks kept natural necessity—all activities concerned exclusively with survival and the needs of the body—in the household, under human control by the paterfamilias and contained within the walls of privacy. Noting the derivation of our word "economics" from the Greek term for household, she holds that, for the Greeks, economics was private. When, in modern times, it went public, it became the social. Thus society is "the public organization of the life process," and "the form in which the fact of mutual dependence for the sake of life and nothing else assumes public significance" (HC 46; see also 29, 45).

The rise of the social, then, seems to mean the development of a complex economy: trade, money, division of labor, a market, eventually the whole extensive, centralized economic system we know, in which people are profoundly interdependent, yet no one is in charge. People are deployed and regulated, but only, as we say, by "the market." When what used to be housekeeping goes large-scale and collective or, in more economic terms, when production is no longer mainly for use, and money and trade begin to generate market forces, natural necessity becomes dangerous: as it reaches beyond the supervision of any human head, people are confronted by the large-scale consequences of what they do as inevitabilities, as if they were the work of some alien force (HC 47, 45).

If the social is people conducting themselves in such a way that the large-scale consequences of what they do are not within anyone's control, then politics must be the effort to control such consequences where they do harm. Politics, then, would mean collective self-governance, supplying the body politic with a head to reassert human control over the socioeconomic forces generated by the mutual dealing of large numbers of people driven by the biological necessities of their bodies.

That might be a Hegelian or a Marxist reading of Arendt, but it won't do. For Arendt's social includes not merely the headless, unregulated market economy, but also central regulation of that market in communist, socialist, or even welfare-state systems, in a sort of "gigantic, nation-wide administration of housekeeping" (HC 28). Replacing the paterfamilias by the administrative state apparently is no solution, but just another extension of the social.[4] Indeed, Arendt complains that modern government is too much *like* a household, where the paterfamilias surely did rule, and she worries that the modern nation-state is too much like "a family," which makes it social, since "society always demands that its members act as though they were members of one enormous family" (HC 28, 39). Arendt here offers another quasi-definition: "the collective of families economically organized into the facsimile of one superhuman family is what we call 'society'" (HC 29).

But what does that mean, and how does it relate to economics? Arendt offers at least three connections. First, a family is a biological unit, and its locus is the household, where one is supposed to tend to biological needs. Thus social may equal familial because "society constitutes the public organization of the life process itself" (HC 46; see also 45). Second, a family is assumed to have "only one opinion and one interest," which, "before the modern disintegration of the family," were represented by the paterfamilias (HC 39). Similarly, in collective life today we assume "one interest of society as a whole in economics . . . [and] one opinion of polite society in the salon." The last phrase, invoking yet another sense of the word "society," introduces a third connection: like the family, society is concerned with "behavior," making all sorts of "demands" to regulate people's conduct: "It is decisive that society, on all its levels, excludes the possibility of action. . . . Instead, society expects from each of its members a certain kind of behavior, imposing innumerable and various rules, all of which tend to 'normalize' its members, to make them behave, to exclude spontaneous action or outstanding achievement" (HC 40). Like an irritated parent, society is out to make us behave ourselves, to regulate and stifle our individuality. (It is surely significant that behavior is related to something called "misbehaving," while there is no comparable term in the vocabulary of action.) "The best 'social conditions,'" that is, the most "social" of social conditions, "are those under which it is possible to lose one's identity" (HC 214).

But again, what is the connection between, on the one hand, suppressing individuality, imposing rules of behavior, the conformity of the salon, and on the other hand, biology, and necessity? Salon behavior and biological urges seem almost polar opposites. Furthermore, all the ways of equating social with familial seem to imply an unhealthy expansion of the private into public life, with the result that some commentators have read Arendt as equating the social with an expansion of the private sphere. But Arendt says very clearly that the social threatens and ultimately destroys privacy, just as it does the public. The social is "neither private nor public," but some kind of "curiously hybrid realm" (HC 28, 35; see also 59, 61).

"Curiously," indeed. Attempting to locate the social in relation to the other central terms deployed in The Human Condition is altogether a frustrating experience. The contrast of social and political holds up fairly well, although even here one is startled to discover that the social finds its own characteristic "political form in the nation-state," its own characteristic "form of government" in bureaucracy, and even its own characteristic, albeit "perverted," version of "acting together" in pressure politics and lobbying (HC 28, 40, 203). Mapping the social onto the distinction between public and private is harder, as just noted. Mapping it and behavior onto the book's central triad of labor, work, and action is still worse. Behavior and the social contrast with action, of course. But action also contrasts with labor and work. In Arendt's version of ancient Greece, labor and work are both private, action is public, and there is no social yet, nor any behavior. The latter are phenomena of the modern world, from which action, politics, the public, the private, and even work have virtually disappeared. That leaves only labor, so perhaps labor, behavior, and the social should coincide.

But if behavior is simply labor, why doesn't Arendt just go on using the word "labor" for it? Also, labor as such is not a bad thing for Arendt. It is one of the eternal, "fundamental human activities" that correspond to "the basic conditions under which life on earth has been given to man" (HC 7). Its elimination would "rob biological life of its most natural pleasures [and] deprive the specifically human life of its very liveliness and vitality" (HC 120). Nothing comparably favorable is ever said about behavior or about the social. Labor, moreover, is the production (and consumption) of what keeps us alive. Behavior does not seem to involve the production of anything tangible. Instead, like action, behavior produces changes in the "web of relationships." Specifically, behavior produces normalized, rule-governed conduct.

Perhaps the social, like so many of Arendt's categories, is best seen not as an objective fact in the world but as a matter of attitude and outlook; not an objectively new mode of conduct or characteristic of modern people, but a modern attitude, even a modern illusion, a *mentalité?*[5] Perhaps instead of changing the adjective into a noun, Arendt should just have used the adverb, "socially," because the social is simply people doing whatever they do in a social way. This move is helpful, but it is also problematic.

Take, for instance, the ambiguous way in which Arendt criticizes Locke and Marx for construing economic growth as inevitable, as an almost biological process beyond human choice. Both of them "wished to see the process of growing wealth as a natural process, automatically following its own laws and beyond willful decisions and purposes" (HC 111). Later, however, Arendt comments that this way of seeing economic growth is in fact "correct," albeit "only in a laboring society" (*HC* 209). A laboring society, however, is exactly what Arendt herself says we have, or are (*HC* 126). So the way that Locke and Marx "wished to see" things is the truth.

More is at stake here than Arendt's assessment of Locke or Marx. She herself writes about the social in exactly the same mode for which she takes them to task: as an irresistible force independent of human "willful decisions and purposes." Ever since housekeeping was permitted to go public, Arendt says, one of the "outstanding characteristics" of the "new realm" that is the social has been "an irresistible tendency to grow, to devour the older realms of the political and private" (*HC* 45). This irresistible growth resulted from the "liberation of . . . a natural process," which indeed is the " 'life process of society,' as Marx used to call it" (*HC* 255). Arendt's society, however, unlike Marx's, is a specifically modern phenomenon rather than our timeless species-being. It had a specific historical onset, and its growth proceeded in a series of "stages" (*HC* 40, 45, 256). In the first stage, "expropriation . . . created both the original accumulation of wealth and the possibility of transforming this wealth into capital through labor" (*HC* 255–56). In that early stage, society "could impose its rules of behavior only on sections of the population and on parts of their activities"; it was confined to the elite in their salons (*HC* 45). Government was even more confined, being the "one-man rule" of a single monarch (*HC* 40).

As the process advanced inexorably, society grew and devoured more and more people, until now, as "mass" society, it "embraces and includes all members of a given community" (*HC* 41). As a corollary, monarchy also became more inclusive, in a series of steps culminating in bureaucracy, "a kind of no-man rule" (*HC* 40, 45). Though this last stage is the rule of no human being, it is not free of domination; the new ruler is called "society." This "stage was reached when society became the subject of the new life process, as the family had been its subject before." Nor is society, "the 'collective subject' of the life process," a merely "intangible entity, the 'communist fiction' needed by classical economics." The social is real now, its power over everyone tangible and evident, "not a matter of theory or an ideology" (*HC* 256, 33; see also 116).

These questions about the meaning of Arendt's concept of the social in *The Human Condition* are not merely idiosyncratic. They were already posed, in somewhat more abbreviated form, by Margaret Canovan in her pioneering *The Political Thought of Hannah Arendt* (1974). Canovan, too, found Arendt's concept incoherent and she, too, sought to make sense of it.[6] She argued that the social consisted of "two separate strands of meaning," whose distinctness and relationship Arendt neither acknowledged nor theorized. In the first strand of meaning, society is the *oikos* enlarged; in the second strand it means "high society with its characteristic manners and vices: the fashionable world, originally composed of only a tiny fragment of the population."[7] This duality is revelatory not only methodologically, with respect to Arendt's "manner of thinking, which is unusually multidimensional." It is revelatory also at the substantive level, engaging "another and deeper ambivalence in Arendt's thought: the problem of "man's power in the modern age and his powerlessness," whether we can or cannot do anything about the mess we are in, which Canovan also called "the general question of the capacity of modern man for action."[8]

Canovan was surely right in these observations, but she took them no further. Nor was she in a good position to do so, since Elisabeth Young-Bruehl's rich biography of Arendt was not available, and Arendt's early essays had not yet been conveniently collected by Ron Feldman.[9] Only recently have a few commentators begun to interpret *The Human Condition* in terms of the circumstances of Arendt's own life and the ideas of her earlier works.[10] This essay builds on their discoveries and on Canovan's insights to locate the origins of the social in Arendt's early life and work.

## "Society" in *Rahel Varnhagen*

Long before society was a Blob for Arendt or connected with economics or housekeeping, it appeared already in a very different sense in her earliest writings (after the dissertation) as meaning "high" or "respectable" or "fashionable society." It was the society we connect with the society pages in the newspaper, into which debutantes emerge at their "coming out parties," the society of social functions and social climbing. Although such things presuppose some wealth, they have little to do with economics, and the issues that concerned Arendt about them were those of status and conformity, not of biological necessity and labor.

Society in this sense is central to *Rahel Varnhagen*, Arendt's biography of an eighteenth-century German Jewish woman, a salonnière, based primarily on her letters. Arendt wrote most of it in Berlin between 1929 and 1933, finished it in 1938 in Paris, but did not publish it until nearly twenty years later.[11] Rahel Varnhagen, as Arendt presents her, was born Rahel Levin, and tried very hard almost her whole life long to assimilate and win acceptance into high society. She tried to do so by marrying a gentile aristocrat, but his family wouldn't let him. She tried to do so by conducting a salon frequented by aristocrats and important personages. For a time she tried to flee the issue by a romantic withdrawal into inner life, but found this also unsatisfactory. She then tried again to assimilate by converting to Christianity and changing her name. Finally she succeeded by marrying a gentile, who even obligingly discovered some aristocratic ancestors in his family tree. And then, having succeeded in her lifelong project, she changed her mind, and decided it had all been a terrible mistake. On her deathbed, Varnhagen reportedly said: "The thing which all my life seemed to me the greatest shame, which was the misery and misfortune of my life—having been born a Jewess—this I would on no account now wish to have missed."[12] Arendt opens the biography with these words, and takes Varnhagen's change of heart as her theme.

The penultimate chapter of the book, called "Between Pariah and Parvenu," introduces a distinction of great significance for Arendt's later work. Following Bernard Lazare, Arendt holds that the Jews are a pariah people, and Varnhagen was a pariah—an outcast, member of a category ascriptively defined as inferior by birth, and excluded.[13] Pariah status, being ascriptive, is something that befalls one. Some pariahs, raised entirely within the subculture of their group, may feel entirely at home there. Others, feeling no pariah cultural ties, may be shocked to find themselves so classified.

Although ascriptive, pariah status is often associated with various markers—stereotypes—some of which can be altered or disguised by sufficient effort, like one's name, dialect, or social manners. Status lines may be more or less rigidly drawn, and the disadvantages of pariah status more or less severe. Most pariahs do have some options within the limits set by the category that has befallen them. A significant option for German Jews in Varnhagen's time was assimilation, which Arendt calls becoming a "parvenu," someone who tries to "climb by fraud into a society, a rank, a class, not [his] by birthright" (RV 199). This word of course is from the French, where it means someone who has arrived, but was particularly used by the French aristocracy to designate those of the nouveau riche middle class who sought, or even achieved, aristocratic status. Thus it connotes only those *recently* arrived, with their crass, pushy manners, their ostentatious display of wealth, their lack of noblesse oblige.

In *Rahel Varnhagen* Arendt applies this originally class-oriented term to Jewish assimilation. Her interest, however, is neither in the acceptance achieved by some parvenus nor in the continuing denial of acceptance implicit in the word's pejorative connotations, but in the *striving* for acceptance that constitutes one of the options open to pariahs. What makes that option attractive is that it sometimes works; where the pariah faces a class rather than a caste system, with demarcation lines not too strictly drawn, he may be able to "pass" into a higher rank. In Varnhagen's milieu, "a personal solution of the Jewish problem, an individual escape into society, was difficult, but not flatly impossible" (7).

Even a successful parvenu, however, rarely manages to achieve full acceptance. The established elite never loses track of who really belongs. When Varnhagen was thirty-nine years old and a social success, her aristocratic "friend," Wilhelm von Humboldt, referred to her as "the little Levin girl," and after she had married into society he wrote, "now at last she can become an Excellency and Ambassador's wife. There is nothing the Jews cannot achieve."[14]

Whatever degree of external success the parvenu achieves, moreover, comes only at a price, and in Arendt's opinion, "the price demanded of the pariah if he wishes to become a parvenu is always too high" (*RV* 213). Becoming a parvenu requires not just some isolated, spectacular act of deception, but a long-term, total commitment affecting every aspect of life and self. The price of success as a parvenu is becoming a parvenu-ish sort of person, and however well he may fool society, the parvenu must live with the one observer whom he cannot fully fool: himself.

Succeeding as a parvenu requires internalizing the standards of those to whom one would assimilate. In theory it might seem that one could be a consummate deceiver toward others while retaining perfect integrity toward oneself, but in practice this is just about impossible. Success as a parvenu requires a passionate desire "to honor [one]self in [one's] superiors, and to track down their good qualities in order to love them." Mere "obedience" or "simple and undisguised servility" may work for a servant, but "for social success and for positions in society," more is necessary: "a strenuous effort to love" (*RV* 199). The parvenu must love his betters and whatever they love, and hate what they hate. And what they hate includes people like himself. In an anti-Semitic society, a successful parvenu must become an anti-Semite. He must endorse existing stereotypes about his pariah group, condemn the stereotypical characteristics in his fellows, and strive to eradicate them in himself.

The parvenu strives to get by as an exception, "to penetrate society solely as [an] individual" (*RV* 85). Success therefore depends on maintaining his exceptionality; he has a stake not only in being different but also in the others' remaining pariahs. Jews who sought to assimilate in Varnhagen's time, Arendt says, shared the Enlightenment's view of traditional Judaism as superstition, of the Jews as "an oppressed, uncultured, backward people who must be brought into the fold of humanity." They "fervently" confessed that the Jews were "a deservedly despised nation" (*RV* 8, 220). Every assimilated, parvenu Jew "felt like a Grand Sultan in contrast to his poor, backward co-religionists. From their degradation, from the great gap that separated him from them, he drew his consciousness of being an exception, his pride in having come so gloriously far" (*RV* 216).

In short, parvenus must not merely separate themselves radically from their pariah group, but also support and join those who condemn it. They must make themselves "unable to distinguish between friend and enemy, between compliment and insult, and [must] feel flattered when an anti-semite assures them that he does not mean them, that they are exceptions" (*JaP* 107). Seeking acceptance from those who despise the likes of him, the parvenu must identify with his oppressors. He "begs from those whom he ought to fight," and appraises his pariah-hood "by the standards of those who have caused it." Thus "he becomes automatically one of the props" supporting the discriminatory social order; in sum: "a scoundrel" (*JaP* 78; *RV* 224).

But severing connections with the people of one's parentage and ancestry is not easy, nor is it accomplished in a single, decisive moment, either. Every sophisticated parvenu Berlin Jew still remained "connected to the Jewish people and the old manners and customs he had discarded," both through his memories and through his "inescapable provincial Jewish relations" (*RV* 216). Here we arrived at a second high price of becoming a parvenu. One must not only become a scoundrel, but also deny a part of oneself, establish a permanent division within oneself, declare war on oneself, become a "battlefield" (*RV* 79). To succeed, the parvenu must commit himself utterly to an inner change that can never be accomplished.

In the opening chapter of Arendt's biography, called "Jewess and Schlemihl," we meet Varnhagen as battlefield, in profound self-disparagement. "Schlemihl" is a Yiddish word meaning an unfortunate who, through no fault of his own, lacks what it takes to succeed, an innocent for whom things never go well. Varnhagen appraises her own limitations: "not rich, not beautiful, and Jewish" (*RV* 25, 9). Of these, the last is "the greatest shame," a "misery and misfortune" that Varnhagen most wants to "flee" (*RV* 3, 223): "The Jew must be extirpated from us, that is the sacred truth, and it must be done even if life were uprooted in the process" (*RV* 120). Jewishness is like a genetic physical defect, "as inescapable as a hump on the back or a club foot," yet the parvenu struggles precisely to escape it, to change it into "a character trait, a personal defect in character," that might be overcome by effort and discipline (*RV* 217–18; see also 13).

This peculiar kind of discipline, however, itself becomes a character trait, an obsession, and the inner struggle is interminable; precisely to overcome this "defect" one must be eternally on one's guard, must in fact keep it alive. In order to "become another person outwardly," Varnhagen could not afford to forget the "shame" of her Jewishness even "for a *single* second. I drink it in water. I drink it in wine, I drink it with the air, in every breath" (*RV* 120). The inner struggle being endless, even when the parvenu meets with outer success, he fails. Construed "as a personal problem the Jewish question was insoluble" (*RV* 221).

One becomes a parvenu, then, at the price of any stable or integrated sense of oneself: one cannot afford to know, yet cannot afford to forget. Varnhagen was highly introspective and enormously preoccupied with herself, yet during most of her life that introspection amounted only to a romantic flight from reality; it did not succeed in producing self-knowledge.

Similarly, the parvenu can achieve no stable, realistic sense of his own powers. Defining himself and his goal in terms of acceptance by certain "superior" others, he fluctuates between delusions of grandeur (being so superior, they can give me and make me into *anything*, once they accept me), and equally delusional helplessness (without them, I am nothing, and besides, I'll never fool them). Thus, "the parvenu's overestimation of himself, which often seems quite mad," is the counterpart of "the tremendous effort, and the straining of all his forces and talents" required for him "to climb only a few steps up the social ladder." His mood, therefore, is totally volatile, fluctuating wildly with the latest sign from on high: "The smallest success, so hard-won, necessarily dazzles him with an illusory: everything is possible; the smallest failure instantly sends him hurtling back into the depths of his social nullity" (RV 202).

In addition, the parvenu must constantly be on guard against any spontaneous personal impulses, perceptions, judgments, or feelings that might betray him. Every personal wish and reaction must be subordinated to the one, central goal of social acceptance, which requires craving what "they"—not oneself—regard as valuable. So the parvenu is "gnawed" by an insatiable craving for "a multitude of things which he [does] not even really want, but which he [cannot] bear to be refused." He must "adapt his tastes, his life, his desires to these things," and thus is required "to sacrifice every natural impulse, to conceal all truth, to misuse all love, not only to suppress all passion, but worse still, to convert it into a means for social climbing" (RV 205, 208). Thus he no longer dares to be himself in anything even for a moment, to perceive or enjoy anything directly, without the mediating others. The parvenu can experience the world "only with the pseudoreality of a masquerade," because he has condemned himself "to lead a sham existence" (RV 225; see also 205).

Here we arrive at a third high cost of the parvenu option: the loss of reality. No more than he can afford a stable sense of his own self, can the parvenu independently assess what is real. For most of her life, Varnhagen's "consciousness of reality was dependent on confirmation by others" (RV 23; see also 177 and JaP 82). The others defined what there was, what it was like, and what it was worth. "The world and reality" had, for Varnhagen, "always been represented by society. 'Real' meant to her the world of those who were socially acknowledged" (RV 177). But this required suppressing her own perceptions and responses, lest they compete or conflict with the social definition of the world. So she had to pay for the social acceptance she sought in the coin of "the 'true realities,'" those simple, personal pleasures and perceptions unrelated to status, which she could not afford: "a bridge, a tree, a ride, a smell, a smile." She won social acceptance "only by sacrificing nature," that is, "green things, children, love, weather" (RV 210, 213).

Along with reality and direct, natural pleasures, truth also had to go. Truth becomes whatever society says is true. The parvenu must focus on impression management; Varnhagen had to master the "art of representing her own life: the point was not to tell the truth, but to display herself; not always to say the same thing to everyone, but to each what was appropriate for him." Consequently there is no such thing as "an honest parvenu." One succeeds in society "only at the price of lying, of a far more generalized lie than simple hypocrisy" (RV 117, 209, 208). To be able to make something true by getting others to believe it is a fabulous power, but also a debilitating constraint: "one is not free when one has to represent something in respectable society."[15] The constant need to manipulate combines with the importance of avoiding any independent perception, to interfere with thinking: if you want to succeed as an exception, it is best not to generalize, not to think. The parvenu becomes "ultimately incapable of grasping generalities, recognizing relationships or taking an interest in anything but his own person" (RV 214). To focus on the task, one may have to wear blinkers.

No wonder, then, that Arendt concluded the costs were too high.

## The Biographical Origins of the Social

Arendt claimed to have written Varnhagen's story as Varnhagen herself might have told it, using her "reflections upon herself," and making no criticism of her that did not "correspond to [her] self-criticism" (RV xv, xvi). No doubt she was able to proceed in this way because Varnhagen's retrospective self-criticism contained the lesson that Arendt wanted to teach, and which probably drew Arendt to Varnhagen's story in the first place.[16] But why did that lesson matter to the young Hannah Arendt? What did it mean to her, in terms of her own life and world? Commentators are quick to note a certain identification of this biographer with her subject, but obviously Arendt's Germany was very different from Varnhagen's, and the two women were not at all alike. Both were Jewish, assimilated, shy, intelligent, and gifted women, to be sure, but Arendt was no social climber anxious for acceptance by respectable society, nor did she experience her Jewishness as a misfortune to be extirpated.

To understand Arendt's interest in Varnhagen's life and retrospective self-criticism, one needs, I believe, to look beyond such actual, objective parallels to more psychological ones, and specifically to Arendt's relationship with her teacher, Martin Heidegger. But that sort of rude, if posthumous intrusion into her personal life requires some advance justification, particularly because Arendt herself so vehemently rejected the modern tendency to personalize, to psychologize, to reduce the public and political to intimacy and introspection. Arendt would have loathed what this essay is about to do to her, as an example of our contemporary illegitimate "eagerness to see recorded, displayed and discussed in public what were once strictly private affairs and nobody's business."[17] Writing Varnhagen's biography, Arendt sought strenuously to "avoid that modern form of indiscretion in which the writer attempts to penetrate his subject's tricks and aspires to know more than the subject knew about himself or was willing to reveal; what I would call the pseudoscientific apparatuses of depth-psychology, psychoanalysis, graphology, etc." For this reason she excluded from consideration in the book an obviously relevant topic that Varnhagen herself, she said, had not addressed: the "Woman Problem, that is, the discrepancy between what men expect of women 'in general' and what women could give or wanted in their turn" (RV xviii).

It is indeed true that a psychobiographical approach to political theory can easily become reductionist, dismissing political doctrines as "really merely" about the theorist's psychic problems or fantasies. But in Arendt's case, almost the reverse is true. Only when the remote, abstract, Grecophile concepts of *The Human Condition* are traced back to their roots in Arendt's life does their true political power and contemporary public relevance emerge.

Hannah Arendt was born in Königsberg, in East Prussia, in 1906. Like so many middle-class, urban German Jews, she grew up assimilated, though aware of her Jewishness. Her parents were not religious, but there were rabbis in their circle of friends, and she was sometimes taken to synagogue by her paternal grandfather. Arendt later said that "the word 'Jew' was never mentioned at home" during her early childhood, that she first encountered it in the anti-Semitic remarks of other children, after which she "became, so to speak, 'enlightened'" (the German word also suggests sexual enlightenment, learning "the facts of life"). Later, as an older child, she was aware that she "looked Jewish," but simply as a fact, she said, "not in a way that made me feel inferior."[18]

The anti-Semitism she encountered did not "poison" her soul, she said, because her mother always "protected" the child's "dignity" by insisting that "One may not duck out of it! [*Man darf sich nicht ducken!*] One must defend oneself!" This sounds more like a moral duty than like protection, however, and the story that Arendt proceeds to tell is not exactly, or not merely, about self-defense, but reflects the complex relations between assimilated German Jews and the embarrassingly un-cultivated Jewish immigrants from the East, relations that also figured in Varnhagen's life:

> when my teachers made anti-Semitic remarks—usually they were not directed at me but at my other classmates, particularly at the Eastern Jewesses—I was instructed to stand up immediately, to leave the class, go home, . . . [where] my mother would write one of her many letters. . . . But if remarks came at me from other children, I was not allowed to go home and tell. That did not count. One had to defend *oneself* against remarks from other children.[19]

Of her mother, Arendt said that, however assimilated, she was "of course Jewish. She would never have had me baptized! I assume she would have slapped my face if she had ever discovered that I had denied being a Jewess myself. Simply out of the question, so to speak."[20]

Arendt's parents' friends were professionals, teachers, and musicians. Her mother had studied music in Paris; she read Proust in French with Hannah. Arendt's father was an engineer. He suffered from syphilis, contracted in his youth and supposedly cured then, but reappearing in its tertiary stage when she was two. She was four when he became bedridden, five when he was institutionalized, seven when he died. She became very close to her paternal grandfather in this period, the one who took her to synagogue, who was also a great storyteller. But then he, too, died, shortly before her father. The next year, so did an uncle with whom she had just vacationed. The year after that, World War I began, and Arendt's mother took her to Berlin, where their life was financially strained, at least until her mother remarried six years later. Arendt was apparently never close to her stepfather, who already had two teenaged daughters of his own. In a short, crucial period, then, Arendt lost her father and two surrogate fathers, along with the familiar, relatively opulent, provincial world of her early childhood. Her mother recorded that the child showed no reaction to her father's death, but that thereafter she turned inward and became "opaque."[21]

Arendt's mother was much influenced by ideas of progressive educa-tion, including the encouragement of "girls to go the education routes long reserved for boys."[22] Later Arendt said that she owed to her mother "above all an education without any prejudices and with all opportunities."[23] Yet her mother seems also to have had quite conventional and traditional ideas about femininity and sexual conduct. Arendt claimed that she herself had never been very interested in "the Woman Question," and her biographer, Young-Bruehl, adds that "she was suspicious of women who 'gave orders.' "[24]

Like Jewishness and gender, Arendt claimed, politics too was of little concern to her in her youth. Her parents were socialists and progressives, active in the Social Democratic movement, though affiliated with its gradualist rather than its radical, Spartacist wing. Nevertheless, her mother was "an ardent admirer" of the Spartacist Rosa Luxemburg, and when the Spartacist uprising began in 1919, excitedly told her daughter to "pay attention, this is a historical moment!"[25] Later Arendt rejected the suggestion by Gershom Scholem that she was among those "intellectuals who came from the German left." Arendt responded, "I was interested neither in history nor in politics when I was young. If I can be said to 'have come from' anywhere, it is from the tradition of German philosophy."[26]

When the eighteen-year-old Arendt came to the University of Marburg, it was primarily to study with Martin Heidegger, to whom (as she explained much later) students flocked from all over Germany, drawn by rumors that in his classes, "thinking has come to life again; the cultural treasures of the past, believed to be dead, are being made to speak. . . . There exists a teacher; one can perhaps learn to think."[27] Arendt encountered this brilliant professor, she later wrote, as "the hidden king [who] ruled in the realm of thinking," a realm to which she had craved admission since reading Kant at age 14.[28] As for what Heidegger saw when he looked at her, a friend and fellow student testifies that Arendt was "shy and turned inward, with striking, beautiful facial features and lonely eyes, [and] immediately stood out as 'unusual' and 'singular.' "[29] Heidegger himself was thirty-five, unhappily married, and already the father of a family, still at work on his first great book, *Being and Time*.

Since Young-Bruehl's biography, everyone knows what happened. The brilliant young professor and the brilliant student half his age had an affair, a romance. It lasted less than a year. Almost nothing is known about who initiated it and how, or how it ended. Heidegger, who later averred that Arendt had been the inspiration for his work in this period, and that she was "*nun einmal* the passion of his life," did not leave his wife. Arendt left Marburg, with a letter of recommendation from

Heidegger, and went first briefly to study with Husserl, then to write a dissertation with Karl Jaspers.[30]

It must have been thrilling, one imagines, to be singled out by this master teacher with his coterie of adoring students, ruler of the realm of philosophy to which she most desired access, this paternal figure who preferred her not only to the other students but also to his wife. Later Arendt came to see the affair in a rather different light. While mostly remaining publicly loyal to and protective of Heidegger, Arendt spoke of him privately with a kind of indulgent contempt, for example finding in his letters "the same mix of vanity and deceit—or better, cowardice—as before."[31] She also came to see her own role with him as deceitful, as a kind of romantic, inauthentic, self-abnegation. After he publicly attacked her book, she wrote in a private letter: "I know that it is intolerable for him that my name appears in public, that I write books, etc. I have really fibbed to him about myself all the while, behaving as . . . if I, so to speak, could not count to three, except when it came to giving an interpretation of his [work, in which] case it was always gratifying to him when it turned out that I could count to three and sometimes even to four."[32]

Under the supervision of Jaspers, who knew nothing of the affair until decades later, Arendt found a dissertation topic through which she could both develop her scholarship and work through her feelings about Heidegger: Saint Augustine's concept of love. She found that Augustine distinguished among love as craving or appetite, love as man's relationship with God, and love of one's neighbor, and she argued for the centrality of the third notion. The essence of love, in effect, is a mutuality between neighbors who perceive each other realistically in both their generic human limitations and their concrete particularity but love each other for who they are, without romance.

Upon completing her dissertation, Arendt moved to Berlin, prepared it for publication, began work on Varnhagen, and married a former fellow student from Heidegger's classes. She also reencountered Kurt Blumenfeld, a friend of her parents, now the head of a Zionist organization, who became her "mentor in politics." Concerning "the so-called 'Jewish Question,'" she later wrote, "Blumenfeld opened my eyes."[33] Of course she had continued to be aware of anti-Semitism and the fact of her own Jewishness, but both seemed altogether irrelevant to what she cared about, her intellectual and scholarly life. The best measure of her obliviousness in this regard is surely her choice of dissertation topic: of all possible thinkers she chose to specialize in a Christian saint. What's a nice Jewish girl doing with a topic like that?

Even without Blumenfeld, however, something else would soon have opened her eyes. In early 1933, after Hitler became chancellor and after the Reichstag fire, there began a wave of illegal "arrests," beatings, torture, and disappearances of radicals, Jews, and people who happened to look Jewish. Arendt wrote later that previously she "had been primarily occupied with academic pursuits. Given that perspective, the year 1933 made a lasting impression on me." Not that she had been blind to the Nazis before: "That the Nazis were our enemies—God knows we did not need Hitler's seizing of power to demonstrate that! It was clear to everyone who was not a little crazy for at least four years prior to 1933." That year, however, these "general political realities transformed themselves into personal destiny as soon as you set foot out of the house," especially if, like Arendt, you looked Jewish.[34]

Of even greater impact than the personal risk, however, was what was happening to other people. What befell those then seized by the Nazis "was such a shock to me that ever after I felt responsible. . . . I no longer felt that [I] could be simply an observer." At this point, Arendt said, "finally it hit me over the head like a hammer, and called me to my own attention."[35] An interesting locution: Arendt was forced to ask herself what she had been doing, what the institutions and people with whom she had been connected, and whose approval she had sought, had been doing. Today we might call it a "consciousness-raising" experience.

Heidegger became, or turned out to be, a Nazi. Later Arendt wrote that what had been hard to come to terms with at the time was not Nazism, but collaboration with it: "the problem, the personal problem was not what our enemies might be doing, but what our friends were doing." People about whom she was accustomed to say "we" were cooperating with the Nazis, at a time when there were not yet any penalties for refusing, when collaboration was still "quite voluntary."[36] That was what was hard to get your head around, what left you feeling "isolated," as if an "empty space" had suddenly opened up all around you.[37]

Arendt's way of understanding it was in terms of the parvenu mentality. But more specifically with regard to intellectuals, academics, philosophers, she reached a conclusion that in effect allowed her to forgive Heidegger even while condemning what he did. Academic intellectuals, and particularly philosophers, are liable to a sort of *déformation professio-*

*nelle,* an occupational disease. The isolation and abstraction required by their professional thinking blinds them to the simple, ordinary realities that are obvious to everyone else ("everyone who was not a little crazy"), and that shape our political lives. Heidegger was "a philosopher's philosopher," and in proportion as he was philosophically brilliant, he "lacked both political judgment and discernment about people."[38]

Academics and abstracted, romantic philosophers, it now seemed to Arendt, were seduced by Nazism because they were in love with their own ideas, unanchored in ordinary reality. Karl Kraus, the celebrated Viennese humorist, was once asked why he did not produce some satire on Hitler and the Nazis. His sad response, widely circulated at the time, was "Mir fällt zu Hitler nichts ein [in connection with Hitler, nothing comes to mind]."[39] Clearly making reference to this witticism, Arendt later said about the academics and philosophers, "Zu Hitler fiel ihnen etwas ein": In connection with the name Hitler, *"ideas came to them.* . . . Quite fantastic and interesting and complicated ideas, and ones that hovered far above the level of the ordinary. . . . They fell into the trap of their own ideas." Arendt found it "grotesque," and drew her own conclusions.[40]

Her husband, involved in radical politics, left Germany a few days after the Reichstag fire. Arendt stayed on, making their apartment available to leftists and others hiding from the Nazis, and undertaking some illegal research for Blumenfeld's Zionist organization. Then she herself was arrested, but released unharmed after eight days. Crossing the border illegally, she too went into exile: "I left Germany dominated by the image—always a little exaggerated, naturally—Never again! I will never again touch any intellectual undertaking. . . . I was of the opinion that it was a matter of this profession, of intellectuality."[41]

Arendt went to Paris, where she found employment with Zionist social service agencies, taking care of Jewish refugee children on their way to Palestine. She wanted nothing more to do with the life of the mind. Still, she took the Varnhagen manuscript along, and finished it in Paris. Re-reading it after the war, she felt distanced from its tone and manner of reflection, but not from its foundation in "the Jewish experience that I acquired for myself with much effort and difficulty." She read that experience as teaching that "When one is attacked as a Jew, one must defend oneself *as a Jew.*" In Paris she began to learn Hebrew and Yiddish.[42]

As Arendt went into exile, seeking to give up not just academic but intellectual life in favor of work that was nurturant, close to traditionally feminine roles, and Jewish, she saw, as she later put it, that "the Jewish problems I was discussing in [*Rahel Varnhagen*] were not my own problems," because in Varnhagen's time Jews "were pariahs only in the *social* sense." Arendt's problem, by contrast, her own "personal problem" she stressed (maybe protesting too much), was "political, purely political! I wanted to do practical work—exclusively and only Jewish work."[43]

The social, I submit, is rooted here, in this setting, not in economics. And *The Human Condition* is also rooted here; not, as it may appear to be, in the Greek polis. At this point "political" seems to mean practical, Jewish, and—although Arendt doesn't say so—nurturant. So "social" presumably means not just parvenu assimilationist but, more broadly, romantic and impractical, unrealistic, abstracted to the point of delusion; it connects with intellectual work and academic aspirations, ambition for an unsuitable job for a woman.

In the period when she was writing the bulk of *Rahel Varnhagen*, then, Arendt made a series of discoveries linked to something like the costs of being a parvenu. She made discoveries about love: the thrills but also the costs of romantic love with its unrealistic fantasies of merger, behind which lie exploitation and inauthentic self-abnegation, and perhaps also about the possibility of a different, more neighborly sort of loving. She made discoveries about ambition and the intellect, and particularly what they might mean for a woman and a Jew in Germany who has a gift for philosophy, with its characteristic *déformation professionelle*, liable to turn her into a political idiot and a scoundrel. She made discoveries about Jewishness and assimilation, about the complex relationship between self-defense and duty in the face of persecution, but also about the possibility of autonomous action and of solidarity. These lessons were profoundly interrelated, and all of them together—political and personal, intellectual and emotional—shaped Arendt's vision of the parvenu, and consequently of the social. Omitting Heidegger from the story would make these links incomprehensible.

But the matter is still more complicated, for the lesson Arendt learned from her romance with Heidegger parallels more than the lesson she thought Varnhagen learned at the end of her life. Both of these lessons also resemble a philosophical doctrine of Heidegger's, developed in *Being and Time*, the book on which he was working during his affair with Arendt, and which they often discussed: the doctrine of *das Man*.

*Das Man* is not easy to translate, since Heidegger invented it. Most commonly *das Man* is translated as "the *they*," although the pronoun *man* can be variously translated as "they," "people," "others," "public opinion," "one," and even "we" ("What will people think?" "They say that . . ." "One wouldn't expect . . ." "We don't do that!"). *Das Man* means other people, in the abstract or generic sense: not as a set of individuals, not as an organization or body, but as the postulated bearers of cultural mores and norms. Heidegger says it means "the Others," but "not *definite* Others." It "is not this one, not that one, not oneself, not some people, and not the sum of them all."[44] It is thus a sort of horizontal version of the parvenu's projected "they, up there": a "they, out there, all around me."

Heidegger maintains that in our ordinary, day-to-day living we conduct ourselves with reference to this projected, generic "they," deferring to it, ascribing to it responsibility for what we do, and seeking fulfillment through it. This way of living Heidegger calls our *"they*-self." It is not, however, our real or authentic self. That can emerge only through philosophy, as the individual isolates himself from "they" to question all conventions and socially imposed assumptions.

This Heideggerian notion is surely one source of Arendt's concept of the social, but that is emphatically not to say that her concept is merely derivative. For one thing, we don't know who influenced whom in their intellectual conversations. For another, Arendt had herself read Kierkegaard and others on whom Heidegger drew. And, most important, Arendt became a *critic* of Heidegger's doctrine.

Both Heidegger and Arendt oppose conformism, and both question the supposed coercive power of the generic, projected "they." Yet Arendt found Heidegger's way of challenging convention and public opinion unsatisfactory. At the personal level, his own disdain for convention evidently reached to an illicit affair with a student, but not to divorce. Politically, his individual philosophical questioning of conventions did not protect him against illusions about the Nazis. And philosophically, *das Man* shared in the general weakness of his approach, perhaps of philosophy itself, with its liability to a *déformation professionelle*: too abstracted, too centered on the individual ego, too romantic. "This whole mode of behavior has exact parallels in German Romanticism," Arendt wrote immediately after the war, and "Heidegger is in fact the last (we hope) romantic."[45] In effect, Heidegger was like Varnhagen, and his proposed solution to the problem of conformism was just as unrealistic, ineffectual, and inauthentic as the *"they*-self."

Arendt's conception of society would have to be different. Where *das Man* is an ontological category, a feature of human life as such, Arendt's society was to be a historically variable phenomenon, humanly created and maintained in concrete, determinate ways at particular times, and humanly changeable—not in the mind, by philosophical insight, but in the world by joint political action. "The circumstances in which we live are created by man," Arendt would soon write in New York, and "insofar as man is more than a mere creature of nature, more than a mere product of Divine creativity, insofar will he be called to account for the things which men do to men in the world" (*JaP* 108, 78).

## "Society" in the New York Essays

By this time Arendt's concept of society is already confusingly multiple, combining several senses with conflicting implications. Often "society" designates what the parvenu has in mind when he talks about society: the all-powerful, privileged "they, up there," who make the rules, set the standards, define everything, and control access. But, like Heidegger on *das Man* and Varnhagen at the end of her life, Arendt is a critic of that outlook, and her critique also employs the words "society" and "social." They stand for what she is criticizing: a social problem is a problem about achieving status as an exception. From this second perspective, the power of society is an illusion, its values fraudulent. Varnhagen discovered at the end of her life that she did not even want the things she had been assuming society kept from her; after that society had no more power over her. Society, in this second sense, is a paper tiger.

But now comes a third sense: Arendt's critique of Heidegger, and thus also of this second view of society. Here society is neither the "they, up there" that parvenus are so anxious to please nor the paper tiger unmasked by Varnhagen and Heidegger; it is something closer to what sociologists talk about. It "embraces and includes all members of a given community," as Arendt says of mass society in *The Human Condition* (41). This is the society that makes people into pariahs: one group (say, Jews) at one time, another group (say, dark-skinned people) at another. It attaches certain penalties to pariahdom at one time, other penalties at another; it is relatively permeable to pariahs who turn parvenu at one time, virtually closed to social climbing at another. Here society is objective and wields real power; it is not a paper tiger. Yet it is not omnipotent; its power is real but limited, and historically changeable. It can be altered by human action.

The tensions among these different ways of thinking about society only get worse and more complicated as Arendt's attention shifts from the eighteenth-century salon to the twentieth-century refugee, in a series of essays written in the 1940s after her arrival in New York. Clearly Jews under Nazi persecution face a pariahdom far more extreme, with consequences far more severe than anything threatening Rahel Varnhagen. No one would want to call the Nazis a paper tiger or suggest that their power is a mere projection of parvenu hopes and fears. While not of course omnipotent, the Nazis wield very real power that will not vanish with philosophic insight, and will not permit Jews to withdraw into any happy pariah privacy among trees and children. Society has shifted from empty foolishness to lethal fanaticism, and it has enlisted the resources of the state. So the parvenu's sense of society's overwhelming power is much closer to the truth in the twentieth century than it was in Varnhagen's time.

At the same time however, the apparently opposite critic's view has also become more persuasive. For the parvenu strategy of deference and conformity has now become quite hopeless. Under the Nuremberg race laws, assimilation is no longer a viable option for Jews. "So long as the Jews were pariahs only in a social sense," Arendt writes in New York, "they could find salvation, to a large extent, by becoming parvenus." Alternatively, they could remain "mere" pariahs in "social isolation." For Jews in Nazi times, by contrast, "social isolation is no longer possible. . . . The old escape mechanisms have broken down." Now the only salvation is in "flight around the globe" (JaP 89–90, 121). So even though the parvenu illusion of society's overwhelming power has become close to true, the parvenu strategy for dealing with that power has become totally unrealistic, not to say pathological.

Yet something very like parvenu conduct was precisely what Arendt now observed among the victims of Nazi persecution she encountered in her own refugee experience. The refugee is of course the pariah par excellence, literally cast out by his society, and a (mostly unwelcome) stranger in his new land: awkward in speech and manner, ignorant of local ways, lacking political rights and often even legal status, without resources or work, often disoriented by recent brutalization, and dependent on the charity of strangers who become less charitable as the flood of refugees mounts. How could the refugee not curry favor with the rich and powerful, not adapt and conform, not compete for scarce and vital resources? How could he survive without some hope of a return to normality? Yet Arendt observed how the plight of twentieth-century refugees constantly pushed them toward the dangerous line where necessary maneuvering turns into collaboration with the oppressor, or where hope turns into pathological denial.

Arendt opens her 1943 essay, "We Refugees" with the words, "In the first place, we don't like to be called 'refugees'" (JaP 55). Those fleeing the Nazis would rather be thought of as ordinary immigrants, who won't be a drain on anyone's resources or cause any trouble, and who are quite ready to forget recent afflictions and settle happily into a new life, already patriots in their new homeland. "After four weeks in France or six weeks in America, we pretend to be Frenchmen or Americans" (JaP 56). This cheerful adaptability rings all the more hollow as it is revised each time the refugee is forced to flee again. Indeed, the refugees adapt so readily and so often "that nobody can find out who we actually are"—least of all the refugees themselves (JaP 62).

Among those fleeing the Nazis, then, Arendt observes a kind of surplus adaptability, a "perfect mania for refusing to keep their identity," whose roots she thinks long antedate Hitler's power, and begin in a parvenu way of life (JaP 64). "We adjust in principle to everything and everybody" (JaP 63). People who have always defined themselves by how others see them become "failures in their own eyes" as soon as the deference to which they have become accustomed is withdrawn or, worse yet, deliberately reversed by Nazi brutalities and humiliations (JaP 60). They respond to external misfortune in the only way they know, by blaming themselves or their fellow victims and trying even harder to conform to the rules and mollify their persecutors.

Like other parvenus, the refugees therefore oscillate between an "insane optimism" and a self-destructive depression, between megalomania and despair. Even as they declare themselves infinitely adaptable and cheerful, something is not quite right about their optimism: "There are those odd optimists among us who, having made a lot of optimistic speeches, go home and turn on the gas or make use of a skyscraper in quite an unexpected way' (JaP 57). No doubt Arendt was thinking not only about the specific tragedy of her friend, Walter Benjamin, but also more broadly of the competitive and self-destructive conduct she observed among the inmates of a French internment camp where, as she later put it, she "had the opportunity of spending some time."[46]

Arendt was in Paris when the Germans invaded in 1940 and France decided to intern all "enemy aliens," mostly in fact German Jewish refugees, but still Germans. She was duly sent to a camp at Gurs, in the south of France. With the aid of a friend as spokeswoman—because she herself was too shy to speak in public—Arendt helped to organize the inmates.[47] At one point, in a discussion of means of resistance, someone suggested a collective suicide pact, "apparently as a kind of protest, to vex the French." When "some of us" pointed out that the French had shipped them there *pour crever* (to croak, or kick the bucket) anyway, the mood promptly changed, as people were brought back to a more realistic sense of who was friend and who enemy. No longer blaming their misfortune on "some mysterious shortcomings in themselves," they instantly regained solidarity and "a violent courage of life." Yet these "same people, as soon as they returned to their own individual lives, being faced with seemingly individual problems," reverted to the parvenu's "insane optimism which is next door to despair" (JaP 59–60).

A few weeks later, when France surrendered to Germany, there came a brief period of administrative chaos when "all communication broke down," and it was possible to get fraudulent "liberation papers" with which one could walk out of the camp. The opportunity was brief, and to take advantage of it, "one had to leave with nothing but a toothbrush, since there existed no means of transportation." Those who still trusted the authorities and deferred to the rules, those who could not walk off into the unknown at a moment's notice and without possessions, stayed in the camp. The opportunity passed. Those who remained were later turned over to the Germans, and most of them died in Nazi extermination camps. Arendt was one of about two hundred women who left, out of some seven thousand in the camp.[48] Young-Bruehl reports that Arendt would tell this story whenever she wanted to illustrate the price paid for indecisiveness and misplaced deference.[49]

A characterological strategy that in Varnhagen's time held fair prospects of paying off for the individual pariah—though even then at a price Arendt considered too high—comes for twentieth-century victims of Nazi persecution to mean "inevitable destruction," and those who nevertheless continue to follow it finally "die of a kind of selfishness" (JaP 76, 60). The personal price of parvenu conduct has gone way up.

So has its cost to other pariahs. The parvenu was always one of the props of the social order that excluded him, but in the eighteenth century his impact was small, not only because Jews were few and anti-Semitism flourished without their help, but also because alternative options were available to fellow pariahs. In the twentieth century, however, the consequences for other pariahs of parvenu conduct have escalated into such horror that "scoundrel" hardly seems the right word. This is particularly true because, even though the Jews are still few and the anti-Semites many, Arendt is now detecting parvenu conduct in many places, not only among Jews.

One did not have to be a Jew or even a pariah to behave as a parvenu; all sorts of people were doing it. Not only did assimilated Jews turn their back on uncultured Eastern Jews, not only did wealthy, established Jews in other countries scorn the refugees from Germany, but gentiles, too, were afflicted by the same disease. They too thought that the Nazis were a threat only to others—to Jews, say—and strove at all costs to dissociate themselves from the victims. Parvenu conduct can be seen in all sorts of conformism, denial, cowardice, and short-sightedness, and it often widens into appeasement: "the outlawing of the Jewish people in Europe has been followed closely by the outlawing of most European nations. Refugees driven from country to country represent the vanguard of their peoples" (JaP 66). It seems that, thanks to the Nazis, history teaches a "moral": failures of solidarity with the victims will soon be punished by one's own victimization (JaP 106). Nonpariah peoples who conduct themselves like parvenus will soon be made pariahs in their turn: "The comity of European peoples went to pieces when, and because, it allowed its weakest member to be excluded and persecuted" (JaP 66).

As parvenu conduct appears among nonpariahs and feeds an evil power that will soon turn them into pariahs, as it persists among pariahs even when it is manifestly senseless, as it seems to become simultaneously more realistic (because the power of the "they, up there" is all too real) and more deluded (because conforming and appeasing cannot possibly work), the tensions in Arendt's configuration of concepts mount. In the New York essays they are not resolved, but only covered over by the simplifying urgencies of war.

## Conclusion: The Blob as Mother?

That is as far as this essay can go. There is a good deal more to be said both about the recurrence of the notion of society and the concepts associated with it in *The Origins of Totalitarianism*—in which the Blob is born as totalitarianism in volume 3—and about how the social comes to replace totalitarianism as Blob in *The Human Condition*. It would be necessary to address the circumstances in which *The Human Condition* was written, the conceptual complexities about "society" and "social" that Arendt ignored, the unconscious symbolic implications of the image of the Blob that Arendt refused on principle to examine, and the enormous logical difficulties of articulating clearly the problem that Arendt's concept of the social was intended to address. All that must be postponed to another time and place, but a few more words are in order here about the unconscious symbolism of the Blob image, because it is so clearly, and so complexly gender-related.[50]

What Arendt designates as parvenu conduct and associates with Jewish assimilationism also clearly resembles the stereotypical feminine role in our society: accommodating, deferential, self-abnegating, but behind the scenes also self-centered, manipulative, and resentful. It is no accident that Arendt's romance with Heidegger seemed to parallel parvenu conduct. The parvenu's experience and the social itself are further characterized by individual isolation and consequent helplessness, loss of reality and natural pleasures, and meaninglessness, all of which sounds a lot like the experience of the suburban housewife, particularly of the 1950s. Moreover, Arendt explicitly links the social with housework and the household. She also links it with labor, but she points out that one of the senses of that word is the physiological effort of giving birth, and her characterization of its other sense, of labor as the production of what is necessary for staying alive, often sounds more like housework than like agriculture or construction.

In ordinary usage, too, the social is in many ways women's realm. On the whole, it is women who are stereotypically supposed to be in charge of "social life," of parties, dinners, weddings, as they once were of salons. Women are stereotypically in charge of reweaving the web of personal relationships when it frays; Carol Gilligan has argued that this tends to make them less inclined to abstract and to generalize than men, more attentive to the particular person they happen to be confronting.[51] Denise Riley has recently shown how, since the nineteenth century, the social has also been supposedly women's province in public life, not only because social welfare and social services involve nurturance, but also because what we now call the "helping professions" were among the earliest to be permissible for women.[52] The welfare state, though mostly run by men like other states, is in important ways symbolically female: mothering, smothering, intruding upon, and regulating to death all who come within its bureaucratic reach. Society, Arendt said, is "the facsimile of one superhuman family"; I am suggesting that she imagined it as a single-parent household, headed by an altogether unpleasant mother, uncontrolled by any counterbalancing paterfamilias.

Speaking psychoanalytically, the Blob is a fantasy of regression, of losing one's separate self and being once more dissolved in—swallowed up by—an engulfing mother. Such fantasies are associated with women because derived from infancy, from a time when all of us were in the hands of women.

None of this should be taken, however, as implying that the problem to which Arendt intended her concept of the social to apply is merely a misogynist myth or a psychological illusion. On the contrary, that problem seems to me preeminently real and urgent, even more so in our time than in Arendt's. The real task is finding a better way of talking and thinking about it, about why we are conducting ourselves *as if* we had been taken over by a Blob. All sorts of dreadful disasters seem to be rushing toward us at ever-increasing speed, from world starvation and nuclear war to the real possibility of rendering the earth uninhabitable. Yet these disasters are not rushing toward us; we are rushing toward them. If they occur, they will have been our doing. The real question is, can we stop? If not, when did we, and how could we, lose that power? Of, if we *can* stop, why don't we? The real task is thinking clearly about those questions. The Blob only gets in the way.

## Notes

1. Hannah Arendt, *The Human Condition* (Chicago: University of Chicago Press, 1974); hereafter cited as *HC*.

2. Dagmar Barnouw, *Visible Spaces: Hannah Arendt and the German-Jewish Experience* (Baltimore: Johns Hopkins University Press, 1990), 22. The passage actually refers to mass culture, which is almost but not quite the same as the social in Arendt.

3. *HC* 23. See also Hannah Arendt, *Between Past and Future* (Cleveland, Ohio: World Publishing, 1969), 199. The social is thus one of those concepts, like revolution but unlike politics, the public, and freedom, whose "earlier" or "original" meaning does not govern their "true" meaning for Arendt.

4. See Arendt's brief history of modern governmental forms (of which, more below), from one-man monarchical rule, analogous to the paterfamilias, to bureaucracy, that "most social form of government," which—like the market—is "the rule of nobody" (*HC* 40, 45).

5. I develop this argument with reference to Arendt's categories of labor and necessity in "Justice: On Relating Private and Public," *Political Theory* 9 (August 1981): 327–52.

6. Margaret Canovan, *The Political Thought of Hannah Arendt* (New York: Harcourt Brace Jovanovich, 1974), 108. See also her *Hannah Arendt: A Reinterpretation of Her Political Thought* (Cambridge: Cambridge University Press, 1992).

7. Canovan, *Political Thought*, 105, 108.

8. Ibid., 109, 108.

9. Elisabeth Young-Bruehl, *Hannah Arendt: For Love of the World* (New Haven: Yale University Press, 1982); hereafter cited as Young-Bruehl, *HA*. Hannah Arendt, *The Jew as Pariah: Jewish Identity and Politics in the Modern Age*, ed. Ron H. Feldman (New York: Grove, 1978); hereafter cited as *JaP*.

10. Judith N. Shklar, "Hannah Arendt as Pariah," *Partisan Review* 50 (1983): 65–77. Elisabeth Young-Bruehl, "From the Pariah's Point of View," in *Mind and the Body Politic* (New York: Routledge, 1989). Barnouw, *Visible Spaces*. Jennifer Ring, "The Pariah as Hero: Hannah Arendt's Political Actor," *Political Theory* 19 (August 1991): 433–52.

11. Hannah Arendt, *Rahel Varnhagen: The Life of a Jewish Woman*, trans. Richard and Clara Winston (New York: Harcourt Brace Jovanovich, 1974), xiii, xx; hereafter cited as *RV*. Young-Bruehl, *HA* 91, 299.

12. Arendt, *RV* 3. Heinrich Schnee has pointed out that Arendt suppressed the closing lines of Varnhagen's deathbed speech, lines in which she identified herself with the suffering of Jesus, said she felt he was her brother, admired the capacity of Mary to bear suffering, remarked that Mary's suffering would have been beyond her own strength to bear, and asked God to forgive her weakness; see his review of *Rahel Varnhagen* in *Historisches Jahrbuch* 80 (1960): 458–59. The suppressed passage does indeed show that Varnhagen did not regret or revoke her conversion, but Arendt was surely right that at this point Varnhagen was no longer a parvenu. She accepted and affirmed as a "nexus of destiny" *both* her Jewish birth *and* her conversion, originally undertaken for parvenu reasons but no longer so regarded. There may be other inaccuracies or distortions in Arendt's account of Varnhagen as well. Compare Heidi Thomann Tewarson, *Rahel Levin Varnhagen* (Hamburg: Rowohlt, 1988).

13. The term was originally brought back by the British from India, where it designated the largest of the low castes, at the bottom of the caste hierarchy. Arendt's source is Bernard Lazare, *Job's Dungheap* (New York: Schocken, 1948), a collection of essays translated into English that Arendt edited and for which she wrote a brief biography of Lazare. See Arendt, *JaP* 32.

14. Gisela T. Kaplan, "Hannah Arendt: The Life of a Jewish Woman," in *Hannah Arendt: Thinking, Judging, Freedom*, ed. Gisela T. Kaplan and Olive S. Kessler (Sydney: Allen and Unwin, 1989), 78. Arendt, *RV* 201.

15. *RV* 213. Young-Bruehl, *HA* 57.

16. See note 12.

17. Hannah Arendt, *Men in Dark Times* (New York: Harcourt Brace and World, 1969), 98.

18. Young-Bruehl, *HA* 11. But compare Jeanette M. Baron, "Hannah Arendt: Personal Reflections," *Response* 39 (1980): 58–63, at p. 58, who claims that as a child Arendt wished that she had been born blond and blue-eyed.

19. Young-Bruehl, *HA* 11–12, 72. Wolfgang Heuer, *Hannah Arendt* (Hamburg: Rowohlt, 1987), 12–13; hereafter cited as Heuer, *HA*.

20. Heuer, *HA* 12.

21. Young-Bruehl, *HA* 23.

22. Ibid., 14.

23. Heuer, *HA* 13.

24. Ibid., 21. Young-Bruehl, *HA* 238. The first passage quoted is all the more striking

because Arendt early published a review of a book on the woman question. Although she told an interviewer, "I am not disturbed at all about being a woman professor because I am quite used to being a woman," she worried when she was the first woman professor invited to Princeton, lest she become their "token woman" (Young-Bruehl, HA 273, 272). Later, a visitor at Berkeley, she integrated the main dining hall of the men's faculty club (personal communication from Norman Jacobson).

25. Heuer, HA 7. Young-Bruehl, HA 27–28.
26. Young-Bruehl, HA 104.
27. Ibid., 49.
28. Ibid., 44. Heuer, HA 15.
29. Heuer, HA 7.
30. Ibid., 20. Young-Bruehl, HA 50. Friedrich Georg Friedman, Hannah Arendt (Munich: Piper, 1985), 114.
31. Heuer, HA 50.
32. Young-Bruehl, HA 307.
33. Young-Bruehl, HA 70–71, 91, 98–99.
34. Ibid., 108. Note that "four years prior" means 1929, the year in which Arendt began work on RV.
35. Ibid., 107. Heuer, HA 29–30.
36. Heuer, HA 29. See also Young-Bruehl, HA 109.
37. Young-Bruehl, HA 108.
38. Ibid., 304, 443. See also 327.
39. Erich Heller, The Importance of Nietzsche (Chicago: University of Chicago Press, 1988), 159.
40. Heuer, HA 29–30; emphasis added. See also Arendt, RV 10.
41. Heuer, HA 29.
42. Ibid., 27. Young-Bruehl, HA 109, 119.
43. Heuer, HA 27, 29. Arendt, JaP 89.
44. Martin Heidegger, Being and Time, trans. John Macquarrie and Edward Robinson (New York: Harper and Row, 1962), sect. 27, 163–68, at 164. Note that the capitalization of "Others" is the translator's; in German all nouns are capitalized. Arendt's view is not entirely fair to Heidegger, who does say that das Man "can become concrete in various ways in history," 167. On some of the difficulties of das Man, compare Hubert L. Dreyfus, Being-in-the-World: A Commentary on Heidegger's Being and Time, Division I (Cambridge: MIT Press, 1991), chap. 8.
45. Arendt, "What is Existenz Philosophy?" Partisan Review 8 (1946): 46–47.
46. Young-Bruehl, HA 160. Arendt, JaP 59.
47. Personal communication from Sara M. Shumer.
48. Young-Bruehl, HA 153–55.
49. Ibid., 160.
50. See my forthcoming The Attack of the Blob: Hannah Arendt's Concept of the Social.
51. Carol Gilligan, In a Different Voice (Cambridge: Harvard University Press, 1982).
52. Denise Riley, "Am I That Name?" Feminism and the Category of 'Women' in History (Minneapolis: University of Minnesota Press, 1988), chap. 3.

# 4

# The Pariah and Her Shadow: Hannah Arendt's Biography of Rahel Varnhagen

*Seyla Benhabib*

## A Methodological Preamble

Hannah Arendt's self-consciousness of herself as a Jew, and her belief that in the twentieth century to be Jewish had become a "political" and unavoidable fact stand in sharp contrast to her almost total silence on

This essay is part of a forthcoming book called *The Reluctant Modernism of Hannah Arendt* (Sage Publications), and was delivered as a paper at the Annual Meeting of the American Political Science Association Convention in September 1993. The research for this project has been supported by an American fellowship from the Leona J. Beckmann and Susan B. Anthony Endowment of the American Association of University Women (January 1991–December 1992). An earlier version of this essay has appeared in *Political Theory* 23, no. 1 (February 1995): 5–24.

the women's question.[1] While the fate of the Jewish people is at the center of her public-political thought, her identity as a woman and the sociopolitical and cultural dimensions of being female in the modern world do not find explicit recognition in her work. We know from her biographer Elisabeth Young-Bruehl that Arendt "was suspicious of women 'who gave orders,' skeptical about whether women should be political leaders, and steadfastly opposed to the social dimensions of Women's Liberation."[2] This perplexing constellation becomes clearer, if also more troubling, when one reads the opening sections of *The Human Condition*. Through these pages one can easily gain the impression that Arendt not only ignored the women's question but that she was almost a reactionary on the issue in that she accepted the age-old confinement of women to the private realm of the household and their exclusion from the public sphere.[3] This was certainly the conclusion drawn by Adrienne Rich in her caustic and powerful comments on *The Human Condition*:

> In thinking about the issues of women and work . . . I turned to Hannah Arendt's *The Human Condition* to see how a major political philosopher of our time, a woman greatly respected in the intellectual establishment, had spoken to the theme. I found her essay illuminating, not so much for what it says, but for what it is. . . . The withholding of women from participation in the *vita activa*, the "common world," and the connection of this with reproductivity, is something from which she does not so much turn her eyes as stare straight through unseeing. . . . To read such a book, by a woman of large spirit and great erudition, can be painful, because it embodies the tragedy of a female mind nourished on male ideologies. In fact, the loss is ours, because Arendt's desire to grasp deep moral issues is the kind of concern we need to build a common world which will amount to more than "life-styles."[4]

Adrienne Rich's verdict on Hannah Arendt is based upon certain heuristic assumptions that lead her to the conclusion that one should read Arendt's work "not so much for what it says but for what it is." Reading Hannah Arendt's work though from the standpoint of a question that she herself did not place at the center of her thought, namely, the woman's question, and examining her political philosophy in this light requires certain innovative hermeneutical and interpretive principles that go beyond those traditionally deployed and shared by Rich as well. One commonly shared principle in the interpretation of texts can be characterized as *historicist indifference.* Historicist indifference requires that we understand a text, a theory, a thinker's views in the context of their genesis. This obvious and unproblematic beginning point of any interpretive effort is inadequate when it is accompanied by the further assumption that to understand can only mean to understand in context and that to pose contemporary questions to historical texts is to fall into anachronism.

The second commonly shared postulate of interpretation, and the one most prominently displayed by Adrienne Rich, can be named the self-righteous dogmatism of the latecomers. In posing questions to the past, this attitude assumes that our already attained answers are the right ones. This kind of reading of past texts is particularly prevalent among activists of social movements who, very often, simply juxtapose the misunderstandings of the past to the truths of the present. For the art of reading and appropriating the past such an attitude is inadequate. If we approach tradition and thinkers of the past only to "debunk" them, then there really is no point in seeking to understand them at all. Such dogmatism kills the spirit and dries up the soul, and it is certainly not conducive to the task of "building a common world which will amount to more than mere 'life-styles.' "

In approaching Hannah Arendt's thought from where we stand today and in probing it from the standpoint of her identity as a German Jewish woman neither principle is adequate: historicist indifference is inadequate since it kills the interests of contemporary readers in past texts by blocking the asking of any questions that transcend the immediate historical context in which these texts were written. The self-righteousness of the latecomers is also misleading in that it would lead us to assume that we can no longer learn from Arendt, that her work has ceased to engage us, that we can treat her as a sociological and psychological curiosity exemplifying the "male-identified" female mind.

Applied to Hannah Arendt's work, this would mean that all questioning of her work, particularly on the women's issue, would be considered anachronistic and insensitive to her own historical concerns. Yet such questioning is neither anachronistic nor insensitive to Arendt's own concerns; on the contrary, it can allow us to pursue certain lines of interpretation that shed unusual light on the initial concerns that motivated Arendt's work. In view of the enormousness of Arendt's contribution to political thought in this century, I resist the conclusion that we should only treat her as a sociological curiosity.

How then should we proceed? Asking the woman's question, as always, signifies a movement from center to margin in the hermeneutic task.[5] We begin by searching in the footnotes, in the marginalia, in the less recognized works of a thinker for those "traces" (*Spuren*) that are left behind by women's presence and more often than not by their absence. For Hannah Arendt's work, this method means that one begins not with *The Human Condition* but with a text that certainly does not occupy a central place in any systematic interpretation of her political philosophy, namely, *Rahel Varnhagen*, subtitled "The Life of a Jewish Woman."

## Rahel Levin Varnhagen's Quest for the "World"

Hannah Arendt's intellectual biography of Rahel Varnhagen, born as Rahel Levin in Berlin in 1771, was begun in 1929, shortly after she completed her dissertation (on Augustine's concept of love) under Karl Jaspers's directorship in Heidelberg. This study appears to have been intended as her *Habilitationsschrift*, to win her the right to teach in a German university.[6] It was completed in 1933 except for the last two chapters, which were finished subsequently during her exile in France in 1938. The book appeared almost twenty years later in 1957 in English translation; the first German edition came out in 1959.[7] *Rahel Varnhagen*, subtitled "Lebensgeschichte einer deutschen Jüdin aus der Romantik" (The life history of a German Jewess from the Romantic period), is a difficult text. An early reviewer found that it "is a relentlessly abstract book—slow, cluttered, static, curiously oppressive; reading it feels like sitting in a hothouse with no watch. One is made to feel the subject, the waiting distraught woman; one is made aware, almost physically, of her intense femininity, her frustration."[8]

"The relentless abstractness" of the book is in part due to Arendt's methodological angle, which she herself admits is "unusual." "It was never my intention," explains Arendt,

> to write a book *about* Rahel; about her personality, which might lend itself to various interpretations according to the psychological standards and categories that the author introduces

from outside; nor about her position in Romanticism and the effect of the Goethe cult in Berlin, of which she was actually the originator; nor about the significance of her salon for the social history of the period; nor about her ideas and her "Weltanschauung," insofar as these can be reconstructed from her letters. *What interested me solely was to narrate the story of Rahel's life as she herself might have told it.* . . . My portrait therefore follows as closely as possible Rahel's own reflections upon herself, although it is naturally couched in different language and does not consist solely of variations upon quotations. (*RV* xv–xvi; my emphasis)

This claim to "narrate the story of Rahel's life as she herself *might have told it*" is astonishing. Arendt's confidence in her judgments about Rahel Varnhagen is so deep that she does not fear correcting Rahel's husband's presentation of her. In fact, at one level the book reclaims Rahel's life and memory from the clutches of her husband—the generous and giving, but upright and boring Prussian civil servant Karl August Varnhagen von Ense, who, Arendt maintains, presented Rahel's life such as to make her "associations and circle of friends appear less Jewish and more aristocratic, and to show Rahel herself in a more conventional light, one more in keeping with the taste of the times" (*RV* xv). One might wish to ask what gives Arendt this confidence that she in fact could know or could claim to know this woman better than her husband? How can Arendt, separated from Rahel's death on 7 March 1833 by almost one hundred years at the time of composing her book on Rahel, claim to narrate Rahel's story as she herself "might have told it?" What hermeneutical mysteries does this little subjunctive phrase, "might have told it," contain?

The facts of Rahel Varnhagen's life story are well known: Rahel was born in Berlin on 19 May 1771 as the eldest child of the well-to-do merchant Markus Levin. She had three younger brothers and a younger sister. Her parental household was still Orthodox Jewish and uneducated in German culture. Rahel's early letters are written in Yiddish, that is, with Hebrew characters.[9] After the death of her father in 1790, her brother Marcus assumes the family business and provides Rahel and her mother with a regular income. Between 1790 and 1806, Rahel holds a salon in the attic room on Jaegerstrasse. Among the guests are the Humboldt brothers (Alexander and Wilhelm), Friedrich Schlegel, Friedrich Gentz, Schleiermacher, Prince Louis Ferdinand of Prussia and his mistress, Pauline Wiesel, the classical philologist Friedrich August Wolf, Jean Paul, Brentano, the Tieck brothers. From 1790 to 1804, Rahel has a series of friendships and love affairs with aristocrats of various European origins, ranging from the Swedish ambassador, Karl Gustav von Brinck-mann, to Count Karl von Finckenstein, and to Friedrich von Gentz (a career diplomat who was to play a significant role in the Vienna Congress of 1815).[10]

With the entry of Napoleon into Berlin on 27 October 1806 Rahel's salon and circle of friends are scattered. A wave of nationalism and anti-Semitism begins to sweep the intellectual and aristocratic circles that had formerly befriended Varnhagen. This period heralds the end of one of the first cycles of "German-Jewish symbiosis." In this period, family and financial difficulties follow suit in Rahel's life. Her mother moves out of the home on Jaegerstrasse and dies shortly thereafter in 1809. Rahel, who had met Karl August von Varnhagen in 1808, now moves from Berlin to Teplitz. After several short separations, she is baptized on 27 September 1814 and marries Varnhagen. Von Varnhagen, who is a career civil servant, moves among several cities, including Frankfurt and Karlsruhe. In 1819 they resettle in Berlin; and from 1821 to 1832, the Berlin salon of the Varnhagens starts. Among the guests are Bettina von Arnim, Heinrich Heine, Prince Pückler-Muskau, G. W. F. Hegel, Ranke, and Eduard Gans. Rahel dies on 7 March 1833.

Arendt's reconstruction of Rahel's story is based primarily upon the unprinted letters and diaries from the Varnhagen collection of the Manuscript Division of the Prussian State Library. In her 1956 preface she indicates that these manuscripts were stored in the eastern provinces of Germany during the war and "what happened to it remains a mystery, so far as I know" (xiii). We know now that the entire collection has turned up at the Library in Kraków, Poland.[11] Arendt herself had to rest content with quoting from old excerpts, photostats, and copies of documents.

There are manifold layers of reading and interpretation that must be disentangled from one another in approaching Arendt's attempt to tell Rahel's story as she herself "might have told it." In the early 1930s Arendt's own understanding of Judaism in general and her relationship to her own Jewish identity were undergoing profound transformations. These transformations were taking her increasingly away from the egali-tarian, humanistic Enlightenment ideals of Kant, Lessing, and Goethe toward a recognition of the ineliminable and unassimilable fact of Jewish difference within German culture. In telling Rahel Varnhagen's story Arendt was engaging in a process of collective self-understanding and redefinition as a German Jew.[12] Her correspondence with Karl Jaspers, who follows the development of Arendt's work on this book with amazement bordering on irritation and bewilderment, is quite revealing in this respect.

On 30 March 1930 Karl Jaspers writes to Hannah Arendt concerning a lecture of hers on Rahel Varnhagen. Unfortunately, this lecture is no longer available. The exchange of letters between Jaspers and Arendt gives the distinct impression that Arendt here is breaking new ground and taking the *Existenzphilosophie* of her teacher Jaspers in new directions. Jaspers indicates that he wants to "get a clearer idea in the give and take of our conversation of what you mean."[13] He continues:

> You objectify "Jewish Existence" existentially—and in doing so perhaps cut existential thinking off at the roots. The concept of being-thrown-back-on-oneself can no longer be taken altogether seriously since it is *grounded* in terms of the fate of the Jews instead of being rooted in itself. . . . The passage from the letters, which you have chosen so well, suggests something quite different to me: "Jewishness" is a *façon de parler* or a manifestation of a selfhood originally negative in its outlook and not comprehensible from the historical situation. It is a fate that did not experience liberation from the enchanted castle. (*Correspondence* 10; emphasis in original)

Jaspers is clearly puzzled by the status of the category of "Jewish existence," and by whether or not Arendt is attributing a more fundamental status to this fact than is allowable by the categories of existential philosophy. Jaspers himself sees "Jewish existence" as a wholly contingent or accidental matter, "a façon de parler," a manner of speaking, or "the manifestation of a selfhood originally negative in its outlook." Neither individually nor collectively, however, can he see in the matter of "being Jewish" more than a contingency of culture and history or an accident of birth.

Arendt's answer is cautious: she indicates that she has not tried

> to "ground" Rahel's existence in terms of Jewishness—or at least I was not conscious of doing so. This lecture is only a *preliminary*

> work meant to show that on the foundation of being Jewish a
> certain possibility of existence *can* arise that I have tentatively
> and for the time being called fatefulness. This fatefulness arises
> from the very fact of "foundationlessness" and can occur *only*
> in a separation from Judaism. (*Correspondence* 11; emphasis
> in original)

Given the perspective of hindsight and what it would signify to be
Jewish in Germany by the end of the 1930s, this exchange is almost
astonishing in its abstractness and aloofness. Neither Jaspers nor Arendt
could have anticipated a situation when the fact of being Jewish would
indeed be the fate for millions and millions. Yet it is interesting that
Arendt is full of premonition, that she seems to be sensing a certain
"uncanniness" (*das Unheimliche*) in Rahel's own attempt to live life as
her "fate." With reference to Rahel, Arendt writes: "What this all really
adds up to—fate, being exposed, what life means—I can't really say in
the abstract (and I realize that in trying to write about it here.) Perhaps
all I can try to do is illustrate it with examples" (*RV* 48). Eventually,
Arendt comes to describe Rahel's own attitude toward her Judaism as a
move away from the psychology of the parvenu to that of the pariah.
Whereas the parvenu denies "fatefulness" by becoming like other members of the dominant culture, by erasing difference and assimilating to
dominant trends, the pariah is the outsider and the outcast who either
cannot or chooses not to erase the fate of difference. The latter is the
self-conscious pariah, who transforms difference from being a source of
weakness and marginality into one of strength and defiance. This is
ultimately what Arendt admires in Rahel. Commenting on Rahel's
reflections on her life as "Friederike Varnhagen," the respectable life of
a Prussian civil servant she writes: "She had at last rid herself of Rahel
Levin, but she did not want to become Friederike Varnhagen, née
Robert. The former was not socially acceptable; the latter could not
summon the resolution to make a fraudulent self-identification. For 'all
my life I considered myself Rahel and nothing else' " (*RV* 212).
    Rahel's Jewish identity and Arendt's own changing understanding of
what this means in the 1930s in Germany are the central hermeneutic
motifs in the Varnhagen story.[14] In telling Rahel's story, Hannah Arendt
was bearing testimony to a political and spiritual transformation that she
herself was undergoing. There is thus a mirror effect in the narrative.
The one narrated about becomes the mirror in which the narrator also
portrays herself.

There is an additional dimension to this narration, and it leads more directly to future themes in Arendt's political philosophy. In telling Rahel's story Arendt is concerned with documenting a certain form of romantic *Innerlichkeit* (inwardness). To live life "as if it were a work of art," writes Arendt, "to believe that by 'cultivation' [*Bildung*] one can make a work of art of one's life was the great error that Rahel shared with her contemporaries" (*RV* xvi). The "claustrophobic" feeling about the book noted above, the sensation that "one is in a hothouse without a watch," derives from Arendt's literary success in conveying this sense of endless expectation, of an endless yearning without fulfillment, of inaction coupled with the wish to live and experience most intensely. "What am I doing?" asks Rahel. "Nothing. I am letting life rain upon me" (*RV* xvi). It is this "worldless" sensibility that Arendt finds most objectionable about Rahel. In the opening chapters of the Varnhagen biography, which deal with romantic introspection, Arendt indicates what she sees as the greatest weakness and ultimately as the "apolitical" quality of romantic inwardness:

> Introspection accomplishes two feats: it annihilates the actual existing situation by dissolving it in mood, and at the same time it lends everything subjective an aura of objectivity, publicity, extreme interest. In mood, the boundaries between what is intimate and what is public become blurred; intimacies are made public, and public matters can be experienced and expressed only in the realm of the intimate—ultimately, in gossip. (*RV* 21)

Romantic introspection leads one to lose a sense of reality by losing the boundaries between the public and the private, the intimate and the shared. Romantic introspection compounds the "worldlessness" from which Rahel Varnhagen suffers to the very end. The category of the "world" is the missing link between the "worldless" reality of Rahel Levin Varnhagen and her contemporaries and Hannah Arendt's own search for a recovery of the "public world" through authentic political action in her political philosophy. Romantic inwardness displays qualities of mind and feeling that are the exact opposite of those required of political actors and that Arendt highly valued. Whereas romantic introspection blurs the boundaries between the personal and the political, the political qualities of distinguishing sharply and precisely between the public good and the personal sphere are extremely important for

Arendt. Whereas the ability to judge the world as it appears to others and from many different points of view is the quintessential epistemic virtue in politics, romantic inwardness tends to eliminate the distinction between one's own perspective and those of others through mood. Finally, an interest in the world and a commitment to sustain it is fundamental for politics, whereas romantic inwardness cultivates the soul rather than sustaining the world.

Varnhagen's search for a place in the "world" was defined not only by her identity as a Jew and as a Romantic but also as a woman. Although Arendt does not place this theme at the center, her story of Rahel begins to reveal an unthematized gender subtext. In Arendt's account, Varnhagen attempts to regain a place in the world for herself by using typically female strategies. In the concluding paragraphs of her 1956 preface to *Rahel Varnhagen* Arendt remarks:

> The modern reader will scarcely fail to observe that Rahel was neither beautiful nor attractive; that all the men with whom she had any kind of love relationship were younger than she herself; that she possessed no talents with which to employ her extraordinary intelligence and passionate originality; and finally, that she was a typically "romantic" personality, and that the Woman problem, that is the discrepancy between what men expected of women "in general" and what women could give or wanted in their turn, was already established by the conditions of the era and represented a gap that virtually could not be closed. (*RV* xviii)

Rahel's strategies for dealing with the fate of her Jewishness were typically female ones: assimilation and recognition through love affairs, courtships, and eventually marriage with gentile males. The female strategy of assimilation through marriage is of course made possible by a gender-asymmetrical world in which it is the husband's public status that defines the woman, rather than the other way around. Rahel Levin Varnhagen's life was full of stories of failed love affairs, broken promises, and unsuccessful engagements. By giving herself to the right man, Rahel hoped to attain the "world" that was denied her as a Jew and as a female.

But "where" is the world, and "who" is it composed of? Interestingly, Arendt's most explicit definition of this category comes much later, in a

1960 essay on Lessing that focuses on his *Nathan der Weise*. "But the world and the people who inhabit it," writes Arendt,

> are not the same. The world lies between people, and this in-
> between . . . is today the object of the greatest concern and the
> most obvious upheaval in almost all the countries of the globe.
> Even where the world is still halfway in order, or is kept halfway
> in order, the public realm has lost the power of illumination
> which was originally part of its very nature. . . . (The) withdrawal
> from the world need not harm an individual; . . . but with each
> such retreat an almost demonstrable loss to the world takes place;
> what is lost is the specific and usually irreplaceable in-between
> which should have formed between this individual and his fellow
> men.[15]

Arendt delivered this speech in 1959, upon receiving the Lessing Prize in Hamburg. Her almost melancholy reflections on the loss of the "world" as that fragile "space of appearances" that "holds men together" stand in interesting contrast with the theme of "worldlessness" that dominates *Rahel Varnhagen*. Rahel and her contemporaries failed to create a world, except in that brief period between 1790 and 1806 when a few exceptional Prussian Jews could emerge into the world of genteel society, only to be pushed back into obscurity with the onslaught of anti-Semitism in Prussia after the victory of Napoleon. The fragility and almost illusory character of the world of the salons that Jewesses like Rahel Varnhagen and Henriette Herz created for a brief moment stand in sharp contrast to the fate of the "stateless" and "worldless" people that the Jews would become in the twentieth century.

The "recovery of the public world" of politics under conditions of modernity is a guiding theme of Hannah Arendt's political philosophy at large. The personal story of Rahel Varnhagen, of her circle of friends, the failure of her salon, the political naïveté of her generation of Jews are a negative utopia. Nonetheless, this cluttered and at times awkward youthful text retains themes, issues, and preoccupations that are much closer to the nerve of Arendt's existential concerns than some of her subsequent formulations.

Arendt's own relentless pessimism about the significance of the salons certainly cannot be separated from the tragic ending of the utopian and optimistic hopes they had initially kindled in the souls of many German Jews. As she notes in the preface to *Rahel Varnhagen*:

> The present biography was written with an awareness of the doom of German Judaism (although, naturally without any pre-monition of how far the physical annihilation of the Jewish people in Europe would be carried); but at that time, shortly before Hitler's coming to power, I did not have the perspective from which to view the phenomenon as a whole. . . . On the other hand, it must not be forgotten that the subject matter is altogether historical, and that nowadays not only the history of the German Jews, but also their specific complex of problems, are a matter of the past. (xvii)

Written in 1956, these melancholy reflections distance Hannah Arendt herself from this biography by "historicizing" Rahel and the fate of the German Jews to whom she belonged. Yet for us, as Arendt's readers, the questions posed by her biography of Rahel Varnhagen cannot be restricted to this tragic-historical context alone. For early works are also beginnings and beginnings frequently are closer to the nerve of a thinker's oeuvre, precisely because time, experience, sophistication, and the apparatus of scholarship have not yet cluttered the existential questions and preoccupations at the origins of thought. When read in the light of this hermeneutic principle, Arendt's early treatment of Rahel Varnhagen suggests a set of issues that go well beyond the fate of German Jewry and of the salonnières among them and that point us to the heart of her political theory.

I suggest that at the beginnings of Arendt's work, we discover a different genealogy of modernity than the one so characteristic of her later writings. As distinct from the analysis of *The Human Condition*, the "rise of the social," in this alternative genealogy of modernity, would not refer to the rise of commodity-exchange relations in a burgeoning capitalist economy, but would designate the emergence of new forms of sociability, association, intimacy, friendship, speaking and writing habits, tastes in food, manners, and arts, as well as hobbies, pastimes, and leisure activities. Furthermore, in the midst of this alternative genealogy of the social is a curious space that is of the home yet public, that is dominated by women yet visited and frequented by men, that is highly mannered yet egalitarian, and that is hierarchical toward the "outsiders" and egalitarian toward its members. What leads Arendt to lose sight of this "other modernity" with which she began and to replace it with a relentless pessimism? Of course, at one level the answer to this question is the Holocaust and the fate of European Jewry, which nullified all the ideals of the Enlightenment and modernity in which Rahel's generation still believed. At another level, though, the answer may be that perhaps Arendt never did lose sight of this other modernity and that her purported "Graecocentrism" is as much a fiction created by us her readers as it is based upon her own texts. Let us re-read the meaning of the concept of the "social" in Arendt's work.

## The Rise of the Social: An Alternative Genealogy of Modernity in Arendt's Work?

Consider the standard reading of Arendt's political philosophy. For many, Arendt is a nostalgic and antimodernist thinker, who sees in modernity the decline of the public sphere of politics and the emergence of an amorphous, anonymous, uniformizing reality that she calls "the social." In this account, the social, by which is meant a form of glorified, national housekeeping in economic and pecuniary matters, displaces the concern with the political, with the res publica, from the hearts and minds of men. The social is the perfect medium in which bureaucracy, the "rule by nobody," emerges and unfolds.

As an account of modernity, this view is jarring in so many ways that it requires a great deal of hermeneutic uncharity to attribute it to a thinker who was as historically grounded and sophisticated as Hannah Arendt was. There are actually three meanings of the term "social" in Arendt's work. At one level, the "social" refers to the growth of a capitalist commodity exchange economy.[16] At the second, the "social" refers to aspects of "mass society."[17] At the third and least investigated level, the social refers to "sociability," to the quality of life in civil society and civic associations.

To explore this last and least discussed meaning of the term, consider now the following passage. "But society equalizes under all circumstances, and the victory of equality in the modern world is only the political and legal recognition of the fact that society has conquered the public realm, and *that distinction and difference have become private matters of the individual"* (HC 41; my emphasis). By "equality" in this passage, Arendt does not mean political and legal equality, but rather the equalization of tastes, behavior, manners and life-styles, which is executed by mass society. Under such conditions "distinction and difference have become private matters of the individual." But have they really? Arendt's historical and political writings on the Jewish question, beginning with her biography of Rahel Varnhagen, reveal quite a different picture. They show that the constant struggle and tension between "equality" and "difference," both in the social and the political domains, is characteristic of modernity. In one of her most illuminating remarks on this dialectic of equality and difference Arendt notes:

> Equality of condition, though it is certainly a basic requirement for justice, is nevertheless among the greatest and most uncertain ventures of modern mankind. The more equal conditions are, the less explanation there is for the differences that actually exist between people; and thus all the more unequal do individuals and groups become. . . . Whenever equality becomes a mundane fact in itself, without any gauge by which it may be measured or explained, then there is one chance in a hundred that it will be recognized simply as a working principle of a political organization *in which otherwise unequal people have equal rights;* there are ninety-nine chances that it will be mistaken for an innate quality of every individual, who is "normal" if he is like everybody else and "abnormal" if he happens to be different. *This perversion of equality from a political into a social concept is all the more dangerous when a society leaves but little space for special groups and individuals, for then their differences become all the more conspicuous.*[18]

Arendt's work as a historian of anti-Semitism brilliantly documents this dialectic of equality and difference, as well as showing how much more complicated and multilayered the dynamics of the social are. Note that the social in this context means *sociability,* patterns of human interaction, modalities of taste in dress, eating, leisure, and life-styles generally, differences in aesthetic, religious, and civic manners and outlooks, patterns of socializing, and forming marriages, friendships, acquaintanceships, and commercial exchanges. Undoubtedly, Arendt's attitude toward even this aspect of the social is somewhat ambivalent. It is within this sphere that the homogenization of tastes, attitudes, manners, and life-styles begins to spread in modernity; this is the sphere in which the parvenu dominates. By contrast, the pariah does not fare well in "society." The pariah is an outsider in matters of taste, manners, habits, and friendships. She breaks social conventions and flouts social norms; she goes against established traditions and plays with social expectations. The self-conscious pariah insists upon the fact of difference and distinction, but does so in a manner that is not wholly individualistic. The complete pariah would be the total outsider, the marginal bordering on suicide, insanity, or criminality. The self-conscious pariah is one who lives with difference and distinctness in such a way as to establish her difference in the "eyes" of society. The self-conscious pariah needs visibility, to be seen "as other" and as "different," even if only by a very small group, by a community of like-minded friends. Paradoxically then, the self-conscious pariah must both reject and affirm the sphere of the social.

This is precisely what Rahel Varnhagen's salon was: a space of sociability in which the individual desire for difference and distinctness could assume an intersubjective reality and in which unusual individuals, and primarily certain highly talented Jewish women, could find a "space" of visibility and self-expression. The Jewish salonnières of Berlin were the daughters and wives of well-to-do Jewish merchants and intellectuals who ran large and complex households and whose fathers and husbands were frequently absent from the house in the world of commerce and community affairs. These women accomplished a triple feat through their social activities. First, they emancipated themselves from traditional patriarchal families. Often they refused to marry their designated Jewish spouses-to-be; some converted to Christianity and lost all ties to the religion of their forebears. Their emancipation as "women" was often coupled with their rejection of traditional Judaism. Second, they helped create high culture in a crucial era at the end of the Enlightenment and the outbreak of Romanticism. They did so by creating a "social space" in which Berlin's intelligentsia—writers, artists, as well as civil servants and aristocrats—could gather together; exchange ideas, views, and texts; mix and mingle with each other; be seen, heard, and noticed by others. In this respect, they acted as the patrons of the intelligentsia in a city that at the time lacked a university, a parliament, and a generous court. Finally, the salons forged bonds across classes, religious groups, and the two sexes, creating the four walls within which new forms of sociability and intimacy could develop among members of an emergent civil society.[19]

What then are the forms of sociability appropriate to the salons? Here a distinction needs to be made between the French and the German versions of this occurrence. In the French salons, which developed in the shadow cast by the courtly regime of the "Roi Soleil," more stylized, ceremonial, and hierarchically defined manners are the norm. In the German salons, developing against the background of a weak aristocracy and a nonexistent courtly public sphere, more spontaneous, less stylized and ceremonial manners are the norms. In both cases, the salons bring to life the Enlightenment idea of "l'homme," "der Mensch," the human being as such. This vision states that when divested of all our social, cultural, and religious accoutrements, ranks, and distinction, we are all humans like each other. There is no greater proof of our common humanity besides the fact that we can communicate with and understand each other. The salons are social gatherings in which the "joy of conversation"[20] (the joy of communication and understanding as well as misunderstandings and lack of communication) is discovered. This is indeed Rahel Varnhagen's strength to which her admirers testify: the magic of her language, her capacity to express herself, her witticisms, her judgments. Rahel opens a world for those with whom she is communicating through her speech.

The joy of speech culminates in friendship, in that meeting of hearts, minds, and tastes between two individuals. Particularly in the case of the German salons, the search for a *Seelensfreund*, a friend of our soul, one who understands us perhaps better than we do ourselves, is predominant. With friends one shares one's soul; to share the soul, though—an entity that itself comes to be discovered in this new process of individuation—one has to project a certain depth of the self; one has to view the self as a being whose public presence does not reveal all. The public reveals and conceals at the same time; it is only in the withdrawal from the public into the sheltered space of a twosome or threesome relationship that one can also move inward, toward who one really is. In this respect as well, the salon is a fascinating space: unlike an assembly hall, a town square, a conference room, or even the family dinner table, the salon, with its large, luxurious, and rambling space, allows for moments of intimacy; in a salon one is with others but must not always be next to others. Salons are amorphous structures with no established rules of entry and exit for those who have formed intimacy; in fact, it may be a sign of good manners to foster and to allow the formation of intimacy among members of the salon. What is important here is the fluidity of the lines between the gathering as one and the gathering as many units of intimacy, and how the salons can be both private and public, both shared and intimate.

A new ideal of humanity, the joy of conversation, the search for friendship and the cultivation of intimacy—these are the ideals and aspirations of the salon phenomena in the age of modernity. Of course, the cleavage between ideals and reality accompany the salons no less than they do other social phenomena: despite their egalitarian humanist rhetoric, class, rank, and religious differences continue to play a role. The salons are not spaces for the whole people, including the laborers, the gardener, the milkmaid, and the coachdriver. They are largely upper-middle-class phenomena. The working and laboring classes of Europe in this period share a different mode of sociability.[21] As Rahel Varnhagen's own experience shows, many of her lovers of noble descent (most notably Count von Finckenstein) are unable to overcome class biases; and, as mentioned, with the defeat of the German armies in the hands of Napoleon and the rise of German nationalism, anti-Semitic feelings immediately come to the fore. Neither are the salons protected spaces of friendship and intimacy; intrigues, jealousies, petty fighting, and even treachery have their place here, as do erotic and sexual jealousy, infidelity, and betrayal.

The phenomenon of the salons, the predominance of the women among them, the kinds of public spaces they are and the forms of interaction, speech, and writing most closely associated with them pose fascinating problems for Hannah Arendt's political philosophy. In almost every respect the salons, as modes of the public sphere, contradict the agonal model of the public sphere of the polis that predominates in *The Human Condition*. Whereas the Greek polis and the public sphere characteristic of it, exclude women (and other members of the household like children and servants generally), the salons are spaces dominated by female presence. Whereas speech in the public spaces of the polis is "serious," guided by the concern for the "good of all," speech in the salons is playful and amorphous, freely taking the best of each. Whereas the public sphere of the polis attempts to exclude and to suppress eros, the salons cultivate the erotic. Of course, the erotic is never silenced in the Greek public sphere either: more often than not, it assumes a homosexual rather than heterosexual form. Whereas the spaces of the polis are governed by the ideals of "visibility" and "transparency," eighteenth-century salons are also governed by "visibility," but not by transparency: self-revelation and self-concealment, even pretending to be quite other than one is, are the norms.

Yet the salons and the polis also have features in common: they are based on assumptions of equality among the participants. In the case of the polis, this is the *isonomia* of political rank as citizen and of economic independence as *oikos despotes*. For the salon participants, equality is an ideal based upon their shared humanity, and their specific talents and abilities as individuals sharing certain tastes and sensibilities. Such equality prevails against otherwise existing social, economic, and even political inequality among salon members. Both the public spheres of the polis and the salons form bonds among their members. According to Aristotle, "friendship" among citizens of the polis is the virtue that good lawgivers try most to cultivate.[22] The salons are also spaces in which friendships are formed: these friendships are more personal than political, but here again the lines are not clear; the salons are spaces in which personal friendships may result in political bondings (what we nowadays refer to as "networking"). In effect, both the polis and the salons contribute to the formation of "civic friendship," either among a group of citizens or among a group of private, like-minded individuals who can gather for a common political purpose.[23]

If we proceed to decenter Arendt's political thought, if we read her work from the margins toward the center, then we can displace her fascination with the polis to make room for her more modernist and woman-friendly reflections on the salons. The "salons" must be viewed as transitory but also fascinating precursors of a certain transgression of the boundaries between the public and the private.[24] Arendt developed her political philosophy to ward off such transgressions, but as a radical democrat she could not but welcome such transgressions if they resulted in authentic political action, in a community of "speech and action."

It is my thesis that the alternative genealogy of modernity suggested by Arendt's *Rahel Varnhagen* leaves its traces throughout her work and suggests a major re-reading of her understanding of modernity and of the place of politics under conditions of modernity. First, as a historian of anti-Semitism and totalitarianism, Arendt focuses on transformations occurring in this sphere of modern societies as they eventually lead to the formation of a mass society. Both the dialectics of identity/difference at the root of modern anti-Semitism and the political power of totalitarianism are located by Arendt, the social and cultural historian, in this domain of modern society. Second, this aspect of the social is important not only for Arendt the historian, but for Arendt the political theorist as well. The kind of revitalization of public life that Arendt envisaged in her later work had at least two salient characteristics. On the one hand, Arendt was a political universalist, upholding egalitarian civil and political rights for all citizens, while supporting nonconformism and the expression of pariahdom in social and cultural life. On the other hand, Arendt's call for a recovery of the public world is anti-statist; indeed, we can complain that Arendt's philosophy as a whole suffers from a certain "state blindness." However, if such revitalization of public life does not mean the strengthening of the state but the growth of a political sphere independent of the state, where must this sphere be located, if not in civic and associational society? Arendt's early biography of Rahel Varnhagen then not only brings to light hitherto unknown dimensions of her treatment of the woman question; it also suggests a major re-reading of one of the central categories in her work—the social—paving the way for a new understanding of what it means to recover the public world under conditions of modernity.

## Notes

1. One of Arendt's earliest publications is a review of a book by Alice Ruehle-Gerstel, *Das Frauenproblem der Gegenwart*, which appeared in the journal *Die Gesellschaft*, affiliated with the Weimar socialists (vol. 10 [1932]: 177–79). In this review, Arendt matter-of-factly reports on the book's findings about continuing discrimination against women in the economic and political realms.

2. Elisabeth Young-Bruehl, *Hannah Arendt: For Love of the World* (New Haven: Yale University Press, 1982), 238.

3. Cf. the following passage from *The Human Condition*: "The fact that the modern age emancipated the working classes and women at nearly the same historical moment must certainly be counted among the characteristics of an age which no longer believes that bodily functions and material concerns should be hidden. It is all the more symptomatic of the nature of these phenomena that the few remnants of strict privacy even in our own civilization relate to the 'necessities' in the original sense of being necessitated by having a body." Hannah Arendt, *The Human Condition* (Chicago: University of Chicago Press, 1973), 73; hereafter cited as *HC*.

4. Adrienne Rich, "Conditions for Work: The Common World of Women," in *On Lies, Secrets and Silence* (New York: Norton, 1979), 212.

5. See bell hooks, *Feminist Theory from Margin to Center* (Boston: South End Press, 1984).

6. See Dagmar Barnouw, *Visible Spaces. Hannah Arendt and the German-Jewish Experience* (Baltimore: Johns Hopkins University Press, 1990), 30–31.

7. I am using the 1974 edition of the English translation by Richard and Clara Winston, *Rahel Varnhagen: The Life of a Jewish Woman* (New York: Harcourt Brace Jovanovich, rev. ed., 1974); hereafter cited as *RV*.

8. Sybille Bedford, "Emancipation and Destiny," in *Book Notes*, 12 December 1958, as quoted in Barnouw, *Visible Spaces*, 48.

9. For the cultural and social background of Rahel Varnhagen and the Jewish salonnières in general, I have benefited greatly from Deborah Hertz, *Jewish High Society in Old Regime Berlin* (New Haven: Yale University Press, 1988), 2.

10. For further discussion on the unusual character of Gentz, his anti-Semitism, and the subversive gender speculations of his letters, see Arendt, *RV* 80–81 and Marlis Gerhardt, "Einleitung. Rahel Levin, Friederike Robert, Madame Varnhagen," in *Rahel Varnhagen: Jeder Wunsch und Frivolität genannt. Briefe und Tagebücher* (Darmstadt: Luchterland, 1983), 22ff. In 1803 Gentz writes to Rahel: "Do you know, my Dear, why our relationship has become so great and perfect? I will tell you why. You are an infinitely producing and I, an infinitely receptive being. You are a great man; I am the first among all females who have ever lived. I know it: had I been a female physically, I had brought the whole world to kneel at my feet." Quoted by Marlis Gerhardt, "Einleitung," 23.

11. See Sybille Wirsing, "Urworte, nicht orphisch, sondern weiblich," review of the *Gesammelte Werke* of Rahel Varnhagen, 10 vols. ed. Konrad Feilchenfeldt, Uwe Schweikert, and Rahel E. Steiner (Munich: Matthes and Seitz, 1983). The review appeared in *Frankfurter Allgemeine Zeitung*, 21 January 1984, no. 18. This edition of Rahel's collected works is based on the early edition from the nineteenth century, originally edited by Rahel's husband, Karl August Varnhagen von Ense.

12. The themes of feeling alien, different, and other; the consciousness of oneself as a "pariah," as an outcast who does not fit in, as they are presented in Varnhagen's as well as Hannah Arendt's own life, are explored by Ingeborg Nordmann in "Fremdsein ist gut. Hannah Arendt über Rahel Varnhagen," in *Rahel Levin Varnhagen: Die Wiederentdeckung einer Schriftstellerin*, ed. Barbara Hahn and Ursula Isselstein (Göttingen: Vandenhoek & Ruprecht), 196–207.

13. *Hannah Arendt–Karl Jaspers Briefwechsel*, ed. Lotte Kohler and Hans Saner (Munich: Piper, 1985), 46; English translation, *Hannah Arendt–Karl Jaspers Correspondence, 1926–1969*, ed. Lotte Kohler and Hans Saner, trans. Robert and Rita Kimber (New York: Harcourt Brace Jovanovich, 1992), 10. On the whole I have used the quite excellent English edition of the correspondence. All future references to the *Correspondence* are to the English edition.

14. The continuing fascination with Rahel Varnhagen's life and letters, particularly as interpretations of her work are influenced by the various authors' perceptions of anti-Semitism and Jewish identity, are explored by Konrad Feilchenfeldt, "Rahel Philologie im Zeichen der antisemitischen Gefahr (Margarete Susman, Hannah Arendt, Käte Hamburger)," in *Rahel Levin Varnhagen*, ed. Hahn and Isselstein, 187–95.

15. Hannah Arendt, "On Humanity in Dark Times," *Men in Dark Times* (New York: Harcourt Brace Jovanovich, 1968), 4.

16. In a trenchant definition, Arendt writes: "Society is the form in which the fact of mutual dependence for the sake of life and nothing else assumes public significance and where the activities concerned with sheer survival are permitted to appear in public" (*HC* 46). The emergence of such a sphere of universal economic exchange and production, in which everything, including labor power, could be bought and sold as a commodity in the marketplace, has been seen by many thinkers before Hannah Arendt as marking an epochal turning point in human history. A century ago G. W. F. Hegel had named this sphere "the system of needs"; namely, the sphere in which economic exchange activities for the sole satisfaction of the needs and interests of the exchangers would become the norm of human

interaction. G. W. F. Hegel, "The System of Needs," in *Hegel's Philosophy of Right*, trans. and with notes by T. M. Knox (Oxford: Oxford University Press, 1973), 126ff.

17. When focusing upon this aspect of the rise of the social, Arendt introduces such contrasts as that between "behavior" and "action." Whereas "behavior" is the ideal typical activities of individuals insofar as they are the bearers of social roles (the bureaucrat, the businessman, the executive, etc.), "action" is individuating and individualizing behavior; it reveals the self rather than concealing him or her behind the social mask. "It is decisive that society," writes Arendt, "on all its levels, excludes the possibility of action, which formerly was excluded from the household. Instead, society expects from each of its members a certain kind of behavior, imposing innumerable and various rules, all of which tend to 'normalize' its members, to make them behave, to exclude spontaneous action or outstanding achievement" (*HC* 40). There is no analysis in Arendt's considerations on these matters in *The Human Condition* of the mechanisms of social control and integration through which such homogenization, leveling, and "normalization" are achieved.

18. Hannah Arendt, *The Origins of Totalitarianism* (New York: Harcourt Brace Jovanovich, 1979), 54. Emphasis added.

19. Commenting on this period in her most comprehensive and illuminating study, *Jewish High Society in Old Regime Berlin*, Deborah Hertz writes: "During the quarter century between 1780 and 1806 the city's Jewish salons caused a stir at home and abroad. Visitors from across Europe hailed the swift assimilation accomplished by the Jewish salonnières, whose social prominence was achieved at a time when the majority of central and eastern European Jews were still poor peddlers and traders, living in small villages, speaking Yiddish and following a traditional way of life. Surely here, in the drawing rooms of Berlin's rich and sophisticated Jewish women, was to be found the realization of the dream of emancipation that was just then being proposed by avant-garde intellectuals. . . . When the French salonnière Madame de Staël visited Berlin in 1804, she found it easier to gracefully entertain princes alongside humble writers than elsewhere in Germany" (3).

20. The discovery of the "joy of conversation" should not lead one to overlook the fact that the salons were fascinating gatherings in which the written and the spoken word often flowed into each other; even private, confidential letters were often written to be read out loud in public. Written texts were often first presented, improvised, and altered in the process. Even the literary creation of the amateurs, and most often of the women, were circulated in this space. See Peter Seibert, "Der Salon als Formation im Literaturbetrieb zur Zeit Rahel Levin Varnhagens," in *Rahel Levin Varnhagen: Die Wiederentdeckung einer Schriftstellerin*, ed. Hahn and Isselstein, 164–72; and Konrad Feilchenfeldt, "Die Berliner Salons der Romantik," in *Rahel Levin Varnhagen*, ed. Hahn and Isselstein, 152–63. The relation of the letter-writing form to "female" expressions of subjectivity is also explored by Petra Mitrovic, "Zum Problem der Konstitution von Ich-Identität in den Briefen der Rahel Varnhagen," master's thesis, University of Frankfurt, Institut für Deutsche Sprache und Literatur (1982). And this is precisely what Rahel Varnhagen has left to posterity of her work: not a literary or philosophical or political text, but her letters, her copious correspondence with her many friends.

21. Geoff Eley, "Nations, Publics, and Political Cultures: Placing Habermas in the Nineteenth Century," in *Habermas and the Public Sphere*, ed. Craig Calhoun (Cambridge: MIT Press, 1992).

22. Aristotle, "Nicomachean Ethics," in *The Basic Works of Aristotle*, ed. and with an introduction by Richard McKeon (New York: Random House, 1966), book VIII, chap. 8, pp. 1068ff.

23. The political dimensions of the salons in the age of the Enlightenment and the French Revolution have been discussed by Jürgen Habermas, *The Structural Transformation of the Public Sphere*, trans. T. Burger and F. Lawrence (Cambridge: MIT Press, 1989) and more recently

from a perspective that takes gender differentials into account by Joan B. Landes, *Women and the Public Sphere in the Age of the French Revolution* (Ithaca: Cornell University Press, 1988). I certainly do not want to suggest that the salons can serve as a normative model of a public sphere for today. Their political, cultural, and gender limitations are all too clear. My point rather is twofold: first, that the kind of public space which the salons represent should lead us to re-read Arendt's concept of the public sphere in a more nuanced way; and second, that whatever revival of the public sphere is possible under conditions of complex and differentiated societies, will take place not only in the sphere of the political but in the domain of civic and associational society as well. The salons are precursors of such civic and associational society; they are not models for its future reconstruction, but past carriers of some of its future potentials. I thank Bonnie Honig for leading me to clarify the political significance of the salons.

24. Deborah Hertz writes: "That the home could be a public as well as private place was obviously one reason why salons were organized by women. The synthesis of the private and the public in salons was evident in the curious, bygone way that guests arrived at the door. . . . That social institutions like salons should ever have appeared in preindustrial Europe, even intermittently, came to seem quite odd. It was odd that private drawing rooms should have been public places, odd that in an age when women were excluded from educational and civic institutions, even wives of rich and powerful men should lead intellectual discussions among the most learned men of their cities. It was odd that men and women should have had important intellectual exchanges during centuries when the two sexes generally had little to say to each other and few public places in which to say it." *Jewish High Society in Old Regime Berlin*, 18.

# 5

# Refiguring the Jewish Question: Arendt, Proust, and the Politics of Sexuality

## Morris B. Kaplan

## Private and Public—Personal and Political

In this essay, I recuperate Hannah Arendt's vision of democratic politics to theorize the reach of a movement for lesbian and gay rights and

I developed this essay during my tenure as the inaugural Rockefeller Foundation Fellow in Legal Humanities at the Stanford Humanities Center, 1993–94, partially funded by President's Junior Faculty Fellowship from Purchase College, State University of New York. It is part of a larger study of lesbian and gay rights, *Sexual Justice*, to be published by Routledge in 1995. My interest in Hannah Arendt goes back almost three decades and has been nourished over the years by conversation with Robert J. Anderson, Seyla Benhabib, Richard Bernstein, Kenley R. Dove, W. Thomas Schmid, William R. Torbert, and James Walsh. Frank Farrell especially encouraged me to pursue the analogy between homosexuality and the Jewish question. At Stanford, Paul Robinson and Pericles Lewis commented on an earlier draft. Ken Dove liberation. Such an effort encounters a formidable obstacle in her definition of the political as a domain necessarily distinct from the private realm of the household and threatened with extinction by the omnivorous demands of the "social" in modern times.[1] It is easy to read Arendt as rejecting implicitly any possibility of a politics organized around issues of sexuality or gender. Nevertheless, Hannah Arendt is almost unique among philosophers of the twentieth century, or perhaps any century, in placing democracy and politics at the center of her thought. She linked them to fundamental aspects of the human situation, most important, the irreducible fact of human plurality and the distinctiveness of our capacity to act. Crucial to her vision was a conception of active citizenship and robust public life especially as manifest in the Athenian polis. In that context she articulated the sharp division between the household and its proper activities, necessary to sustain life, and the city in which common action aimed at a glory transcending self-preservation. The starkness of this boundary between private and public appears to exclude not only a wide range of concerns and activities but also large numbers of persons from public life. Arendt acknowledges that the freedom of citizens to act in the polis was utterly dependent on the labor of others—women, slaves, artisans, resident aliens—who provided for life's necessities. Although her view of the polis is to some extent mythical and idealized, she does not conceal the flaws in its foundation that today make it unacceptable as a form of political life. She seeks rather to retrieve from her historical narrative an image of democratic citizenship and public life increasingly hard to discern among the institutions and practices of modernity.

Despite her turn to the ancient polis for inspiration, Arendt believed that the continuity of tradition was irretrievably broken, disrupted, and shattered by events for which it had somehow also prepared the way. Precisely this gap "between past and future" enables us to examine the fragments of tradition in the light of current historical circumstances and perhaps find some material with which to construct anew.[2] Her effort to redeem some moments from the fatally troubled political and philosophical history of the modern West led her to write about the great democratic revolutions of the eighteenth century,[3] the French

---

provided a timely and pointed critique that proved very helpful in clarifying my argument. Bonnie Honig has earned very special thanks for her intensive efforts as an engaged, sympathetic, and critical editor to bring this essay to fruition.

Resistance,[4] the revolts in Hungary and East Berlin,[5] and the civil rights and anti–Vietnam War movements in the United States, and the student movement in Europe and the United States in the 1960s.[6] In these studies, she displayed greater sympathy for the egalitarian aspirations of modern democracy. The historical specificity of these works requires us to recontextualize the division between private and public formulated in *The Human Condition*. In this essay, I turn to Arendt's analysis of the Jewish question in modern Europe, which she saw as intertwined with the fate of the modern nation-state, to investigate fundamental dilemmas of modern democracy, especially the tensions between the aspiration to political equality and the facts of social difference.

It is perhaps especially appropriate to begin this reading of Hannah Arendt's understanding of the connections between the personal and the political with passages from a letter she wrote to her friend and mentor Karl Jaspers on 26 January 1946, shortly after they had resumed a relationship that had been interrupted by the war. In the course of catching him up on the conditions of her life in America, Arendt makes a number of comments bearing on her attitude toward the Jewish question and more generally, on the connections among the personal, political, and intellectual dimensions of her life. Matter-of-factly, she reports: "I continue to use my old name. That's quite common here in America when a woman works, and I have gladly adopted this custom out of conservatism (and also because I wanted my name to identify me as a Jew)."[7] In another letter later that year, she declared: "Politically, I will always speak only in the name of the Jews when circumstances force me to give my nationality."[8] The decision to retain her "own name" is a political one; it is a way of identifying herself as a Jew under historical circumstances when being a Jew had become a fateful and dangerous condition. By announcing herself a Jew, Arendt is neither revealing some deep truth about her personal identity nor making a declaration of religious faith. Retaining her "Jewish name" is a sign of affiliation and solidarity with a people who have suffered mightily the burdens of twentieth-century European history.

However, this political gesture is necessitated by something besides Arendt's birth in a Jewish family: she has married a non-Jew. Both of these facts of her life, putatively "private" in the extreme, are taken by Hannah Arendt to have important political and social consequences: "If I had wanted to become respectable, I would either have had to give up my interest in Jewish affairs or not marry a non-Jewish man, either option equally inhuman and in a sense crazy" (*Correspondence* 29). Arendt's political and intellectual engagement with "Jewish affairs" lasted nearly a lifetime. Moreover, her analysis of the anomic consequences of Jewish attempts at assimilation in nineteenth-century Europe focuses importantly on the displacement of the strains of unequal political status onto private life, especially in the context of "mixed marriages." The question of "respectability" echoes Arendt's later critique of the tyranny of the social. Equally important, her rejection of respectability aligns her with the "conscious pariah," a term that she adopted from the French Jewish thinker Bernard Lazare.[9] For Arendt, Jews in nineteenth-century Europe who were in a position to assimilate to gentile society were forced to choose between a parvenu conformism to standards of behavior by which they were always found wanting and an abject status outside of society as members of a pariah people. In both cases, the individual was reduced to a function of her social status. The "conscious pariah" refuses this choice and insists on thinking for herself.

In this letter to Jaspers, Arendt alludes with some irony to her sense of the importance of remaining outside of society for preserving one's integrity: "As you see, I haven't become respectable in any way. I'm more than ever of the opinion that a decent human existence is possible today only on the fringes of society where one then runs the risk of starving or being stoned to death" (*Correspondence* 29). The importance of maintaining a thoughtful independence of social convention is central in Arendt's work right up to her thesis on "the banality of evil" in *Eichmann in Jerusalem* and her portrayal of thinking as dialogue of the soul with itself in *The Life of the Mind*. The connection between this withdrawal into conversation with one's self and "a decent human existence" is made explicit in the latter work: "When everybody is swept away unthinkingly by what everybody else does and believes in, those who think are drawn out of hiding because their refusal to join in is conspicuous and thereby becomes a kind of action."[10]

The relationship between Arendt's intellectual work and her political commitments is especially illuminated by remarks in this letter. She defines her writing and thought in these terms: "My literary existence, as opposed to my existence as a member of society, has two major roots: First, thanks to my husband, I have learned to think politically and see historically; and, second, I have refused to abandon the Jewish question as the focal point of my historical and political thinking" (*Correspondence* 31). In describing her current work to her former teacher Jaspers, she invokes her husband as mentor.[11] Her thinking is itself dependent on the conversations of friendship and intimacy, perhaps even, on the sharing of a household. The juncture of the private domain of thought with the public world of writing becomes a site of tension in her friendship with Jaspers as she explains her ambivalence about contributing work to a new German journal as he has urged her to do: "It is not an easy thing for me to contribute to a German journal. . . . It seems to me that none of us can return (writing is surely a form of return) merely because people again seem prepared to recognize Jews as Germans or something else. We can return only if we are welcome as Jews. That would mean that I would gladly write something if I can write as a Jew on some aspect of the Jewish question" (Correspondence 31–32). As these passages from her letter to Jaspers should indicate, the Jewish question had a complex resonance in the intellectual, political, and personal aspects of Arendt's life. Indeed, one of the most fascinating aspects of her correspondence with Jaspers is the interplay among their sustained, reflective exchanges on the politics of the twentieth century; their ongoing dialogue about the complexities of Jewish, German, and German Jewish identities; and the unfolding of a rich and rewarding friendship that came to include two couples, each composed of a non-Jewish German man and a German Jewish woman.

From the outset of her engagement with the Jewish question in *Rahel Varnhagen*, Arendt insisted that the great mistake of European Jewry and its friends was to treat as a social question what was inherently a political question about equal citizenship. Arendt's concern for the pressures on personal lives generated by the strains of legal emancipation and social assimilation focused particularly on marriage and the family. Restrictions on intermarriage and the stigma attached to "mixed marriages" by both gentile and Jewish communities were important factors in maintaining Jewish difference and subordination. Arendt addressed the political significance of restrictions on marriage in other contexts as well: already in the 1950s, she identified the anti-miscegenation laws in the southern United States as a major component enforcing racial inequality.[12] She was similarly critical of religious restrictions on marriage in the State of Israel.[13] If we think with Arendt against Arendt on the issue of the relation between private households and the public arena of citizenship, we see that the capacity to establish and maintain a household affects both the personal and the political domains.[14] Drawing the boundaries between private and public and ensuring that all democratic citizens have a place in both is an issue, not of normal politics, but of the politics of founding celebrated in her work of the 1960s.[15] The construction of domesticity on egalitarian terms becomes a crucial piece of the unfinished business of democratic revolution. Might Arendt's recognition of the mutual penetration of the personal and the political adumbrate a politics of gender and sexuality?

The legal status of homosexuality in the United States today effectively constructs lesbians and gays as second-class citizens. Consider the following: the criminalization of same-sex activities in one-half the states and the denial to homosexuals of constitutional privacy rights that are well established for heterosexual citizens; the failure of most states and the federal government to protect lesbian and gay citizens from retaliation for the exercise of political freedom in their efforts to attain full equality; the stigmatization as demands for "special rights" of efforts to attain constitutional equality; and the systematic denial of legal recognition to same-sex couples and queer families who want to establish lasting relationships.[16] Arendt's conception of the centrality of the status of citizenship for guaranteeing human rights helps to focus the range of issues raised by a movement for lesbian and gay emancipation. Her insistence that human rights can be actualized only through equal membership within a political society,[17] and her belief that political freedom depends on a capacity to establish private households suggests that she would support the claims of lesbian and gay citizens to protection against social retaliation for the exercise of political rights and to the recognition of rights to marry or otherwise establish legally recognized domestic partnerships.[18]

The great power of Arendt's analysis of the problematic history of modern democracy is to direct our attention to the broader historical and cultural matrix within which rights-claims and political differences are contested and adjudicated. Here too Arendt's analysis of the Jewish question has implications for the politics of sexuality. In what follows, I shall pursue this analogy more fully, probing Arendt's analysis of anti-Semitism and of the ambiguous situation of assimilated Jews in gentile society in the nineteenth century to shed light on two central phenomena of lesbian and gay life: homophobia and the closet. I shall then turn to Arendt's reading of Proust to show how the racial construction of Jews and homosexuals as "natural" essential identities in the nineteenth century worked to foreclose the individual and collective agency of both groups. Finally I shall turn to recent work by Sander Gilman on

"Jewishness" to attend more fully than Arendt herself does to the interpenetration of race with sexuality and gender within scientific discourse.

# The Jewish Question

At least as old as Proust, the analogy between the Jewish question and the situation of homosexuals has been deployed quite recently by Larry Kramer in *Reports from the Holocaust*[19] and Eve Kosofsky Sedgwick in *Epistemology of the Closet*.[20] Kramer explicitly invokes Arendt's analysis of anti-Semitism from *The Origins of Totalitarianism* and her critique of Jewish leadership during the Final Solution from *Eichmann in Jerusalem*.[21] He uses Arendt to establish an analogy between anti-Semitism and contemporary homophobia and to criticize the efforts of leaders within the gay community for their responses to the AIDS epidemic. His argument focuses almost exclusively on Arendt's contention that modern European Jews were made vulnerable to anti-Semitism because some enjoyed highly visible wealth without the responsibilities of political power. Kramer compares this situation with that of contemporary gay men whom he casts as conspicuous consumers in the pursuit of their own pleasures. Kramer's picture of lesbian and gay realities is distorted and inaccurate, although it may capture a widespread perception. As for Arendt's *Eichmann* book, Kramer's reading misses her nuance and continually crosses the line from identifying the complexities of agency in totalitarian contexts to simply blaming the victims. Kramer uses the comparison of gays with Jews to support his own aggressive intervention in the AIDS crisis relying on the hyperbolic and misleading analogy between the epidemic and the Nazi attempt at genocide.[22] But there is more to the analogy between anti-Semitism and homophobia, Jewish history and lesbian/gay existence, than Kramer's example suggests.

Eve Kosofsky Sedgwick's *The Epistemology of the Closet*, opens with a reading of the story of Queen Esther (as refracted by Racine's play and Proust's allusions), as a "coming out" story in which Esther's concealment of her Judaism from king and court figures as a metaphor of the closet.[23] For Sedgwick, the comparison between homosexuals and Jews turns on the possibility of concealment, of passing, and is reinforced in Racine by his figuring of the Jews as "an unclean people" and "an

abomination against nature." The closet is central to Sedgwick's interpretation of the emergence of homosexuality in the nineteenth century
in contrast with a pervasively homosocial order where close ties among
men perpetuated male domination. She argues that homophobia protected homosocial men from the dangerous proximity of an expressed
and threatening homo-*sexuality*. Homosexuals were marked as abject,
marginal "others," yet invested with powers of invisibility and disguise.
According to Sedgwick, the "minority politics" of the story of Esther
and its conservative treatment of gender suggests a complex relationship
between gender as a universal category and homosexuality as a minority
identity that does not easily permit systematization or the establishment
of priority. Rather, Sedgwick marks a vacillation, within both homopho-
bic and emancipatory discourses, between "minoritizing" views of homosexuality that define a distinct group with a common identity and
"universalizing" views that link homosexuality to tendencies shared by
all human beings. That vacillation may be read as expressing in general
theoretical terms an analogy with the social dilemmas of assimilation
and difference generated by Jewish emancipation.

Hannah Arendt's own engagement with the Jewish question was in
large part a response to the contingent historical developments that
made the issue a central concern in twentieth-century European politics,
with life-or-death implications for those affected. In an interview in
1964, Arendt reflected on her turn away from scholarship after 1933: "I
realized what I then expressed time and again in the sentence: If one is
attacked as a Jew one must defend oneself as a Jew. Not as a German,
not as a world-citizen, not as an upholder of the rights of Man, or
whatever. . . . [B]elonging to Judaism had become my own problem, and
my own problem was political. Purely political!"[24] These attitudes are
fully developed in Arendt's unrelenting investigation of the question of
what it has meant to be a Jew in modern Europe: "It has been one of the
most unfortunate facts in the history of the Jewish people that only its
enemies, and almost never its friends, understood that the Jewish
question was a political one."[25] Arendt insists that one can understand
this tragic history only by focusing on both the actions of those with
power and the responses of Jews themselves to the conditions they faced.
She rejects the claim that anti-Semitism is necessarily an eternal,
recurrent theme in the history of the West, and she dismisses more
general scapegoat theories, because neither attends to the specificities of
historical circumstance and political agency among Jews.

Treating the Jewish question as a social issue resulted in a double movement by which Jews were characterized in psychological rather than religious or national terms and Jewish difference was attributed to inherent racial characteristics. This racial construction of Jewishness, together with the refusal of European Jewish communities to engage in collective political action, combined to increase Jewish vulnerability to the forces of anti-Semitism within modern totalitarianism. The modern nonpolitical and, increasingly, nonreligious and non-national under-standing of Judaism displaced the burdens of inequality onto personal and family life. Ultimately, Judaism was transformed into "Jewishness": the effects of a common history and collective political status were attributed to individual Jews as immutable racial characteristics. This tendency was reinforced by the chauvinism with which some secularized Jews continued to cultivate a sense of "chosenness" despite the eclipse of their traditional faith. "Jewishness" became part of the self-under-standing of individual Jews: "And the more the fact of Jewish birth lost its religious, national and socio-economic significance, the more obses-sive Jewishness became; Jews were obsessed by it as one may be by a physical defect or advantage, and addicted to it as one may be to a vice" (OT 84). By the time genocidal anti-Semites came to power, many throughout society were prepared to accept the characterization of "Jewishness" as an essential trait that could not be changed but only accepted or eliminated.

The specifics of the Jewish question were deeply implicated in the transition to modernity and the emergence of the nation-state in Western Europe. Throughout the Middle Ages, the political and social rights and privileges of Jews, like those of other groups, were defined by their collective status in relation to a web of interlocking historical and legal relationships. Because they were not members of Christendom, the Jews were always outside the boundaries of traditionally defined classes and communities. Periodically exiled from various parts of Europe, Jewish families became extended across conventional boundaries and maintained ties that made them useful as sources of both funds and information. As powerful princes worked to consolidate territory and to centralize administration in national states, Jewish financial support became for them an alternative to feudal ties. Jewish status and privilege became closely linked with consolidating national monarchies, without Jews themselves playing a political role in these transformations. Jews were increasingly dependent on nation-states without becoming part of

the nation. Because of their relative powerlessness, Jewish communities
became an easy target for those forces that opposed the end of feudalism
and the consolidation of nation-states. The extended Jewish family
figured importantly in the perception of Jews as having no loyalty to
local communities. Resentment of this alien and self-enclosed entity
within the body politic was heightened by the visibility of a small
number of banking families that financed the new order.[26] When modern
racial ideologies appeared with the "pan" movements in Germany and
eastern Europe, this widespread conception of Jewish existence, together
with the biblical notions of chosenness adopted by these movements,
made anti-Semitism a political issue.[27] For Arendt, the history of the
Jews as a people outside the nation-state but implicated in its development positioned them as models for movements eager to ground politics
in ties of "blood" rather than citizenship and as targets for these same
movements whose real adversary was the nation-state. Just as Jews came
to represent the modern democratic nation-state in the eyes of its
discontents, so too homosexuals may bear the weight of a range of
dissatisfactions with liberal society, especially as homosexuality is taken
to threaten traditional institutions of religious or family life.

The French Revolution and the Napoleonic Wars made legal equality
and Jewish emancipation an issue throughout Europe. This situation
reflected more general incoherence in nation-states that established legal
and political equality against the background of an increasingly stratified
class society. Arendt argues that Jewish emancipation had different
ramifications for distinct classes within Jewish society as well. Access to
non-Jewish society was available to "exceptional" Jews willing to separate
from the "Jew in general" and the collective life of the Jewish people.
Wealthy or educated Jews faced a choice between remaining in solidarity
with a people stigmatized as pariahs or embracing the status of parvenus
in a larger society that condemned their fellow Jews. Often, these
"exceptions" joined in condemning some segment of the Jewish people—
the poor or immigrants from Eastern Europe—in the same terms applied
by the larger society to all Jews. The conditions of their assimilation
were highly ambiguous. Although expected to forgo identification with
the Jewish community, these few were admitted to high society *as Jews*
recognized as interesting precisely because of their questionable origins:
"under no circumstances were they allowed simply to disappear among
their neighbors" (OT 65). This description of the situation of assimilated
Jews bears an uncanny resemblance to that of homosexuals whose lives

are structured by "the closet." The contradiction between public persona and personal existence falsifies both domains; trying "to be a Jew at home and a man in the streets" generated intolerable strains. Homosexuals "in the closet" are analogous to the parvenus, while "out" gays become pariahs.

The interaction of "exceptional" Jews, non-Jewish society, and the political environment of the nation-state led to the construction of "Jewishness" as a *racial* category: "Instead of being defined by nationality or religion, Jews were being transformed into a social group whose members shared certain psychological attributes and reactions, the sum total of which was supposed to constitute 'Jewishness' " (*OT* 66). This increasingly sharp focus of the Jewish question on the most private and intimate details of individual life among assimilated Jews produced a recognizable "Jewish type" that exercised an ambiguous fascination for a society increasingly plagued by boredom: "Jews became people with whom one hoped to while away some time. The less one thought of them as equals, the more attractive and entertaining they became" (*OT* 67). For Arendt, "Jewishness" was itself an effect of complex political, social, and psychological interactions: "As long as defamed peoples and classes exist, parvenu- and pariah-qualities will be produced anew by each generation with incomparable monotony, in Jewish society and everywhere else" (*OT* 66). However, the interplay between political equality and social difference led to the eventual "racialization" of marginal groups in the course of the nineteenth century. Those qualities that defined some groups as social exotics were "naturalized," in popular opinion and in scientific discourse, to become identified with inherent biological or racial conditions that individuals could not escape. This historical social, political, and ideological configuration gave rise to both "Jewishness" and "homosexuality" in late nineteenth-century Europe.

Hannah Arendt's analysis of the impact of anti-Semitism on newly emancipated, assimilating Jews in European society in the nineteenth century resonates richly with Sedgwick's work on the dynamics of the closet in organizing the discourses of homophobia; lesbians and gays are consigned to a regime of silence and discretion, subjected to a knowing social gaze that defines us as both radically "other" and perfectly transparent. Arendt's portrayal of the peculiar combination of attraction and repulsion that fueled the exoticization of Jews and homosexuals in fin-de-siècle France evokes a sense of uncanny repetition in a world where clean-cut lesbians hold hands on *Newsweek* covers, queer *menages à trois* stage lovers' quarrels on the Oprah Winfrey show, and supermarket tabloids detail the last days of the actor Raymond Burr (*Perry Mason, Ironside*) with his longtime male lover. All of this at the same time that same-sex activities remain criminal in half the states, only eight states protect homosexual citizens against discrimination and nowhere in the United States may same-sex lovers establish socially and legally recognized households. Arendt's lesson from the history of nineteenth-century anti-Semitism: celebrity is no substitute for political equality.

## "Accursed Race," "New Species"

JACK: Yes, but you said yourself that a severe chill was not hereditary.
ALGERNON: It usen't to be, I know—but I daresay it is now. Science is
  always making wonderful improvements in things.
    (Oscar Wilde, *The Importance of Being Earnest* [1895], act 2)

Hannah Arendt introduces the comparison between Jews and homosexuals in *The Origins of Totalitarianism* with a reading of Proust: "There is no better witness, indeed, of this period when society had emancipated itself completely from public concerns, and when politics itself was becoming a part of social life" (OT 80). Proust dramatized the "racial" conceptions of "Jewishness" and "homosexuality" that emerged from complex negotiations between demands for conformity and assertions of difference:

> Proust's "innate disposition" is nothing but this personal, private obsession. . . . Proust mistook it for "racial predestination," because he saw and depicted only its social aspect and individual reconsiderations. . . . Both [Jews and homosexuals] felt either superior or inferior, but in any case proudly different from other normal beings; both believed their difference to be a natural fact acquired by birth; both were constantly justifying *not what they did, but what they were;* and both, finally, always wavered between such apologetic attitudes and sudden, provocative claims that they were an elite. (OT 84; my emphasis)

Arendt uses Proust to portray the interplay between political and social factors that transformed Jews and homosexuals into exotic specimens.

She situates this exoticization of Jews and homosexuals in the triumph of bourgeois society: "The victory of bourgeois values over the citizen's sense of responsibility meant the decomposition of political issues into their dazzling, fascinating reflections in society" (OT 80). Groups associated with transgression offered a locus of fascination and a promise of passion. This shift did not reflect a new tolerance for acts and conditions previously linked to crime or sin. Rather, crime itself had become attractive and was savored by a society grown sated with respectability. Here, what Eve Kosofsky Sedgwick, in her essay on Proust, calls the "spectacle of the closet" is identified as the social condition of both assimilated Jews and closeted homosexuals. Each is distinguished by his "open secret":[28] "This in turn resulted in the typically equivocal situation in which the new members could not confess their identity openly, and yet could not hide it either. . . . [O]nly one's Jewishness (or homosexuality) had opened the doors of the exclusive salons, while at the same time they made one's position extremely insecure" (OT 82). Arendt's characterization of this effect on Jews resonates with the ambiguities of the closet: "In this equivocal situation, Jewishness was for the individual Jew at once a physical stain and a mysterious personal privilege, both inherent in a 'racial predestination' " (OT 82).

Arendt's handling of the Jewish question converges with Michel Foucault's account of the formation in the nineteenth century of "perverted" sexual identities as biologically grounded and medically defined conditions. Foucault describes a shift in nineteenth-century medicine from a universalizing discourse of sexual acts, potentially criminal or sinful but within the capacity of any ordinary person, to the minoritizing construction of "perverted" sexual identities for which behavior became "symptomatic"; that is, revelatory of an inner truth about fundamentally different kinds of persons. This discursive shift also marked a transition from controlling individual behavior primarily through religious and juridical prohibitions on conduct to an effort to produce "normal" individuals through newly dominant medical, pedagogic, and therapeutic professions and practices. For Foucault, this transition marked the emergence of a new species: "Homosexuality appeared as one of the forms of sexuality when it was transposed from the practice of sodomy onto a kind of interior androgyny, a hermaphroditism of the soul. The sodomite had been a temporary aberration; the homosexual was now a species."[29]

Arendt's analysis of the comparison between Jews and homosexuals supports Foucault's emphasis on the contingent historical and fundamentally political character of the construction of sexual identities. According to Arendt, the complex and ambivalent shift "from crime to vice," in social attitude toward Jews and homosexuals put each in a precarious position: "Human wickedness, if accepted by society, is changed from an act of will into an inherent, psychological quality which man cannot choose or reject but which is imposed upon him from without and which rules him as compulsively as the drug rules the addict" (*OT* 80). For Proust, the transformation of criminal action into an inherent vicious behavior results in a denial of human dignity, as moral responsibility is displaced by the language of racial predisposition or medical pathology. Arendt describes his insight in these terms:

> "Punishment is the right of the criminal," of which he is deprived if (in the words of Proust) judges assume and are more inclined to pardon murder in inverts and treason in Jews for reasons derived from . . . "racial predestination." It is an attraction to murder and treason which hides behind such perverted tolerance, for in a moment it can switch to a decision to liquidate not only all actual criminals but all who are "racially" predestined to commit certain crimes (*OT* 80–81).

For Arendt, this insight foreshadows the grim reality of the concentration camps, where Nazi racial ideology led to the incarceration and eventual murder of "racially" defined groups independent of any actions of individuals, and where convicted criminals, punished for specific violations, benefited from legal status denied to the innocent (*OT* 447–57). Jews and homosexuals were finally undone by this revaluation of the stigmas by which they had been historically defined, the sins or crimes of rejecting Christ and Christendom or of practicing sodomy. Jews were still suspected of harboring a tendency to treason; homosexuals were still seen as threatening religious and family values with their transgressive passions. These associations with treason and illicit passion, which made them exotics, were reified as immutable qualities by nineteenth-century racial ideology: "Jews had been able to escape from Judaism into conversion; from Jewishness there was no escape. A crime moreover, is met with punishment; a vice can only be exterminated" (*OT* 87).

Arendt uses Proust's text to focus on the construction of Jews and of homosexuals in racial terms that perpetuated historical stigmas. I develop this analogy further by reading some passages from the section of Proust's *Cities of the Plain* called "the accursed race" (*la race maudite*). The narrator Marcel has been spying on a serendipitous assignation between M. de Charlus, a middle-aged aristocratic queen, and Jupien, a retired tailor. His observation of the flirtation and subsequent sexual encounter between the two leads to an extended meditation on homosexuals and their place in the world. The narrator describes his "discovery" of the Baron's homosexuality:

> Although in the person of M. de Charlus another creature was coupled, as the horse in the centaur, which made him different from other men, although this creature was one with the Baron, I had never perceived it. Now the abstraction had become materialized, the creature at last discerned had lost its power of remaining invisible, and the transformation of M. de Charlus into a new person was so complete.[30]

Critical to this transformation is a shift in the narrator's view of the Baron's *sex*: "I now understood, moreover, why earlier, when I had seen him coming away from Mme. de Villeparisis's, I had managed to arrive at the conclusion that M. de Charlus looked like a woman: he was one!" This moment in Proust powerfully illuminates several of Foucault's insights into the emergence of the "homosexual" as a new species. The narrator has witnessed an act of sodomy; what he describes is a "transformation" of the Baron into "a new person." Here is Foucault's description of the emergent "homosexual":

> Nothing that went into his total composition was unaffected by his sexuality. It was everywhere present in him: at the root of all his actions because it was their insidious and indefinitely active principle; written immodestly on his face and body because it was a secret that always gave itself away. It was consubstantial with him, less as a habitual sin than as a singular nature. . . . [A] certain way of inverting the masculine and feminine in oneself.[31]

M. de Charlus is not only exotic, but monstrous, in the narrator's eyes. His strangeness is somewhat clarified by uncovering his inner femininity, identified as the truth that explains the Baron's earlier ambiguity: he really was a woman all along. However, in Proust's text, there is a further turn in this dialectic of concealment and revelation. After all, Marcel discovers the Baron's "inner truth" only as a result of a fairly complicated effort to spy and eavesdrop on the two men. The elaborate account of M. de Charlus's dalliance with Jupien and of the revelation of the Baron's nature also exposes its narrator as a voyeur.

Arendt does not comment on this complex erotic dynamic nor on its feminization of the homosexual. However, sexual ambiguity and gender inversion are central to Proust's portrayal of the "race" of homosexuals.[32] We are in the presence of the "third sex," defined most famously as a "female brain in a male's body."[33] The new medical conception of homosexuality combined an earlier notion of gender inversion with inversion of sexual object. Proust's deployment of that rhetoric defines the Baron's inner femininity in terms of (hetero)sexual object choice:

> He belonged to the race of beings, less paradoxical than they appear, whose ideal is manly precisely because their temperament is feminine, and who in ordinary life resemble other men in appearance only; there where each of us carries, inscribed in those eyes through which he beholds everything in the universe, a human form engraved on the surface of the pupil, for them it is not that of a nymph but that of an ephebe. A race upon which a curse is laid and which must live in falsehood and perjury . . . (636)

This passage further illustrates the ambiguity that pervades this entire section as a result of the problematic position of its narrator.[34] Figuring homosexuality in terms of the forms inscribed in the gaze of desire serves to remind the reader of the narrator's own intensely interested observation of the encounter between two men. His ambiguous rhetoric joins the discourse of racial science with biblical and Greek myth and the language of medical pathology: "what they have been calling their love . . . springs not from an ideal of beauty which they have chosen but from an incurable disease" (639). Later, "psychical hermaphroditism," femininity, and the primitive are joined in a phantasmagoria of evolutionary biology: "In this respect the race of inverts . . . might be traced back further still, . . . to that initial hermaphroditism of which certain rudiments of male organs in the anatomy of women and of female organs in that of men seem still to preserve the trace" (653). This deployment of the languages of science and pathology works to provide some cover for the voyeurism of the narrator. His construction of himself as the disinterested observer is already at work earlier in the section where he describes himself passing time as a "botanist" studying the sex life of flowers when he happens to witness the encounter of the Baron and Jupien. Ruminations on the erotic language of flowers are threaded throughout Marcel's portrayal of the mores of the "accursed race," positioning the narrator in a stance of scientific detachment that preserves the distance between an acceptable homosociality and a pathological homosexuality, between the narrator's "disinterested" gaze and the amorous glances exchanged by the men on whom he spies.

Soon after, Proust introduces "the dark comparison" between the race of homosexuals and the Jews. Jews and homosexuals, as members of stigmatized groups, internalize the social gaze that abjects them. They come to reject each other and to identify themselves with their deep desires for those with power, Christians or "normal" men, "shunning one another, seeking out those who are most directly their opposite, who do not want their company, forgiving their rebuffs, enraptured by their condescension" (638). Both combine the parvenu's anxious search for acceptance by others with the self-hatred that divides him from others of his kind. Here Proust moves from an essentialist to a historical conception of both homosexual and Jewish identity, noting the tendency of each to claim Socrates and Jesus as forebears, "without reflecting that there were no abnormal people when homosexuality was the norm, no anti-Christians before Christ, that the opprobrium alone makes the crime because it has allowed to survive only those who remained obdurate to every warning, to every example, to every punishment, by virtue of an innate disposition" (639). The paradox is inescapable: this "innate disposition" results in "Jewishness" or "homosexuality" only under social conditions of Christian orthodoxy or compulsory heterosexuality.

Insistent in his use of metaphors of race to portray their condition, Proust likens homosexuals not only to Jews, but to blacks as well, suggesting that this accounts for the persistence among them of dangerous desires that distinguish them from "the other race" among which they live: "Perhaps, to form a picture of these, we ought to think, if not of the wild animals that never became domesticated, of the lion cubs, allegedly tamed, which are still lions at heart, then at least, of the negroes whom the comfortable existence of the white man renders desperately unhappy and who prefer the risks of life in the wild and its incomprehensible joys" (647). Proust pervasively associates the trope of race with references to "primitive" nature (including animals and plants), to the "feminine," and to the discourses of science and medicine. At once, male homosexuality is identified with femininity and figured as a threatening animality. We are not far from the rhetoric by which gays in the military are imagined as both lacking in the manliness to be good soldiers and posing a predatory threat to their fellows in the showers.

But the rhetoric of science does not completely displace politics. Proust presents a playful variation on the biblical account of the origins of "the accursed race" in Sodom and Gomorrah. It appears that the angels charged with destruction of the "cities of the plain," not being themselves sodomites, were easily fooled by the disguises and deceptions perpetrated by those sinful folk: "they allowed all the shameless Sodomites to escape. . . . With the result that they engendered a numerous progeny . . . established themselves throughout the entire world" (655). The narrator rejects one "political solution" to the Sodomite diaspora: "I have thought it as well to utter here a provisional warning against the lamentable error of proposing (just as people have encouraged a Zionist movement) to create a Sodomist movement and to rebuild Sodom. For no sooner had they arrived there than the Sodomites would leave the town so as not to have the appearance of belonging to it, would take wives, would keep mistresses in other cities where they would find, incidentally, every diversion that appealed to them" (655–56). Proust has inverted the relations between the hidden race and that larger society among which they live. It appears that not all deception is laid at the door of that minority of sexual intermediates who harbor souls with desires at odds with those proper to their biological sex. It would seem that the boundary between these "psychical hermaphrodites" and the "other race" that dominates society is not so easy to draw. Indeed, diversity and fluidity of desires and sexual identities may be the real "open secret" of Proust's world. In recognizing that the descendants of Sodom would continue their diaspora even after the rebuilding of their city, the narrator notes that "everything would go on very much as it does to-day in London, Berlin, Rome, Petrograd or Paris" (656). Once again like the Jews of Europe in the nineteenth century, contemporary

Sodomites are denizens of its major cities. In fact, they may be no different from their fellows after all.

Proust's text exhibits and problematizes the rhetoric of race in figuring both Jews and homosexuals. But Arendt's reading does not attend to the moment of problematization, and it occludes Proust's attention to the dynamic of feminization and the role of scientific and medical discourse in racializing Jewishness and homosexuality. Proust shows the extent to which at the turn of the twentieth century, racial characterization employed the language of science and pervasively linked difference to the "feminine" and the "primitive." Perhaps these insights were more available to him because of his own interest in the discourses of sexology and the specificities of homosexual existence. Taken together, Arendt and Proust provide a complex genealogy of the production of "natural" identities as an attempt to stabilize an order disturbed by tensions between equality and difference. By marking as inherent qualities the effects of shared historical circumstance, racialized identities served to naturalize and internalize the subordination of marginal groups, subject-ing them to continuing social control as distinct, transparent, and permanent minorities. The construction of Jewishness and homosexual-ity as essential identities in the nineteenth century worked to foreclose the individual and collective agency of both, limiting their capacity to determine what they were and who they might become. Arendt and Proust alert us to the disempowering effects of accepting naturalized definitions of sexuality and race that are in fact produced and maintained by a history of political oppression and social abjection.

## The Politics of Sexuality

I now supplement Hannah Arendt's reading of Proust with Sander Gilman's recent work on "Jewishness" as a racial concept in nineteenth-century medicine. My argument will push Arendt's analysis toward greater attention to the role of science in the discourse of racism and toward recognition of the historical imbrication of race with gender and sexuality. I conclude with some reflections on the implications of these genealogies of "Jewishness" and "homosexuality" for theorizing a contemporary politics of sexuality. The comparison between Jews and homosexuals becomes even more salient when we note the extent to which the rhetoric of political anti-Semitism deployed the discourse of science in its racial construction of "the Jew," especially the male, as a feminized and sexually primitive figure. Sander Gilman has articulated the intimate links among race, gender, and sexuality in this discourse.[35] His account complements Arendt's portrayal of the historical interactions through which Judaism as a religious, national, or collective socioeconomic status became "Jewishness" understood as an innate psychological attribute of individuals. Gilman contends that racial conceptions of Jewish identity were pervasive in late nineteenth-century Europe, although the details were sometimes contested; Jewish physicians and scientists worked within the prevailing paradigm, seeking to alleviate its more negative consequences, especially those bearing on their own capacity to achieve "objective" knowledge.

Although the focus of Gilman's inquiry is the construction of a "Jewish body," such a concept was always fraught with implications for the intellectual, psychological, and, especially, sexual status of Jews. The "Jewish body" was defined in terms of a diverse collection of qualities and dispositions, most carrying a negative valence within contemporary culture and society. These included distinctively marked languages and linguistic competence, skin and hair color and texture, facial structure and characteristics, general physical appearance and capacity, propensity to mental illness and physical disease, tendencies to sexual excess and perversion. With the passing of a political and social system explicitly grounded in Christianity, the intimate if problematic link between Judaism and the dominant religion was severed: "Jewishness" as a racial type was contrasted not with the Christian faith but with the "Aryan race." Gilman argues that all of the components of "Jewishness" presumed the Jewish male as their object; at the same time, the "Jew's body" was feminized and linked to a threatening sexuality. The practice of ritual circumcision with its resultant genital marking of Jewish men played a central role in medical research on Jews, in the culture of anti-Semitism, and in debates within Jewish communities. Lamarckian theories about the inheritance of acquired characteristics licensed the identification of circumcision as a "racial" characteristic of the male Jew despite the fact that it was a result of ritual practice. This stereotype, together with the association of Jews with a propensity for mental illness and syphilis, combined to mark Jews as infectious agents of sexual corruption within the body politic. These tendencies were "explained" in terms of the Jewish practice of endogamy, which was conflated with incest. The Jewish family became the site of a pathological difference that bred elements threatening to the mental, physical, and sexual health of "normal families." Thus, anti-Semitism as a political movement and social attitude gained credence from the racial science of the day: "racial models of the Jew . . . are found not only in the 'crackpot' pamphlet literature of the time; they were present in virtually all discussions of pathology published from 1880 to 1930. It is in the 'serious' medical literature . . . [that] these ideas of Jewish difference appear."[36]

Gilman's material amply demonstrates the affinities between the racial rhetoric of "Jewishness" and that associated with constructions of homosexuality as a "third sex." Homosexual men were similarly feminized; and lesbians characterized as masculine women. Moreover, closer examination of the figures deployed regarding Jews reveals a whole cluster of family resemblances. Like homosexuals, Jews were understood in terms of biologically based inherent characteristics, and yet thought to be capable of a dissembling invisibility (like the Baron de Charlus). They shared access to a "hidden language" understood only by others of their kind; possession of a distinctive pattern of speech that involuntarily revealed their "inner nature"; propensities to mental illness and physical disease, especially those linked with sexuality; identification with urban living and with the ills of urban civilization; perception as sources of danger to normal families; incapacity to discharge the (manly) duties of citizens, especially military service; and a tendency to debilitating self-hatred. Jewish physicians themselves accepted many of these characterizations, while emphasizing the role of historical oppression in creating such conditions; defenders of homosexual rights advanced the immutable, biological basis of that condition as an argument against criminal penalties and discrimination. The medicalized discourse of race was treated by both homosexual rights advocates and Jewish activists as a given with potentially emancipatory implications, while anti-Semites used it in their campaigns against Jewish civil rights, and medical authorities worked to develop techniques for the control or cure of deviant sexualities. Gilman's work on the medical discourse of race joins Arendt's more political treatment of racism to show that the production of inherent naturalized identities is very much a function of historical configurations of power and that those identities, once produced, can be pressed into service equally by both progressive and reactionary forces.

Gilman's material also indicates the need to integrate discussions of race and sexuality with an analysis of the rhetoric of feminization, the construction of gender, and the political status of women.

At this point, we may step back to examine the distinctive contributions of Hannah Arendt and of other theorists to our understanding of this complex genealogy of race and sexuality. First, Arendt's analysis of the Jewish question is emphatic in attending to its contingent historical character. There is no master discipline or Archimedean point from which to grasp the significance of questions regarding the status of Jews in modern nation-states. Rather, Arendt developed and revised a series of historical narratives—from *Rahel Varnhagen* to *Origins* to *Eichmann*—interpreting the specific configurations of political, social, and ideological factors that gave shape to modern anti-Semitism and the vicissitudes of Jewish history in Europe. Underlying the historical questions is her understanding that racial categories of collective behavior of whatever sort emerge from complex interactions among various groups under specific political conditions. Second, Arendt sees that the particular character of racial thought derives from both the ideological stereotypes of dominant groups and the diverse responses of those so labeled. She reminds us that analyses that deny all agency to oppressed groups reiterate racist reductions of collective activity to the behavioral outcomes of inherent natural conditions. She insists that the distinctively political dimension of human life is the capacity to initiate actions in concert with others, through which we share in defining who we are to become. Thus any attempt to define persons in terms of inherent essential qualities, with reference not to "what they did, but what they were" (*OT* 84), whether in the service of racist oppression, scientific explanation and control, or emancipatory identity politics, risks a radical distortion of the human condition.

Arendt teaches us "to see historically" and "to think politically." She practices a historical specificity that interrogates the claims of all general theories of human action by locating them in relation to the concrete exigencies of particular circumstance. In that spirit, we have challenged her rigid theoretical dichotomy between private and public by examining her own sensitive portrayal of the interpenetration of the two in the history of Jewish persecution and emancipation. Similarly, Gilman's discussion of "Jewishness" as a concept in nineteenth-century medicine and racial science suggests that Arendt's account of anti-Semitism and modern Jewish existence must be developed further to include the role of scientific theory and medical practice in its articulation and institutionalization. Arendt was perhaps too uncritical in separating "pseudo-scientific" propaganda from the discourses of established science. Her genealogy of race must be supplemented by Foucault's emphasis on the appearance in modernity of new forms of disciplinary power deploying scientific knowledge and related techniques of social control. This kind of historical analysis, which Gilman has performed for the Jewish question and which has informed much work in lesbian and gay studies,[37] complements and extends the reach of the kind of concrete political reflection practiced by Arendt, specifically with reference to totalitarianism. Foucault presses that sort of reflection into practice, tracing the pervasive reach and institutional manifestation of normalizing practices that shape an individual's very sense of self and produce the subjectivities they function to control.[38] He is especially acute in seeing that discourses of sexuality have informed a range of pedagogic and therapeutic practices through which individuals are brought to understand themselves as bearers of an inner truth marked as a biologically grounded "sexual identity." His analysis of sexuality as a mode of social control calls for a politics that contests the definition of the very sexual identities it seeks to mobilize.

Neither Arendt nor Foucault theorizes the role of gender in modern society and politics. Arendt's analysis of anti-Semitism proposes in part that the attribution of inherent biological differences to minority groups is an attempt to reintroduce in naturalized terms social differences that have been banished from modern democratic political discourse. But she does not seem to recognize that the single most pervasive "natural" difference recognized in modern societies is that between men and women. Some account is required, especially given the extent to which racial groups and sexual minorities have been subordinated through strategies of "feminization." Already imbricated in racial accounts of "Jewishness," gender is pervasively at work in the construction of "sexual identities." A politics of sexuality must be thought in tandem with a politics of gender that directly confronts and analyzes the identification of femininity as a primary figure of abjection in Western culture.[39] Why did Hannah Arendt fail (refuse?) to think the place of gender in politics? This is not the place to hazard a full explanation of her silence, but it is certainly linked to the exclusions that are effected by her rigid containment of household and social matters in The Human Condition. It may be that Arendt accepted uncritically a naturalized and essentialist view of gender at odds with the entire spirit of her critique of race thinking and racism. Arendt's hostility toward Freud and psychoanalysis may be at work here as well. In part motivated by a rejection of the scientific claims of psychoanalysis, Arendt also expressed a deep discomfort with the project of theorizing the intimacies of personal life. She clearly preferred the indirection of literature. Only in the early *Rahel* do we see her engage with an individual life in all of its messiness; she even wrote about Rahel's dreams. It is no surprise that her later distance from this book included a rejection of its "psychology." But under the conditions of modernity, as Arendt's own rich treatment of the Jewish question reveals, one cannot understand politics and history without reference to family life, to subjectivities and to the social and ideological matrices that shape them. Gilman's account of "Jewishness" in medical discourse and Foucault's narrative of the emergence of "sexuality" as a mode of social control provide additional incentive, in contexts relevant to Arendt's work, for a more radical thinking of the politics of the personal, with a sharp focus on the question of gender.

If Arendt's own thinking must be tested and reformulated to confront gender, so too, the question of gender must be reworked by Arendt's political and historical thinking. Some feminists have argued that essentialism about gender or sexual orientation has occluded differences that shape identities and ways of life different from the projections of dominant groups; such theorists have been especially sensitive to the ways that race, social class, religion, ethnicity, and nationality refract the experiences of contemporary women, challenging the right of any single group to speak for all women, or all lesbians, or all women of color.[40] This critique displays a deep affinity with Arendt's practice regarding the Jewish question, her insistence on the differences among Jewish notables and masses, rich and poor, West and East Europeans, financiers and intellectuals, parvenus and pariahs. Arendt's genealogy of anti-Semitism and Jewish existence is refracted through the prisms of religion, nationality, political status, and social class. The demand to see historically and to think politically mandates rejection of the project of discovering a master category that holds the key to understanding historical contingency and political difference. Among contemporary theorists of gender and sexuality, Judith Butler has expressed this imperative with special cogency:

> To prescribe an exclusive identification for a multiply constituted subject, as every subject is, is to enforce a reduction and a

paralysis, and some feminist positions, including my own, have problematically prioritized gender as the identificatory site of political mobilization at the expenses of race or sexuality or class or geopolitical positioning/displacement. And here it is not simply a matter of honoring the subject as a plurality of identifications, for these identifications are invariably imbricated in one another, the vehicle for one another.[41]

Arendt's genealogy of Jewishness and Foucault's genealogy of homosexuality combine to suggest that essentialized collective identities are best understood as the products of complex political and social interactions. Butler's deployment of psychoanalysis demonstrates a similar dynamic at work in the formation of personal identities from individual histories within the intersubjective contexts of early life. These identities are shaped by excluding those aspects of existence that threaten the self's unity and by treating them as an abject other against which one comes to define oneself. Butler sees this dynamic at work in the construction of shared political identities as well—in the processes that mark designated groups as marginal and in the emancipatory movements that work to resignify their marginality and transform their social status.

The task becomes to disarticulate the politics of sexuality and the emancipation of sexual minorities from the politics of "exclusive identification." Arendt and Proust on the Jewish question, Proust and Foucault on homosexuality, Butler on the dynamic of identification more generally—these perspectives converge to emphasize the imbrication of personal and collective identities with the socioeconomic, political, juridical, and moral imperatives governing any particular culture and historical period. As Arendt recognized in her correspondence with Jaspers, personal life is deeply situated in political contexts, the private mutually implicated with the public. In modernity, "identity" functions as a highly ambiguous sign, alternately and sometimes simultaneously indicating personal and political processes and outcomes. This is no accident. Personal and group identities emerge from a setting of interacting, sometimes conflicting, affiliations and desires. Self-formation is an inherently political process: identities are formed by negotiating a plurality of forces and relations, affirming some, excluding others, to reach provisional settlements, themselves subject to repudiation, revision, and transformation. The materials available for self-making are themselves conditioned by particular cultures and their histories; they include specific configurations of race, gender, sexuality, class, religion, nationality. The identities of both individuals and communities are contingent, provisional, and often precarious accomplishments; they are established by defining the boundaries of individuals and groups, dividing the world into self and other, friends and enemies, neighbors and strangers, citizens and aliens, allies and adversaries. Hegemonic entities like the nation-state and minority communities like the Jews in Europe each reenact these founding gestures and interact in reinforcing or contesting their borders. If nineteenth-century bourgeois society defined normality for assimilating Jews, these "exceptional" Jews secured their inclusion by projecting stereotypes used to mark all Jews onto a segment of the Jewish population—East European or poor Jews. Similarly, just as dominant institutions enforce compulsory heterosexuality by pathologizing homosexuality, contemporary lesbian and gay movements have themselves sometimes pathologized or marginalized other sexual nonconformists such as transvestites, transsexuals, pedophiles, or bisexuals.

The genealogies in this essay demonstrate how essential naturalized identities were ascribed to subordinate groups by dominant social attitudes supported by established science in the racial and sexual politics of the nineteenth century. The efficacy of this move depended in part on obscuring its political origins by invoking the alleged neutrality of science and indifference of nature. Contemporary "essentialist" defenses of homosexuality as an inherent natural condition that is biologically determined, over which individuals have no control, and for which they ought not to be penalized, may reiterate that history.[42] Capitalizing on an analogy with race made attractive by the promise of constitutional equality, these essentialist defenders of homosexual rights do not account for the history of racial oppression that necessitated the development of such remedial doctrines, nor are they alert to the fact that essentialism is a double-edged sword. There is nothing essentially progressive or emancipatory about the essentialist maneuver, as Arendt well knows. Her account provides a much-needed cautionary note, reminding us that the most insidious effects of racial thinking resulted from its acceptance even by those it marked as inferior. The point is reiterated by Judith Butler: such "exclusive identifications," accomplished through their own constitutive negations and disavowals, may lead to reduction and paralysis. For both Arendt and Butler, the politics of naturalized identities is at odds with democratic commitments to plurality and contestation. The production of marginalized sexual subjects is linked with a diversity of other normalizing practices that produce and maintain inequalities throughout late modern societies. Not simply "lesbians and gays," but particular communities and individuals characterized by class, race, nationality, and religion as well as gender and sexuality make up the complex, pluralized cultures in which we live. There is no single factor or comprehensive theory by which to order or rank the contending political and psychic forces. However, as a pervasive dimension of modern normalizing power, sexuality provides a promising and much-needed strategic site for political organization. Informed by the processes of sexuality's historical production, a democratic politics of sexuality must forgo the temptations of exclusive identification and forge alliances for common action from intersecting and multiple identifications and communities. The crucial task is to secure the public space and shared purpose necessary for action without inscribing new exclusions and foreclosing future agencies. This democratic politics of sexuality requires an ongoing willingness to contest boundaries of community, redefine coalitions for concerted action, and reconfigure relationships between personal and political identities. Hannah Arendt's conception of the political as a domain where diverse individuals interact to realize themselves and to construct a shared world is in the service of that task.

## Notes

1. See Hanna Fenichel Pitkin's essay (Chapter 3) in this volume.

2. Cf. Seyla Benhabib, "Hannah Arendt and the Redemptive Power of Narrative," *Social Research* 57 (Spring 1990): 167–96.

3. Hannah Arendt, *On Revolution* (New York: Viking, 1962).

4. Hannah Arendt, *Between Past and Future*, enl. ed. (New York: Penguin Books, 1968).

5. Hannah Arendt, *The Origins of Totalitarianism*, 2d enl. ed. (New York: Meridian Books, 1958).

6. Especially "Civil Disobedience" and "On Violence," included in Arendt, *Crises of the Republic* (New York: Harcourt Brace Jovanovich, 1972).

7. *Hannah Arendt–Karl Jaspers Correspondence, 1926–1969*, ed. Lotte Kohler and Hans Saner (New York: Harcourt Brace Jovanovich, 1992), 29; hereafter cited as *Correspondence*.

8. *Correspondence*, 17 December 1946.

9. "The Jew as Pariah," in Hannah Arendt, *The Jew as Pariah*, ed. Ron Feldman (New York: Harcourt Brace Jovanovich, 1978).

10. Hannah Arendt, *The Life of the Mind* (New York: Harcourt Brace Jovanovich, 1977), 192.

11. Heinrich Blücher was a professor of philosophy at Bard College.

12. In the controversial essay on the school-desegregation crisis, "Reflections on Little Rock," some of which she later repudiated as a result of conversation with Ralph Ellison. *Dissent* 6:1 (1959).

13. *Eichmann in Jerusalem: A Report on the Banality of Evil* (New York: Viking Press, 1963), 8–9.

14. Hanna Pitkin, "Justice: On Relating Private and Public," *Political Theory* 9 (August 1981): 327–52.

15. Cf. Bonnie Honig, *Political Theory and the Displacement of Politics* (Ithaca: Cornell University Press, 1992), 96–104.

16. In *Bowers v. Hardwick*, the United States Supreme Court held that constitutional privacy rights did not protect homosexuals from prosecution under Georgia's sodomy laws for acts performed by consenting adults in the privacy of the home. 478 U.S. 186 (1986). For a more extended analysis, see Morris B. Kaplan, "Autonomy, Equality, and Community: The Question of Lesbian and Gay Rights," *Praxis International* (July 1991): 195–213.

17. This understanding was based on her study of the effects of "statelessness" on those Jews and others who were stripped of citizenship rights before being exiled, interned, or murdered by the Nazis and their collaborator regimes in Europe. The first step in the loss of human rights was consignment to a status of second-class citizenship; for Jews in Germany by the Nuremberg laws of 1935. It is a sober reminder of the history and continued vitality of racism in Western culture that these laws were based in part on the Jim Crow laws that mandated racial segregation in the southern United States after the failure of Reconstruction in the latter quarter of the nineteenth century.

18. For the argument that civil rights laws work as a "civil shield" protecting the exercise of political rights by lesbians and gays, see Richard Mohr, *Gays/Justice* (New York: Columbia University Press, 1989), chaps. 5–7; for an extended treatment of same-sex marriage in the context of constitutional privacy rights, see Morris B. Kaplan, "Intimacy & Equality: The Question of Lesbian and Gay Marriage," *Philosophical Forum* (Summer 1994): 333–60.

19. Larry Kramer, *Reports from the Holocaust* (New York: St. Martin's Press, 1989).

20. Eve Kosofsky Sedgwick, *The Epistemology of the Closet* (Berkeley and Los Angeles: University of California Press, 1990).

21. I am indebted to David Bianco for calling Kramer's essay to my attention and for sharing with me his unpublished paper, "Eichmann in Washington? The AIDS/Holocaust Metaphor and Larry Kramer's Reading of Hannah Arendt."

22. Kramer has been both founder and critic of the Gay Men's Health Crisis (GMHC) and the AIDS Coalition to Unleash Power (ACT UP). His pre-AIDS novel *Faggots* was deeply critical of contemporary gay life and his plays "The Normal Heart" and "The Destiny of Me" address the AIDS epidemic.

23. See also Eve Kosofsky Sedgwick, *Between Men* (New York: Columbia University Press, 1985).

24. Hannah Arendt, *Essays in Understanding, 1930–1954*, ed. Jerome Kohn (New York: Harcourt Brace, 1994), 11–12.

25. Hannah Arendt, *The Origins of Totalitarianism* (New York: Harcourt Brace Jovanovich, 1968), 56; subsequent references in text are to this edition, cited as *OT*.

26. "Intermarriage between leading families soon followed, and culminated in a real international caste system . . . numerically no more than perhaps a hundred families. But since these were in the limelight, the Jewish people themselves came to be regarded as a caste" (*OT* 63).

27. "But what drove the Jews into the center of these racial ideologies more than anything else was the even more obvious fact that the pan-movements' claim to chosenness could clash seriously only with the Jewish claim" (*OT* 240).

28. D. A. Miller, *The Novel and the Police* (Berkeley and Los Angeles: University of California Press, 1988), 207, quoted in Sedgwick, *Epistemology*, 67.

29. Michel Foucault, *The History of Sexuality*, vol. 1, *An Introduction*, trans. Robert Hurley (New York: Vintage Books, 1990), 43.

30. Marcel Proust, *Remembrance of Things Past: Cities of the Plain*, trans. C. K. Scott Moncrieff and Terence Kilmartin (New York: Vintage Books, Random House, 1981), 636; page references in text are to this edition.

31. Foucault, *The History of Sexuality*, 43.

32. The narrator's definition of the "accursed race" deploys the conception of sexual intermediates introduced into nineteenth-century discourses of sexuality by Karl Ulrichs, developed by Otto Weininger in his misogynist *Sex and Character*, and promoted by the sexologist Magnus Hirschfeld in defense of homosexual and women's rights.

33. This formulation derives from Karl Ulrichs. Jeffrey Weeks, *Sexuality and Its Discontents* (London: Routledge and Kegan Paul, 1985), 93, 153. See also Sigmund Freud, *Three Essays in the Theory of Sexuality* (New York: Basic Books, 1975), 8.

34. See Sedgwick, *Epistemology*, 233ff.

35. Sander Gilman, *The Jew's Body* (New York: Routledge, 1991); *Difference and Pathology* (Ithaca: Cornell University Press, 1985).

36. Sander Gilman, *Freud, Race and Gender* (Princeton: Princeton University Press, 1993), 5.

37. See Jeffrey Weeks, *Sexuality and Its Discontents*; and his *Coming Out* (London: Quartet Books, 1977); John D'Emilio, *Sexual Minorities, Sexual Communities* (Chicago: University of Chicago Press, 1983); John D'Emilio and Estelle B. Freedman, *Intimate Matters* (New York: Harper and Row, 1988).

38. But then, something like this insight is at work in the account of a bureaucratic mentality in *Eichmann in Jerusalem*.

39. Julia Kristeva, *Powers of Horror* (New York: Columbia University Press, 1982); Luce Irigaray, *An Ethics of Sexual Difference* (1993); *Speculum of the Other Woman* (1985); *This Sex Which Is Not One* (1985) (all published Ithaca: Cornell University Press).

40. Elizabeth Spelman, *Inessential Woman* (Boston: Beacon, 1988), among many others.

41. Judith Butler, *Bodies That Matter* (New York: Routledge, 1993), 116.

42. Janet Halley has recently argued that this popular opinion does not reflect accurately the state of constitutional doctrine. To the contrary, she shows that the status of an "immutable condition" is neither a necessary nor a sufficient condition to secure constitutional equal protection of a minority. Janet E. Halley, "Sexual Orientation and the Politics of Biology: A Critique of the Argument from Immutability," *Stanford Law Journal* 46 (February 1994): 503–68. See also Edward Stein, ed., *Forms of Desire* (New York: Routledge, 1992) for materials relating to the essentialist/social constructivist controversy about sexual orientation. Stein's concluding essay, "The Essentials of Constructionism and the Construction of Essentialism," demonstrates that the debate has tended to conflate distinct philosophical issues about realism and nominalism; nature and nurture; and voluntarism and determinism. More recently, Stein has persuasively argued that the ethical status of homosexuality is independent of scientific explanations of its origin, "The Relevance of Scientific Research about Sexual Orientation to Lesbian and Gay Rights," *Journal of Homosexuality*, forthcoming. Daniel R. Ortiz makes a strong case that the debate is primarily a political struggle over the definition of lesbian and gay identities in "Creating Controversy: Essentialism and Constructivism and the Politics of Gay Identity," *Virginia Law Review* 79 (October 1993): 1833–57. See also Cheshire Calhoun, "Denaturalizing and Desexualizing Lesbian and Gay Identity," *Virginia Law Review* 79 (October 1993): 1859–75; and Morris B. Kaplan, "Constructing Lesbian and Gay Rights and Liberation," *Virginia Law Review* 79 (October 1993): 1877–1902.

# 6

# Toward an Agonistic Feminism: Hannah Arendt and the Politics of Identity

## Bonnie Honig

Hannah Arendt is an odd, even awkward figure to turn to if one is seeking to enrich the resources of a feminist politics. Notorious for her rigid public/private distinction, Arendt protects the sui generis character of her politics and the purity of her public realm by prohibiting the politicization of issues of social justice and gender. These sorts of occupations belong not to politics but to the traditional realm of the household as Aristotle theorized it. In short, the "Woman Problem," as she called it, was not one that Arendt thought it appropriate to pose, politically.[1]

First published in *Feminists Theorize the Political*, ed. Judith Butler and Joan Scott (New York: Routledge, 1992), this essay has been moderately revised and expanded to include a new Afterword that responds to feminist critiques of agonism.

Why turn to Arendt, then? I turn to her not as a theorist of gender, nor as a woman, but as a theorist of an agonistic and performative politics that might stand a feminist politics in good stead. I turn to Arendt because of what she does include in her vision of politics, and also because (not in spite) of what she excludes from it. The terms of that exclusion are instructive for a feminist politics that engages entrenched distinctions between a public and a private realm. In spite of Arendt's insistent reliance on her public/private distinction, the resources for its politicization are present within her account of politics and action. A reading of Arendt that grounds itself in the agonistic and performative impulse of her politics must, for the sake of that politics, resist the a priori determination of a public/private distinction that is beyond augmentation and amendment. This resistance (for the sake of perpetu- ating the possibility of augmentation and amendment) is itself an important and component part of Arendt's account of politics and political action.

I begin by arguing that resistibility (not necessarily resistance) is a sine qua non of Arendt's politics. Next, I briefly examine the terms of her exclusion of the body from the realm of politics, focusing first on the univocal, despotic, and irresistible character of the body, as Arendt theorizes it, and then on the multiplicity of the acting self whose performative speech-acts win for it the politically achieved identity that Arendt valorizes. On Arendt's account, identity is the performative production not the expressive condition or essence of action. This feature of Arendt's work, combined with the public/private distinction upon which it is mapped, have led feminist critics of Arendt to fault her for theorizing a politics that is inhospitable to women and women's issues.[2] In my view, however, it is precisely in Arendt's rejection of an expressive, identity-based politics that her value to a feminist politics lies. The problem is that Arendt grounds that rejection in a refusal to treat private-realm identities, like gender, as potential sites of politiciza- tion. I note, however, that Arendt's famous engagement with Gershom Scholem over the terms of her Jewish identity and its responsibilities illustrates her failure in practice to contain (so-called) private identities to a "prepolitical" realm and suggests the need for alternative strategies of resistance and resignification that are more empowering because more directly engaged with the politics of identity.

I conclude that Arendt's politics is a promising model for those brands of feminism that seek to contest (performatively and agonistically) the prevailing construction of sex and gender into binary and binding categories of identity, as well as the prevailing binary division of political space into a public and private realm. Arendt herself would undoubtedly have been hostile to this radicalization of her work but I believe that, as an amendment of her (founding) texts, it is very much in keeping with her politics.

## Political Action and Resistibility

Arendt's briefest and most pointed discussion of her vision of politics and action comes to us by way of her reading of the American Declaration of Independence. Here we have all the basic elements of Arendt's account. The Declaration is a political act, an act of power, because it founds a new set of institutions and constitutes a new political community; it "brings something into being which did not exist before," it "establishes new relations and creates new realities."[3] It is a "perfect" instance of political action because it consists "not so much in its being 'an argument in support of an action' " as in its being an action that appears in words.[4] It is a performative utterance, a speech-act, performed among and before equals in the public realm.

Focusing on the famous phrase, "We hold these truths to be self-evident," Arendt argues that the new regime's power, and ultimately its authority, derive from the performative "we hold" and not from the constative reference to self-evident truths.[5] Both dramatic and nonreferential, the performative brings a new political community into being; it *constitutes* a "we." This speech-act, like all action, gives birth, as it were, to the actors in the moment(s) of its utterance (and repetition).

In contrast to the performative "we hold," the constative reference to self-evident truths expresses not a free coming together but an isolated acquiescence to compulsion and necessity. A self-evident truth "needs no agreement"; it "compels without argumentative demonstration or political persuasion"; it is "in a sense no less compelling than 'despotic power.' " Constatives are "irresistible"; they "are not held by us, but we are held by them" (OR 192–93). For the sake of free political action, Arendt cleanses the Declaration and the founding of their violent, constative moments, of the irresistible anchors of God, self-evident truth, and natural law. There is to be no "being" behind this doing. The doing, the performance, is everything.[6]

In Arendt's account the real source of the authority of the newly founded republic was the performative not the constative moment, the action in concert not the isolated acquiescence, the "we hold" not the self-evident truth.[7] And the real source of authority in the republic, henceforth, would be the style of its maintenance, its openness to refounding and reconstitution: "Thus, the amendments to the Constitution augment and increase the original foundations of the American republic; needless to say, *the very authority of the American Constitution resides in its inherent capacity to be amended and augmented*" (OR 202; my emphasis). A regime so favorably disposed to constitutional amendment and augmentation, to refounding, must reject the foundational anchors of God, natural law, and self-evident truth because it knows that God defies augmentation, that God is what does not need to be augmented. God, natural law, self-evident truth are, all three, irresistible and complete. These devices petrify power. Their reification of performativity into constation closes the spaces of politics and deauthorizes a regime by diminishing its possibilities of refounding and augmentation. Resistibility, openness, creativity, and incompleteness are the sine qua non of this politics. And this is why Arendt insists on the inadmissibility of the body, and its needs, to the public realm.

## The Single, Univocal Body

The human body is, for Hannah Arendt, a master signifier of necessity, irresistibility, imitability, and the determination of pure process. As Arendt puts it:

> The most powerful necessity of which we are aware in self-introspection is the life process which permeates our bodies and keeps them in a constant state of a change whose movements are automatic, independent of our own activities, and *irresistible*—i.e., of an overwhelming urgency. The less we are doing ourselves, the less active we are, the more forcefully will this biological process assert itself, impose its inherent necessity upon

us, and overawe us with the fateful automatism of sheer happening that underlies all human history. (OR 59; my emphasis)

One of the reasons for action in the public realm, then, is to escape the
pure process that afflicts laboring, working, and (most of all) impover-
ished beings in the private realm. At least this is what Arendt says in On
Revolution where she documents the horrific failures of the French
Revolution and attributes them to the fact that "the poor, driven by the
needs of their bodies, burst onto the scene" and effectively closed the
spaces of politics by making the "social question" the center of political
attention (OR 59). When demands are made publicly on behalf of the
hungry or poor body, then the one individuating and activating capacity
that humans possess is silenced. There can be no speech, no action,
unless and until the violently pressing, indeed irresistible, needs of the
body are satisfied.
     Elsewhere, in The Human Condition, Arendt's emphasis is different.
Here her hostility to the political consideration of the "social" is
unabated but the "rise of the social" is theorized in terms of the
usurpation of political space by behaviorism, mass society, and the
administration of "housekeeping" concerns that are no less obtrusive
than the body's urgency but that seem to be less urgently irresistible.
Here, the social rises, it does not burst, onto the scene.
     In contrast to On Revolution, The Human Condition tends not to
discuss the body directly. And when things of the body are addressed,
the emphasis is less on the body's irresistibility than on its imitability.[8]
For example, Arendt says that in the political speech and action
that distinguish him, man "communicate[s] himself and not merely
something—thirst or hunger, affection or hostility or fear" (HC 176).
Thirst or hunger are "merely something" because they are common,
shared features of our biological existence and as such they are incapable
of distinguishing us from each other in any significant way. This
commonality is exaggerated in modernity as the social develops into a
strongly conformist set of arrangements that "by imposing innumerable
and various rules, . . . tend to 'normalize' its members, to make them
behave, to exclude spontaneous action or outstanding achievement"
(HC 40). Here, the reason to act is not situated in a need to escape the
body and be freed, episodically, from its urgency; instead, Arendt focuses
on the need to escape or contain the normalizing impulse of the social
through the antidotal but also sui generis goods of politics and action.

The reason to act is situated in action's unique, individuating power, and in the self's agonal passion for distinction, individuation, and outstanding achievement.

When they act, Arendt's actors are reborn (HC 176). Through innovative action and speech, they "show who they are, reveal actively their unique personal identities and thus make their appearance in the human world" (HC 179). Their momentary engagement in action in the public realm engenders identities that are lodged forever in the stories told of their heroic performances by the spectators who witness them. Prior to or apart from action, this self has no identity; it is fragmented, discontinuous, indistinct, and most certainly uninteresting. A life-sustaining, psychologically determined, trivial, and imitable biological creature in the private realm, this self attains identity—becomes a "who"—by acting. For the sake of "who" it might become, it risks the dangers of the radically contingent public realm where anything can happen, where the consequences of action are "boundless" and unpredictable, where "not life but the world is at stake."[9] In so doing, it forsakes the comforting security of "what" it is, the roles and features that define (and even determine) it in the private realm, the "qualities, gifts, talents and shortcomings, which [it] may display or hide," and the intentions, motives, and goals that characterize its agency.[10] Thus, Arendt's actors are never self-sovereign. Driven by the despotism of their bodies (and their psychologies) in the private realm, they are never really in control of what they do in the public realm, either. This is why, as actors, they must be courageous. Action is spontaneous, it springs up ex nihilo and, most disturbing, it is self-surprising: "[I]t is more than likely that the 'who' which appears so clearly and unmistakably to others, remains hidden from the person himself."[11]

There is nothing interesting nor distinct about "what" we are, nothing remarkable about the psychological and biological self. The features of the private self are, like our inner organs, "never unique" (HC 206). Arendt says of the biological self: "If this inside were to appear, we would all look alike."[12] Here the silence that is opposed to the performative speech-acts valorized by Arendt is not the muteness provoked by violently urgent bodily need, but rather a kind of silent communication, a constative speaking that is strictly communicative and narrowly referential, so narrowly referential that it need not even be spoken. Here, "speech plays a subordinate role, as a means of communication or as a mere accompaniment to something that could also be achieved in silence" (*HC* 179; my emphasis). Since the point of language in the private realm is "to communicate immediate identical needs and wants" (of the body), this can be done mimetically. The single, univocal body is capable of handling this task without the aid of speech: "signs and sounds," Arendt says, "would be enough" (*HC* 176).

## The Multiple, Acting Self

By contrast with the single, univocal body, the acting self is multiple. This bifurcated self maps onto the bifurcated constative and performative structure of the Declaration of Independence. Constatives and bodies are both despotic, irresistible, univocal, and uncreative. Both are disruptive, always threatening to rise, or burst, onto the scene and close the spaces of politics. Because of this ever-present threat, we must be vigilant and guard the public realm, the space of performativity, against the intrusion of the bodily or constative compulsion.

The acting self is like the performative moments of the Declaration: free, (self-)creative, transformative, and inimitable. Arendt's performatives postulate plurality and her actors postulate multiplicity. The power of the performative "we hold" is actualized by distinct and diverse individuals with little in common prior to action except a care for the world and an agonal passion for distinction (*OR* 118, passim). Likewise, Arendt's actors do not act because of what they already are, their actions do not express a prior, stable identity; they presuppose an unstable, multiple self that seeks its, at best, episodic self-realization in action and in the identity that is its reward.

This multiple self is characterized by Arendt as the site of a struggle that is quieted, temporarily, each time the self acts and achieves an identity that is a performative production. The struggle is between the private and the public self, the risk-aversive stay-at-home and the courageous, even rash actor in the contingent public realm. This bifurcation between its private and public impulses marks the self but does not exhaust its fragmentation. In the private realm alone, this self is also animated and conflicted by three distinct, rival, and incompatible mental faculties—thinking, willing, and judging—each of which is also internally riven, "reflexive," recoiling "back upon itself." Always, Arendt says, "there remains this inner resistance."[13] This is why Arendt insists that autonomy is an impositional construction. It imposes a univocity on a self that is fragmented and multiple; it involves "a mastery which relies on domination of one's self and rule over others"; it is a formation to which the self, on Arendt's account, is resistant (HC 244). This self is not, ever, one. It is itself the site of an agonistic struggle that Arendt (sometimes) calls politics.[14] And Arendt approves of this because, like Nietzsche, she sees this inner multiplicity of the self as a source of its power and energy, as one of the conditions of creative performative action.[15]

These bifurcations, between the univocal body and the multiple self, are presented as attributes of individual selves but they actually operate to distinguish some selves from others in the ancient Greece that is Arendt's beloved model. Here the experience of action is available only to the very few. The routine and the urgency of the body are implicitly identified in The Human Condition, as they were explicitly in ancient Greece, with women and slaves (but also with children, laborers, and all non-Greek residents of the polis), the laboring subjects who tend to the body and its needs in the private realm where "bodily functions and material concerns should be hidden."[16] These inhabitants of the private realm are passively subject to the demands that their bodies and nature make upon them, and to the orders dictated to them by the master of the household to which they belong as property. As victims of both the tiresomely predictable, repetitious, and cyclical processes of nature and the despotism of the household, they are determined incapable of the freedom that Arendt identifies with action in the public realm. Free citizens, by contrast, could tend to their private needs in the private realm (or, more likely, have them tended to) but they could then leave these necessitarian, life-sustaining concerns behind to enter the public realm of freedom, speech, and action. Indeed, their ability to leave these concerns behind is the mark of their capacity to act. In politics, after all, "not life but the world is at stake."

This passage, made periodically by free citizens from the private to the public realm, indicates that the chasm between the two realms is not nonnegotiable (HC 24). But this is true only for citizens, only for those who are not essentially identified with their condition of embodiment, for those who can be other than only, and passively, embodied beings. This is, in effect, the criterion for their citizenship. For "others," whose very nature prevents them from ever becoming citizens because their identity is their embodiment (and this is the criterion for their barbarism), there is no negotiating the public/private impasse.

This problematic feature of political action is certainly one that Arendt attributes to the polis, but is it right to attribute it to Arendt herself?[17] Arendt does often speak as if her private realm and its activities of labor and work were to be identified with particular classes of people, or bodies, or women in particular. But, as Hanna Pitkin points out, at other times the private realm and its activities of labor and work seem to represent not a particular class or gender but "particular *attitude[s]* against which the public realm must be guarded."[18] Labor, for example, "the activity which corresponds to the biological process of the human body," is a mode in which the necessitarian qualities of life and the instrumental character of a certain kind of rationality dominate us so thoroughly that the freedom of politics and its brand of generative performativity cannot surface (*HC* 7). Since Arendt's real worry about labor and work is that they require and engender particular sensibilities that hinder or destroy action, Pitkin suggests that "Perhaps a 'laborer' is to be identified not by his manner of producing nor by his poverty but by his 'process' oriented outlook; perhaps he is driven by necessity not objectively, but because he regards himself as driven, incapable of action."[19]

Or, better, perhaps it is the laboring sensibility that is excluded from political action, a sensibility that is taken to be characteristic of laboring as an activity but which may or may not be characteristic of the thinking of any particular laborer, a sensibility that is certainly not taken to signal a laboring nature or essence that is expressed when the laborer labors. There is no "being" behind this doing. The same analysis applies to work. In this account, there is no determinate class of persons that is excluded from political action. Instead, politics is protected from a variety of sensibilities, attitudes, dispositions, and approaches all of which constitute *all* selves and subjects to some extent, all of which engage in a struggle for dominion over the self, and all of which are incompatible with the understanding(s) of action that Arendt valorizes. In short, the construal of labor, work, and action as sensibilities could de-essentialize or denaturalize them. Each would be understood as itself a performative production, not the expression of the authentic essence of a class, or a gender, but always the (sedimented) product of the actions, behaviors, norms, and institutional structures of individuals, societies, and political cultures.[20]

This reading of labor, work, and action as (rival) sensibilities is compatible with Arendt's view of the self as multiplicity. And it might point the way to a gentle subversion of Arendt's treatment of the body as a master signifier of irresistibility, imitability, and the closure of constation. Labor is, after all, a bodily function, in Arendt's account, as well as being the mode in which the body is tended to, the mode that is preoccupied with things that are "needed for the life process itself" (*HC* 96). If labor (that determining sensibility by which all are sometimes driven) can be a performative production, why not the body itself? Why not allow this reading of labor, work, and action as sensibilities to push us to de-essentialize and denaturalize the body, perhaps pluralize it, maybe even see *it* as a performative production, a possible site of action, in Arendt's sense?

## Distinguishing Public and Private

If there is one thing in the way of this radicalization of Arendt's account, it is Arendt's reliance on that series of distinctions that I have grouped together under the heading of performative versus constative. Arendt treats these distinctions as binary oppositions, nonnegotiable and without overlap, and she maps them onto a (historically invidious) public/private distinction that lies at the (shifting) center of her work. Indeed, as it turns out, there is more than one thing in the way since Arendt secures her public/private distinction with a multilayered edifice. The distinction spawns numerous binaries, each one a new layer of protective coating on the last, each one meant to secure, that much more firmly, the distinction that resists the ontologizing function that Arendt assigns to it. Performative versus constative, "We hold" versus "self-evident truth," multiple self versus univocal body, male versus female, resistible versus irresistible, courageous versus risk-aversive, speech versus mute silence, active versus passive, open versus closed, power versus violence, freedom versus necessity, action versus behavior, extraordinary versus ordinary, inimitable versus imitable, disruption versus repetition, light versus dark, in short: public versus private.

Why so many? In the very drawing of the distinction, where the drawing is an extraordinary act in Arendt's sense (it has the power to create new relations and new realities), Arendt is caught in a cycle of anxious repetition. Binary distinctions and adjectival pairs are heaped, one upon another, in a heroic effort to resist the erosion of a distinction that is tenuous enough to need all of this. Tenuous, indeed. There are, in Arendt's account, numerous instances of the permeation of these distinctions. Arendt is quite straightforward about the fact that the public realm is all too easily colonized by the private and turned into the social (it is to this problem that she responds in *The Human Condition* and in *On Revolution*). Her candor tempts us to think that these distinctions are, above all else, drawn to protect the public from the private realm's imperialism. But the converse is also true. It is equally important to Arendt to protect the private realm's reliability, univocality, and ordinariness from the disruptions of action and politics.[21] In short, Arendt domesticates not only behavior but also action itself. She gives action a place to call home and she tells it to stay there, where it belongs. But, of course, it refuses.

Here is the real risk of action: in this refusal. The self-surprising quality of action is not limited to the fact that action does not always turn out as we would have intended it to; nor even to the fact that we, as actors, are never quite sure "who" it is that we have turned out to be. Action is self-surprising in another sense as well, in the sense that it happens to us. We do not decide to perform, then enter the public realm, and submit our performance to the contingency that characterizes that realm. Often, political action comes to us; it involves us in ways that are not deliberate, willful, or intended. Action produces its actors; episodically, temporarily, we are its agonistic achievement. In Arendt's account, the American Revolution happened to the American revolutionaries: "But the movement which led to the revolution was not revolutionary except by inadvertence" (*OR* 44). And, sometimes, particularly in her account of willing, action happens to the private self, initially in the *private* realm.

Arendt treats willing as an antecedent of action but it is a funny kind of antecedent because it actually defers action. Caught in a reflexive, internal, and potentially eternal dynamic of willing and nilling, a dynamic it is incapable of arresting, the will awaits redemption. And when that redemption comes, it comes in the form of action itself. *Action* liberates the self from the will's paralyzing "disquiet and worry" by disrupting the compulsive repetitions of the will. Action comes in, as it were, to the private realm; it happens to the as yet unready and not quite willing (because still also nilling) subject in the private realm. Like a coup d'état, action "interrupts the conflict between *velle* and *nolle*," and redeems the will. "In other words," Arendt adds, "the Will is redeemed by ceasing to will and starting to act and *the cessation cannot originate in an act of the will-not-to-will* because this would be but another volition."[22]

Examples of public/private realm cross-fertilizations abound; they are as manifold as the distinctions that are supposed to account for their impossibility, their perversion, their monstrosity. What is to prevent us, then, from applying "performativity to the body itself," as one feminist theorist of sex/gender performance does?[23] What prohibits the *attenuation* of the public/private distinction? What would be the punishment for unmasking the private realm's constative identities as really the (sedimented) products of the actions, behaviors, and institutional structures and norms of individuals, societies, and political cultures? What is at stake?

At stake, for Arendt, is the loss of action itself, the loss of a realm in which the actionable is vouchsafed. This is a real cause of concern, especially given the astonishing and disturbing success of the "innumerable and various rules" of the social in producing normal, well-behaved subjects. But in order to vouchsafe it, Arendt empties the public realm of almost all content. Things possessed of content are constatives, after all, sites of closure in Arendt's theorization, irresistible obstacles to performativity. Hence Hanna Pitkin's puzzled wonderment at what those citizens "talk about together in that endless palaver of the *agora.*"[24] Arendt's effective formalization of action, her attempts to safeguard action with a nonnegotiable public/private distinction, may contribute more to the loss or occlusion of action than any rise of the social, than any bursting forth of ostensibly irresistible bodies.

The permeability, inexactness, and ambiguity of the distinction between public and private, however, are not reasons to give it up. Instead, they suggest the possibility of attenuation. What if we took Arendt's own irresistibly lodged public/private distinction to be a line drawn in the sand, itself an illicit constative, a constituting mark or text, calling out agonistically to be contested, augmented, and amended? And what if we began by dispensing with the geographic and proprietary metaphors of public and private? What if we treated Arendt's notion of the public realm not as a specific *topos*, like the ancient Greek agon, but as a metaphor for a variety of (agonistic) spaces, both topographical and conceptual, that might occasion action? We might be left with a notion of action as an event, an agonistic disruption of the ordinary sequence of things that makes way for novelty and distinction, a site of resistance of the irresistible, a challenge to the normalizing rules that seek to constitute, govern, and control various behaviors. And we might then be in a position to identify sites of political action in a much broader array of constations, ranging from the self-evident truths of God, nature, technology, and capital to those of identity, of gender, race, and ethnicity. We might then be in a position to *act*—in the private realm.

Arendt would no doubt be concerned that these amendments of her account politicize too much, that (as Nancy Fraser puts it on her behalf) "when everything is political, the sense and specificity of the political recedes."[25] For Fraser, Arendt's theorization of politics highlights a paradox: If politics is everywhere then it is nowhere. But not everything *is* political in this (amended) account; it is simply the case that nothing is ontologically protected from politicization, that nothing is necessarily or naturally or ontologically *not* political. The distinction between public and private is seen as the performative product of political struggle, hard-won and always temporary. Indeed, the paradox is reversible. The impulse to secure, foundationally, the division between the political and the nonpolitical is articulated as a concern for the preservation of the political but is itself an antipolitical impulse. Arendt knew this: it was the basis of her critique of the constative, foundational ground of the Declaration of Independence. This is what motivated her to apply performativity to the self-evidence of the Declaration. And the same impulse can motivate the application of performativity to Arendt's public/private distinction itself.

This dispersal of the agon is also authorized by another, somewhat different moment in Arendt's theorization of politics. Arendt understood that there were times in which the exigencies of a situation forced politics to go underground. She looks to the underground politics of occupied France, and valorizes its proliferation of sites of resistance, its network of subversive political action.[26] Occupation might not be a bad term for what Arendt describes as the "rise of the social" and the displacement of politics by routinized, bureaucratic, and administrative regimes. In the absence of institutional sites, a feminist politics might well go underground, looking to locate itself in the rifts and fractures of identities, both personal and institutional, and doing so performatively, agonistically, and creatively, with the hope of establishing new relations and realities.

## Acting in the Private Realm

This notion of an agonistic politics of performativity situated in the self-evidences of the private realm is explored by Judith Butler, who focuses in particular on the construction and constitution of sex and gender. Butler unmasks the private realm's constations—described by Arendt as the mindless, tiresome, perfect, and oppressive repetitions of the cycles of nature—and redescribes them as performativities that daily (re-) produce sex/gender identities. These performances, Butler argues, are the enforced products of a regulative practice of binary gender constitution centered on and by a "heterosexual contract." But these acts are "internally discontinuous"; the identities they produce are not "seamless." The "multiplicity and discontinuity of the referent [the self] mocks and rebels against the univocity of the sign [sex/gender]." There are "possibilities of gender transformation" in these spaces of mockery and rebellion, "in the arbitrary relation between such acts, in the possibility of a different sort of repeating."[27] A subversive repetition might performactively produce alternative sex/gender identities that would proliferate and would, in their proliferation (and strategic deployment), contest and resist the reified binaries that now regulate and seek to constitute, exhaustively, the identities of sex/gender.

The strategy, then, is to unmask identities that aspire to successful constation, to deauthorize and redescribe them as performative productions by identifying spaces that escape or resist identitarian administration, regulation, and expression. In Arendtian terms, this strategy depends upon the belief that the sex/gender identities that "we hold" can be amended and augmented in various ways through action. Political theory's task is to aid and enable that practice of (re-)founding by widening the spaces (of tension, undecidability, and arbitrariness) that might be hospitable to new beginnings.[28] These are spaces of politics, spaces (potentially) of performative freedom. Here action is possible in the private realm because the social and its mechanisms of normalization consistently fail to achieve the perfect closures that Arendt attributes to them too readily. This failure of the social to realize its ambitions means that it is possible to subvert the concretized, petrified, reified, and naturalized identities and foundations that paralyze politics and to broaden the realm of the actionable, to resist the sedimentation of performative acts into constative truths and to stand by the conviction that in matters of politics and in matters of identity, it is not possible to get it right, over and done with. This impossibility structures the needs and the repressions of Arendt's public and private realms. And it provides good reasons to resist and to problematize any politics of identity.

Hanna Pitkin energetically criticizes Arendt's refusal to theorize politics as a practice or venue of the representation of interests, and of shared material needs and concerns.[29] She rightly worries that Arendt's politics is so formal as to be left without import or content. But Pitkin fails to appreciate the promise in Arendt's vision. There is promise in Arendt's unwillingness to allow political action to be a site of the representation of "what" we are, of our reified private-realm identities. In Arendt's view, a politics of representation projects a false commonality of identity and interests that is impositional, and ill-fitting. Further, it obstructs an important alternative: a performative politics that, instead of reproducing and re-presenting "what" we are, agonistically generates "who" we are by episodically producing new identities, identities whose "newness" becomes "the beginning of a new story, started—though unwittingly—by acting [wo]men [and] to be enacted further, to be augmented and spun out by their posterity."[30]

## Identity Politics

The centrality of performativity to Arendt's theory of action stems from Arendt's opposition to attempts to conceive of politics as expressive of shared (community) identities such as gender, race, ethnicity, or nationality. Performativity and agonism are not coincidentally connected in Arendt's account. Arendt's politics is always agonistic because it resists the attractions of expressivism for the sake of her view of the self as a complex site of multiplicity whose identities are always performatively produced. This agonism eschews the complacent familiarities of the what-ness of subjectivity and it rejects the seductive comforts of the social for the sake of action and its exhilarating capacity to generate new relations and new realities.

From Arendt's perspective, a political community that constitutes itself on the basis of a prior, shared, and stable identity threatens to close the spaces of politics, to homogenize or repress the plurality and multiplicity that political action postulates. Attempts to overcome that plurality or multiplicity, Arendt warns, must result in "the abolition of the public realm itself" and the "arbitrary domination of all others," or in "the exchange of the real world for an imaginary one where these others would simply not exist" (HC 220, 234). The only way to prevent such an exchange is by protecting the spaces of politics in the nonidentity and heterogeneity of political communities, and also in the resistances of the self to the normalizing constructions of subjectivity and the imposition of autonomy (and perhaps also to the formation of sex/gender identities into binary categories of male and female, mascu-line and feminine). The self's agonistic ill-fittedness to the social, psychological, and juridical categories that seek to define it is a source of the generation of power, a signal that there are sites from which to generate (alternative) performativity(ies).

It is this care for difference and plurality as conditions of politics and action that accounts for Arendt's hostility to the nation-state, whose repugnant "decisive principle" is its "homogeneity of past and origin" (OR 174). And it might also account for her silence on the subject of a feminist politics: Arendt would have been quite wary of any proclamation of homogeneity in "women's experience," or in "women's ways of knowing." She would have been critical of any feminist politics that relies on a category of woman that aspires to or implies a universality that belies (or prohibits, punishes, or silences) significant differences and pluralities within—and even resistances to—the bounds of that (so-called) identity.

These remarks are speculative because Arendt did not address the issues of feminism or a feminist politics in her theoretical work. I myself have been reluctant to pose gender questions to Arendt directly because those questions tend to be posed by Arendt's feminist critics in a moralistic mode. The assumption is that, as a woman, Arendt had a responsibility to pose the "woman question" or at least to theorize a politics that showed that she had women in mind. Her failure to do so marks her as a collaborator. The charge is made most bluntly and forcefully by Adrienne Rich who describes The Human Condition as a "lofty and crippled book," exemplary of the "tragedy of a female mind nourished on male ideology."[31] I am less certain about the responsibilities assumed here and so I seek to pose these questions, but not in that mode; that is, without assigning or even implying that responsibility. In fact, I feel a certain respect for Arendt's refusal to be a joiner, for her wariness of identity politics and of membership in identity communities, for the startling perversity that led her to say of Rosa Luxemburg (but also, I think, of herself) that "her distaste for the women's emancipation movement, to which all other women of her generation and political convictions were irresistibly drawn, was significant. In the face of suffragette equality, she might have been tempted to reply, *'Vive la petite différence.'* "[32]

An odd remark; certainly unfair to the suffragists whose political dedication is dismissed as a product of an "irresistible" identification with a "movement," not a politics; but an intriguing remark nonetheless. What is this *petite différence* that Arendt imagines Luxemburg celebrating? It is not sexual difference—that is *la différence,* nothing petite about it. *La petite différence* is an intra-sex/gender difference (albeit one that is itself gendered by Arendt's significant choice of phrasing). It is the difference that sets Luxemburg apart from these other women. Arendt admires in Luxemburg a quality that she herself strove for: the refusal of membership, the choice of difference or distinction over a certain kind of equality.[33] The "suffragette equality" to which she refers in this passage is not the civic equality with male voters for which these women were still striving; it is the equality among the suffragettes, their devotion to a common cause in the name of which (Arendt alleges) differences among them are effaced. Arendt constructs and celebrates a Rosa Luxemburg who was "an outsider," a "Polish Jew in a country she disliked," a member of a political "party she came soon to despise," and "a woman," the sort of excellent woman who resisted the "irresistible" allure of a women's movement, called other contests her own, and won for herself, thereby, an identity of distinction, not homogeneity (*MDT* 45).

The same sentiments, the same distancing techniques and distaste for identity politics are evident in Arendt's exchange with Gershom Scholem, an exchange that professed to be about Arendt's controversial book on Eichmann but that was really or also a contestation of the terms of Arendt's (would-be private-realm) identity as a Jew.[34] This short exchange is an instructive and provocative study in identity politics. Scholem's letter to Arendt is an exercise in identification and politicization. He tells Arendt that her book has little in it of the "certainty of the believer," that it manifests "weakness" and "wretchedness, and power-lust," that it leaves "*one* with a sense of bitterness and shame . . . for the compiler," that he has a "deep respect" for her and that that is why he must call to her attention the "heartless" and "almost sneering and malicious tone" of her book. He can find "little trace" in her ("dear Hannah") of any "*Ahabath Israel:* 'Love of the Jewish People,' " and this absence is typical of "so many intellectuals who came from the German Left." What licenses Scholem to say all of these things, and to mark them as moral failings? The fact that he regards Arendt "wholly as a daughter of our people and in no other way."[35]

Arendt responds with two strategic refusals: First, she contests Scholem's claim that she is "wholly" Jewish and is neither riven nor constituted by differences or other identities. Second, she contests Scholem's assumption that Jewish identity is expressive, that it has public effects and carries with it certain, clear responsibilities. She resists the claim that particular sorts of action, utterance, and sentiment ought necessarily to follow from the fact that she is Jewish. Throughout, however, she assumes, as does Scholem, that Jewish identity is an "indisputable," univocal, and constative "fact" (like the other facts of her multiple but private identity), "not open to controversy" nor to "dispute." Thus, she can say that many of Scholem's statements about her "are simply false" and she can correct them. For example, she is not "one of the 'intellectuals who come from the German Left' "; if Arendt "can be said to 'have come from anywhere,' it is from the tradition of German philosophy."

To Scholem's "I regard you wholly as a daughter of our people, and in no other way," Arendt responds cryptically: "The truth is I have never pretended to be anything else or to be in any other way than I am and I have never even felt tempted in that direction." The point is not that she has not pretended to be anything other than "a daughter" of the Jewish people; she has simply not pretended to be anything other than what she is. But Arendt never says what she is, she never identifies herself affirmatively. All she says is that to pretend "to be anything . . . other than I am . . . would have been like saying that I was a man and not a woman—that is to say, kind of insane." Again, there is no affirmative identification of herself, in this case as a woman, just the claim that to assert its contrary would be "insane." (What would it be to assert it affirmatively?)[36]

Where Scholem regards her "*wholly* as a daughter of our people and in no other way," Arendt has "always regarded" her own "Jewishness as *one of* the indisputable factual data of my life." She does not regard her Jewishness as the "wholly" constitutive identity that Scholem projects it to be. Arendt is constituted by other "facts," as well, two of which she mentions here—sex/gender, and her schooling in German philosophy.[37] Thus, Arendt says, Scholem's depiction of her as "wholly" a "daughter of our people," is a "label" that he "wish[es] to stick" on her, but it has "never fitted in the past and does not fit now."[38] The label is a label, ill-fitting and stuck on, because Arendt's Jewishness is a fragment of a complex and conflicted identity.

For Arendt, nothing follows from the fact of her Jewishness as she understands that fact. Her Jewishness is a private matter; because it is a fact, it is not at all actionable. And for that, for its facticity, Arendt is grateful: "There is such a thing as a basic gratitude for everything that is as it is; for what has been given and was not, could not be, made; for things that are *physei* and not *nomoi*," for things that are "beyond dispute or argument." This insistence on her ethnic, religious, cultural identity as a given, private fact, not to be made or acted upon, is structurally figured in Arendt's letter to Scholem. Arendt begins the letter with a discussion of the facts of her private identity, presented as a series of corrections aimed at what she treats as factual errors. These matters of fact are uninteresting, "not open to controversy." Arendt sets this part of the letter up as a prepolitical preamble, separate from the political debate that follows. Only the latter treats "matters which merit discussion" and speech. She underscores this distinction by beginning the paragraph that marks the end of the identity-centered preliminaries and the start of the political debate with the phrase: "To come to the point."

But the very thing for which Arendt expresses her gratitude in this letter is the one thing that Scholem will not grant her in this encounter. Scholem will not treat her Jewish identity as a private affair. For Scholem, certain identifiable and incontestable public responsibilities and implications follow from the indisputable and univocal fact of Arendt's Jewishness. This is why Arendt resists Scholem's inclusions, this is why she resists his writing of her "wholly as a daughter" of the Jewish people. She treasures difference, even a *petite différence*, over and above the equality or sameness that Scholem ascribes to and demands from Jews. She sees in his identity politics insidious resources for the homogenizing control of behavior and the silencing of independent criticism. And that is why she resists. Her resistance, however, is not all it could be.

Instead of insisting on the privacy of Jewish identity, a privacy that is already problematized by Scholem's charges and by this very public, highly politicized, identity debate, Arendt would have done better to contest the terms of Scholem's construal of Jewishness as identity. This strategy was not available to Arendt, however, because she agrees with

Scholem on the most important point. Both she and Scholem treat Jewish identity as a univocal, constative fact. They disagree on whether it is a public or a private fact,[39] on whether any prescriptions or requirements for action follow from it, but both agree that Jewishness is a fact that "could not be made," nor indeed, unmade; it is unaffected by what the actor does. This is why Scholem can regard Arendt, in spite of all the things that she has written, in spite of her apparently total lack of any Ahabath-Israel, as "wholly" a "daughter of our people." Arendt could not deny or subvert her authentic identity as a Jew no matter what she did. With this, Arendt is in perfect agreement. Her defense strategy mimes the basic premise of Scholem's accusations: nothing she does can call into question or subvert the indisputable, constative fact of her Jewishness.

In treating Jewish identity as constative, Arendt relinquishes the opportunity to engage or even subvert Jewish identity performatively, to explore its historicity and heterogeneity, to dislodge and disappoint its aspirations to univocity, to proliferate its differentiated possibilities. This leaves her without any resources with which to respond critically to Scholem's portrayal of Jewishness as a homogeneous, univocal identity that implies certain incontestable responsibilities and claims certain loyalties. Scholem's constative criterion for distinguishing good Jews from bad is left intact. The same would be true of Adrienne Rich's strategy for distinguishing healthy from crippled women, loyal women from those who are treasonous. After all, Rich's approach mirrors Scholem's: It is because she regards Arendt "wholly as a [woman] and in no other way," that she can treat Arendt's other constituting identities (like her schooling in German philosophy) as betrayals of Arendt's authentic and univocal identity—as a woman.

The more powerful and empowering defense against Scholem or Rich or, indeed, against any identity politics is to resist the irresistible, not by privatizing it but by unmasking the would-be irresistible, homogeneous, constative and univocal identity in question as a performative production, fractured, fragmented, ill-fitting, and incomplete, the sedimented and not at all seamless product of a multitude of performances and behaviors, the naturalized product of innumerable repetitions and enforcements. This is Arendt's strategy for empowering the "We hold" of the Declaration against the coercive violence of that document's "self-evident truths." Why not usurp this strategy of empowerment to unmask, engage, subvert, or resist the violent closures of univocity and self-evidence assumed by some Jewish and feminist politics of identity?

The strategy here is to interrupt established identities, to theorize and to practice a Jewishness that is not homogenizing and a feminism that does not efface difference for the sake of an equality of sameness. The strategy here is to proliferate and explore differences rather than reify them and the result might be the empowering discovery or insistence that there are many ways to do one's Jewishness, many ways to do one's gender.[40] The homogenizing effects of some (so-called) private-realm identities would be weakened and that would allow for greater differentiation and contestability within the frame of the "identities" themselves.

This strategy of interruption constitutes an important alternative to the notions of a pariah, and a pariah perspective, so celebrated by Arendt.[41] Arendt treats the conscious pariah's position of outsider (personified by Rosa Luxemburg as well as by others whom Arendt admired) as a privileged site from which one can secure the distance necessary for independent critique, action, and judgment. But Arendt's location of the pariah position is fueled by her problematic assumption that there is no critical leverage to be had from inside formed identities. Arendt celebrates the pariah's outsider status because she believes that identities succeed, that they do attain seamlessness and closure, that they are necessarily homogenizing. The agonistic politics of performativity that I extend and explore here assumes instead that identities are never seamless, that there are sites of critical leverage within the ruptures, inadequacies, and ill-fittednesses of existing identities. It assumes, therefore, that the position of the pariah is itself unstable, that the pariah is never really an outsider, and that its sites are multiple. These multiple sites decenter the privileged public space of Arendtian politics and proliferate the sites of action beyond the single public realm to explore a broader range of spaces of potential power and resistance.[42]

This agonistic feminism also departs from the implied individualism of Arendt's pariah by postulating agonism as a kind of action in concert.[43] The identities engaged by agonistic feminists are shared, public practices not merely markers of individual personalities. While any particular agonistic action may be performed by one or many actors, the point of the action is to offset the normalizing effects of the social by opening up and founding new spaces of politics and individuation for others to explore, augment, and amend in their turn. This feminist politics presupposes not an already known and unifying identity of "woman" but agonistic, differentiated, multiple nonidentified beings that are always becoming, always calling out for augmentation and amendment. Agonistic (resistant but always also responsive to the expressive aspirations of any identity) and performative, this politics seeks to create new relations and establish new realities, as well as to amend and augment old ones . . . even in the private realm.

## Afterword: Agonism versus Associationism?[44]

Political theorists and feminists, in particular, have long criticized Arendt for the agonistic dimensions of her politics, charging that agonism is a masculinist, heroic, violent, competitive, (merely) aesthetic, or necessarily individualistic practice.[45] For these theorists, the notion of an agonistic feminism would be, at best, a contradiction in terms and, at worst, a muddled and, perhaps, dangerous idea. Their perspective is effectively endorsed by Seyla Benhabib who, in a recent series of powerful essays, tries to rescue Arendt for feminism by excising agonism from her thought.[46] Juxtaposing agonism to "associationism," Benhabib argues that these are two alternative "models of public space"[47] and that, of the two, the associative model is to be preferred because it is "the more modernist conception of politics" and a better model for feminism as well. Rather than reassess the meaning of agonism and its possibilities for feminism, Benhabib accepts and even expands upon earlier feminist genderings of agonism as the provenance of male action. Privileging the associative model of individuals acting with each other in concert, she deprives feminism of a much-needed appreciation of the necessarily agonistic dimension of all action in concert, in which politically engaged individuals act *and* struggle both with *and* against each other.

In "Feminist Theory and Hannah Arendt's Concept of Public Space," Benhabib constructs agonism and associationism as perfect, mirror opposites. In contrast to the agon, which presupposes a "morally homogeneous and politically egalitarian, but exclusive community," the modern public space is heterogeneous: "neither access to it nor its agenda of debate can be predefined by criteria of moral and political homogeneity." While the agon located freedom in a stable public space, the associative model treats freedom as a practice not a space: it "emerges from action in concert" wherever and whenever that occurs. "The agonal space is based on competition rather than collaboration," focused on "greatness, heroism, and pre-eminence" not on action in concert. It "individuates those who participate in it and sets them apart from others," rather than binding them together.[48]

This rejection of agonism in favor of its supposed opposite, association-ism, depends upon a problematic series of contestable definitions and elisions. First, agonism is defined strictly in classical terms, while associationism is revised and updated for modernity. This depiction of the Arendtian agon as essentially and necessarily a site of classical heroic individualism flies in the face of Arendt's own resignification of agonism as a practice of concerted action. (Arendt makes it quite clear that on her account, action—even in its most agonal forms—is always, always in concert.)[49] Benhabib then moves on to revise and update Arendtian associationism in order to produce the more modern conception of the public sphere she wants to endorse. Pointing out that Arendt "limit[s] her concept of public space in ways which are not compatible with her own associative model," Benhabib eases the incompatibility by amending Arendt's associationism to include concerns that Arendt rejected as antipolitical (no such amendment is forwarded for agonism) and to identify associationism, again contra Arendt's own account, with "not a substantive but a procedural" model of public discourse.[50]

The problem is not that Benhabib amends Arendt's account. She quite clearly positions her project as one that proceeds by "thinking with Arendt against Arendt."[51] The problem lies in her bifurcation of Arendt's complex vision of political action into two distinct, separable, and mutually exclusive types of public space, in her insistence that we must choose between them, in her loading of that choice with her asymmetric treatment of the pair, and in her (at this point, unsurprising) conclusion that associationism is the better, because more modernist, notion of the two.

In another essay, "Hannah Arendt and the Redemptive Power of Narrative," the agon is again devalued, this time by contrast with discursive (associative) public space. Once again proceeding asymmetri-cally, Benhabib metaphorizes the discursive moment in Arendtian action but leaves its agonistic other behind, arguing that agonistic public space is a "topographical or institutional" *place*, while insisting that discursive public space, Arendt's more "modernist" notion, "emerges whenever and wherever men act together in concert."[52] This limitation of the metaphorization is arbitrary, however. There is nothing in Arendt's account of the various more and less agonistic and associative public spaces to suggest that the latter are any more amenable than the former to the dispersal sought by Benhabib. If we are to say, "with Arendt against Arendt," that associative public space emerges whenever people act together in concert, why may we not also say that agonistic public space emerges whenever people act and struggle with and against each other in concert?

In her most recent essay, "The Pariah and Her Shadow: Hannah Arendt's Biography of Rahel Varnhagen," Benhabib further genders the agonism/associationism binary, juxtaposing male agonistic space to a now explicitly feminized associationism, here modeled by the salon. Drawing boldly on *Rahel Varnhagen*, Arendt's early biography of a Romantic era, Jewish German salon hostess, Benhabib champions the salon as an associative, female-dominated semipublic space that enables association, intimacy, conversation, friendship, and female agency. Agonal space, by contrast, is said to exclude women and to generate struggle and competition.[53]

But the salon is less supportive of Benhabib's feminized associationism than it is of efforts (like my own) to attenuate the oppositions that Benhabib seeks to secure, such as those between agonism and associationism or male- and female-friendly models of public space. Women did have more power in the salons than in other public spheres but their power depended upon public and private patriarchal power. The salons hosted by women were owned by temporarily absent fathers and husbands. The brief success of Rahel's salons derived partly from the fortuitous and temporary absence of any competing, male, cultural centers like a university, parliament, or royal court.[54] Moreover, the salons were famous for generating not only friendship, communication, and intimacy but also gossip, intrigue, competition, and struggle; one is even tempted to say . . . agonism.

Benhabib concedes all of this but argues that these imperfections in the salons' representation of her associative ideal do not pose a problem because she is not interested in recuperating the salons as such, but in treating them as "precursors" of associationism, as "past carriers of some of its future potentials."[55] Fair enough. But might not the salons' imperfections as models of a feminized associationism raise questions nonetheless about Benhabib's deployment of the salon as a figure through which to gender the agonism/associationism binary?[56] The salons' complicated combination of agonistic and associative dimensions might unsettle (rather than support) the mutually exclusive opposition that Benhabib seeks to ground in the salons' example.

The brand of agonism explored in this essay is not the agonism rejected by Benhabib. It models a kind of action in concert that resists or exceeds her binary. Neither a heroic individualism nor a consensus-based associationism, this agonism models an action in concert that is also always a site of struggle, a concerted feminist effort that is always with *and* against one's peers because it takes place in a world marked and riven by difference and plurality. This agonism takes as its point of departure Arendt's resignified agonism not the classical polis experience. It does not map neatly onto any male-female oppositions; it takes those conventional oppositions as its adversaries. And it is centered not on excellence and theatrical self-display, but on the quest for individuation and distinction against backgrounds of homogenization and normalization. Benhabib sees agonism as a practice in which actors compete "for distinction and excellence."[57] She is not wrong. But her immediate identification of agonism's distinction-awarding effects with a craving for fame and excellence forecloses an alternative reading of "distinction" that is no less true to classical agonism but that may also have more (post-) modern dimensions. The agonal passion for distinction, which so moved Arendt's theoretical account, may also be read as a struggle for individuation, for emergence as a distinct self: in Arendt's terms, a "who" rather than a "what," a self possessed not of fame, per se, but of individuality, a self that is never exhausted by the (sociological, psychological, and juridical) categories that seek to define and fix it.

What makes this passion an *agonal* passion once it is no longer tethered to the fame and excellence that only the classical agon could award? The feminist practices endorsed here are agonistic because they are tied to struggle; specifically, to a political struggle to (re-)found, augment, and amend governing practices of sex/gender. Just as the combatants in the agon individuated themselves in a publicly supported relation of struggle with and against an Other, so too agonistic feminists support the struggles of their peers to individuate and position themselves with and against various feminisms, dominant practices and identities of sex-gender, and those others who practice and enforce them.[58] Agonistic feminists achieve and enable individuation and distinction by interrupting conventional practices of sex/gender and decentering the would-be primacy of conventional sex/gender binaries.[59] This process of individuation is not *for* an audience, though any set of actions or performances may be witnessed by one. It is for the self who in concert with others like herself gains individuation, and for others who are enabled to do the same by way of these shared, if also always conflicted, practices of support and struggle. Agonistic individuation need not be the goal of political or feminist action. As Arendt well knew, individuation tends, rather, to be one of the by-products of political engagement. Through the acid test of political action in concert, Arendtian actors find out who they are. This self-discovery or transformation need not be shunned as mere boyish posturing; it may just as well be taken to signal the development of character and individuality in worldly settings.

The emphasis of agonistic feminism on the development of individuality as an effect of participation in concerted political action restores Arendt's original partnering of agonism and associationism.[60] The restoration is important for contemporary feminisms at this time because our recent focus on difference and plurality in response to the deployment by some feminisms of the homogenizing and disciplinary category of "woman" has led some to wonder how, in the absence of a unifying identity, cause, or ground, any future feminism might motivate concerted action. Arendt helps us to answer the question (albeit not for feminism in particular) by theorizing an agonistic action in concert that postulates difference and plurality, not identity, at its base. By insisting that action not take the what-ness of subjectivity as its point of departure, she (unwittingly but nonetheless valuably) provides a model for those feminisms that seek to put "woman" into question rather than take that figure to signify an identity that is always already known. By theorizing an action in concert that is riven by differences (both within and among the agents of action), Arendt invites us to think of concerted action as a practice of (re-)founding, augmentation, and amendment that involves us in relations not only "with" but also always simultaneously "against" others. In short, once we stop thinking of agonism and associationism as mutually exclusive alternatives, we are empowered to develop, "with Arendt against Arendt," an (augmented and amended) vision of agonistic, feminist political action that is well positioned to engage rather than simply redeploy the dominant sex/gender binaries that feminists have always sought to decenter, resist, or transcend.[61]

# Notes

1. *Rahel Varnhagen: The Life of a Jewish Woman*, rev. ed., trans. Richard and Clara Winston (New York: Harcourt Brace Jovanovich, 1974), xviii.

2. The most hostile charges are in Adrienne Rich's *On Lies, Secrets and Silence: Selected Prose, 1966–1978* (New York: Norton, 1979) and Mary O'Brien's *The Politics of Reproduction* (Boston: Routledge and Kegan Paul, 1981). I discuss Rich's charges briefly below and take up the issues surrounding feminist rejections of agonism in the final section of this essay.

3. *The Human Condition* (Chicago: University of Chicago Press, 1958), 155, 200; hereafter cited as *HC*.

4. *On Revolution* (New York: Penguin Books, 1963), 130; hereafter cited as *OR*.

5. Henceforth, I allow J. L. Austin's terms, performative and constative, to play an integral role in my reading of Arendt. As I have argued elsewhere, Austin's distinction usefully and aptly adumbrates arguments that Arendt herself makes about the illicit tension between two moments in the founding document: the "we hold" versus the "self-evident truths." That tension, which is ultimately ineliminable (in spite of Arendt's effort to resolve it in favor of the performative "we hold") makes it impossible for institutions to legitimate themselves "all the way down." Arendt effectively affirms that impossibility when she responds to it by brilliantly theorizing authority as a nonfoundational, *political* practice of augmentation and amendment. I argue here that that practice also covers the engagements and interruptions of identity that I identify with an agonistic feminism.

My use of Austin's distinction is not, as Seyla Benhabib argues, an attempt to use a "linguistic" distinction to settle the problem of legitimacy nor does it amount to a defense of "Derrida's thesis of the ultimate arbitrariness of all power" (this is not, in any case, his thesis). If it looks that way to Benhabib, that is because she assumes that the problem of political legitimacy must be solvable within the domain of theory. From that perspective, it is no surprise that my own project should appear either as a failed attempt to solve the problem of legitimacy or as a theoretical claim that the problem of legitimacy is unsolvable (or, as in this case, somehow both). But Benhabib's perspective and her project are different from mine. The lesson I draw from Arendt's reading of the Declaration, with help from Austin and Derrida, is that the resolution of the problem of legitimacy is itself an ongoing, never-ending project of political work, a perpetual practice of democratic augmentation and amendment, not a philosophical problem to be solved. The attempt to solve the problem of legitimacy at a philosophical level (or the belief that it is susceptible to philosophical resolution) is distinctively un-Arendtian in spirit and symptomatic of political theory's generally problematic tendency to displace politics. More to the point, her assumption that legitimacy is a philosophical rather than a political problem unhelpfully limits Benhabib's diagnostic options to only two: that of total legitimacy versus total arbitrariness. In my view, one of the main attractions of Arendt's theorization of authority as a political practice of augmentation is that it escapes and unsettles this binary. See Seyla Benhabib, "Democracy and Difference: Reflections on the Metapolitics of Lyotard and Derrida," *Journal of Political Philosophy* 2 (1994): 11 n. 24; and Bonnie Honig, "Declarations of Independence: Arendt and Derrida on the Problem of Founding a Republic," *American Political Science Review* 85 (1991): 97–113. On political theory's tendency to displace politics, see my *Political Theory and the Displacement of Politics* (Ithaca: Cornell University Press, 1993).

6. I am paraphrasing Nietzsche, to whom Arendt is greatly, albeit ambivalently, indebted here. See Friedrich Nietzsche, *On the Genealogy of Morals*, ed. Walter Kaufmann, trans. Walter Kaufmann and R. J. Hollingdale (1887; New York: Vintage Books, 1969), 1, xiii.

7. I criticize and amend this essentialist component of Arendt's reading of the Declaration

in "Declarations of Independence" and argue, following Jacques Derrida, that the success of the Declaration actually depends not on its really performative character but on its structural undecidability, on the fact that we cannot tell for sure whether this founding speech-act is a performative or a constative utterance. My argument here, that agonistic feminism should proceed by redescribing would-be constative identities as performatives, aims not to suggest that all identities are up for grabs and available for easy reenactments. Instead, the point is to recapture the undecidability (between constative and performative) that touches all regimes, identities, and foundings but that is then hidden and disguised as pure constation (of nature, the body, or God). That structural undecidability is a space of augmentation and amendment. It enables not a free-floating set of performances but a series of political engagements and struggles with the estimable forces of constation and naturalization.

8. Hanna Pitkin notes this difference, too; see her "Justice: On Relating Public and Private," *Political Theory* 9 (1981): 303–26. However, she reads it differently, arguing that *On Revolution* is "franker," presumably a more genuine expression of Arendt's real views on the body and the social (334). But this conclusion is unwarranted: it implies that *The Human Condition* is reticent in a way that is uncharacteristic of any of Arendt's texts. Moreover, Pitkin's treatment of one of Arendt's accounts of the body as a thin veil for the other obscures the fact that Arendt *layers* distinct characterizations of the body, one on top of the other. In a more recent essay, "Conformism, Housekeeping, and the Attack of the Blob: The Origins of Hannah Arendt's Concept of the Social" (Chapter 3 of this volume), Pitkin adopts a less essentialist approach, seeking to denaturalize Hannah Arendt's concept of the social by tracing its complex transformations through several of Arendt's texts.

9. Hannah Arendt, "What Is Freedom?" in *Between Past and Future,* enl. ed. (New York: Penguin, 1977), 156.

10. Arendt, *HC* 179; and "What is Freedom?" 151–52. Arendt reads these attributes of agency behaviorally, as *causes* of action that compromise its freedom.

11. Arendt, *The Human Condition,* 179. I borrow the term "self-surprising" from George Kateb's treatment of Arendt, *Hannah Arendt: Politics, Conscience, Evil* (Totowa, N.J.: Rowman and Allanheld, 1984).

12. Hannah Arendt, *Thinking,* vol. 1 of *The Life of the Mind,* ed. Mary McCarthy (New York: Harcourt Brace Jovanovich, 1978), 29. This claim is clearly false. Arendt may have meant not that all "insides" look identical but that biological differences are not interesting or significant: as bodies we are all alike.

13. Hannah Arendt, *Willing,* vol. 2 of *The Life of the Mind,* 69. Arendt makes this claim specifically with reference to willing but it is characteristic of a recoiling that affects all three of the mental faculties.

14. I mean to say that Arendt terms "political" the phenomenon of agonistic struggle, not that she herself would use the term "political" to describe these internal struggles. She would not.

15. Elisabeth Young-Bruehl is the only reader of Arendt to note the multiplicity of Arendt's self but she does not pursue the connections between this view of the self as multiplicity and Arendt's treatment of action as performative, not expressive. Nor does Young-Bruehl see this multiple self as a site of agonistic struggle. On the contrary, she refers to the "checks and balances existing within an individual," implying an overarching unity that is inapt in this context. See Elisabeth Young-Bruehl, *Mind and the Body Politic* (New York: Routledge, 1989), 23.

16. Arendt, *HC* 73. In *The Human Condition,* Arendt describes "the laborers who 'with their bodies minister to the bodily needs of life' [here quoting Aristotle's *Politics* 1254b25] and the women who with their bodies guarantee the physical survival of the species" (72).

17. Arendt often fails to distinguish clearly her (admittedly admiring) descriptions of the

practice of agonal politics in the polis from her own vision of politics; and her critics often mistake the first for the second. For example, Pitkin notes that Arendt's account of action is "individualistic" but the citation upon which Pitkin relies (from HC 41) is one in which Arendt describes the agon of the polis. Where Arendt describes her own view of action, even in the early, some say too agonal, *Human Condition*, she says that it is always, always "in concert."

18. Pitkin, "Justice," 342.

19. Pitkin, "Justice," 342. I borrow the term "sensibilities" from Shiraz Dossa, who makes a case quite similar to Pitkin's. Both he and Pitkin, however, stop short of arguing that, as sensibilities, labor, work, and action are characteristic of *all* selves. See *The Public Realm and the Public Self: The Political Theory of Hannah Arendt* (Waterloo: Wilfred Laurier University Press, 1989), chap. 3; and my review of Dossa in *Political Theory* 18 (1990): 322.

20. This call to denaturalize labor, work, and action so as to see their effects as the products of our own doings parallels the position that informs Hanna Pitkin's essay in this volume. Pitkin puzzles over the incredible power that Arendt assigns to the social: "Coming from a thinker whose main effort was to teach us our powers—that we are the source of our troubles and should stop doing as we do—the science-fiction vision of the social as Blob ["intent on taking us over, gobbling up our freedom and our politics"] is truly astonishing" (53).

21. Arendt insists that the "whole sphere of" politics be "limited," that it not "encompass the whole of man's and the world's existence" (Arendt, "What is Freedom?" 264).

22. Arendt, *Willing*, 37–38, 101–2; my emphasis. I have argued elsewhere that, on Arendt's account, the will is both self-generating *and* capable of bringing its own activity to an end; see "Arendt, Identity, and Difference," *Political Theory* 16 (February 1988): 81. However, the phrase highlighted in the text here has persuaded me that Arendt did not attribute the latter feature to the will, but to action.

23. Judith Butler, "Performative Acts and Gender Constitution: An Essay in Phenomenology and Feminist Theory," in *Performing Feminisms*, ed. Sue-Ellen Case (Baltimore: Johns Hopkins University Press, 1990), 273.

24. Pitkin, "Justice," 336.

25. Nancy Fraser, *Unruly Practices: Power, Discourse, and Gender in Contemporary Social Theory* (Minneapolis: University of Minnesota Press, 1989), 76.

26. Arendt, "Preface," in *Between Past and Future*, 3–4.

27. Butler, "Performative Acts," 276, 271, 280, and 271.

28. See note 5 for my defense of this view of political theory's task against the view that the proper mission of theory is to provide a comprehensive justification of political institutions.

29. Pitkin, "Justice," 336.

30. Arendt, OR 47. Cf. Judith Butler, "Performative Acts," 274.

31. Adrienne Rich, *On Lies, Secrets and Silence*, 211–12. Arendt's readers have been recirculating this citation for some time. Less often noted is that Rich's essay "On the Conditions of Work" also opens with a citation from Arendt's *The Human Condition*, which is, after all, a "lofty" even if also a "crippled" book.

32. Hannah Arendt, *Men in Dark Times* (New York: Harcourt Brace Jovanovich, 1968), 44; hereafter cited as MDT. Arendt never considers the possibility that politically active women were drawn to suffragist activities because the suffragist movement was one of the few available opportunities for political action open to women at the time.

33. The story is probably apocryphal but Arendt is reported to have refused to appear at an American Political Science Association Women's Caucus panel devoted to her work, saying "I do not think of myself as a woman."

34. The controversy surrounding the publication of Arendt's *Eichmann in Jerusalem* is well

documented in Dagmar Barnouw's *Visible Spaces: Hannah Arendt and the German-Jewish Experience* (Baltimore: Johns Hopkins University Press, 1990).

35. Gershom Scholem, " 'Eichmann in Jerusalem:' An Exchange of Letters between Gershom Scholem and Hannah Arendt," *Encounter* (January 1964): 51–52 (my emphasis). All citations from Scholem henceforth are from 51–52. All citations from Arendt in this section are from 53–54.

36. Even when she identifies herself with "the tradition of German philosophy," the identification is conditional: "*If* I can be said to have come from anywhere, it is from the tradition of German philosophy." More broadly, the phrasing suggests that Arendt would have preferred that the question of her origins simply not be a subject for speech; that is, that she not be "*said* to have come from anywhere" (my emphasis).

37. And so is Scholem, of course, constituted by differences and identities other than his Judaism and Zionism. Arendt reminds him of this—and retaliates in kind for his projections of her identity—by addressing her letter to "Dear Gerhard" even though Scholem signs his letter to her with his Hebrew name: "Gershom Scholem."

38. My emphasis. I treat Scholem's use of the term "daughter" in this context less as a recognition that Arendt is distinctly constituted by sex/gender difference than as a means of invoking a sense of obligation to the paternal figure, "our people." In short, the term "daughter" in Scholem's phrase seeks to assimilate Arendt's sex/gender *unproblematically* into her Jewish identity.

39. Arendt's claim that identity is a fact is unchanging. Her claim that it is a *private* fact does change, however, depending on the context. There are times, she says, when one has to defend oneself "in terms of the identity that is under attack." At other times, though, positioning oneself in terms of one's identity can be no more than a pose (see Dietz, 48 n. 106, in this volume). Given the strategy's context-dependence, one has always to diagnose the situation and decide whether to accede to the (for Arendt, unfortunate) relevance of identity in the space of action or to insist on its privacy or irrelevance. (This diagnostic debate is one that feminism regularly confronts.) My argument is that, in the case of her exchange with Scholem, Arendt misdiagnosed the situation. She should have responded in terms of the identity that was under attack, her own way of being Jewish. I suspect that her failure to do so stemmed partly from her identitarian assumption that since she and Scholem were both Jews, her Jewish identity could not be the one that was under attack and so neither could it be a ground from which to respond.

40. I borrow the notion of "doing one's gender" from Judith Butler, "Performative Acts," 276.

41. Hannah Arendt, *The Jew as Pariah*, ed. Ron H. Feldman (New York: Grove, 1978).

42. I track the multiple sites of political space in Arendt's account in *Political Theory and the Displacement of Politics*, 116–17.

43. In fact, the implied individualism of Arendt's pariah perspective contributes to the weakening of her position in relation to Scholem's. Scholem repeatedly invokes the communal figure of the Jewish people to which he aims to restore Arendt, whom he figures as a renegade. Arendt accepts these terms and responds from within their frame. But she need not have done so. She could have forged coalitions with others (past or present) who might have been sympathetic with her views and she might have positioned herself vis-à-vis the Jewish community as part of an alternative Judaic history of intra-Jewish criticism. Arendt uses this last strategy in her Lessing Address when—as Lisa Disch argues (Chapter 12, this volume)—Arendt reclaims Lessing from the German Enlightenment tradition and positions him as part of an alternative intellectual genealogy to which she, herself, is heir.

44. My thanks to Linda Zerilli and Morris Kaplan for their comments on earlier drafts of this section.

45. Hanna Pitkin, for example, accuses Arendt's political actors of "boyish posturing" and of membership in a "romanticized" and "agonistic male warriors' " club ("Justice"). See also Patricia Springborg, "Hannah Arendt and the Classical Republican Tradition," in *Thinking, Judging, Freedom*, ed. G. T. Kaplan and C. S. Kessler (Sydney: Allen and Unwin, 1989); and Wendy Brown, *Manhood and Politics* (Totowa, N.J.: Rowman and Littlefield, 1988).

46. In short, Benhabib effectively reprises the 1970s and early 1980s debates, which charged Arendt with being either a phallocentric (agonistic) or a gynocentric (associative) thinker. Benhabib's innovation inheres in her refusal to identify Arendt exclusively with either one of these dimensions of her thought, in her acknowledgment of the presence of both in the Arendtian schema. But like those earlier feminists, she goes on to position these two dimensions oppositionally and hierarchically and to insist that we must choose between them. (For more detailed discussions of these early feminist receptions of Arendt, see my "The Arendt Question in Feminism," and Mary Dietz's "Feminist Receptions of Hannah Arendt," Chapters 1 and 2, this volume.)

47. Seyla Benhabib, "Feminist Theory and Hannah Arendt's Concept of Public Space," *History of the Human Sciences* 6 (1993): 97–114.

48. Ibid., 103–4, 102.

49. See note 18. Benhabib ignores Arendt's resignification of agonism in this context only. Elsewhere she clearly attends to one dimension of it, arguing that Arendt "subdues and, yes, 'domesticates' the Homeric *warrior-hero* to yield the Aristotelian *deliberative citizen*" (ibid., 103; emphasis in original).

50. Ibid., 104, 105.

51. Ibid., 100.

52. Seyla Benhabib, "Hannah Arendt, and the Redemptive Power of Narrative," *Social Research* 57 (1990): 193–94.

53. "The Pariah and Her Shadow," this volume, 94–95, 97–100.

54. Ibid., 87–88, 93, 97. The very temporary success of Varnhagen's salon and its dependence upon this fortuitous and temporary vacuum in patriarchal institutional power suggest that the real lesson of this example is that those who would champion associationism must also learn and affirm agonism if they are going to preserve their valued alternative spaces of action against the hegemonic aspirations of the state and/or the patriarchal public realm.

55. Ibid., 104 n. 23.

56. In short, my goal here is not to debate the merits of the salon as a model of associative or feminist public space but briefly to note the role of the salons in Benhabib's larger effort to position—and to gender—agonism and associationism as binary opposites in order to develop a feminism and an Arendt capable of meeting on the common ground of a discourse and consensus model of politics.

57. "Feminist Theory and Hannah Arendt's Concept of Public Space," 103.

58. For an account of the agon as a site of both concerted action and struggle, see my "The Politics of Agonism," *Political Theory* 21 (August 1993): 528–33.

59. For some examples of this (shifting coalitional) practice, see Melissa Orlie's essay, Chapter 14, this volume. Orlie valuably highlights the ways in which a politics of sex/gender is also always imbricated in a politics of race, class, and sexuality.

60. Insofar as this agonism departs from Arendt's to broaden her realm of the actionable and include so-called social concerns and so-called constative facts, it ought not (contra Mary Dietz, 36, this volume) to be taken to treat identity as its necessarily *central* concern. It does so merely in this essay. If this agonism is always to some extent interested in the politics of identity, that is because it knows that identity—specifically, the formation and production of subjectivity under the (juridical or social) law—is always *an* effect or instrument of social-political-juridical orders and, therefore, *an* indispensable site of political engagement.

61. Notably, this phrase, "with and against," is the one that Benhabib uses to describe her own relation to Arendt as a reader ("Feminist Theory and Hannah Arendt's Concept of Public Space," 100). In so doing, she describes an *agonistic* relation and this is apt; her reading of Arendt is a concerted action that simultaneously individuates Benhabib's own position. It should also be noted that Benhabib herself seems to recognize, if only momentarily, that agonism and her variety of associationism are not really mutually exclusive: "While all genuine politics and power relations involve an agonistic dimension, in the sense of vying for distinction and excellence, agonal politics also entails an associative dimension based on the power of persuasion and consensus. In this sense the sharp differentiation between these two models needs to be softened" (103). Having said this, however, Benhabib goes on further to specify the terms of the opposition and does nothing to soften it.

# 7

# The Arendtian Body

## Linda M. G. Zerilli

*The Arendtian Body. To speak about this body in public, to make this body
speak, to write it. Is this not outrageous, scandalous, indecent?*

*I confront the Arendtian body as an interpretive law that has been erected
by at least two generations of traditional scholarly commentators; I confront
this body as an interdict that has been issued by Hannah Arendt herself; I
confront this body as a terrible, terrifying desire-in-language that I, a putatively
female political theorist, imagine myself duty-bound to conceal.*

*I am sitting at my desk, staring at a monitor screen whose vast emptiness I
must fill with words about the Arendtian body. The very thought of giving*

Thanks to Lisa Disch, Gregor Gnädig, and especially Bonnie Honig for their help with
this essay.

Hannah Arendt, New York, 1944 (photo by Fred Stein)

*voice to the unutterable in Hannah Arendt's intellectual corpus fills me with dread. On a shelf next to the blank screen I have placed a 1944 photo of the theorist. Reclined on what appears to be a bed, she is cut off at the waist, dressed in black, and looking very existential. Here is the model of the thinking woman: high forehead, short hair, serious and sad eyes that reflect the weight of the world. Framing this curiously disembodied image of female intellect is the shadow that her impressive head has cast upon the wall. I can't decide whether this haunting shadow confirms or contests the disappearance of the body in the pose of the thinker. Then I notice that she is smoking a cigarette. Judging from the ashtray, she has smoked several. For a fleeting moment, this paper seems possible.*

## Whose Body?

Whose body, indeed: that is precisely the question I faced when, at the request of the editor of this volume, I delivered an earlier version of this paper as part of a panel discussion on feminist approaches to Hannah Arendt at the 1993 American Political Science Association Meeting. After the panel—which had incited a heated debate about Arendt's intellectual legacy and had made quite clear the political stakes of interpretation for readers of diverse theoretical persuasions—I retreated to the bar in order to ponder the unusual intensity of academic emotion. Upon entering I encountered a table occupied by a group of my esteemed and senior male colleagues. Upon seeing me, one of them—or was it all of them?—shouted: THE BODY, LINDA! THE BODY! This outburst generated a rather loud and nervous fraternal laughter in the group and, I must admit, in myself as well.

How was this hysterical ejaculation to be accounted for? How had my public performance become an occasion to debate, not the discursive figure of the Arendtian body (which I took to be *my* topic), but, rather, the question: *Whose body?* In a flash I recognized my colleagues' answer to *their* own (if also disowned) question: not Hannah Arendt's body and certainly—or rather by extension, as I shall explain—not ours. It is *your* body, Linda, your obsession with the body that you now attribute to poor Hannah Arendt, one of the few women to have been admitted to our little club, the canon of political thought.

What was at stake for my masculine interlocutors in keeping the legacy of Hannah Arendt untainted by the question of the body, now redefined as the problem of my body? How had I become the very problem that I was trying to pose?

> *Ladies and Gentlemen:*
>     Throughout history people have knocked their heads against the riddle of the nature of femininity. . . . Nor will *you* have escaped from this problem—those of you who are men; to those of you who are women this will not apply—you are yourselves the problem.[1]

Where was Freud when I needed him? Had I recalled those words, I might have escaped the exposure that attended my effort to enunciate the very problem that I, a "woman," apparently am.[2] I might have anticipated the eclipse of my status as a speaking subject on the (Arendtian) body by my symbolic status *as* the body for putatively masculine subjects, my esteemed colleagues. Failing to heed the words of psychoanalysis, I transgressed the great sexual divide. If "one is a woman," to *enunciate* rather than to be the problem (of femininity, of the body) is to make of oneself a spectacle; it is to lose one's symbolic placement by walking through the wrong restroom door—and just as embarrassing.[3]

This would not have happened to Hannah Arendt. She knew how to keep straight her identity, her doors, her sex—didn't she?

> The truth is I have never pretended to be anything else or to be in any way other than I am, and I never even felt tempted in that direction. It would be like saying that I was a man and not a woman—that is to say, kind of insane. . . . There is such a thing as a basic gratitude for everything that is as it is; for what has been *given* and was not, could not, be *made*; for things that are *physei* and not *nomǭ*.[4]

Were my colleagues right? Was this the lesson of Hannah Arendt for a feminist like myself? To be thankful for things that are "beyond dispute or argument," to know and walk through the right door, to accept the facts of identity, of sexual difference?

What would it mean to dispute or argue those facts? Does one have to be "kind of insane," and if so, what, exactly, induces that madness? Is it the imagined identification with masculinity ("like saying I was a man"), the imagined *dis*identification with femininity ("and not a woman"), or something else?

Posing these questions I am struck by the rhetorical features of Arendt's prose: the repetitive, insistent denial of any wish to argue the facts of identity; the claim that those facts are indisputable in any case; and the figuration of the challenge to gender identity as a psychic trauma, insanity.[5] These features are significant for two reasons: (1) they suggest parallels with the psychoanalytic account of hysteria, which also reads the female subject's disidentification with "woman" as a psychic trauma; and (2) they intimate that a stable subjectivity requires absolute clarity about one's sex/gender, an impossible clarity that is both enabled and threatened by a deep silence about "what has been given and was not, could not, be made."

In *On Revolution* and *The Human Condition*,[6] that silence takes the form of a prohibition on speaking (about) the body in public, an Arendtian taboo of sorts that includes but never directly names sexuality and barely broaches the question of, just as it appears to assume, (hetero)sexual difference. Mute and shrouded in secrecy, the Arendtian body exhibits the curious mixture of uncanny, dangerous, forbidden, and sacred attributes that Freud associates with the fundamentally ambivalent structure of taboo. The latter, he writes, is not different "in its psychological nature from Kant's 'categorical imperative,' which operates in a compulsive fashion and rejects conscious motives."[7] Drawing on psychoanalytic accounts of the body as the site of cultural prohibitions, I suggest that the Arendtian taboo on the body too has something unspeakable about it, something that remains unsymbolized, perhaps foreclosed, and in this specific sense appears to be, in Freud's terms, "resistant to analysis" or, in Arendt's terms, "beyond dispute or argument"—that is, beyond contestation or speech.[8]

At stake in the Arendtian taboo on the body is the future of the speaking, common world, which risks total annihilation or, to use Arendt's telling word, "engulfment" by the mute, "devouring," and insatiable body of *animal laborans*. This body, often figured as ravenous and oral, poses an immanent threat to Arendtian plurality.[9] It violates the boundaries that vouchsafe plurality, on Arendt's account. One of those boundaries distinguishes male from female. Arendt attempts to ground plurality in it, explicitly appealing to the naturalized sexual difference given in Genesis: "We know only 'male and female created he *them.*' "[10] This plurality is endangered by the embodied subject who follows an illicit desire, who dares to question what has been given (male and female), to seek the forbidden fruit. To the extent that the heterosexually differentiated body guarantees human plurality as the human condition for Arendt, then, it would appear to function, as all foundations do, as "the unquestioned and unquestionable" in her political thought.[11] But does it? Why forbid something that is already impossible? If what is *physei* is by definition not *nomǭ*, and if no dispute or argument can change those facts, then why demand that we remain silent?[12]

## Nature's Body

To approach this paradox—why prohibit speech on a body that no word could (re)signify—consider first the Arendtian body not as a sexed but as a generic and natural object. For this is the body that we encounter in Arendt's major political texts. It is a body marked more by its mortal destiny than by its sex, a body fated to return, as *The Human Condition* tells us, "into the overall gigantic circle of nature herself, where no beginning and no end exist and where all natural things swing in changeless, deathless repetition" (96). The body's passage from linear to cyclical time is a move from the time of language (syntax and enunciation) and the speaking subject to a temporality characterized by an eerie silence, which Arendt elsewhere calls "the eternal quiet of being-forever that rests or swings within itself."[13] It is also a passage that menaces mortal man as *animal laborans*, the living being whose bodily functions tie him to "the recurring cycles of nature," binding him to a silent, daily struggle for existence and an endless battle against decay (*HC* 98). Here, in the infinite time or rather mute space of "nature's household," there is neither birth nor death, neither beginning nor end, but only "changeless eternal recurrence, the deathless everlastingness of the human as of all other animal species" (*HC* 97).

" 'Father's time, mother's species', as Joyce put it; and indeed, when evoking the name and destiny of women, one thinks more of the *space* generating and forming the human species than of time, becoming or history."[14] So begins Julia Kristeva's controversial essay, "Women's Time," an essay whose psychoanalytic approach to the body and the speaking subject offers a productive tension with Arendt's stony, forbidding silence on sexual difference. In stark contrast to *The Human Condition,* "Women's Time" insists on the specificity of the feminine subject's corporeal and psychical relation to nature; a relation character-ized, in Kristeva's words, precisely by "cycles, gestation, and the eternal recurrence of a biological rhythm which conforms to that of nature and imposes a temporality whose stereotyping may shock, but whose regular-ity and unison with what is experienced as extra-subjective time, cosmic time, occasion vertiginous visions and unnameable *jouissance*" (191).

And shock it has, this Kristevan account of feminine subjectivity. In the view of Judith Butler, Kristeva's cheery alignment of the feminine body with nature and the eternal recurrence of the biological life processes is evidence of her heterosexism and essentialism. Kristeva adopts Plato's figuration of the *chora* as a mother, characterizes it as "matrix space, nourishing, unnameable, anterior to the One, to God, and consequently defying metaphysics," and ignores his counterclaim that this receptacle, "the dynamic nature *(physis)* that receives all the bodies that there are," has itself, as Butler writes, "no proper shape and is not a body."[15] Rather than read the *chora* as formless and sexually undecidable, Kristeva reads it as feminine and maternal and so courts the danger of mystifying the female body's cultural status as the mysteri-ous eternal maternal, a cosmic natural object.

Without attempting to adjudicate the complicated case of Kristeva, I want to raise a related charge about Arendt, despite and because of her failure (or refusal?) to specify, in *The Human Condition,* the body as sexed. Is not the putatively generic Arendtian body an instance of biologism, ahistoricism, and even mysticism? How else shall we interpret a body that, from birth to death, is ruled by "the devouring processes of life" (*HC* 141) and condemned to the "deathless repetition" that defines its return to the "gigantic circle of nature herself"? And isn't this very figuration of "nature *herself*" as a mute, feminine receptacle of sorts akin to and just as troubling as Kristeva's identification of the Platonic *chora* with the maternal body?

There is surely evidence in Arendt's texts for an affirmative answer to these questions. But if she seems at times to be beholden to a feminized conception of nature and a naturalized conception of the body,[16] Arendt, contra Kristeva, does not focus on the female and/or maternal body's relationship to the cyclical life processes—in Kristevan terms, to the drives that throw the transcendental subject back into the semiotic *chora.* Treating the body as genderless, Arendt highlights neither maternity nor femininity but the sheer terror associated with mortality, with having a body. Arendt brings men's bodies into question, too, reminding us that they are also entangled in processes beyond the transcendental subject's control. She thus opens a conceptual space for thinking about how the flight from the body and the asymbolic *chora* has been managed in Western culture, partly through the very process of naming bodies masculine or feminine. But at a price. Arendt's genderless characterization of the body ignores the whole question of the cultural association of the cyclical life processes with the feminine body. As Mary Dietz remarks, "It is certainly curious that Arendt never makes this central feature of the human condition an integral part of her political analysis."[17]

Curious indeed. But we would be mistaken to think that this oddity can be normalized by, and Arendt rescued for, feminism by producing with Dietz "an Arendtian analysis enlightened by gender." This approach can generate important critical insights—as Dietz's reading does—but the attempt to compensate for "Arendt's gender blindness" risks blinding us to what is gained by a theory that does not symbolize the laboring and generative body in clear, unchanging, and all-too-familiar gendered terms (although it sometimes participates in such symbolization).[18] If Arendt has something important to say to feminists, it is not because her work can be reread to include the category of gender, but because (her appeal to Genesis notwithstanding) Arendt also fails (or refuses) to treat gender as the primary, already given category for thinking about the human body. She offers instead a powerful if problematic account of the subject's terror of embodiment and loss of symbolic mastery. This account can be used by feminists to rethink the Kristevan *chora,* which unsettles the transcendental, speaking subject and which Kristeva too quickly maps onto the female body, thereby risking the occlusion of the *chora*'s sexual undecidability.

Instead of rushing to correct Arendt's gender-blindness, then, we might pause and consider what she makes visible: namely, the terror of having a body, an anxiety about mortality and loss of symbolic mastery that, on her account, haunts every speaking subject in Western culture. Arendt neither ascribes this terror to men only nor assumes that women escape it by dint of their supposedly unique relationship to what Kristeva calls "cycles, gestation, and the eternal recurrence of a biological rhythm." Instead, Arendt's prose stages and amplifies the terror of embodiment and of the asymbolic *chora* for readers of both sexes. In doing so she both confirms *and* contests, secures *and* attenuates, the symbolic order that barely conceals the sexually undecidable *chora* with the very notion of two sexes, each in its proper place. In this Arendtian staging of terror we witness a recalcitrant, desiring and polymorphous body that ruptures the very boundaries (private/public) and identities (woman/man) that Western culture and Hannah Arendt herself frantically secure in an effort to keep the body in its place. But we also witness the violence, injustice, and, finally, the futility of that effort.

Rather than resolve these deep tensions, I want to amplify them by reading the Arendtian body, not as the site of curious (feminist) oversights or regrettable (and correctable) omissions, but as a site of fundamental ambivalence, as both symptom and symptomatic: symptom in the psychoanalytic sense "as the space where the Word fails, where the circuit of the Symbolic communication is broken,"[19] and symptomatic in the discursive sense as the complex site of displacement, a dumping ground for those elements in Arendt's political thought that remain un- or undertheorized. As symptom, the Arendtian body serves not as a figure of biological necessity but as resistance to symbolic necessity; as symptomatic, however, it serves as a reinscription of naturalized sexual difference. That may be why Arendt's political thought seems to exhibit or share the enormous anxiety about the body that it rhetorically stages, and why the Arendtian body is always in excess to the terms of its containment. Arendt evades the body but she does not try to escape it and she even acknowledges pleasure in it. She refuses to embrace the abstract transcendental subject—who is nobody and has no body.[20] In short, Arendt does not deny the subject as embodied, but she does not know quite what to do with the body. This tension puts her in a difficult but productive relationship with both feminist political theories and the Kristevan subject-in-process.

## The Semiotic Body

The Arendtian body as symptomatic appears not only in Arendt's appeal to Genesis but also in her deep reverence for ancient philosophy and the city-state, whose conceptions of nature, the body, and the public/private distinction she seems to adopt. In *The Human Condition*, Arendt is obsessed with re-membering and remapping this ancient distinction as the long-lost difference between the realm of biological necessity and that of political freedom, the space of the mute body and that of the speaking subject. In light of feminist critiques of the polis, it seems incredible that Arendt, who notes but does not explicitly criticize the place of free women and slaves, should express admiration and even nostalgia for ancient Greece.

Does Arendt reinscribe the very distinction that feminist theory would dismantle? In Arendt's view, modernity has beaten feminists to the task, blurring the great ancient gulf between private and public, and replacing both realms with that amorphous and unbounded creature that Arendt calls "the social." With the rise of the social, says Arendt, "the two realms [public and private] indeed constantly flow into each other like waves in the never-resting stream of the life process itself" (33). But how should that "flow" be figured? In the second chapter of *The Human Condition*, she figures it as continuous with the biological necessity that animates the body of *animal laborans* and that the Greeks wisely kept hidden from the eyes of others.

Here the social is the flow of the biological into the political, a flow that sweeps away the solid, common world of citizens (*HC* 97–100). Elsewhere, however, Arendt treats the social as profoundly unnatural and destructive of the borders between public and private and between nature and culture. As she moves to map the laboring body onto biological necessity and to contain both within the private sphere, Arendt figures nature via labor not as destructive and devouring but, rather, as irrepressibly productive and generative. The moment labor was emancipated (not the working class but the laboring body), she writes, "it was as though the growth element inherent in all organic life had completely overcome and overgrown the processes of decay by which organic life is checked and balanced in nature's household. The social realm, where the life process has established its own public domain, has let loose an unnatural growth, so to speak, of the natural" (*HC* 47). *Animal laborans* is the accomplice of a nature that threatens the man-made world, not with natural decay, but with an unnatural growth.

Arendt's staging of the "unnatural growth of the natural" (*HC* 47), wherein nature, working through the body of *animal laborans*, is in a kind of generative excess to herself, profligate and unbounded by organic decay or death, bears an uncanny resemblance to what Mikhail Bakhtin calls the "grotesque body," an "ever unfinished, ever creating body" that "outgrows itself, transgresses its own limits." Indeed this unnatural growth, this grotesque body, stands both as a reminder that nature is always already culture—what else can an unnatural nature mean?—and as an incitement to resurrect ancient borders against the body that knows none. This body, as Bakhtin writes, "is not separated from the world by clearly defined boundaries."[21] But like the mythical Pandora's jar that, once opened, could not be closed—and out of which came *animal laborans*, as Arendt herself tells us—there is no border that could possibly (re)contain such a body and put it back in its place.[22] This body transgresses all human borders, including those between public and private, nature and culture.

The Arendtian body—grotesque, mute, oral, desiring, and engulfing—is symptomatic, the space where the Word fails. It is Kristeva's semiotic: a body of drives that retains its relation to the protean and generative *chora*. It is a body, moreover, whose polymorphous heterogeneity never disappears from the signifying process that produces the speaking subject. It is a body or "signifying disposition" that, in Kristeva's terms, "introduces wandering or fuzziness into language" and is opposed to, but coexists with, "the symbolic function of significance," that is, "of meaning, sign, and signified object." This disruptive body of *jouissance*, argues Kristeva, unsettles the Cartesian speaking subject and makes it "a questionable *subject-in-process.*"[23]

Arendt refuses the transcendental, disembodied subject, but she is not exactly ready to embrace this Kristevan subject-in-process and, it seems, would happily send it back into the darkness whence it came.[24] And yet this subject-in-process haunts the notes and margins of the very text that seeks to exclude or shelter it in a privacy that is dark but also sacred. Writes Arendt, "The sacredness of this privacy [of the household or private property] was like the sacredness of the hidden, namely of birth and death, the beginning and end of mortals who, like all creatures, grow out of and return to the darkness of the underworld [ruled by Pluton and, for a third of the year, his abducted bride Persephone, daughter of Demeter]." This realm, she continues, "must be hidden from the public realm because it harbors the things from human eyes and impenetrable to human knowledge. It is hidden because man does not know where he comes from when he is born and where he goes when he dies" (HC 62–63). Arendt elaborates in a footnote:

> It seems as though the Eleusinian Mysteries provided for a common and quasi-public experience of this whole realm, which, because of its very nature and even though it was common to all,

needed to be hidden, kept secret from the public realm: Everybody could participate in them, but nobody was permitted to talk
about them. The mysteries concerned the unspeakable, and
experiences beyond speech were non-political and perhaps antipolitical by definition. . . . That they concerned the secret of
birth and death seems proved by a fragment of Pindar: oide men
biou teleutan, oiden de diosdoton archan (frag. 137a), where the
initiated is said to know "the end of life and the Zeus-given
beginning."[25]

Arendt cites Zeus, but Zeus was not at the center of the Eleusinean
Mysteries: the reunion of Demeter (goddess of fertility) and her daughter
Persephone was.[26] Arendt's substitution of Zeus for Demeter rewrites the
Mysteries as a celebration of the paternal rather than maternal character
of human beginnings; it effaces the maternal body with the proper name;
and it neglects the whole question of the mother-daughter drama, the
violent separation and joyful reunion of Demeter and Persephone.[27]

This remarkable set of elisions is symptomatic of Arendt's failure to
theorize the place of sexual difference in the social, cultural, and
political practices of the ancient city-state. But Arendt's silence on the
fertility rites of Demeter—which were financed by the polis but carried
out with a great deal of autonomy by women—entails more than her
gender-blindness. Arendt's erasure of Demeter with Zeus reasserts the
symbolic law of the father against the unnameable, *jouissant* body of the
mother.[28] Could it be that the maternal body is itself blinding? Is this
what Arendt means when she says that the Mysteries were unspeakable?
What cannot be uttered is the mother's sex.[29]

This sacred mystery, this *physis* (which in Greek also means genitals)
must be shut up in the darkness of the private realm and guarded by law
(*nomos*).[30] It must never be spoken in public, even though, as Arendt
observes of the Mysteries, it is an open secret. The phrase is perfect for
that place that Freud called an *unheimlich* place, the "entrance to the
former *Heim* [home] of all human beings, to the place where each of us
has lived once upon a time."[31] When Arendt says, citing Heraclitus,
that "the people should fight for the law as for a wall"—"the wall that
separates them from others"—she marks the wall that secures separation
from and prohibits access to the mother. This was the law of the city-
state, not "a catalogue of [conscious] prohibitions resting, as all modern
laws do, upon the Thou Shalt Nots of the Decalogue. It was quite

literally a wall"—a taboo that had been spatialized ("two buildings were never permitted to touch"). "And this wall-like law was sacred, but only the inclosure was political." On the other side was "the biological life process of the family" (HC 63–64), the unutterable, the maternal body.

Arendt does more than describe the wall that secures the border between public and private, nameable and unnameable, symbolic and semiotic; she rebuilds it. The rebuilding is symptomatic of the untheorized place of and unspoken anxiety about the maternal body in Arendt's account of the city-state. But if Arendt aligns herself with the paternal law of "Zeus Hereious, protector of border lines" (HC 30) and against the *jouissant* body of Demeter, she also endorses a signifying practice that mobilizes the drive-force of the semiotic body against the stultifying dictates of symbolic law. That practice is Arendtian action, a practice in which the body is not symptomatic, reinscribed in the symbolic, but symptom, open to the semiotic, to pleasure that exceeds the proper name.

## Bodies in Action

Although it appears that, for Arendt, the desiring, semiotic, and private body is at odds with the bounded, symbolic space of the public world, she also shows that the law that maintains this opposition (and keeps the difference between the sexes) was sustained in the city-state through violence and the repudiation of life itself: an abjection of the body and with it of the human condition. Man's flight from embodied existence not only forces "one part of humanity into the darkness of pain and necessity" but also substitutes "vicarious life for real life" (HC 119–20). The man who compels another to bear the burden of his body thereby gains free-citizen status but he is also thereby condemned to the alienated existence that Arendt finds in the haunting words of Herodotus: "We walk with alien feet; we see with alien eyes; we recognize and greet people with an alien memory; we live from alien labor" (HC 120n).

Arendt not only sees the violence in these borders. She also sees the need to transgress or attenuate them. Intimating that the slave stood as the disavowed, embodied part of the free (masculine) subject, Arendt contests the very meaning of that subject's freedom and, by extension, the borders that he erects to secure it. "Man cannot be free if he does not know that he is subject to necessity," she writes. Inasmuch as "his freedom is always won in his never wholly successful attempts to liberate himself from necessity" (HC 121), it is always partial and, when bought at the price of disavowal, both illusory and empty. To repudiate one's embodied existence, says Arendt, "would not only rob biological life of its most natural pleasures but deprive the specifically human life of its very liveliness and vitality."[32]

Arendt acknowledges and even celebrates the pleasures of the body, emphasizing the subject's sheer bliss in being alive. But she also insists that "our trust in the reality of life and the reality of the world is not the same." Whereas the latter "derives primarily from the permanence and durability of the world," the former derives from "the intensity with which life is felt." And this intensity, experienced through the body, "is so great and its force so elemental that wherever it prevails . . . it blacks out all other worldly reality."[33] Here the body is symptom, the space where the Word fails. The subject is so riven with bodily drives that it refuses the symbolic and is dangerously indifferent to the common speaking world of citizens. But if an exclusive focus on and lack of distance from the body eject one from the world, so too does a repudiation of the body. Such repudiation results in a kind of worldlessness—a "lifeless life" or a deadened and, as Herodotus suggests, vicarious existence in which the reality of the world is itself derealized, deprived of the animating force of life, of the semiotic body. The world (locus of great words and deeds) and life (locus of the body), then, are not in fact so much opposed as interdependent. For Arendtian action and speech would be empty without the bodily drives that animate them, just as, on Kristeva's account, the semiotic animates the symbolic and puts desire and pleasure in language.

As the locus of radical heterogeneity and vitality, the body is not the limit point but rather the condition for the nonsovereign subject of Arendt's action. "If men wish to be free," Arendt declares boldly, "it is precisely sovereignty that they must renounce."[34] This rejection of self-sovereignty and selfsame identity presupposes the very semiotic subject-in-process whose bodily drives Arendt otherwise denounces. The language of the speaking subject of action is composed of both meaning and nonmeaning, and it is more pleasurable than instrumental. "The actor, the doer of deeds, is possible only if he is at the same time the speaker of words" (HC 178–79), writes Arendt, and the words he speaks are more than a means of "communication and information," different from "sign language" which is ends-oriented and used to "convey certain meanings, as in mathematics and other scientific disciplines" (HC 179). The speech of action resists such formalisms because it is fundamentally ambiguous and in excess of symbolic significance, although always in sight of it. In contrast to sign-language, Arendtian speech remains close to the body as symptom, to the semiotic, that which is "*heterogeneous* to meaning and signification."[35]

Insofar as the speech of action is related but resistant to communicable meaning, it is the vehicle of self-disclosure, of "who" in contradistinction to "what" one is. "In acting and speaking, men show who they are, reveal actively their unique personal identities," writes Arendt, "while their physical identities appear without any activity of their own in the unique shape of the body and the sound of the voice" (HC 179). Whereas the "what" not only *can* be symbolized by the subject but also is fixed or (over)determined by symbolic categories (such as "man" or "woman"), the *jouissant* "who" exceeds those categories and is even "hidden from the person himself" (HC 179). Indeed, in action and speech, the subject is ex-centric, radically other to itself.[36] Arendt claims that the voice and the body are not party to that surplus of identity and meaning because they situate the subject within the rigid symbolic universe of the "what." But her own account of speech (oral language or voice) and Kristeva's account of the body (locus of the semiotic heterogeneity we found in Arendtian speech) suggest that both body and voice are in fact actively present in the symbolically transgressive practice of action, of self-disclosure. Voice and body, then, just as they indubitably signify "what" one is, are also vehicles for the signifying practice of action, which resists meaning proper and discloses "who" one is.

The "who" that action and speech disclose, says Arendt, "can almost never be achieved as a willful purpose." It is rather "like the *daimon* in Greek religion which accompanies each man throughout his life, always looking over his shoulder from behind and thus visible only to those he encounters" (HC 179–80). This daimon or divine power, as Jean-Pierre Vernant and Pierre Vidal-Naquet observe, stands in relation and contradistinction to man's ethos or character. "Since the origin of action lies in both man himself and outside him, the same character appears now as an agent, the cause and source of his actions, and now as acted upon, engulfed in a force that is beyond him and sweeps him away."[37] The radical otherness that haunts the subject unsettles it. From a Kristevan perspective this daimon is not outside but inside the subject, it is the semiotic, bodily drive-force that disrupts the transcendental ego.

Action—ineffable, fleeing, and futile—demands a story. Its subject achieves immortality but never stability through the narratives that others construct to name him and give meaning to his words and deeds. The subject of this story, of action, is never its author. In this sense too, then, he is a subject-in-process, unable to control his self-disclosure and the human meanings and worldly consequences of what Arendt calls his "second birth": the "insert[ion] of himself into the human world through action and speech." The "who" is like an open text, a narrative authored by no one and subject to resignification, re-readings, and reinterpretations. That which exceeds the rational, willful subject, however, also exceeds the sign language that others employ to name his essence. "The manifestation of who the speaker and doer unexchangeably is," says Arendt, "retains a curious intangibility that confounds all efforts toward unequivocal verbal expression." This "who" cannot be captured by the signifier: it is impossible "to solidify in words the living essence of the person as it shows itself in the flux of action and speech." Refusing that which exceeds meaning proper, the fluidity of identity that exceeds the proper name, we try to affix a name to action, for "action without a name, a who attached to it, is meaningless."[38]

The asymbolic character of action, then, incites a symbolic panic in subjects who, confronting the bodily desire in language and the limits of significance, reassert the categories that collapse difference into sameness. As Arendt explains, "The moment we want to say who somebody is, our very vocabulary leads us astray into saying what he is; we get entangled in a description of qualities he necessarily shares with others like him; we begin to describe a type or 'character' in the old meaning of the word, with the result that his specific uniqueness escapes us" (HC 181). Frightened at the loss of the referent, we are driven to reify the logic of either/or: a symbolic order in which subjects must take up their proper place and proper names, in which the body marks subjects as nameable and as identical in their difference (masculine or feminine, man or woman). The frightening arbitrariness of action leads us, not only to name the unnameable, to efface the who with the what of our being, but also to fetishize the whole realm of human affairs, ascribing to it an intending agent, agency, or process ("invisible hand, Nature, the world spirit"), in a frantic attempt to halt the endless play of signification. Often enough, says Arendt, our quest leads us back to metaphysics with its overdetermined notion of process and "definition of man" (HC 181).

Arendt celebrates action's "inherent tendency to force open all limitations and cut across all boundaries" (*HC* 190), its protean capacity to establish relationships and to yield the unexpected, but she also worries about it. Thus action, which creates the "web of human relationships," the intangible "in-between which consists of deeds and words," must be supported by "a physical, worldly in-between," by objective worldly interests that constitute "something which inter-est, which lies between people and therefore can relate and bind them" (*HC* 182). What relates and binds also separates us, and counteracts the boundary-transgressing forces of action.

Stressing the need for a durable, worldly space that keeps men both related *and* separate, Arendt warns against action that, like the semiotic body, respects no boundaries yet requires them. Without these boundaries, which secure the common world, action itself would vanish without a trace (*HC* 198). The common world that gives symbolic support to the asymbolic "who" of action exists only to the extent that we "have different locations in it, and the location of one can no more coincide with the location of another than the location of two objects" (*HC* 57). This plurality of perspectives on a common object is the public realm, which "gathers us together and yet prevents our falling over each other, so to speak." Mass society, says Arendt, is characterized by "the fact that the world between [people] has lost its power to gather them together, to relate and separate them. The weirdness of this situation resembles a spiritualistic séance where a number of people gathered around a table might suddenly, through some magic trick, see the table vanish from their midst, so that two persons sitting opposite each other were no longer separated *but also would be entirely unrelated* to each other by anything tangible" (*HC*; my emphasis). This collapse of the border-object (figured as a table produced by *homo faber*) that keeps us not only separated but also related is in turn the collapse of speech. Subjects tumble, first, into an undifferentiated space of bodies without borders and, then, into the speechless prison of "the subjectivity of their own singular experience" (*HC* 58). The necessary distance from oneself, from others, and from one's own body has vanished.

Arendt is so concerned to keep subjects distinct and bodies separate that it leads her often enough to align herself with Zeus, the protector of borders, and against the unnamed Demeter, whose body marks the continuity between subjects and their corporeal pleasure. From a Kristevan perspective, Arendt is implicated in a rigid defense of the symbolic order that keeps the difference between subjects and between the sexes.

But Arendt's account of mass society, in which such differences are attenuated or obliterated, suggests otherwise. Mass society, which marks the disappearance of the common world, is akin to "mass hysteria, where we see all people behaving as though they were members of one family, each multiplying and prolonging the perspective of his neighbor."[39] In contrast to the psychoanalytic account of hysteria, the hysteria Arendt writes about consists not in a refusal of symbolic law but in a rigid adherence to it. Arendt's defense of the borders that keep us distinct, then, is not simply a tribute to the symbolic but a safeguard against its rigidity. Like the table functions in Arendt's image of a séance, those borders ensure that we remain related to each other *because* we remain separated. Without such separation there is no relation to others but only hysterical unanimity that collapses difference into sameness and leads subjects to fetishize symbolic law. In Arendt's figuration of mass society as mass hysteria, the human condition is an odd combination of symbolic homelessness (the absence of a common world) and symbolic reification (conformity). It is the condition where the "what" has overwhelmed the "who" of our being. The mass subject has lost its relation to the world and to the semiotic component of the word, support of the plural and ineffable "who."

Where does the body figure in Arendt's critique of mass society? Arendt claims that the body is the locus of sameness, but she also shows that the plural subject of action is animated by a semiotic drive-force that resists the formalization of meaning and conformity Arendt deplores. Action and the body stand in a mutually imbricated heterogeneity that preserves plurality in the word and the world. Arendt is right to insist that the body, like action, requires borders in order to function as a safeguard against the rigidity of the symbolic. Just as the semiotic needs the symbolic, so does the body need markers of difference and separation, without which it would have nothing to work on or against. Arendt finds and fears that absence of difference in the hermaphroditic body, which figures Arendt's horror of the world citizen, mass society on a global scale.

## The Hermaphroditic Body

In a short essay, "Karl Jaspers: Citizen of the World?" Arendt contests the idea of world citizenship, while agreeing that it is our sameness or humanity that binds us to others: "Just as man and woman can be the same, namely human, only by being absolutely different from each other, so the national of every country can enter this world history of humanity only by clinging stubbornly to what he is. A world citizen, living under the tyranny of a world empire, and speaking and thinking in a kind of glorified Esperanto, would be no less a monster than a hermaphrodite."[40]

Arendt's figuration of the world citizen links the collapse of sexual difference to a presumably natural monstrosity, the hermaphrodite, and to the symbolic singularity of an "artificial" universal language, Esperanto. Just as the world citizen is nobody by dint of being everybody, so too is the hermaphrodite no (natural) body by dint of including every body or rather the bodies of both sexes. For Arendt, the world citizen is not a meaningful composite of various cultures but a cipher—an empty, lifeless, and dangerous global fantasy. This citizen's body is likewise devoid of the markers of cultural difference, which for Arendt are foremost those of sexual difference. The hermaphroditic body lacks definition: it is not multiple, it is undifferentiated, it is nothing.

But for what kind of symbolic order is the hermaphroditic body sexually monstrous and culturally meaningless? Genesis says: "Male and female created He them." Arendt cited this phrase to defend her conception of human plurality and she repeats its message here to attack world citizenship. It would appear that this binary conception of naturalized sexual difference is to safeguard us against the monstrous hermaphroditic body that presumably looms on the horizon of global society and threatens to engulf the Arendtian subject of action.

But if the categories "male" and "female" correspond to the "what" rather than the "who" of our being, as Arendt herself argues, how could they possibly support Arendt's plural subject of action against the univocal citizen of a world empire? Arendt's claim that by clinging stubbornly to *what* one is the subject can retain its difference is at odds with her own account of the uniqueness of persons. For this "what" signifies not difference but that which one shares with others. To cling to this "what" is to remain caught in the signifier, which, as Arendt herself suggests, can never capture the "who," the plural and political subject of action. The symbolic representation of universal sexual difference in Genesis (which defines "what" one is, man or woman), moreover, is a metalanguage not unlike the scientific signifying practice of Esperanto (whose universal grammar quite literally cuts the speaking subject off from the psychic and cultural plurality of its body). Insisting that one hold fast to what one is, male or female, Arendt reinscribes a universalism that she otherwise denounces.

Arguing that we cling to what we are, figured as a gendered bodily identity, Arendt fastens here, as she does elsewhere, onto the body, as a hysterical patient fastens onto a symptom. Arendt is at odds with her own critique of conformist imperatives when she insists that we accept what has been given, not speak about the body, and take it as the ground for political relations, citizenship. The very stubbornness with which Arendt clings to the body, however, refusing to give its difference over to the univocal world citizen and its symbolic practice (Esperanto), suggests that this passage might be read against the grain and interpreted not as a reinscription of masculine and feminine but as a resistance to a too rigid symbolic order.

If we read the Arendtian body as symptom through the lens of psychoanalysis, another interpretation becomes possible. The symptom exhibits the subject's refusal to yield its *jouissance* to the symbolic logic of either/or. Clinging to its symptom, its body, the subject holds fast to what Kristeva calls the "semiotic disposition" and thus to "his [or her] capacity for renewing the order in which he [or she] is inescapably caught up; and that capacity is, for the *subject*, the capacity for enjoyment."[41] In hysteria, such clinging entails both a refusal of the symbolic aspect of language (its capacity to signify and to name the body) and an unwillingness to take up residence in a symbolic order organized around a binary conception of sexual difference. As Ellie Ragland-Sullivan observes, "The hysteric's gender question—Am I a man or a woman?—links sexuality to identity: her discourse reveals the fundamental impossibility of reducing identity to gender in the first place."[42]

Arendt's horror at the hermaphroditic body would seem to be more symptomatic than symptom, more a reinscription of sexual difference than a resistance to it. Arendt appears to refuse the bisexuality that characterizes the subject of hysteria. Arendt clings not to the unsymbolizable body but to the sexed body. To ask the hysteric's gender question would be, in Arendt's words, "like saying I was a man and not a woman—that is, kind of insane." One must cling to the body as sign, to the Word of Genesis, as one must cling to sanity. One must affirm, confirm the symbolic order that naturalizes and keeps the differences between the sexes. But this imperative does not square with Arendt's subject of action and her plural account of identity. Just as the hysteric's question shows that identity cannot be reduced to gender, Arendt's account of the subject of action shows that identity always exceeds the symbolic terms that name it, including "male" and "female."

Notwithstanding her appeal to Genesis, then, Arendt herself demonstrates that "who" someone is cannot be captured by the signifier, by the terms of gender difference. The words "male" and "female," "men" and "women," stand at best as markers of "what" a person is. And that "what" is, in Arendt's own account, a symbolic crutch; we fall back on it in a desperate and futile attempt to stabilize that which escapes sign language, the "who" of action that precisely cannot be signified and that is at the core of Arendtian politics. The body of the unnameable "who," moreover, is semiotic and thus in excess to the binary logic of Genesis, of naturalized sexual difference. And this semiotic Arendtian body that animates the plural subject of action is at odds with Arendtian interpretation, at least as it is practiced by some of my colleagues, including some of those whose work is explicitly feminist.

## Whose Body Indeed?

In conclusion, I return to the scene of the American Political Science Association conference. When I dared to question rather than to be the problem of the body, I lost my symbolic placement and mistakenly walked through the wrong restroom door. Perhaps it was not I, however, but my colleagues, those chivalric defenders of Hannah Arendt, who were thereby exposed. Defending the Arendtian body against the "phallic" assault of my feminist reading, their fraternal laughter worked to protect the fantasy of their own body-as-sign, as the signifier of a common brotherhood. Perhaps it worked to conceal the terror of inadvertent exposure on the part of those who like to think that there are only two doors ("Ladies" or "Gentlemen"), that they know which door to walk through, and that so too did Hannah Arendt. It is the kind of exposure that reveals as illusory the sexed body as the naturalized ground of signifying practices, including that of Arendtian action. In that moment of exposure we find with a distraught Freud that "what constitutes masculinity or femininity is an unknown characteristic which anatomy cannot lay hold of."[43]

If it is true that the body cannot serve as the indisputable biological referent for one's enunciative status and signifying practice, then my colleagues' answer to the question, "Whose body?" is undecidable. The urgency that characterized their need to answer, "Your body, Linda," belies an anxiety about the undecidability of sexual difference. It also indicates the cultural imperative to take up a position in the symbolic order as either a man or a woman; to (be forced to) choose the correct door all the better to maintain the illusion of a natural correspondence between anatomy and destiny. Perhaps it reflects as well the sheer terror of embodiment that Hannah Arendt makes all too visible. If gender assuages this terror by assigning stable meanings to undefined, semiotic bodies, we might read my male colleagues' answer as an attempt to fix the body, to gender it female (as *my* body), and thereby to be rid of it.

When feminists rush to correct Arendt's "gender-blindness," they too can become implicated in the reinscription of sexual difference, which all too often serves as a screen over the uncanny experience of having a body. Reading gender back into Arendt's "nonfeminist" account of the city-state, for example, feminists cite sexual difference as if it were always already historically real and symbolically meaningful. But is it? If Judith Butler is right when she says there is no reference to a body "that is not at the same time a further formation of that body,"[44] feminist references to the missing sexed bodies of the Arendtian city-state are descriptive and *as such* performative: feminists give form to the very bodies they describe and thereby materialize sex. But feminist criticism, as I understand it, ought to loosen the hold that gender has on both our interpretive frameworks and cultural imaginary. And Hannah Arendt's gender-blindness may actually aid us in that difficult task.

Arendt's inattentiveness to gender is surely symptomatic of her failure to theorize gender in all its historical variability *and* predictability. But the blind spot in Arendt's political theory is also the space of the body as symptom: where the Word (of Genesis and the paternal law) fails, gender difference is attenuated, and alternative symbolic practices, like action, become possible. Critics may insist that Arendt holds fast (don't most of us?) to the sexed body in her flight from the sheer terror of embodiment. As for me, I imagine her walking, in a rather determined fashion, through the wrong restroom door, laughing and smoking a cigarette, perhaps a cigar.

## Notes

    1. Sigmund Freud, "Femininity," in *New Introductory Lectures on Psychoanalysis*, trans. James Strachey (New York: Norton, 1965), 100.

2. As Shoshana Felman interprets: "To the extent that women *are* the question,' they cannot *enunciate* the question; they cannot be the speaking *subjects* of the knowledge . . . that the question seeks." "Textuality and the Riddle of Bisexuality," in *What Does a Woman Want?: Reading and Sexual Difference* (Baltimore: Johns Hopkins University Press, 1993), 43.

3. In "The Agency of the Letter in the Unconscious or Reason since Freud," Lacan sketches two restroom doors, each marked by its respective signifier: Ladies and Gentlemen. Every speaking being, he argues, must choose one door, line up on one side of the sexual divide. *Écrits*, trans. Alan Sheridan (New York: Norton, 1977), 151.

4. Hannah Arendt, " 'Eichmann in Jerusalem': An Exchange of Letters between Gershom Scholem and Hannah Arendt," *Encounter* (January 1964): 53–54. In her letter to Scholem, Arendt is concerned primarily with her identity as a Jew which, like her identity as a woman, she tells us: "is one of the indisputable factual data of my life." Arendt belongs to the two social groups called women and Jews "as a matter of course, beyond dispute or argument" (54).

5. Arendt, as Bonnie Honig argues, "never says what she is, she never identifies herself, affirmatively." Honig, "Toward an Agonistic Feminism: Hannah Arendt and the Politics of Identity," in *Feminists Theorize the Political*, ed. Judith Butler and Joan Scott (New York: Routledge, 1992), 215–35, 229. How is Arendt's refusal to identify herself as a member of a socially specified group to be squared with her forceful and repetitive denial of wishing to deny "what" she is? I suggest below that, for Arendt, identification with "what has been given" (*physei*), even when she denies denying it, is never totalizing; *physei* includes the "what" but never the "who" of our being. To belong to Jews and women as a matter of course (see note 4) does not entail an explicit identification with either. One cannot deny one's socially ascribed membership in either group without denying one's very existence. But one can critically negotiate that membership, not by denying it but by refusing to affirm it. Arendt can say, "I have never denied being a woman or a Jew" without saying "I am a woman and a Jew." She can resist the closure of socially ascribed subjectivities, keeping them undecidable.

6. Hannah Arendt, *On Revolution* (New York: Viking [1963] 1965); and *The Human Condition* (Chicago: University of Chicago Press, 1958); hereafter cited as HC.

7. Sigmund Freud, *Totem and Taboo*, trans. James Strachey (New York: Norton, 1950), 18, x. "The meaning of 'taboo,'" writes Freud, "diverges in two contrary directions. To us it means, on the one hand, 'sacred,' 'consecrated,' and on the other 'uncanny,' 'dangerous,' 'forbidden,' 'unclean.' . . . Thus 'taboo' has about it something unapproachable, and it is principally expressed in prohibitions and restrictions." Ibid., 18.

8. In the preface to the Hebrew translation of *Totem and Taboo*, Freud asks the reader to consider "the emotional position of an author who is . . . completely estranged from the religion of his fathers—as well as from every other religion—and who cannot take a share in nationalist ideals, but who has yet never repudiated his people, who feels that he is in his essential nature a Jew and who has no desire to alter that nature." If asked "what is there left to you that is Jewish," says Freud, "he would reply: 'A very great deal, and probably its very essence.' He could not now express that essence clearly in words; but some day, no doubt, it will become accessible to the scientific mind." Ibid., xi.

Like Arendt, Freud too expresses a weak identification with the Jews without denying his identity as a Jew. And Freud, like Arendt again, claims that this identity is beyond dispute and even beyond language, but Freud hopes that it may someday become accessible to the "talking cure." Gender identity is as radically entangled with Jewish identity in Freud's as it is in Arendt's work. Sander Gilman shows that Freud displaces the unknowable essence of the Jew onto woman and tropes femininity as the "dark continent," with all its racialized resonances. See *Freud, Race, and Gender* (Princeton: Princeton University Press, 1993).

9. For Arendt, *the* body is just that: generic, uniform, univocal, a virtual prison-house. Nothing is less common, less communicable, less public than the body. So private are our bodily needs and sensations, says Arendt, that "they cannot be voiced, much less represented"; see HC 112, 147. On the distinction between the univocal body and the plural subject see

Honig, "Toward an Agonistic Feminism," esp. 217–20. For an excellent account of the narrative construction of the body in Arendt's thought see Norma Moruzzi, "Speaking Through the Mask: The Construction of the Body in the Political Thought of Hannah Arendt," Ph.D. diss., Johns Hopkins University, 1990.

10. Arendt's comment on Genesis follows a discussion of the death of God and metaphysics. This, she says, led the eighteenth-century revolutionaries "back scrambling for antiquity. . . . They were in all nakedness confronted with the fact that men exist in the plural. And no man knows what *man* in the singular is. We know only 'male and female created he *them*'—that is, from the beginning this plurality poses an enormous problem." Hannah Arendt, "On Hannah Arendt," in *Hannah Arendt and the Recovery of the Public World*, ed. Melvyn A. Hill (New York: St. Martin's Press, 1979), 313.

11. The phrase "unquestioned and unquestionable" comes from Judith Butler, "Contingent Foundations," in *Feminists Theorize the Political*, ed. Judith Butler and Joan Scott (New York: Routledge, 1992), 7.

12. The question I raise here is borrowed from Slavoj Žižek's interrogation of the paradox of Wittgenstein's *Tractatus*: "Whereof one cannot speak, thereof one must be silent." "Immediately," says Žižek, "the stupid question arises: If it is already stated that it is *impossible* to say anything about the unspeakable, why add that we *must not* speak about it?" *The Sublime Object of Ideology* (New York: Verso, 1989), 164.

13. Hannah Arendt, "The Concept of History," in *Between Past and Future* (New York: Viking, 1968), 42.

14. Julia Kristeva, "Women's Time," in *The Kristeva Reader*, ed. Toril Moi (London: Blackwell, 1986), 190.

15. Judith Butler, *Bodies That Matter: On the Discursive Limits of "Sex"* (New York: Routledge, 1994), 40. Judith Butler's account of the *chora* is fascinating but her critique of Kristeva is disputable. Kristeva says that the *chora* is maternal, but the maternal, in her view, cannot be assimilated to a clearly bounded body (which, from the infant's perspective, already assumes entry into the symbolic); it is rather a radically heterogeneous space, anterior to, subversive of, but coexisting with sign and syntax. Butler accuses Kristeva as well of treating the semiotic as a prediscursive reality and thus of essentialism. But Kristeva insists that the semiotic is not prediscursive (neither before nor wholly distinct from the discursive) since it already harbors the "ordering principle" that functions later both to enable and threaten the structure of signification. We find in the semiotic (which has neither existence nor meaning apart from the symbolic) the most primary "modality of significance in which the linguistic sign is not yet articulated as the absence of an object." Kristeva repeatedly stresses this "regulated aspect of the *chora*." See "Revolution in Poetic Language" in *The Kristeva Reader*, 94. For a sympathetic reading of Kristeva and critical response to Butler, see Kelly Oliver, *Reading Kristeva: Unravelling the Double-Bind* (Bloomington: Indiana University Press, 1993). Note that Arendt's figuration of nature *(physis)* as the protean space of eternal recurrence both converges with Plato's conception of a "dynamic nature *(physis)*" and contrasts with Arendt's appeal to "what has been given *(physis)*." For Arendt, then, nature is both the space of a formless dynamism (the Platonic *chora*) and the reliable, stable ground of sexually differentiated bodies (the Word of Genesis).

16. *The Human Condition* also suggests that our experience of nature is itself a symbolic, cultural construction. Thus, writes Arendt, "it is only within the human world that nature's cyclical movement manifests itself as growth and decay. Like birth and death, they, too, are not natural occurrences, properly speaking" (97). It is rather "the man-made world" that attributes to those not quite natural occurrences the cultural meanings that symbolize our experience of nature and our bodies in terms of linear time. Extending Arendt's argument about the cultural status of the "natural," the same might well be said for her figuration of

nature. The very metaphor of "nature's household" establishes between nature and culture a likeness that Arendt herself puts into question.

17. Mary G. Dietz, "Hannah Arendt and Feminist Politics," in *Feminist Interpretations and Political Theory*, ed. Mary Lyndon Shanley and Carole Pateman (University Park: Pennsylvania State University Press, 1991), 240.

18. Ibid., 240, 244, 242.

19. The citation is from Žižek, *The Sublime Object of Ideology*, 421.

20. Compare this reading with Thomas F. Tierney's claim that Arendt's attitude toward the body is one of contempt and even disgust. Arendtian politics, he argues, is a flight from the body. *The Value of Convenience: A Genealogy of Technical Culture* (Albany: State University of New York Press, 1993), 20–22.

21. Mikhail Bakhtin, *Rabelais and His World*, trans. Hélène Iswolsky (Bloomington: Indiana University Press, 1984), 26, 27.

22. Citing Hesiod, Arendt distinguishes work, "which is due to Eris, the goddess of good strife," from "labor [which], like all other evils, came out of Pandora's box and is a punishment of Zeus because Prometheus 'the crafty deceived him'. Since then, 'the gods have hidden life from men' and their curse hits 'the bread-eating man' " (HC 83). According to Jean-Pierre Vernant, Hesiod casts Pandora as "an insatiable belly devouring the *bios* or nourishment that men procure for themselves through their labor." Pandora is also a trap: her bestial nature is disguised by her virginal appearance. But this "double-nature is, as it were, the symbol of the ambiguity of human existence," of man's status as neither beast nor god. The figure of Pandora stands for, indeed is, the human condition. *Myth and Society in Ancient Greece*, trans. Janet Lloyd (New York: Zone Books, 1990), 194, 199.

23. Julia Kristeva, "From One Identity to Another," in *Desire in Language*, ed. Leon S. Roudiez (New York: Columbia University Press, 1980), 136, 134, 135.

24. Although Arendt tries to contain the body, she also seeks to protect it. She worries about the vulnerability of bodies in totalitarian and mass societies. Arendt's strategy for shielding the body is crucial to her critique both of the disembodied subject of Enlightenment humanism and of modern mass society, see HC, esp. 26, 31, and 59.

25. HC 63. Contra Arendt's reading, not everyone could participate in the core practices of the Mysteries: only those who were properly initiated through a ritual prescribed by tradition—aimed at purification and cleansing from defilement—and who had solemnly promised not to divulge the secret rites, which "no one may in any way transgress or pry into or utter." *Homeric Hymn to Demeter*, vv. 473–79 (trans. H. G. Evelyn-White, in Hesiod, *The Homeric Hymns and Homerica*, Loeb Classical Library [Cambridge: Harvard University Press, 1914]).

26. A more accurate translation of Pindar reads: "god-given beginning." Zeus is more closely associated with political life than with fertility, and (contra Arendt) the latter was in fact debated as a practical matter in the polis. The Mysteries center not on Zeus but on the mythical abduction of Persephone by Pluton, Demeter's grief and stay in Eleusis, and the recurring separation and reunion of mother and daughter. Zeus is relevant to the Mysteries inasmuch as it was he who worked out a compromise between Demeter and Pluton after the goddess, in her grief, had let the earth fall fallow. See George E. Mylonas, *Eleusis and the Eleusinian Mysteries* (Princeton: Princeton University Press, 1961).

27. Erasing Demeter with Zeus, Arendt also elides the figure of Baubô. In the Orphic account of the Mysteries, Baubô made the grieving Demeter laugh by lifting her skirts and showing the goddess her genitals and her belly (on which was drawn Iaachos, the child of Demeter, sometimes associated with Dionysus). In one version of the legend the sacred objects that were revealed to the initiated were Baubô or the female pudenda. See Mylonas, *Eleusis and the Eleusinian Mysteries*, 296. In Sarah Kofman's retelling of the Orphic account,

Baubô's body, open and conceiving, blends with the world. Baubô—the name for "protean life" and "the equivalent of *koilia*, another of the improper words used in Greek to designate the female sex"—affirms the eternal return of all things and mocks the logic of either/or. Baubô's sexuality is equivocal. She evades the binary opposition of masculine and feminine. Sarah Kofman, "Baubô: Theological Perversion and Fetishism," in *Nietzsche's New Seas*, ed. Michael Allen Gillespie and Tracy Strong (Chicago: University of Chicago Press, 1988), 175–202, 198, 107.

28. According to John J. Winkler, the Demetrian festivals, from which men were more often than not excluded, were characterized by "ribald laughter." In the Thesmophoria, Stenia, and Haloa, celebrant women engaged in obscene speech and a variety of lewd acts (akin to Bakhtin's account of the carnivalesque in *Rabelais and His World*). See "The Laughter of the Oppressed: Demeter and the Gardens of Adonis," in *The Constraints of Desire: The Anthropology of Sex and Gender in Ancient Greece* (New York: Routledge, 1990), 188–209.

29. Perhaps this is what Pindar means when, to quote that part of the fragment that Arendt omits, he exclaims: "Happy is he who, *having seen* those rites [Demeter], goes below the hollow earth; for he knows the end of life and he knows its god-sent beginning." Quoted in Mylonas, *Eleusius and the Eleusinian Mysteries*, 299.

30. See John J. Winkler, "Phusis and Natura Meaning Genitals," in *The Constraints of Desire*, 217–220.

31. Sigmund Freud, "The Uncanny," in *The Complete Psychological Works of Sigmund Freud* (London, 1971), 17:245.

32. HC 120. According to Drucilla Cornell, "Arendt insists that for the realm of freedom to exist, the realm of necessity must be conquered. But she also assumes that *conquering* must take place in the private realm, in the household, if it is not to contaminate the realm of freedom." *Transformations: Recollective Imagination and Sexual Difference* (New York: Routledge, 1993), 162. This reading both neglects Arendt's own claim that necessity can never be fully conquered and does not take proper account of her critique of the flight from necessity that characterized and qualified the Greek masculine subject's freedom.

33. Arendt, HC 120. This is especially true of the body in pain, which, says Arendt, induces worldlessness. Arendt's discussion converges in intriguing ways with Freud's account of the subject's libidinal and narcissistic investments in pain. These investments, he argues, lead to a radical rejection of the world or what he calls the refusal to transfer libido to objects. Narcissism is negative for Freud because it leads to a psychic withdrawal of the subject that is akin to what Arendt calls worldlessness. Arendt associates worldlessness with "hedonism, the doctrine that only bodily sensations are real," and with "all theories that argue against the world-giving capacities of the senses"; see HC 112–13; Sigmund Freud, "On Narcissism: An Introduction," *The Standard Edition of the Complete Psychological Works of Sigmund Freud*, trans. and ed. James Strachey (London: Hogarth, 1961), 14:67–104.

34. Arendt, "The Concept of History," 165.

35. It is this semiotic component of language, writes Kristeva, that "scientific discourse, . . . aspiring to a metalanguage, tends to reduce as much as possible." "From One Identity to Another," 133, 134. On a similar point, see Arendt's critique of statistics in HC 42–43.

36. On Arendt's ex-centric subject see Fred Dolan, "Political Action and the Unconscious: Arendt and Lacan on Decentering the Subject" (paper delivered at the Eighty-eighth Annual Meeting of the American Political Science Association, Washington, D.C., September 1992).

37. Jean-Pierre Vernant and Pierre Vidal-Naquet, *Myth and Tragedy in Ancient Greece*, trans. Janet Lloyd (New York: Zone Books, 1988), 77.

38. Arendt, HC 181. Compare this reading of speech with Dagmar Barnouw's claim that Arendtian speech-acts "presuppose the speaker's intention to speak to others in order to be

understood and . . . are meaningful only in the realization of this intention." *Visible Spaces: Hannah Arendt and the German-Jewish Experience* (Baltimore: Johns Hopkins University Press, 1990), 205.

39. HC 58. Hannah Arendt, "To Save the Jewish Homeland: There is Still Time," quoted in Dagmar Barnouw, *Visible Spaces,* 121.

40. Hannah Arendt, "Karl Jaspers: Citizen of the World?" in *Men in Dark Times* (New York: Harcourt, Brace and World, 1968), 89.

41. Julia Kristeva, "The System and the Speaking Subject," in *The Kristeva Reader,* ed. Toril Moi (New York: Columbia University Press, 1986), 24–33, 29.

42. Ellie Ragland-Sullivan, "Hysteria," in *Feminism and Psychoanalysis: A Critical Dictionary,* ed. Elizabeth Wright (Cambridge, Mass.: Blackwell, 1992), 163–66, 163–64. See also Monique David-Ménard, *Hysteria From Freud to Lacan,* trans. Catherine Porter (Ithaca, N.Y.: Cornell University Press, 1989).

43. Sigmund Freud, "Femininity," 101.

44. Judith Butler, *Bodies That Matter,* 10.

# 8

## *Novus Ordo Saeclorum:*
## Gender and Public Space in Arendt's
## Revolutionary France

### *by Joan B. Landes*

*On Revolution* is a paradoxical work, at once affirmative and deeply pessimistic. Arendt celebrates the spaces of political freedom and equality in which citizens talk and act in concert to create a common world. She commemorates historical instances of the founding of new political orders; and she insists that political freedom "means the right 'to be a participator in government,' or it means nothing."[1] Yet, her aim is not to write history, nor to extol its results. Rather, she meditates on the failures of modern politics and revolutions. Even Arendt's moving invocation of the council tradition, the revolution's "lost treasure," serves as an occasion for a series of nostalgic reminiscences on the

I thank Bonnie Honig for her expert editorial advice, and astute contributions to this piece.

evanescent status of genuine citizenship in the modern world. In our times, she believes, politics has been reduced to "representation" and the sway of public opinion; society has invaded the public realm. Arendt concludes *On Revolution* on a note of pathos, recalling the once-glorious Athenian polis as a "space of men's free deeds and living words, which could endow life with splendor." Quoting Sophocles' *Oedipus at Colonus*, she warns of the conditions of natality and mortality to which human and political life are equally subject: "Not to be born prevails over all meaning uttered in words; by far the second-best for life, once it has appeared, is to go as swiftly as possible whence it came" (*OR* 285).

Despite (or perhaps because of) her appreciation of the transitory nature of physical and political life, Arendt does believe in the possibility of new beginnings. She holds that "men are equipped for the logically paradoxical task of making a new beginning because they themselves are new beginnings and hence beginners . . . [T]he very capacity for beginning is rooted in natality, in the fact that human beings appear in the world by virtue of birth" (*OR* 213). Thus, *On Revolution* is a book about political foundations and the human capacity to achieve them, in the profoundly eighteenth-century American sense of a *novus ordo saeclorum*, "an absolutely new beginning" (*OR* 212). Such beginnings are not made by violence or force, but arise from the common delibera-tions and mutual promises whereby citizens bind themselves to each other and to a set of shared principles. Yet, without remembrance and thought, actions alone cannot secure freedom's permanence. For Arendt, only "talking over and over again" about "living words and living deeds," only putting into concepts these same remembrances, might make it possible to achieve and secure once again what in eighteenth-century language was called public freedom, public happi-ness, or public spirit (OR 222–23). It is in this respect that history most impresses Arendt. As James Miller has observed, Arendt follows Walter Benjamin in "constructing revolutionary history as an episodic set of stories needing to be remembered and told again, lest the true revolution-ary spirit, with its redeeming commitment to freedom, be lost 'through failure of thought and remembrance.' "[2]

In modern times, the work of remembrance must proceed without the aid of tradition or religious authority; remembrance in modern times can never achieve closure or a complete sense of the past. Following Benja-min, Arendt focuses on the fragments, ruptures, and displacements in history. Additionally, she takes from Heidegger the notion of a "destructive hermeneutics" of the Western philosophical tradition, hoping to recover the lost origins of Western philosophical concepts from their distorted "incrustations of tradition." As Maurizio Passerin d'Entrèves suggests, together these two hermeneutic strategies enable Arendt to redeem from the past its "lost" or "forgotten treasure": "Only by means of this critical reappropriation can we discover the past anew, endow it with relevance and meaning for the present, and make it a source of inspiration."[3]

For our purposes, however, *On Revolution* is best viewed not merely as an exercise in "destructive" hermeneutics. Rather, it is a challenging contribution to political argument, one that envisions an alternative set of political practices to those that dominate "a world overcome by a preoccupation with mass consumption and the ritualized spectacles of mass politics." Defending Arendt against frequent accusations of anti-democratic elitism, Jeffrey C. Isaac characterizes her ideal as an "insurgent politics, rooted in civil society, that would invigorate rather than replace mass democratic politics." To this end, Arendt aims to retrieve the "lost treasure" of modern revolution: a genuinely participatory, egalitarian, and democratic (counter)tradition in which political agents are empowered and self-governing. She is determined to free politics and our political imagination from the grips of liberalism and Marxism. She charges modernity's two great political traditions with having failed "to understand the distinction between liberation (the removal of impediments to action) and freedom (the exercise of capacities for participation in collective self-government)."[4] Both liberation and freedom are essential to a more robust idea of freedom, one capable of producing the special "pathos of novelty" that resides in the "lost treasure" of modern revolutions: "Only where this pathos of novelty is present and where novelty is connected with the idea of freedom are we entitled to speak of revolution" (*OR* 27). *On Revolution* is an account of those fragile moments of participatory democracy within the American and the French Revolutions, as well as in the workers' councils that briefly flourished in Russia, Germany, and Hungary in the twentieth century.

Proceeding from Walter Benjamin's historiographical method, Arendt selectively appropriates marginal fragments from the past in order to recover lost meanings, concealed and repressed moments. Her history is stubbornly partial; at best, she aims to seize hold of a memory that would otherwise be lost, repressed, or distorted. Now, there is much to recommend this approach, but it comes at a price. As James Miller has noted regarding Arendt's versions of the revolutionary record, not only can the meanings Arendt derives from the past be misleading, they often "sound like so much wishful thinking."[5] And, this is not all! For all her perspicacity, Arendt's compelling counterreadings of modern revolutions are marked by a stunning blind spot: a marked resistance in her writings to the question of gender, and (in her own terms) to the stories of women.[6] These absences are all the more surprising with respect to the history and philosophy of revolutionary France in which, at least since Burke's *Reflections* and Michelet's *History*, women's stories have figured so prominently.[7]

Perversely, Arendt's silence might be greeted with relief: At least she doesn't burden women with added responsibility for the unhappy tale she recounts of the Revolution's failure in the face of "the social question."[8] Nevertheless, her insouciance in this regard contrasts markedly to other salient dimensions of *On Revolution*. For instance, Arendt's anti-Jacobin reading of the revolutionary tradition comes remarkably close to the revisionist historiography and philosophy of recent decades in its regret over the missed opportunities of the Girondins and other partisans of liberty.[9] Yet, because she misses the register of women's political agency, she overlooks *another* failed revolution in France, one that promised a new beginning for women as political actors. Also, she ignores the paradox of women's self-constitution as political subjects of the republic *despite* their exclusion from political rights, their subordinate status in civil and political law, and, during the height of the radical Revolution, their banishment from the political to the domestic sphere.[10] The stories of women's attempts to achieve political agency and, correspondingly, of masculine rights (the constitution of a masculine-gendered political subject and a masculinized public sphere) during the French Revolution are not easily accommodated in Arendt's model of revolutionary democracy. I intend neither a wholesale defense nor rejection of Arendt's political theory. Rather, I shall consider some interesting interruptions—and, I hope, expansions—of her thought deriving from an appreciation of what Joan Wallach Scott has aptly termed "gender as a category of history."[11] In particular, I am interested in exploring the way in which a consideration of women's political agency works to disrupt the stability of the binary oppositions Arendt draws: e.g., as between freedom and necessity, spontaneity and determinism, political rights and human rights, freedom and equality, public and private. I see the entire project of feminist historiography—to recover women's agency in the Revolution—as completely Arendtian in spirit, however paradoxical, constituting in effect the search for another "lost treasure" that she herself did not seek even though it was doubly lost: initially, within the revolutionary movement, and later in the historiography of the Revolution.

## Arendt's Story: "The People" and "The Citizens"

The story of the French Revolution, as told by Arendt, is a violent tale about the abandonment of freedom. Oddly, however, the violence that most concerns Arendt is not simply the predictable one of the devolution of politics into Terror. Arendt presents the Terror as unfolding alongside the potentially more ominous story of "the poor, driven by the needs of their bodies, burst[ing] onto the scene of the French Revolution" (*OR* 54). In the eruption of what she otherwise calls "the social question," Arendt discovers the source of "the politically most pernicious doctrine of the modern age, namely that life is the highest good, and that the life process of society is the very center of human endeavor" (*OR* 58). In one respect, then, what most troubles Arendt is a kind of speechless human crowding onto the political realm: Thus, she describes the revolution of Paris as

> the upheaval of the populace of the great cities inextricably mixed with the uprising of the people for freedom, both together irresistible in the sheer force of their number. What from then on has been irrevocable, and what the agents and spectators of revolution immediately recognized as such, was that the public realm—reserved, as far as memory could reach, to those who *were* free, namely carefree of all the worries that are connected with life's necessity, with bodily needs—should offer its space and its light to this immense majority who are not free because they are driven by daily needs. (*OR* 41)

Arendt distinguishes here between two groups and two absolutely contrasting motives: "the populace" or "immense majority" who are "driven by daily needs," and "the citizens" (in this instance called "the people") who are motivated by the love of public freedom.[12] Indeed,

Arendt believes that the very conditions of freedom are threatened when the majority, driven by the force of biological needs, sweeps into the public realm. In place of speech, unanticipated actions, and "the factual plurality of a nation or a people or society," there appears a multitude "in the image of one supernatural body driven by one superhuman, irresistible 'general will' " (OR 54). The multitude speaks, as it were, in one voice. Its "opinion" is unified. There is no room for disagreement, deliberation, or debate. What weighs most heavily on the will so conceived is the irresistible force of biological needs. In effect, Arendt links the disastrous outcomes of the French Revolution to the collapse of a boundary separating the private from the public or the body from the political realm. In the absence of such boundaries, the univocal demands of "private misery" drown out all other voices. Thus, the Revolution's most horrific aspects seem to derive from the escape of the body's demands from their proper containment within the private sphere.

> Poverty is more than deprivation, it is a state of constant want and acute misery whose ignominy consists in its dehumanizing force; poverty is abject because it puts men under the absolute dictate of their bodies, that is, under the absolute dictatorship of necessity as all men know it from their most intimate experience and outside all speculations. It was under the rule of this necessity that the multitude rushed to the assistance of the French Revolution, inspired it, drove it onward, and eventually sent it to its doom, for this was the multitude of the poor. When they appeared on the scene of politics, necessity appeared with them, and the result was that the new republic was still born; freedom has to be surrendered to necessity, to the urgency of the life process itself. (OR 54)

In a related fashion, Arendt recalls the revolutionary leadership's fateful turn away from freedom toward the goal of human happiness, the happiness of the people. Not only does she reject happiness or welfare as a dangerous substitute for the principle of freedom, but (in what appears to be a profoundly undemocratic gesture) she scorns the very notion of "the people" as well as any virtue claimed by those who serve its cause:

> The words le peuple are the key words for every understanding of the French Revolution, and their connotations were determined

by those who were exposed to the spectacle of the people's sufferings, which they themselves did not share. For the first time, the word covered more than those who did not participate in government, not the citizens but the low people. The very definition of the word was born out of compassion, and the term became the equivalent for misfortune and unhappiness—*le peuple, les malheureux m'applaudissent,* as Robespierre was wont to say; *le peuple toujours malheureux,* as even Sieyès, one of the least sentimental and most sober figures of the Revolution would put it. (*OR* 70)

Arendt objects to a politics driven by a compassionate concern for justice and social equality; in her estimation, a politics of absolute goodness and morality. She contemptuously refers to compassion as "that imperious impulse which attracts us towards *les hommes faibles.*"[13] At best, she regards poverty—and the unequal distribution of economic and social resources—as posing problems amenable only to technical *not* political solutions. On this point, she parts company with social reformers, who seem to share Marx's "obsession with the social question" (*OR* 262). Remarkably, she finds support for her own radically antisocial, antiadministrative view of politics in Lenin, who once described the aim of the October Revolution as "electrification plus *soviets.*" Arendt is emphatic on this score: "the problem of poverty is not to be solved through socialization and socialism, but through technical means; for technology, in contrast to socialization, is of course politically neutral; it neither prescribes nor precludes any specific form of government. In other words, the liberation from the curse of poverty would come about through electrification, but the rise of freedom through a new form of government, the *soviets*" (*OR* 60). Having praised Lenin for his insight into the *soviets* as new institutions of freedom, Arendt is careful however to repudiate his more conventional Marxist, post–French Revolution faith in the party as the means to solve the social question. In her view, the latter is (and will always remain) a purely administrative problem.

## Reconsidering "The People"

Who, then, are the people who in the French context inappropriately demanded citizenship on the basis of their needs, and thereby produced a spectacle of misery and poverty in the revolutionary public realm? Arendt is curiously vague about the composition of this social group. Sometimes she refers to the people as the *sans-culottes*. In one note she adopts the sociological-historical definition of *le peuple* as the *menu* or *petit peuple*, consisting of "small businessmen, grocers, artisans, workers, salesmen, servants, day laborers, *lumpenproletariat*, but also poor artists, play-actors, penniless writers" (OR 293–94). Yet, even this last categorization is imprecise, insofar as it obscures women's presence among the *menu peuple*, as well as within the active citizenry. In fact, women of the popular classes participated in the most important revolutionary *journées* leading up to and following the constitution of the Republic. From the outset and through the popular manifestations in Germinal and Prairial of Year III, women were a visible part of the revolutionary crowd.

In 1789, women participated in the events at the Bastille Prison— symbol of ministerial despotism and rumored arsenal for royalist troops— though they likely did not plan the operation. Some days after 14 July women took bouquets to the newly elected mayor of Paris, Bailly, and the commander-in-chief of the National Guard, Lafayette.[14] Barely three months later, marketwomen initiated the October March to Versailles, which prompted the establishment of a constitutional monarchy. The October Days are, to be sure, the revolutionary event with which women are most often associated or about which attributions regarding the character of women's revolutionary participation are commonly made, by Arendt as well as others. Typically, women's participation is depoliticized, or interpreted as an instance of the urban poor's protest over urban provisioning, high prices, and shortages. Early modern European women, in particular, are deemed to be chief instigators in bread riots due to their management of their family's income and their place as consumers and sellers in the marketplaces, especially of bread, the dietary staple. Thus, because marketwomen chanted about returning to Paris the nation's chief baker, along with his family—that is, the king and the royal family—we are led to believe that their horizons were limited and their actions traditional or economic in motivation. To recall Arendt's formulation, this is surely an instance of the people consumed by "needs." Noting that whatever hopes then existed for quickly resolving the bread crisis, it continued for another month and that women were active participants in these further protests at the markets and over the food supply, George Rudé has characterized this sort of explanation as follows: "The traditional account of the women's march to Versailles has it that, as they marched, the women chanted, 'Allons chercher le boulanger, la boulangère et le petit mitron!' It was supposed that the king would, by his very presence among his subjects, ensure a plentiful supply of bread."[15]

However, Rudé also argues persuasively that the spring of 1789 marked a dramatic break from popular manifestations in the Old Regime in that the laboring poor now acquired an understanding of the implications of their actions for national politics; a political rhetoric from pamphleteers and journalists; and later, a base for their efforts in popular societies and Section assemblies.[16] Darline Gay Levy and Harriet Applewhite make a similar case with respect to women's actions in the crucial autumn months of 1789. "In October 1789, the women comprehended that the deputies at Versailles were their representatives, not their rulers, and that they could playact at being their own representatives. They were holding a dress rehearsal for their performance as the sovereign people." More generally, Levy and Applewhite claim:

> On some occasions, women made traditional subsistence de-
> mands for plentiful food at acceptable prices, but also adopted
> new tactics of democratic participation in a framework of revolu-
> tionary institutions along with extrainstitutional protest. . . . At
> other times, women combined subsistence demands with broader
> demands for public recognition of their rights as democratic
> citizens. Not only did women claim redress of individual griev-
> ances, but they also made occupational group claims and claims
> based on patriotic or republican interests. The principal agencies
> of these transformations in women's political roles were political
> journals, clubs, elected assemblies, and popular societies, all
> functioning to mobilize women for political activities.[17]

In other words, women were certainly counted by others *and* counted themselves as members of the mobilized, articulate, democratic citizenry! There is evidence, as well, that though women in 1789 and thereafter did enter the public sphere to demand bread, sugar, or soap (that is, to call for economic redress), and though they certainly acted spontaneously on countless occasions, their actions—as during the October Days—were not entirely spontaneous nor unrehearsed. This is important to underscore, especially because Arendt separates spontaneous from unspontaneous actions, and counts only the former as instances of free political practices.

Yet, when the actual circumstances are considered, her view is difficult to sustain. As Jennifer Dunn Westfall discovered, women of the people were participating in almost daily processions of thanksgiving to Sainte Geneviève, patron saint of Paris during August and September 1789 following the popular insurrection that culminated with the fall of the Bastille and the reorganization of municipal government in Paris. In these events, women expressed both their subsistence concerns and their new interest in "justice." Westfall cites one report of a young woman representing the female secondhand clothes dealers of the Halles and vendors from the Cimitière des Innocents lauding Lafayette, the commander-general of the newly formed bourgeois National Guard, in these words: "We have come to offer you the homage which you most like, that of our hearts. It is to your sublime virtue, to your profound wisdom that we owe our safety. We can only look upon you as an angel that was sent from Heaven to save his people. We are confident that you, as the common father of so large a family, will find a way to replace scarcity with abundance, arbitrary despotism with enlightened justice, troubles and disorders of which we have so long been the victims with calm and peace."[18]

Many of the women who recruited National Guardsmen to march alongside them to Versailles came from the same market districts and *faubourgs* where the summer thanksgiving processions had occurred. Certainly, their physical presence in the streets of Paris helped them to make an alliance with the militia. At Versailles, moreover, it is reported that women occupied the meeting place of the National Assembly, voted with the deputies on motions and amendments relating to legislation on the circulation and distribution of grains, and "exercised . . . the function of the legislative power and the executive power."[19] Certainly, women were consciously supportive of the movement for political change promoted in the Assembly by the delegates of the Third Estate, and in the streets of Paris by the revolutionary crowd. Again, in the spring and summer of 1792, women were a visible presence in the insurrectionary movement leading to the fall of the monarchy, augmenting significantly the numbers of those challenging the political status quo:

> They engaged in decisive collective demonstrations of force and acts of violence; they were key actors in the cooptation of the armed force available to authorities who supported the constitutional monarchy. These acts, in combination with women's discourse—everything from shouts and slogans denouncing ty-

rants, proclaiming liberty, and validating the *sans-culottes* to formal addresses before the Legislative Assembly demanding women's right to bear arms—contributed to the delegitimation of constitutional monarchy, a reformulation of rights and respon- sibilities of citizenship, and a redefinition of sovereignty as the will and power of the people.[20]

Whereas Arendt is intent on distinguishing force from speech, women and men of the mobilized citizenry were apt to mix the one with the other in their discourse and their actions. In 1791 Cordeliers Club member Pauline Léon (in 1793, she served as president of the Society of Revolutionary Republican Women) petitioned the National Assembly for the right of women to bear arms ("pikes, pistols, and sabres—even muskets for those who are strong enough to use them"), to assemble on festivals and Sundays to practice maneuvers on the Champs de Mars or other suitable places. Defying Arendt's privileged boundary between the private and public spheres, Léon calls for legislative authorization for a women's militia so that women might defend their homes against aristocrats; she links this, in turn, to a defense of women's rights. Unlike Arendt, Léon directly confronts the gender contradictions in republican philosophy that refused women the right to join militias and to act in defense of the patria, and expected them to act virtuously only through their domestic roles. While claiming the right to bear arms, Léon does so on republican not individualistic grounds; most important, she ties women's political rights to their domestic duties:

> Do not believe, however, that our plan is to abandon the care of our families and home, always dear to our hearts, to run to meet the enemy.
>
> No, Gentlemen. We wish only to defend ourselves the same as you; you cannot refuse us, and society cannot deny the right nature gives us, unless you pretend the Declaration of Rights does not apply to women, and that they should let their throats be cut like lambs, without the right to defend themselves. For can you believe the tyrants would spare us? No, no—they remember October 5 and 6, 1789. . . . But, you say, men are armed for your defense. Of course, but we reply, why deprive us of the right to join that defense, and of the pleasure of saving their days by using ours? Do they know the number and strength

of our hidden enemies? Have they but one fight to fight? Is our life dearer than theirs? Are our children not orphaned by the loss of their fathers as much as their mothers? Why then not terrorize aristocracy and tyranny with all the resources of civil effort [*civisme*] and the purest zeal, zeal which cold men can well call fanaticism and exaggeration, but which is only the natural result of a heart burning with love for the public weal?[21]

Whereas Arendt would have us believe that women's concern was only with bread, Léon—and she was not alone in this perspective—spoke from a deeply held conviction that women must participate actively in order to constitute and preserve the (always endangered) public realm of liberty and virtue.

Arendt dismisses the actions of the people as a kind of mob rule, reducing their demands to the dictates of a unified "opinion." However, as participants in the militant citizenry, women were not all of one mind. They did not speak in one voice. Indeed, politically active women were just as likely as men to identify with the political positions of groups and factions within the revolutionary movement as a whole. Yet this did not mean that they were mere ciphers of others' opinions. At her trial, Charlotte Corday's interrogators questioned her repeatedly but unsuccessfully for proof of a conspiracy by the enemies of Marat, holding that "a person of her age and sex" could not have acted alone, nor formed her own political judgments; and, yet, she had.[22] Two examples from spring and fall 1793 are also revealing. In May, the former courtesan and revolutionary militant Théroigne de Méricourt was accosted by republican women, among whom were many Jacobin and Enragé sympathizers and supporters. The latter were intent on preventing Girondin supporters from gaining access to the Convention's galleries. After an altercation in which she was accused of being a moderate and a Brissotin, Théroigne was publicly whipped by these women in front of the doors to the Convention, only to be rescued when Marat took her under his protection. In the autumn, another series of confrontations divided women, and proved fateful to the fortunes of all politically active women. After street clashes in the markets over the wearing of the revolutionary cockade, marketwomen demanded the government's closing of the Society of Revolutionary Republican Women. The club's closing was followed by bans on all women's clubs and associations, and later proscriptions against all political activity by women.

Arendt's description of the multitude belies the complexity of social identifications among the populace. Like the men of *le peuple*, politically involved women occupied different social occupations and social locations. They came from different social classes, and from different groups within similar classes. The female citizenry included actresses (Claire Lacombe of the Society of Revolutionary Republican Women), playwriters (Olympe de Gouges, author of the *Declaration of the Rights of Woman*), producers (chocolate-maker Pauline Léon of the Society of Revolutionary Republican Women, and salonnières (Théroigne de Méricourt, Mme de Roland, Mme de Condorcet, and Etta Palm d'Aelders, founder of the women's section of the "Cercle Social").[23] Arendt failed to recognize women's plurality. However, in their persons, words, and actions, the women who interjected themselves into the public arena during the Revolution manifested a plurality of perspectives: precisely what Arendt deems to be "the basic condition of both action and speech"; that is, equality, individuality or difference (rather than "otherness") among persons.[24] Not only were revolutionary women activists heterogeneous, but the activists *tout court* were more heterogeneous than Arendt allows. Whereas Arendt imposes a strict division between necessitarian concerns and the practice of freedom, it is apparent that women's marches for bread, sugar, and other necessities were an essential condition of their politicization. Additionally, an important side effect of their participation in the public realm for these demands was a quest for such perfectly Arendtian political goals as citizen rights. Whereas republicans (not unlike Arendt) were intent on imposing a strict public/ private divide on women such that they were deprived of access to the public sphere, women activists such as Léon reconstrued the public/ private divide in such a way as to honor it but, at the same time, to demonstrate its elasticity. Home is not something apart from the "public [which] signifies the world, in so far as it is common to us and thus distinguished from our privately owned place in it," as in Arendt's conception.[25] Rather, for Léon, women's and men's location in the private sphere and their active engagement in domestic responsibilities is also potentially a site of "worldliness" and concern for a common realm.

## Freedom and Equality; Freedom and Bodies

It is striking that Arendt remains indifferent to, and even troubled by, the French passion for equality and justice. Likewise, she has little to say about the Revolution's achievement of universal male citizenship. Indeed, she upbraids the French for confounding political and social equality, and for conflating political and natural equality when, in the Declaration of the Rights of Man and of the Citizen, they locate human (inalienable) rights in nature. Like other adherents of natural law, they mistake the most consummately human sphere of action for the direct, biological necessities of bodily function. According to Arendt, freedom cannot be reduced to a pre-political condition, nor can equality be derived from the condition of birth: "Inalienable political rights of all men by virtue of birth would have appeared to all ages prior to our own as they appeared to Burke—a contradiction in terms. And it is interesting to note that the Latin word *homo,* the equivalent of 'man,' signified originally somebody who was nothing but a man, a rightless person, therefore, and a slave" (*OR* 39).

Arendt insists that human rights are not natural; they are not secured by "moral sense"; nor are they necessitated by the conscious reasoning of all humans as free subjects. Instead, she argues, human rights are conventional. They reflect the human condition and the forms of agreement and recognition that result from human interaction.[26] Likewise, freedom is animated by the specifically human activities of seeing, judging, and remembering; it is not a synonym for some naturally ordained condition of equality. Arendt locates freedom, rights, and equality entirely in the political sphere. She deems "human" rights as such—without political entities to enforce or protect them—to be meaningless. In contrast, she celebrates freedom's spaces, the locales where freedom and equality reside and rights have content. Furthermore, for Arendt, equality is strictly speaking only political equality: "isonomy" or the condition of nonrule. She relates the problem of inequality to the despotism of rule, or the division between rulers and ruled. She especially despises the hypocrisy of those who would rule over others in the name of equality.

Given Arendt's unorthodox position on the subject of natural rights— granting for the moment her presentiment that too generic a category of rights can have no content—it is curious to find her faulting the French for submitting to transcendental arguments, while finding confirmation of her own views in eighteenth-century America. She applauds the colonial Americans for seeming to understand this ancient Greek "truth": that "the life of a free man need[s] the presence of others. Freedom itself need[s] therefore a place where people [can] come together—the agora, the marketplace, or the polis, the political space proper" (*OR* 24). She praises the American Bill of Rights for instituting permanent restraints upon all political power. Whereas the French are characterized as insisting naively on natural rights, Arendt believes that the Americans from the outset presupposed the existence of a body politic and the functioning of political power.

However, the transcendent language of natural rights detected in the French Declaration of the Rights of Man and of the Citizen was not kept so carefully at bay in America as Arendt might like. She herself admits that the Preamble to the Declaration of Independence contains a deistic appeal characteristic of Enlightenment thought: "When in the Course of human events, it becomes necessary for one people to dissolve the political bands which have connected them with another, and to assume among the Powers of the earth, the separate and equal station to which the Laws of Nature and of Nature's God entitle them, a decent respect to the opinions of mankind requires that they should declare the causes which impel them to the separation." Yet, she is at pains to explain this matter in terms of competing, contradictory and excessive languages, principles, and practices. Clearly, we need to consider the possibility that Arendt was apt to draw strong oppositions where perhaps there are none. The discourse of rights in eighteenth-century Europe and America was one in which nature figured as an alternative to traditional, religiously derived transcendent, transmundane sources of authority in the body politic and as an explanation of the unconventional, precontractual origin of human freedom. References to God and nature and human rights occur in French *and* American documents; Arendt cleanses the one constitution of the offending moments, but not the other, and then celebrates the difference between them.

Had she not overlooked the claims of equality, Arendt might not have been able to insist upon so great a difference between the two revolutionary traditions. Both the French and Americans articulated the principle of equality. Still, only the French went so far as to abolish slavery and to eliminate the principle of property as the requirement for citizen rights. In this respect, at least, they confronted the fact of institutionalized power, and power's ability to constrain both equality and liberty. Yet neither nation advanced the rights of women, instead inscribing in law the inequality of the sexes in the political sphere; and, at least in France to a lesser extent, in the civil sphere.[27] Although she did return to the issues of slavery and racial issues as a piece of unfinished constitutional business in essays written in the 1960s, here in *On Revolution* Arendt omits any consideration of the slavery question or property in the American constitutional debates, while highlighting the impact of the poor in the French context. She maintains her own ideological distinction by counterposing the (supposedly and oddly contentless) American philosophy of freedom and work of constitution-making to the French practice of democratic citizenship and socioeconomic reform.

Also, Arendt never addresses the radical implications of the discourse of natural rights when embraced by advocates of women, slaves, or the poor. Had she done so, she might have noticed the dilemma posed when those who sought to claim universal rights on the basis of their status as reasoning beings were reminded of their marked, bodily differences, concerning skin color or sexual anatomy.[28] Because she seems to accept uncritically the relegation of slaves, women, and laborers to the pre-political sphere, Arendt never worries about the ways in which republican discourse in the modern world worked to associate freedom only with masculinity, and to connect women to particularity. Arendt, in other words, evades the dilemmas posed for a philosophy of freedom by the presence of embodied subjectivity.

In contrast, the writings of the playwright, actress, pamphleteer, and condemned royalist Olympe de Gouges bear consideration as a compelling attempt to reconcile rights with the demands of the body and the particularities of female subjectivity. On the one hand, in her 1791 *Declaration of the Rights of Woman* Gouges follows the more predictable course of making an immanent critique of the *Declaration of the Rights of Man and the Citizen.* By a single standard of justice, she finds it wanting; by virtue of race and sex it deprives people of the rights to which they are entitled by nature. Linking the cause of slaves and women, Gouges insists on equality for all sentient beings. On the other hand, Gouges disrupts the discourse of universality by continually inserting herself and (the needs of) her sex into what might otherwise be an impartial argument. To begin with, the mimicry of the original document is upset by Gouges's dedication to the queen who was, by this point in time, extremely unpopular. Defying public "opinion" Gouges interjects this personal note from a republican female subject, one who takes it upon herself to speak freely to her political and social superiors: "My purpose, Madame, is to speak frankly to you." She declares her loyalty to the queen even "when the whole empire accused you and held you responsible for its calamities," but she warns that her allegiance will end abruptly if the queen is found to be plotting with foreigners to bring arms into France. She calls on the queen as a wife and a mother (the "particular" circumstances that women share) to lend her weight to the rights of women.[29] Gouges refused the easy, but ultimately unsatisfactory solution, of securing woman's status as an abstract individual in the face of its masculine embodiment. As Joan Scott observes, "In order to claim the general status of 'human' for women, she insisted on their particular qualifications; in the process of insisting on equality, she constantly pointed out and acknowledged difference."[30]

In the course of enumerating women's rights—to liberty, property, security, justice, political and civil freedom, speech and assembly, employment and offices—Gouges unexpectedly adds another: woman must be free, too, to "name" the father of her child. She linked this in turn to a guarantee of paternal obligation, that is, that fathers would (be made to) recognize their children. Acknowledging women's subjection to men in the family, Gouges connects the right of speech to women's ability to enforce paternal duty. Simultaneously, she makes a claim on masculine prerogatives and exposes the abuses of patriarchal power. Yet, precisely because it is in the area of pregnancy "that a woman's speech is simultaneously most authoritative and most open to doubt," Scott observes that "the terms by which de Gouges claims the rights of speech for women . . . raise the spectre of the unreliable feminine, the devious and calculating opponent of rational, truth-speaking man, and so they are literally fraught with uncertainty."[31] Moreover, while extolling the mothers, daughters, and sisters of the nation, Gouges remains ambivalent about ("actually existing") women. She scorns "the nocturnal administration of women" that characterized Old Regime practice, and requests that prostitutes be placed in designated quarters. She prophesies that in the new Republic "the powerful empire of nature" would lead women to disavow their former illicit and immoral behavior, their former "empire."[32]

How, then, does nature figure for Gouges? Scott proposes that while Gouges reinterpreted nature's meaningfulness as a ground for rights, she nonetheless adhered to the notion of "natural" justifications for political arrangements. For example, she rejected the differentiation of bodies into fixed binary categories, insisting on "multiplicity, variety, ranges of difference, spectra of colors and functions, confusion of roles—the ultimate undecidability and indeterminacy of the social significance of physical bodies."[33] This led Gouges to challenge not only the fixity of sexual nature, but also the terms of racial division. Among other things, she argued on the basis of the undecidability of color against the prerogatives of whites and the enslavement of blacks. Yet, like many of her age, she also sought in nature the grounds for the legitimization of universal, human rights. Consequently, because Gouges held rights to be at once embodied and universal, she never resolved the paradox in her thinking whereby physical differences were at the same time irrelevant and essential to the meaning of equality. For this very reason, though, she comes closer than her male counterparts—and certainly closer to Arendt, in that regard—to appreciating the dilemmas that trouble rights discourse down to the present. Moreover, it may have been the paradoxical nature of her thinking about these matters that enabled her to articulate, however messily, the marginalizing and politicizing effects of marked bodies in the social and political spheres. On the one hand, Gouges's discourse underscores Arendt's point about the limitations of abstract, transcendent political rights. On the other hand, she undercuts the very division between human and political rights to which Arendt is so committed by appealing to both in her "feminine" discourse of freedom.

## Gendered Republics

Not least because of her antipathy toward social equality, Arendt never derives any explicit principles of gender equality from her general perspectives on the *vita activa*, on the one hand; nor, on the other hand, from the evidence of women's actions during the revolutionary era.[34] She represents the French Revolution, like the American, as a wholly man-made series of events. The stories she recounts are by and about men. Whereas in the past, authority was anchored in God, king, and tradition, men, by establishing democracy in France, established a new source of authority in the republic. As we have seen, Arendt does recognize the implications of the specifically political capacity for change that accompanied the movement for democratic sovereignty. Moreover, she embraces a performative concept of politics. She applauds the eighteenth-century invention of a *novus ordo saeclorum*. What she fails to appreciate, however, is the novelty of women's presence in the revolutionary public sphere, and the powerful claims made by some on behalf of women's civil freedom and political equality. By not even registering women's presence as "participators" in revolutionary public space, Arendt obscures what should count as another "new beginning"— one that was truly no less fragile than that introduced by the organs of popular government such as the Paris Commune or the section assemblies whose eclipse under the circumstances of political centralization and socioeconomic goals Arendt decries. Women never wholly succeeded in undermining the new gendered boundaries of public and private life. Yet, in the public spaces of the revolutionary public sphere and within feminist counterdiscourses, a radical performativity by women did exist, overriding at least temporarily the constraints imposed on women by republican morality and laws. Militant women's discordant, egalitarian words and actions expressed the contingent, fragile, yet expansive possibilities within the political practice of democracy. They foreshadow the movements for women's emancipation of the nineteenth and twentieth centuries. Echoing Arendt's own principles, Claude Lefort's explanation of democratic action aptly fits: "without the actors being aware of it, a process of questioning is implicit in social practice . . . no one has the answer to the questions that arise, and . . . the work of ideology, which is always dedicated to the task of restoring certainty, cannot put an end to this practice."[35]

To an important extent, however, Arendt's democratic commitments are packaged within a republican wrapper.[36] There is no question that Arendt's arguments for democratic civic initiative hold considerable promise. Yet, it is also possible that because she is committed to basic republican premises she failed to examine explicitly the gendered outcomes of the Revolution, or to acknowledge that the leadership she holds most responsible for leading the Revolution astray on "the social question" was also those most responsible for the *repression* of women's political actions and women's rights. While she observes how the Girondins' defeat by the Jacobins signified the moment when the institutions and constitution of the republic were supplanted by "the natural goodness of a class" (OR 70); it is odd that she never congratulates the Girondins for their early support of the political and civil rights of women, mulattoes, and slaves, nor does she link their political demise to the subsequent suppression of women's political initiatives. It is as if she shared the ancients' indifference to women's invisibility in the public sphere. Or, could it be that she unwittingly echoes republicans' fears of the invasion of the political sphere of freedom by particularity, sexuality, and women? Despite her powerful critique of the failures of French republicanism, she seems to share with republicans a set of commitments and blindnesses regarding freedom, public and private life, the body, and, above all, gender difference.

However, these commonalities do not prevent Arendt from being relentlessly critical of the eighteenth-century war upon hypocrisy and its endless quest for authenticity and sincerity: having "unmasked the intrigues of the Court [the Revolutionaries] proceeded to tear off the mask of its own children . . . the mask of hypocrisy" (OR 103). What the revolutionaries thought they had liberated was natural man, man shorn of all disguise; what they were left with, in Arendt's estimation, was not some pre-social truth but the hypocrite's endless deceptions. Arendt concludes that "the men of the French Revolution had no conception of the persona [the rights-and-duty-bearing person, created by the law], and no respect for the legal personality which is given and guaranteed by the body politic." Rather than emancipating nature or the natural man, the Reign of Terror succeeded only in leaving "all inhabitants equally without the protecting mask of a legal personality." Arendt makes a powerful point, but again her argument is curiously abstract. She insists that equality is sui generis, a consequence not of nature but of the emancipation of citizens, each of whom is "equally entitled to his legal personality, to be protected by it, and at the same time, to act almost literally 'through' it" (OR 104). But she fails to notice the demands of women for civil and political rights; that is, to achieve a legal personality, a legal persona. Nor does she address their successes or failures, even when those French movements for civic equality fit her own model of nonidentitarian politics. Likewise, she ignores the debates over mulatto rights and slave abolition during the Revolution. She is unimpressed by the historic removal of the property barrier to citizenship. Not until her later essays does she attempt to account for the fact that American slavery was ultimately abolished by a presidential decree, the Emancipation Proclamation, an act by which the political state reached deep into the master's household in order to rectify injustice.

## Lost Treasures and Possible "Futures"

Reading On Revolution in the mid-1990s, some thirty years after its original publication, is a chastening experience. By reintroducing another "lost treasure"—the too-often erased story of women's political agency—we have observed the fragility of the oppositions that Arendt has drawn: between citizens and need-driven subjects, freedom and equality, rights and bodies, public and private, political rights and human rights. Certainly, Arendt's failure to acknowledge the registers of revolutionary action traced here has led her into misleading categorizations and bifurcations that fail to capture the full range of revolutionary action and possibility; worse yet, it even suggests approval of the revolutionary government's assignment of women to the home. Yet Arendt would be the first to acknowledge that retold stories of actions will reverberate in the aftermath of action, and that judges—including historians—will introduce new visions of the past. Especially in the case of founding stories, such re-visioning (including revisionist history) works, as Arendt said it should, to augment and amend the terms of the original founding.[37] By recovering another "lost treasure," that of women's political agency in revolutionary France, we are led to the possibility of future new beginnings that Arendt might have invited but did not. As Arendt herself knew from her studies of the radical beginnings of both revolutionary France and America, actors who initiate something new politically invariably take their bearings from those whom they take to be their predecessors. For that reason, future women activists—those who struggle for political and social reform, and for the grass-roots democratization of civil society—will be empowered by the successful recovery of such "lost treasures" as the story of women's political agency during the French Revolution.

## Notes

1. Hannah Arendt, *On Revolution* (New York: Viking, 1965), 221; hereafter cited as *OR*.

2. James Miller, "The Pathos of Novelty: Hannah Arendt's Image of Freedom in the Modern World," in *Hannah Arendt: The Recovery of the Public World*, ed. Melvyn A. Hill (New York: St. Martin's Press, 1979), 183.

3. Maurizio Passerin d'Entrèves, *The Political Philosophy of Hannah Arendt* (New York: Routledge, 1994). Seyla Benhabib offers a contrasting, but equally plausible reading of the two sources of Arendt's thought. Unlike d'Entrèves, she sees the Benjaminian method of fragmentary historiography as being in conflict with the phenomenological approach of Husserl and Heidegger, "according to which memory is viewed as the mimetic recollection of the lost origins of phenomena as contained in some fundamental human experience." Benhabib acknowledges that Arendt's thought "is not free from aspects of an *Ursprungphilosophie* that posits an original state or temporal point as the privileged one. As opposed to rupture, displacement, and dislocation, this view emphasizes the continuity between origin and the present and seeks to uncover at the privileged origin the lost and concealed essence

of the phenomena." Thus, Benhabib explains how it is that Arendt appears to be arguing, as in *The Human Condition*, for an "original meaning of politics"; i.e., the lost distinction between "public" and "private." Seyla Benhabib, "Hannah Arendt and the Redemptive Power of Narrative," in *Hannah Arendt: Critical Essays*, ed. Lewis P. Hinchman and Sandra K. Hinchman (Albany: State University of New York Press, 1994), 127. D'Entrèves is also aware of the problems raised by Arendt's efforts to retrieve primordial experiences (*Urphänomen*) and original meanings from the philosophical record. However, for his defense of Arendt against the charge of "hermeneutic naïveté" leveled by some critics, see *The Political Philosophy of Hannah Arendt*, 33–34; on Arendt's historical method, see 28–34.

4. Jeffrey C. Isaac, "Oases in the Desert: Hannah Arendt on Democratic Politics," *American Political Science Review* 88, no. 1 (March 1994): 156–57.

5. Miller, "The Pathos of Novelty," 181.

6. Arendt's indifference to the category of gender in revolutionary historiography is perhaps best compared to her sidestepping of the question of slavery in the American Revolution. One could speculate further that if, in Arendt's view, the question of poverty involves the unfortunate intrusion of the realm of necessity and the demands of the body into the political sphere of freedom, how much worse if politics were given over to the seemingly irresistible demands of the biosphere.

7. Admittedly, women are much less prominently featured in the more "scientific," analytical, even discursive histories of the twentieth century (Marxist and revisionist, Annales and post-Annales). It is almost as if these historians, like the revolutionaries themselves, were seeking to secure their own legitimacy by repudiating the feminine aura of their predecessors' work. Of course, Arendt has read very widely in certain primary sources—the speeches and writings of Robespierre, Saint-Just, Condorcet, as well as Soboul and Markov's compilation of documentary sources on the sans-culottes and the Parisian popular movement—and she refers to the writings of twentieth-century historians R. R. Palmer, J. M. Thompson, L. R. Gottschalk, G. Jellinek, G. Lefebvre, A. Soboul, W. Markov, as well as to earlier contributions by A. Sorel and K. Marx. Yet, taken together, the authors she consults most frequently were not so concerned as their nineteenth-century predecessors with the presence of women in the Revolution.

8. As Arendt states: "It was the men of the French Revolution who, overawed by the spectacle of the multitude, exclaimed with Robespierre, 'La République? La Monarchie? Je ne connais que la question sociale'; and they lost, together with the institutions and constitutions which are 'the soul of the Republic' (Saint-Just), the revolution itself" (*OR* 50).

9. Strikingly, the authors François Furet, Lynn Hunt, Claude Lefort, Ferenc Fehér, Roger Chartier, and Keith Baker echo aspects of Arendt's account. Yet Arendt is rarely acknowledged in the subsequent history and theory of the French Revolution. Lefort (perhaps because he is a philosopher rather than a historian) is an exception. For his estimation of this absence, and his own evaluation of Arendt's contribution, see his *Democracy and Political Theory*, trans. David Macey (Minneapolis: University of Minnesota Press, 1988). On the themes in recent historical writing, see Sarah Maza, "Politics, Culture, and the Origins of the French Revolution," *Journal of Modern History* 61 (December 1989): 704–23; Jack R. Censer, "Commencing the Third Century of Debate," *American Historical Review* 94, no. 5 (1989): 1309–25; idem, "The Coming of a New Interpretation of the French Revolution?" *Journal of Social History* 21 (Winter 1987): 295–309; two forums, "The Origins of the French Revolution: A Debate" and "François Furet's Interpretation of the French Revolution," *French Historical Studies* 16, no. 4 (Fall 1990): 741–802.

10. Changes in secular law during the First Republic were of particular significance to women. Marriage was declared a civil contract and divorce was permitted on an equal basis for both partners; inheritance rights for women and illegitimate children were declared, along

with the right of youths of both sexes over twenty-one to marry without parental permission. However, under the Napoleonic Civil Code many of these reforms—most especially in marriage and divorce law—were reversed.

11. See Joan Wallach Scott, "Gender: A Useful Category of Historical Analysis," in *Gender and the Politics of History* (New York: Columbia University Press, 1988), 28–50.

12. Actually, Arendt's terminology is imprecise and shifting. Generally, she uses "the people" to refer to the multitude or immense majority who are driven by needs and speak in one voice (its " 'opinion' is unified," as she states). In contrast, she refers to "the citizens," plural subjects who speak and act spontaneously. The latter are committed to freedom, the former to happiness. Arendt sometimes also substitutes the term "people" for citizens, as in the quotation just discussed. However, she uses it in the sense of the "uprising of the people for freedom," underscoring that the people are committed to freedom not to life's necessities or bodily needs. In general, then, I shall maintain the overall distinction she draws between citizens and people in order not to confuse the matter further.

13. *OR* 70. Arendt has a knack, it should be noted, for drawing from her opponents support for her own views. Here, she is citing Robespierre, in his "Adresse aux Français" of July 1791, who is made to appear just a bit contemptuous of those who would usurp power on the basis of a presumed shared "suffering" and "compassion" with the poor. Arendt, of course, objects most strenuously to Robespierre's greatest crime, his effort to raise compassion to the "rank of the supreme political passion and highest political virtue" (70).

14. Darline Gay Levy, Harriet Branson Applewhite, and Mary Durham Johnson, eds., *Women in Revolutionary Paris, 1789–1795: Selected Documents, Notes and Commentary* (Urbana: University of Illinois Press, 1979), 14.

15. George Rudé, *The Crowd in the French Revolution* (Oxford: Oxford University Press, 1959), 78.

16. For competing interpretations of the popular movement, stressing either the change or continuity of popular movements in the early modern and revolutionary period, see Jeffrey Kaplow, *The Names of Kings* (New York: Basic Books, 1972) and George Rudé, *The Crowd in History* (New York: Wiley, 1964), on the one hand, and Steven L. Kaplan, *Bread, Politics and Political Economy in the Reign of Louis XV*, 2 vols. (The Hague: Martinus Nijhoff, 1976), on the other. While Kaplan defends the continuity of protest, he nonetheless rejects the implication that the urban poor were "prepolitical." Instead, he holds that they were motivated by a "subsistence mentality" or "moral economy" according to which governmental officials (at all levels) are obligated to intervene in the grain markets to police the people's food supply and protect their livelihood and security when shortages occur. Cf. Edward P. Thompson, "The Moral Economy of the Crowd in the Eighteenth Century," *Past and Present* 50 (1971):76–136.

17. Darline Gay Levy and Harriet B. Applewhite, "Women of the Popular Classes in Revolutionary Paris," in *Women, War and Revolution*, ed. Carol R. Berkin and Clara M. Lovett (New York: Holmes and Meier, 1980), 15, 12.

18. Jennifer Dunn Westfall, "The Participation of Non-Elite Women in the Parisian Crowd Movements of the Opening Year of the French Revolution," honors thesis, Mount Holyoke College, 1976, 79–80, cited in Levy and Applewhite, "Women of the Popular Classes," 13.

19. Cited in Levy and Applewhite, "Women of the Popular Classes," 15.

20. Darline G. Levy and Harriet B. Applewhite, "Women, Radicalization, and the Fall of the French Monarchy," 81, in *Women and Politics in the Age of the Democratic Revolution*, ed. Harriet B. Applewhite and Darline G. Levy (Ann Arbor: University of Michigan Press, 1990).

21. Pauline Léon, "Addresse individuelle à l'Assemblée nationale, par des citoyennes de la Capitale, le 6 mars 1791 (Paris, n.d.) in *Women in Revolutionary Paris*, 73.

22. Jacqueline Dauxois, *Charlotte Corday* (Paris: Albin Michel, 1988), 241.

23. See Darline Gay Levy et al., *Women in Revolutionary Paris;* Harriet Applewhite and Darline Gay Levy, "Women, Radicalization and the Fall of the French Monarchy," in *Women and Politics in the Age of Democratic Revolution,* 81–107; Dominique Godineau, "Masculine and Feminine Political Practice during the French Revolution, 1793—Year III," in *Women and Politics in the Age of Democratic Revolution,* 61–80; Godineau, "Daughters of Liberty and Revolutionary Citizens," in *A History of Women in the West,* vol. 4, ed. Geneviève Fraisse and Michelle Perrot, trans. Arthur Goldhammer (Cambridge: Harvard University Press, 1993), 15–32; Judith Vega, "Feminist Republicanism: Etta Palm-Aelders on Justice, Virtue and Men," *History of European Ideas* 10 (1989): 333–51; Elisabeth Roudinesco, *Théroigne de Méricourt: A Melancholic Woman during the French Revolution,* trans. Martin Thom (London: Verso, 1991); Suzanne Desan, *Reclaiming the Sacred: Lay Religion and Popular Politics in Revolutionary France* (Ithaca: Cornell University Press, 1990); Joan B. Landes, *Women and the Public Sphere in the Age of the French Revolution* (Ithaca: Cornell University Press, 1988).

24. Hannah Arendt, *The Human Condition* (Garden City, N.Y.: Doubleday, 1958), 155.

25. Ibid., 48.

26. I am greatly indebted to Jeffrey C. Isaac for sharing his work-in-progress, "A New Guarantee on Earth: Hannah Arendt on Human Rights," from which I have gained a fuller appreciation of Arendt's view of human rights.

27. See Lynn Hunt, *The Family Romance of the French Revolution* (Berkeley and Los Angeles: University of California Press, 1992).

28. See Joan Scott's excellent account of Olympe de Gouges's dilemma with respect to the questions of women's rights as well as racial equality: Joan Wallach Scott, " 'A Woman Who Has Only Paradoxes to Offer': Olympe de Gouges Claims Rights for Women," in *Rebel Daughters: Women and the French Revolution,* ed. Sara E. Melzer and Leslie W. Rabine (New York: Oxford University Press, 1992), 102–20. More generally, Dorinda Outram addresses the question of sexual difference in her *The Body and the French Revolution: Sex, Class and Political Culture* (New Haven: Yale University Press, 1989). Finally, for a discussion of sexuality in relationship to modern contract theory, see Carole Pateman, *The Sexual Contract* (Stanford: Stanford University Press, 1988).

29. Olympe de Gouges, *The Declaration of the Rights of Woman,* in *Women in Revolutionary Paris,* 87–88. Cf. Olympe de Gouges, *Oeuvres,* ed. Benoite Groult (Paris: Mercure de France, 1986). For a biographical account, see Olivier Blanc, *Olympe de Gouges* (Paris: Syros, 1981).

30. Scott, "A Woman Who Has Only Paradoxes to Offer," 108.

31. Ibid., 110.

32. As I have argued elsewhere, what is remarkable is that these pleas for the rights of wives and mothers of the new republic were proffered by a woman whose very occupation and way of being in the (public) world were in tension with the republican revolutionary code of female domesticity to which she appealed; as, for example, when she spoke of the relationships between the Assembly and the monarchy as "two powers [executive and legislative], [which] like man and woman, should be united but equal in force and virtue to make a good household." Gouges, *The Declaration of the Rights of Woman,* cited in Landes, *Women and the Public Sphere,* 126–27.

33. Scott, "A Woman Who Has Only Paradoxes to Offer," 112.

34. For an overview of women in this period, see the anthology *Women and Politics in the Age of the Democratic Revolution.*

35. Claude Lefort, *Democracy and Political Theory,* trans. David Macey (Minneapolis: University of Minnesota Press, 1988), 19.

36. For example, Jeffrey C. Isaac, in a recent defense of Arendt's conception of democratic politics, endorses her vision of "a robust civil society of [plural] elementary republics"; "Oases in the Desert," 165.

37. On this significant dimension of Arendt's thought, see Bonnie Honig's "Toward an Agonistic Feminism: Hannah Arendt and the Politics of Identity," in *Feminists Theorize the Political*, ed. Judith Butler and Joan W. Scott (New York: Routledge, 1992); and *Political Theory and the Displacement of Politics* (Ithaca: Cornell University Press, 1993), chap. 4.

# 9

## On Nationalism: Frantz Fanon, 1925–1961; Rosa Luxemburg, 1871–1919; and Hannah Arendt, 1906–1975

*Joan Cocks*

The great reinterpretation of Hannah Arendt at the end of the century makes one suspect that this theorist has been overmined, and that if she is to have anything left to say to the next generation, she should be sealed off from the further comments of this one. The suspicion could not come at a more unfortunate time. History just has thrown up a new combination of "political catastrophes" and "moral disasters"[1] resembling the interwar stimulus to some of Arendt's most fertile political reflections. Once again capitalist expansion and imperial collapse have precipitated the uprooting of whole populations, waves of ethnonational identification and aggression, the creation of stateless

I would like to thank Bonnie Honig for her perceptive comments on earlier drafts of this essay.

peoples and despised minorities, and intellectual coteries formed in the crucible of social homelessness and political estrangement.

The light Arendt could shed on our own predicaments is blocked not just by unfortunate timing but by an unfortunate text. Arendt inspects what can be called, for short, "the national question" most minutely in "Imperialism," the second part of *The Origins of Totalitarianism*. But she pursues there a line of thought on Africa and Africans that not only reveals but instantiates the phenomenology of European racism, making sections of the work distasteful to the contemporary palate. The confluence of political theory's near-overdose on Arendt as a subject of inquiry, a Zeitgeist that finds it easier to spit out "Imperialism" than to savor it, and the practical resurgence of rootlessness, ethnonationalism, and sociopolitical estrangement about which "Imperialism" above all has so much to say, demands that Arendt's attention to nationalism be approached . . . but with delicacy.

It is for delicacy's sake that I highlight Arendt on nationalism by setting her alongside Rosa Luxemburg and Frantz Fanon, who share with her a critical interest in the subject and at least a foothold in the twentieth century. This commonality of interest and epoch, as well as a commonly hybrid national-cultural identity of exactly the kind that nationalism in its rightward turn tries to stamp out, forms a thread connecting these disparate figures. Following the thread, we can move back and forth between Luxemburg's treatment of nationalism as an important if secondary political problem (important in part because it gets in the way of the primary problem, class division),[2] Fanon's wary celebration of struggles for national liberation, and Arendt's dissection of national identity, imperialism, and statelessness. If the national question that consumes Luxemburg, Fanon, and Arendt during the first sixty years of the century slides into obscurity almost at the stroke of Fanon's death, it returns to prominence almost at the stroke of Arendt's.[3] Ultimately it takes center stage as the most romantic and brutal version of the drama of collective identity—the obsessive drama of our age.

One key ingredient in Arendt's analysis of the witches' brew of modern nationalism is the bourgeois pursuit of private profit, which ultimately corrupts the nation's public life and geographical limitations. In emphasizing the contradiction between the boundedness of the European polity and the unboundedness of capital, Arendt in "Imperialism" is an explicit successor to Luxemburg in *The Accumulation of Capital*, although Luxemburg sees the bourgeoisie as founding the modern nation-state and then using it as its instrument of economic consolidation and expansion, while Arendt sees the bourgeoisie as capturing the state and undermining the national community, morally and territorially, through forsaking the public business of the nation for private profit all over the globe. In emphasizing the poisonous effects of the chase for infinite wealth in the colonial territories—the sole beneficial effect being colonialism's provocation of movements for national independence—Arendt in "Imperialism" anticipates Fanon in *The Wretched of the Earth*, although Arendt is preoccupied with the self-aggrandizement and self-corruption of the colonizer, and Fanon, with the misery and militance of the colonized.[4]

Two other main ingredients in Arendt's analysis of nationalism are the rise of the pan-movements in Central and Eastern Europe, to which she is singularly attuned, and the intolerance of nationalism toward the feature of modern sociopolitical life that today goes by the name of "difference," which Luxemburg and Fanon also spy and decry from their own vantage points. Luxemburg notes how national self-determination degenerates into national tyranny, the impulse toward national independence giving rise, for both logical and historical reasons, to attempts to crush such impulses on the part of other nationalities. Fanon notes how anticolonial nationalism can turn into "ultra-nationalism, to chauvinism, and finally to racism," if national consciousness, which is alert to who people are and how they are distinguished from other sorts of people, is not replaced by social and political consciousness, which is alert to what people do in relation to one another, and how greater justice between them can be brought about.[5] It is Arendt, however, rather than Luxemburg or Fanon who is bothered by the monochromatic effects of nationalism as a problem in itself, distinct from the problem of group persecution. Arendt shows us how both republican nationalism and ethnonationalism are driven to supplant social plurality with singularity, if for reasons that are diametrically opposed. Republican nationalism raises the identity of all citizens to the highest political principle; consequently it seeks to obliterate all symptoms of group particularity in society. Ethnonationalism raises group particularity to the highest political principle; consequently it seeks to rid society of all particular groups except one.

Their criss-crossing ideas on the national question notwithstanding, Luxemburg, Arendt, and Fanon are enough "unlike each other" intellectually, politically, and, shall we say, spiritually, that they would probably protest "against being gathered into a common room."[6] They not only belong to "different generations" but are contemporaries only in pairs, and Luxemburg and Arendt only at one edge of their lifespans. Luxemburg is sparked to think, agitate, and write on the national question by the period preceding, and Fanon by the period succeeding, the period sparking Arendt. Luxemburg's interest in nationalism stems from her commitment to socialist internationalism; Fanon's, from his commitment to anticolonial liberation. Arendt is not moved by a political, forward-looking commitment at all, but by a historical, backward-looking determination to trace the chain of events leading to the specific destruction of the European Jews and the general destruction of freedom in the West.

In three obvious ways Luxemburg and Fanon are not merely different but severed from Arendt. First, they are active revolutionaries, Luxemburg in and Fanon against Europe—although Luxemburg looks forward to the entire world's release from material exploitation and political subalternity, and Fanon, to a worldwide transvaluation of values.[7] Second, they stand on the side of the popular masses against the ruling classes in society. Third, their habits of thought are orthodoxly Marxist in Luxemburg's case (Arendt's weird "doubt" of Luxemburg's Marxism notwithstanding) (MDT 38), and Marxist in the traveling-theory sense in Fanon's. Against them both, Arendt strikes a strictly intellectual attitude toward revolution no less than toward nationalism, seeking to understand it critically, but not in the midst of, or as an immediate prelude to, acting politically either for it or against it. Moreover, Arendt is unruffled by class distinction, despises Marxism, and accuses movements that aim to change "the fabric of society" for the sake of satisfying the material needs of the multitude, of ruining the chances for individual distinction, plurality, debate, and the ability "to embark on something new" (OV 82). Arendt is kinder to liberation movements but still is wary of them, for the struggle against oppression or what she terms the constraint on free movement is at best only an antecedent to the project of building "a new house where freedom can dwell" and "excellence can shine."[8]

On the other side, Luxemburg and Arendt are, not in thinking or acting but in being, twice separated from Fanon. First, Luxemburg and Arendt are members of a diaspora minority in Europe, historically poised between eliciting Europe's attraction and contempt, and between desiring from Europe differentiation and assimilation. Fanon is a member of a majority outside Europe transformed by Europe into a pariah population in its own land and, together with all other colonized peoples, across the earth. Second, Luxemburg and Arendt are women, although this does not prevent them from refusing much more absolutely than Fanon does to acknowledge the importance of what once went by the misnomer of "the woman question."[9] In addition, all sorts of unpleasant assumptions about sexuality, gender, and bodily life can be found to operate implicitly in Arendt's work. My purpose here, however, is not to chastise any of these extraordinary figures for such sins of omission or commission. Instead, I want to see how the national difference is as burning a difference for Luxemburg, Arendt, and Fanon as the difference of sexuality and gender has been for us, until the national question began to burn as our question too.

## Fanon and Arendt

Quite apart from whatever feminist charges might be leveled against them, our theorists have been vulnerable to certain prejudices on the part of writers on ethnicity and nationalism. The prejudice against Luxemburg alone is that she has nothing to teach us about ethnicity and nationalism because of her fixation on class division, and because her defense of working-class internationalism against bourgeois nationalism bypasses nationalism's popular force.[10] The prejudice against Luxemburg and Arendt together is that they have nothing to teach us about nations and nationalism because, as members of a deracinated Jewish intelligentsia, they are unable to appreciate territorially-based experiences of national community.[11] The prejudice against Arendt alone, almost the reverse of this one, is that Arendt's eagerness to implicate Jews in the making of modern anti-Semitism reveals her to be a self-hating Jew who can have nothing to teach us about nationality in the nonterritorial sense of ethnic or ethno-religious feeling.

The complaints against Luxemburg and Arendt are best left to stand or fall on the basis of how useful these theorists' answers to the national question actually prove to be.[12] But we will have to look directly into the complaint against Fanon, because it is Arendt who files it. Arendt suggests that Fanon has nothing to teach us, not only about nationalist politics but about politics per se, above all because he glorifies violence.

Arendt makes an implicit argument against the author of *The Wretched of the Earth* in her impressive *On Revolution*. There, while noting the legendary connection between the origins of political community and violence, she stresses violence's incapacity for speech, its marginality to politics, and its unsuitability as subject matter for political theory, which "can only follow the articulations of the political phenomena themselves, it remains bound to what appears in the domain of human affairs; and these appearances, in contradistinction to physical matters, need speech and articulation" (OR 9). She confronts Fanon directly, however, only in *On Violence*, an admittedly much weaker work. Here she argues that violence is antipolitical even though it belongs to "the political realm of human affairs." This combination of ideas is less peculiar than it seems, for Arendt can charge violence with being antipolitical—that is, at odds with argument and persuasion, and destructive of "the world of appearances and . . . the company of our fellow men"—only if she also can establish that violence belongs to the realm of human contingency and artifice, not the realm of biological necessity and natural forces, where charges against anything are beside the point (OV 82 and 67). Arendt denies that violence has an instinctual or organic origin in part by fiat, stipulating that human violence occurs in the sociopolitical realm, and that biological factors never can explain anything there. But she also denies that violence is instinctual or "vital" by tracing violence to rage, and rage not to unreason but to an offended sense of justice or a reaction against the hypocrisy of lying speech.[13] In addition, Arendt rejects the equation of violence with automatic impulses or bodily reflexes by defining violence as strategic or "instrumental by nature," so that it is assimilated to rational calculation and is rational "to the extent that it is effective in reaching the end that must justify it."[14] Finally, she states that violence does not repeat some natural cycle but brings into being something new, even though what this type of action brings into being is most probably only "a more violent world" (OV 80).

One of Arendt's aims in *On Violence* is to discredit all thinkers who embrace bloodshed as either an inescapable element of politics or a positive good. She focuses special attention on Fanon because of what she sees as his lamentable influence on the spirit of her age. If she admits in a footnote that Fanon is "much more doubtful about violence than his admirers,"[15] she does not significantly lower the pitch of her complaint against him anywhere else.

What must be said at once on Fanon's behalf, then, is that his attitude toward violence only erroneously can be taken as great enthusiasm dampened by a small doubt. Indeed, his entire treatment of nationalism is more aptly seen as a canvas painted in certain colors and then brushed over with different colors again. This self-revising method of argument does not reflect either an ambivalence toward violence on Fanon's part or his belief in a contradiction between the appearance of nationalism and its reality. Rather, that method reflects the dynamic quality of the struggle for national liberation, the explosive effects of decolonization on the entire social environment, the instability of every aspect of life during "a program of complete disorder." In short, the sudden thawing out of a world that had been previously frozen requires a corresponding fluidity in the conceptualization and assessment of that world's constitutive elements. Thus, in response to changes nationalism itself helps produce in its sociopolitical milieu, and without ever being self-contradictory, Fanon moves from celebrating to criticizing to repudiating national consciousness, culture, and politics. Thus, too, he raises the curtain on colonialism as a two-person drama between the native and the settler, and then gradually brings onto the stage peasants, towndwellers, a parasitical native bourgeoisie, Senegalese and Sudanese, black Africans and Arabs, and even sympathetic Europeans. This multiplication of characters does not at all signal a mistake in his original casting but mimics the actual process by which decolonization replenishes a world colonialism had "cut in two."[16]

In the same way, Fanon calibrates his judgment of violence to suit torrential changes in the political landscape. In his first essay he condemns the colonial order for speaking "the language of pure force" but declares that against such an order, the " 'thing' which has been colonized" must exert a counterforce in order to become "man." In his second essay, he insists that spontaneous mass uprisings must give way to thought and action tempered by political education, if a popular movement against tyranny is not to become either tyrannical itself or open to a new kind of tyranny through having too naive a notion of the world. Fanon's startling final essay exhibits the psychiatric case studies of torturers, soldiers, resistance fighters, and civilian victims of brutality, all suffering the aftershocks of anticolonial war. In their psychological disintegration, these figures reach an eerie equality with one another, being most clearly distinguishable not as Algerian or French, and not as the active agents or passive targets of violence, but rather as individuals plagued by this or that nightmarish neurosis or psychosis (38 and 37).

In "Concerning Violence," Fanon praises violence for making subjects out of human objects. In "Colonial War and Mental Disorders," he reveals that violence shatters human subjectivity. The two essays to-gether confirm the following truth: that the slave who "at the moment he realizes his humanity . . . begins to sharpen the weapons with which he will secure its victory," can win freedom from the master/slave relation with those weapons but not freedom from the reverberations of his own acts (43). If Fanon treats the question of violence with greater complexity than Arendt admits, he also treats it with greater complexity than Arendt musters—a difference between them that should remind us that intellectual intricacy does not always guarantee political depth.

First, Fanon represents violence in the colonial context as antipolitical in its original thesis but as pre-political in the antithesis to that. The imposition of colonial rule by "bayonets and cannons" and its maintenance by "the policeman and the soldier" are antipolitical be-cause, as Arendt would put it, they prohibit the emergence of a sphere for public speech and action. The rebellion of the colonized against colonial rule is pre-political because, as Fanon does put it, it catapults those who are oppressed from the position of "spectators crushed with their inesssentiality into privileged actors." This is not to say that he is sanguine about whether these newly privileged actors can make their way from violence to politics. That depends, for a start, on whether they manage to escape being psychologically "crushed with" the horror of what they have violently done and what has been violently done to them (36, 38).

Second, Fanon conceives of violence as expressive of somatic feelings no less than ideas about injustice or intentions to achieve specific ends. Fanon highlights the bodily aspects of violence not because he sees violence as belonging to a biological rather than sociopolitical zone, but because he does not ever divide off the body from sociopolitical life, and also because he believes the bodily aspects of violence loom large in the colonial setting. The world into which the colonizer herds the popular masses—unlike the world of magic the people traditionally inhabit, unlike the world of Western culture into which the native intellectual is lured, and unlike the world of bourgeois consumption that has seduced the European working class—is not so much ideologically mystified as it is physically claustrophobic. It is a "narrow world, strewn with prohibi-tions," a "motionless, Manicheistic world," a world in which "[t]he first thing which the native learns is to stay in his place, and not to go beyond certain limits." Because colonial power operates on the masses by brute force and physical containment rather than by cultural and political suasion; because the native's sense "that his life, his breath, his beating heart are the same as those of the settler" fuels in him a resentment that is as visceral as it is cerebral; and because the muscles of the native are "always tensed," violence against the colonizer offers the colonized a physiological as well as psychological release from the effects of servitude. This is why Fanon can understand violence "at the level of individuals" as a "cleansing force" that "frees the native from his inferiority complex and from his despair and inaction" (37, 51, 52, 45, 53, 94).

Is Arendt right, or wrong, to find Fanon politically irresponsible for advocating violence as a part of national liberation? The answer depends in part on whether Fanon is right or wrong that the colonized cannot escape either the external rule of the colonizer or his own internal situation of being permanently "tensed" without a physical explosion. But the answer just as centrally depends on whether Arendt is right or wrong that violence is antipolitical and yet part of the political, not the biological, realm. It is important to realize that Arendt's claims are animated by a primary antagonism to the presence of the body in politics rather than by a primary antagonism to the political infliction of bodily pain.[17] The first antagonism, not the second, lies behind her insistence that the language of politics is exclusively verbal, never physical, so that violence must be counted as speechless and incapable of speech. It also lies behind her presumption that no somatic experience ever pressures a subject to act with physical force, so that it always is possible, and (for the sake of protecting, not the body, but speech) almost always desirable, to forswear the "use" of violence through the use of reason.

Conversely, while Fanon may disturb contemporary sensibilities because he does not bristle at the thought of spilling blood (how drastically the spirit of our age differs from the spirit of Arendt's!), he has much in his favor to recommend to us. Fanon is unprejudiced against the body and consequently is not compelled to pry the realm of the body and the realm of speech and action apart. Thus he can see violence as a feature simultaneously of visceral and political experience, as a means of detonating the master/slave relation, and so as a provider of one crucial pre-condition of a democratic public sphere. He also is able to appreciate the paradoxical consequences of a system of rule that, in speaking the language of pure force, invites its subordinates to use the same language in return. Fanon would find it perverse to call "antipolitical" a conversation in which "the violence of the colonial regime and the counter-violence of the native . . . respond to each other in an extraordinary reciprocal homogeneity" (88). Through that conversation, the native achieves the status of an active subject in history that a monologue of violence had precluded before. Nonetheless, Fanon shows us that the violence that emancipates the self socially can destroy the self "humanly." In that unfortunate case, the free self will be too tormented to enjoy politics or any other human pleasure.

## Luxemburg and Arendt

Fanon pinpoints greater threats to the popular enjoyment of political speech and action in the new nation than the psychological breakdown of individuals. There is the dictatorial political leader, the corrupt official machine, the rule of the country on behalf of a single family or tribe. There are the collective hatreds that nationalist ideology can stir up the day after independence from the settler is won—which Fanon believes have their basis in the different economic functions different ethnic groups perform, even though such groups experience their animosities as originating in their very "beings." Finally, there is the great disparity in wealth between the native elite and the vast majority of the people. If Fanon's critique of dictatorship and ethnonational hatred brings him into harmony with Arendt, his allegiance to what Gramsci would have called the "simple people" of the nation, and his call for a political struggle against poverty, illiteracy, and a parasitical bourgeoisie, put him at odds with her again. Arendt has no great love of the bourgeoisie, but she loathes the conquest of the political realm by the poor. "[T]he cry for bread will always be uttered with one voice," she complains; the "misery of the people" imposes the dictates of necessity on a realm that is meant for freedom (OR 89 and 90).

But at this point we must shift our sights from Frantz Fanon to Rosa Luxemburg, whose comments on nationalism, ethnonational persecution, and class rule can be taken more aptly than Fanon's as a prelude to Arendt's own line of thought. To be sure, Luxemburg plays the class card so intently that she brings into relief on the one hand the presumption she shares not with Arendt but with Fanon that the nation must be made to serve the common people; and on the other hand the presumption Arendt shares with Fanon and not with Luxemburg that nationality, ethnicity, and race rather than class pose the most arresting political problems for the century. Nevertheless, Luxemburg is allied with Arendt in these important respects: both begin their musings on the national question inside Europe, both see the trajectory of the European nation-state as shaped by the activities of the bourgeoisie, and both believe that trajectory concludes more regularly in domination than in liberation.

According to Luxemburg, the nationality not as an ethnic or cultural group (for such "national particularities had already existed for centuries"), but as a national movement aspiring to its own nation-state, is a product of the bourgeois era. The ascendent bourgeoisie lends its weight to the unification of a particular territory, language, and set of customary practices in order to secure "an internal or domestic market for its own commodity production." Two contradictions, one of time and one of space, follow from this relation of nation to class. First, the sanctifying idea of the nation as founded in an age-old rural tradition, an unchanging peasant people, and a folkloric culture, is contradicted by the nation-state's reality as the site on which capital ushers into being the universal characteristics of modernity: "the big city," technical progress, industrialization, speedy transportation and communication, "a new social class: the professional intelligentsia," and so on. Second, the geographical limitation of the nation-state is contradicted by the fact that the bourgeoisie's economic appetite is "so elastic and extensive that it always has the natural tendency to include the entire globe."[18] Luxemburg gives a new inflection to Marx's view that capital becomes world-historical when she argues that the accumulation process requires not simply capital's ceaseless expansion but its forceable and parasitical interaction with noncapitalist economies.[19] Luxemburg is typical of early twentieth-century European Marxists in viewing imperialism as an imperative of capital at a certain stage in its development, although many of the technical reasons she gives for that view are her own. But unlike other Marxists, she so darkly underlines the ensuing destruction of whole ways of life with their own integrity and value, that one is struck much more by the world wreckage that capital produces than by its part in unconsciously advancing the dialectic of world history.[20]

Luxemburg's great hostility to nationalism is grounded in her convictions that the nation-state is a creature of the bourgeois class rather than "the people";[21] that nationalism severs whole working classes that had mingled in the old multinational dynastic states, binding each instead to its national ruling class;[22] and that the nation-state provides the administrative and coercive apparatus for capital's consolidation domestically and its expansion abroad. These convictions do much if not everything to explain Luxemburg's assault on the principle of national self-determination—an assault the contemporary reader is sure to see as antithetical to both democracy and difference but that in fact is unassailable from a democratic if not always from a "difference" point of view.

Luxemburg takes a hard-headed but not hard-hearted stance when she notes that the trajectory of modern life does not "tend to return to each nationality its independent existence, but moves rather in the opposite direction," working against the self-determination of most peoples and for the self-determination of the great capitalist states.[23] Luxemburg also asks who the self *is* that national self-determination is to make self-determining, and wherever she looks she finds an antipopular answer. In the old multinational European empires, nationalists appear to be fighting for their people's freedom, but their preoccupation with political independence and their lack of interest in democratizing the existing society show that they are really fighting to become their people's new rulers.[24] In Bolshevik Russia, party leaders embrace the right to national self-determination for all peoples as "a jewel of democratic policy" (in the hope, claims Luxemburg, that those peoples will choose to be determined inside the Bolshevik regime); the same leaders display a "cool contempt" for the "whole apparatus of the basic democratic liberties of the people" on which true self-determination depends.[25] In capitalist countries, the idea of national identity is belied by the reality of social division, and the national self is given its actual content by the particular will and interests of the bourgeoisie.

If in each of these cases "national self-determination" turns out to mean the determination of a people by a master, at least that master is, nationally speaking, the people's "own." But Luxemburg also attacks the impulse of the nation to assert the right to self-determination for itself while crushing that assertion by other national, ethnic, and racial groups.[26] One obvious source of the "antinational" impulse of nationalism with respect to peoples outside the borders of the nation-state is the propensity of the European nation-state for colonial adventures. Since nationalism as a general principle can be coupled with colonialism only if "the European peoples are regarded as nations proper, while colonial peoples are looked on as 'supply depots,'" colonialism betrays nationalism as "a theory of the ruling races" originating in "'European' cretinism" no less than in "bourgeois liberalism."[27] By overlaying a socioeconomic interest in nationalism and colonialism with a cultural-racial interest, Luxemburg takes a first step toward transforming an analysis of class relations in which an opposition between bourgeoisie and proletariat develops in Europe and then reverberates everywhere else, into an analysis of regional inequality and exploitation within a global capitalist system, in which whole peoples are the primary antagonists.[28]

However, Luxemburg's most telling remarks for us, given the bloodiest brutalities at our own end of century, concern the way ethnonational self-determination turns into ethnonational oppression in any social context characterized by the mingling of peoples—which in the modern age is synonymous with the human context. As a result of a long history in which, as Luxemburg puts it, nationalities "were constantly moving about geographically . . . joining, merging, fragmenting, and trampling one another," nationalities have become everywhere an entangled inter-mixture.[29] This entanglement has been intensified by modern capital, which knits small, parochial communities into large, highly integrated units.[30] Given the fact that a melange of peoples inhabits a single geographical space, the bid for national self-determination on the part of any one of them will be a bid to consign the rest to a fate on that continuum of unhappy fates ranging all the way from political inconsequence and social discrimination to persecution, expulsion, and genocide.

What makes movements for ethnonational self-determination so decentralizing and democratic vis-à-vis the political unities they are moving against, and so centrist and tyrannical toward their own ethnic and racial minorities? Part of the answer lies in the logic of "self-determination," whenever the "self" is particular, not universal, and possesses the material means to try to impose its will on the world.[31] Hegel exposes this logic when he states that the self-determining self must seek to determine everything outside itself that otherwise would determine *it* as an alien force. It is because the quest for self-determination inevitably degenerates into a quest for domination that Arendt refuses to equate freedom with self-determination at all. She conceives of freedom instead as the ability of the self to begin something new in the world, setting off a chain of other unpredictable and uncontrollable actions on the part of other selves, so that all selves are, in their very freedom, radically un-self-determining.[32] Alas, it is the nature of every ethnonational movement to understand freedom in Hegelian, not Arendtian, terms: to view its own identity as made not through a process of creative self-composition and self-combustion with other identities, but through the assertion of a rigidly separate substance over and against all other substances. Alas, too, the degeneration of the quest for self-determination into domination is nowhere more catastrophic than when the self in question is a nationality aspiring to acquire a state with its own military and police force.

If Hegel assures us that the struggle for domination is not the final resolution of the search for subjective freedom, Luxemburg warns us that the reciprocal recognition of equally independent and self-determining subjects isn't either, at least not when those subjects are ethnic nationalities. The equal independence and self-determination of ethnonational subjects is exactly what the geographical intermixture of peoples rules out, by making the independent self-determination of any one of them a prelude to the domination of the rest. Not mutual recognition on the part of autonomous peoples, each fortified inside its own territorial nation-state, but a community's composition of itself as an ethnoculturally multiple political identity is for Luxemburg the only democratic path that modern polities can take. She supports political identity against political separation out of a realistic assessment of the tendency toward the economic integration of larger and larger geographical areas in the modern age, and out of an idealistic faith in the potentially universal expansion of human identification, as well as the belief that, once class domination has been brought to an end, human identification *should* expand until it reaches the limits of the whole human race. She supports ethnic difference against ethnic domination not out of a respect for difference but rather out of a repugnance for domination, as well as out of an appreciation for specific traditional cultures that are, in comparison with capitalist society, cooperative and unexploitative.

As appealing as Luxemburg's formula of a unity of political identity and ethnic difference may be, it is easy to suspect it of hinging on the substitution of a dream of ethnic harmony for the reality of ethnic conflict. It is also easy to suspect it of hinging on a presumption that ethnic differences in the long run will not be very great. Certainly the spread of bourgeois political liberties and the eventual triumph of social democracy that Luxemburg views as the road to interethnic peace and understanding, she also portrays as part and parcel of the general shift in the world from traditional cultural particularities to the universal characteristics of modern social life. Then, too, from the angle of minority peoples, any attempt to extend the ties of solidarity to cover the entire human race is likely to appear as a threatening move by a large and morally arrogant but still particular people dressed up in universal-culture disguise. Her passionate hatred of all forms of subjugation notwithstanding, even Luxemburg cannot escape suspicion on this last count.

# Arendt

In "Imperialism," Arendt follows Luxemburg in underlining the suitability of the European nation-state for the early development of capital, the bourgeoisie's later interest in overseas expansion, and that class's use of nationalist ideology to obscure social divisions at home. But while Luxemburg sees the nation-state as a creature of the bourgeoisie from the beginning, and the bourgeoisie as pitted with the state against the working class, Arendt sees the nation-state initially as having an independent integrity to it, and the bourgeoisie as pitted against that integrity. Both thinkers idealize their favored antinomies to the bourgeoisie. For Luxemburg, empirical members of the working class might be blinded by nationalist ideology, but the "most advanced segment" of that class is conscious that its true connections are with other oppressed workers around the world. Consequently, when Luxemburg speaks of the proletariat in its relation to nationalism, she always calls it "internationalist." Arendt for her part refers to the original Western European nation-state not as it is in reality but as it is in conception: a rule of law protecting all people equally; an authority derived from popular sovereignty; a citizen body inclusive of all of those who participate in the nation's history and destiny; a bounded territory, within which "private property" is understood as the possession of a specific place of one's own in the world. The nation-state in conception also combines national identity, political equality, and social plurality, with politics having primacy in national life over economics.

Arendt shows us how each of these good characteristics is undone as the bourgeoisie presses for an expansion of public political power to serve its global search for private gain. Economic motivation takes primacy over politics. The nation-state rules over foreign peoples by violence and without their consent. Property conceived as the infinite accumulation of wealth undermines the stability of property as place and contributes to mass rootlessness everywhere. The nation discovers its identity in the distinctiveness and superiority of its race—a discovery legitimating the colonization of other peoples and reassuring the lower classes at home that while they may be socially and economically inferior to others there, they are biologically and culturally superior to everyone everywhere else.

Ironically, racial solidarity unites the nation at the moment that the nation-state becomes, in its imperialism, "antinational." Ironically, too, racial solidarity corrodes the significance of the nation by making preeminent broader distinctions between European and non-European civilizations, and white and colored or black races. We should add that the awkward fit between "nation" and "race" comes to haunt nationalist movements against Western domination too. In these cases, however, nationalists are prone to protest that nation-state allegiances corrode racial-civilization solidarities rather than the other way around. That is, they see the line of degenerative movement as running from the unities of "the African people" or "Arab civilization" to legalized and militarized divisions between "Senegal" and "Kenya," or "Syria" and "Egypt," dreamed up by the West and serving the interests of native political elites.

While Arendt does not turn her sights to twentieth-century pan-Africanism and pan-Arabism, she studies in detail the nineteenth- and twentieth-century pan-movements in Europe and their devastating impact on modern history. These pan-movements are born out of the situation of oppressed minorities in Central and Eastern European multinational states and give rise to what Arendt terms "continental imperialism." Unlike overseas imperialism, continental imperialism is the work not of capital but primarily of the "mob"—the déclassé, the unemployed, the criminal elements at the top and bottom of society— and secondarily of the intelligentsia. Its principle of expansion is not  economic gain but an "enlarged tribal consciousness" with a commit-ment to unify all individuals of the same "blood" or "spiritual" origin and to elevate this distinctive "folk" above all other people. It threatens the established European nation-states through its disregard for settled political borders; its elaboration of a compensatory myth in the absence of a real state, a real territory, a real public life; and its location of the criteria for belonging to a people in "being," not "acting." Still, Arendt warns us, the tribal or ethnonational idea of the people is not utterly at

odds with the republican idea, which implies through its own hyphen-
ation of "nation" and "state" that before acquiring an artificial state, the
people had a naturalistic existence.[33]


The less than airtight separation of republican- and ethno-nationalism
is on display whenever racial images are used to conjure up the "French"
or "English" people, and whenever the cultural creations of language[34]
and literature are used as evidence of a "Slavic" or "Germanic" soul.
Moreover, while in theory republican nationalism is unlike ethnonationalism in extending the possibility of citizenship to individuals of any
origin who accept the nation's law and public life as their own, in
practice the republican nation-state is twice capable of ethnic persecution. In the service of ensuring the national identity and equality of its
citizens, the state is driven to suppress public signs of ethnocultural
difference, which in effect means the suppression of ethnic minority
difference. In the service of limiting its citizen body to a particular
subsegment of the whole human race, that state also will resort to
exclusionary policies as soon as it is besieged by refugees from elsewhere
en masse. It follows that precisely the peoples ethnonational states select
out to despise and expel will be treated as stateless and rightless by
republican nation-states. Arendt holds that from the end of World War
I to the end of World War II, republican nation-states reiterate the racial
judgments of ethnonational states, consigning peoples condemned by
ethnonationalism as nonnational to the extralegal authority of their own
police forces and the extraterritorial limbo of their own concentration
camps. In short, "Those whom the persecutor had singled out as scum
of the earth . . . were received as scum . . . everywhere" (OT 269).
   A gloom pervades "Imperialism" about the outcome of nationalism in
politics that Luxemburg and Fanon never even distantly match. Why are
their spirits higher than Arendt's? After all, Luxemburg sees her position
on nationalism attacked from every side and finally is forced to witness
social democracy's ignominious consent to World War I on nationalist
grounds. For his part, Fanon finds nationalism a dubious means to any
good end except decolonization and spends many of his pages in The
Wretched of the Earth denouncing the iniquities of nationalist parties
and leaders.
   Certainly Luxemburg and Fanon preserve an optimism about the
possibilities for the political world in general as a consequence of their

own engagement in revolutionary movements. However exasperating those movements may be, they spare Luxemburg and Fanon the isolation Arendt describes in *The Origins of Totalitarianism* and regrets on behalf of herself and others like her in her personal letters. Those movements also save Luxemburg and Fanon from the despair of being unable to make a dent in the overarching political situation, by multiplying a hundred thousandfold the force of individual words and deeds. Certainly, too, the times are more hopeful for Luxemburg and Fanon than for Arendt. In comparison with the 1930s and 1940s, the two decades leading up to the Russian Revolution are open-ended enough that barbarism *or* socialism can strike Luxemburg as history's likely denouement. In turn, the two decades after the defeat of Nazism have something heartening about them, in that each year transports one part of the world further and further away from the collapse of its own civilization, and another part closer and closer to independence from that civilization's rule.

Yet Arendt is also bleak about the national question because, unlike our other two thinkers, she sees it as a riddle with no solution. Above and beyond her alienation from collective political action and the extraordinary darkness of her times, it is her view of the national question as a conundrum that makes Arendt so well-suited a thinker for us. She emphasizes that once modern rootlessness (Luxemburg would add "historic rootlessness too!") undermines the organic homogeneity of peoples in every region, all answers to the national question are bad: the nation as a society of heterogeneous strangers joined only by the same central state, or the nation as a unified culture created and imposed by state authority; the formal distinction, separation, and protection of ethnic minorities, or the disappearance of minorities through their cultural assimilation or physical liquidation; the exclusion of "nonnationals" by the nation-state, or its indiscriminate inclusion of them until "the nation" swells up to universal size; the domination of a minority people by a national majority, or the minority's acquisition of its own separate nation-state, with the domination of some new minority people and the further political fracturing of the human race as inescapable results.

In a world that is socially an intermixture of peoples and politically all sewn up by established nation-states, the "worst factor" in the tangle of bad factors to do with nationalism, Arendt tells us, is the fine-sounding conviction that "true freedom, true emancipation, and true popular sovereignty [can] be attained only with full national emancipation" (*OT*

272). That conviction, in that setting, is a recipe for claustrophobia: not Fanon's colony-claustrophobia, in which native populations are restricted from moving beyond narrow limits, but a world-claustrophobia, in which peoples turned by the politics of national self-determination into "natives of nowhere" can find nowhere on earth to go to be free without setting off a new chain of discriminations, coercions, and exclusions.

Why doesn't Arendt opt for Luxemburg's counterproposal to national self-determination as a way out of these various dead ends? Clearly Arendt finds "the unity of political identity and ethno-cultural distinction" a sympathetic phrase.[35] If she refuses to second Luxemburg's proposal, it is because Arendt, unlike Luxemburg, is alert to the difference between what it is possible to do in words to transcend the dilemmas of nationalism and what it is possible to *do*. Given the slip between our own fond ideas about the unity of identity and heterogeneity, and real collective antagonisms of every sort, shouldn't we be alert to that difference too?

## Fanon, Luxemburg, Arendt, and Contemporary Feminism

Feminism plainly has lessons to teach our three authors about the interplay of gender, sexuality, and nationalism. Let me conclude my remarks, however, by noting a few lessons our authors have to teach us. The first lesson is that historical circumstances always will conspire to press certain questions to the forefront of the consciousness of a given age. Future generations, formed by different circumstances, are likely to look back in amazement that other questions that should have been glaring to the past generation weren't. The surprise of the future at the limitations of the past, in combination with the impulse of the future to teach the past what it should have known about itself, contains more than a pinch of self-satisfaction. "Look how blind *they* were—and how insightful, and so how politically and morally superior to them—*we* are!" Alas, modern intellectual history is full of examples of the delusion in the view that critical intelligence and political-moral virtue make great leaps forward from one generation to the next. To pick a single example in honor of Luxemburg: while we can congratulate ourselves today for underlining the question of gender and sexuality as Luxemburg never did, the question of material class distinction, so consuming for her, has almost entirely evaporated for us, without the actual distinction at all evaporating. Thus if the future, with its special sensibilities, can see the questions that were overshadowed in the past by the prominence of other concerns, the questions that the past did see can slide into obscurity in the future, not because the future has answered them in practice but because its own preoccupations have pushed them out.[36]

That every complex of insights suppresses some other possible complex suggests that insight and blindness always appear as a couplet. It also suggests that critical theory is unable to produce a cumulative kind of knowledge over the long run. There is an unsettling sense in which critical theory can be said to gaze at the world in the same way a viewer gazes into a kaleidoscope: as if the world suddenly were given a quick turn, old patterns disappear; new patterns glitter before the appreciative and forgetful eye.

It would take another essay to sort out the complicated reasons why nationality and nationalism, so significant in the first half of the century, became a matter of relative indifference to many intellectuals until almost the last decade of the second half. One obvious contributing factor is that the most explosive political faultline in the world from the end of World War II to the late 1980s was the single "difference" between capitalism and communism, not the multiple differences among ethnonationalities or nation-states.[37] Even anticolonial movements for national liberation received their greatest significance during the cold war through being struggles against imperialism in a larger context of the opposition between two antagonistic economic systems, rather than struggles for the self-determination of peoples in a larger milieu of heterogeneous nation-states.

The intellectual indifference to the national question except when it dovetailed with efforts of decolonization (and even then, the interest in it as a subsidiary of the question "capitalism or communism?") was overdetermined in the feminist case. In addition to ignoring the various conundrums of nationality and nationalism for the same reasons that other critical thinkers did, feminism ignored those conundrums for reasons of its own. Feminism repudiated the synonymity of politics with the public life of nation-states, proclaimed the division between the sexes to be more fundamental than national divisions, and alienated itself in practice from the affairs of nation-states as entities organized and ruled by men.

The sheer strength of ethnic and communal passions at the end of our century has compelled critical thinkers to turn to the national question once again. Here, too, feminism's own turn has been doubly compelled. For the national question currently is posed in terms feminism likes best: not the external, institutional terms of state formation, but the internal, psychocultural terms of the construction of collective identity. Having probed the fixities and fluidities of masculine and feminine, heterosexual and lesbian, transvestite and transsexual; having recognized racial and cultural differences as fracturing the category "woman"; having traded in a declaration of the true analysis of socio-sexual life and the right way of revolutionizing it for an acceptance of a multiplicity of gender narratives, sexual practices, and modes of resistance, feminism is perfectly set up to see nationality and nationalism as another field for the absorbing play of identity and difference.

It is precisely at this point that we would do well to return to our authors for a second lesson. We have seen that at least Fanon and Arendt emphasize some positive moment in national identity—the experience of felt community and solidarity, the expression of a local desire for democracy against a dictatorial center, the transformation of subordinated masses into a united and independent people. We also have seen that all three warn of nationalism's underside: the insularity and nativism of any particularist community, the drive of a newly emancipated nation to forge a cohesive national identity by suppressing differences inside itself, the will to power at the heart of the quest for national self-determination. But what Fanon, Luxemburg, and Arendt also show us, if obliquely, is that multiculturalism, which feminists along with other contemporary critics tout as the resolution of the contradiction between identity and difference, produces a new and stubborn contradiction. Multiculturalism seeks to mesh a respect for difference with a value on multiplicity and heterogeneity in identity. But a respect for difference prompts one to shy away from making authoritative judgments about how different identities see the world and what they seek to do in it, and so also to shy away from attacking identities that refuse to see multiplicity and heterogeneity as positive goods. The paralysis of judgment and action that can set in just at the crucial moment is troubling in any identity-politics context. It is tragic in the nationalist context, where identities not only have the will but also have or are out to acquire a legal-military apparatus to enforce the singularity and homogeneity of a people in a territory, a culture, a society. The paralysis is ironic as well as tragic when intellectuals in one place happily chatter away about multicultural community, while in another place, as if separated from the chatterers by a universe instead of an ocean, a people actually defining itself in multiple terms is left to withstand on its own an ethnonationalist drive to wipe it off the face of the earth.

Our authors would have found incomprehensible such a break between intellectual discourse and political practice, such squeamishness before the need for fighting words and deeds. Their personal temperaments— Fanon's compassionate anger, Luxemburg's fiery impetuousness, Arendt's arrogance—help explain why, but so do their theoretical dispositions. Fanon and Luxemburg can judge and act with self-certainty because they see situations as having a truth to them rather than being made of multiple stories, because they have a concept of humanity that overarches all particular identities and provides a standard to which all identities can be held, and because they make clear-cut distinctions between the forces of oppression and the forces of emancipation, so that they can throw in their cards with one set of forces against the other. Arendt presents us with a more complicated case. On the one hand, she is contemptuous of the idea of a single good that it is the task of history or politics to realize, and she champions the idea of a plurality of ends in human life. On the other hand, she affirms a truth not of ends but of beginnings, by insisting that plurality can flourish only under quite particular conditions. Consequently Arendt can and does make imperious pronouncements about the worth of different social orders on the basis of whether they secure those conditions or not.

The final lesson, from Fanon, concerns feminism's beloved subject, the body, but in a posture that feminism abhors: the body as it is poised to lash out in violence against the world. While Luxemburg and Arendt as well as current nationalist brutalities warn us to proceed with the utmost delicacy and caution, Fanon prompts us to qualify our opposition to violence in politics in two ways.

First, Fanon suggests that, against power that works through physical coercion rather than through the manufacture of consent or the normalization of selves, violent rebellion is an eminently suitable response. This is not to say that it is the only suitable response[38] or that it has no malignant consequences, but it *is* to refuse to condemn political violence in a flat, blanket way. Second, Fanon suggests that the same importance feminism attributes to bodily sensation, sexual desire, and the concrete pains and pleasures of intimate life, also must be attributed to the bodily component of resentment, indignation, and rage, and hence to the visceral pressures to violence against a social order that is felt to be unjust. To admit the physicality of certain forms of domination and the visceral aspect of the fury at injustice is also to admit that under certain circumstances, the absence of the impulse to violence must be counted as a puzzle, not a virtue.

In short, our authors' first lesson is that we should alert ourselves to the insights and aptitudes we have forsaken that they had attained. Their second lesson is that we should search for a way to fuse our affection for multiplicity with their hard political edge. Their third lesson is that we should consider whether the lack of a desire to lash out forcefully against domination is itself a domination effect.

## Notes

1. Hannah Arendt, *Men in Dark Times* (New York: Harcourt Brace Jovanovich, 1955), vii; hereafter cited as *MDT*.

2. In the severity of that insistence, Luxemburg stands out from all the other prominent Marxists debating the national question in her day.

3. Arendt has glimmers of that return by the end of the 1960s. She describes—as a reaction against the centralization, anonymity, and monopolization of power (all frustrating "the faculty of action in the modern world")—"the recent rise of a curious new brand of nationalism, usually understood as a swing to the Right, but more probably an indication of a growing, world-wide resentment against 'bigness' as such. While national feelings formerly tended to unite various ethnic groups by focusing their political sentiments on the nation as a whole, we now watch how an ethnic 'nationalism' begins to threaten with dissolution the oldest and best-established nation-states." Hannah Arendt, *On Violence* (New York: Harcourt Brace Jovanovich, 1969), 83 and 84–85; hereafter cited as *OV*. This is precisely the line that many critical theorists of nationalism will take by the late 1980s and early 1990s, although their characteristic defense of the "ethnos" in ethnonationalism as a basis of the polity puts them at an unbridgeable distance from Arendt.

4. A less kind way to put the point about Arendt is the way Said does when he describes Conrad, "the precursor of the Western views of the Third World which one finds in the work of . . . theoreticians of imperialism like Hannah Arendt," as a man "whose *Western* view of the non-Western world is so ingrained as to blind him to other histories, other cultures, other aspirations." Edward Said, *Culture and Imperialism* (New York: Knopf, 1993), xvii–xviii.

5. Frantz Fanon, *The Wretched of the Earth* (New York: Grove, 1963), 156.

6. Arendt, *MDT* vii. Arendt probably would not protest against being in a common room with her own idea of Luxemburg, which is a different matter.

7. Thus Fanon begins his concluding remarks on anticolonial struggles for national liberation with the line "Leave this Europe where they are never done talking of Man, yet

244 Feminist Interpretations of Hannah Arendt

murder men everywhere they find them," and ends those remarks with the line "For Europe, for ourselves, and for humanity, comrades, we must turn over a new leaf, we must work out new concepts, and try to set afoot a new man." Fanon, *The Wretched of the Earth*, 311 and 316.

8. Arendt, *On Revolution* (New York: Viking Press, 1965), 28 and 63; hereafter cited as *OR*.

9. Fanon attends to the complex interplay of sexuality and racism in *Black Skin, White Masks* (New York: Grove Weidenfeld, 1967).

10. As one neo-Marxist (who later turns neo-nationalist) puts it, Luxemburg on nationalism is "heroic" but entirely unrealistic: she strikes a pose of "defiant moral grandeur, in perpetual rebuke of a fallen world." Tom Nairn, *The Break-Up of Britain* (London: New Left Books, 1977), 84.

11. Arendt's involvement in Zionist political affairs, and her allegiance to the idea of a Jewish homeland and the growth of Jewish culture, are not enough to exempt her from the general association of the European Jewish intellectual with a universalist mentality. Arendt may not be so blunt as Heinrich Blücher when he writes in 1956 that "it has become impossible to be both a human being and a German, a Frenchman, or a Jew (in Israel, in any case) . . . as a representative of this or that nationality, one will be forced sooner or later to become an inhuman monster." *Hannah Arendt–Karl Jaspers Correspondence, 1926–1969*, ed. Lotte Kohler and Hans Saner (New York: Harcourt Brace Jovanovich, 1992), 280. Nonetheless, Arendt shows a definite antagonism to nationalism in her discussions of Zionism, where she emphasizes "the dangerous tendencies of formerly oppressed peoples to shut themselves off from the rest of the world and develop nationalist superiority complexes of their own." Hannah Arendt, "To Save the Jewish Homeland (May 1948)," in *The Jew as Pariah*, ed. Ron Feldman (New York: Grove, 1978), 186. She counts as one of the worst political costs of the Jewish state "the creation of a new category of homeless people, the Arab refugees" and urges Jewish-Arab cooperation in Palestine, a goal she links to "non-nationalist trends in Jewish tradition—the universality and predominance of learning and the passion for justice." Hannah Arendt, "Peace or Armistice on the Near East? (January 1950)," in *The Jew as Pariah*, 215 and 212.

12. The last complaint against Arendt happily is no longer current in any case.

13. Arendt even defends the limited use of enraged violence: "under certain circumstances violence—acting without argument or speech without counting the consequences—is the only way to set the scales of justice right again" (*OV* 64).

14. *OV* 79. That is, the end of "multiplying natural strength," which she defines in turn as "the property inherent in an object or person," belonging "to its character, which may prove itself in relation to other things or persons, but is essentially independent of them" (*OV* 46 and 44).

15. The first and foremost admirer is Sartre, whom she clearly loathes here (*OV* 14 n. 19).

16. Fanon, *The Wretched of the Earth*, 36 and 38; subsequent page references are to this text.

17. To get a sense of the difference the different antagonism makes, see Elaine Scarry's *The Body in Pain* (New York: Oxford University Press, 1985).

18. *The National Question: Selected Writings by Rosa Luxemburg*, ed. Horace B. Davis (New York: Monthly Review Press, 1976), 160, 159, 251–53, and 161.

19. Rosa Luxemburg, *The Accumulation of Capital* (London: Routledge and Kegan Paul, 1963).

20. Compare Luxemburg's bleak final chapters of *The Accumulation of Capital* with Marx's always half bitter but also half triumphant portrayal of the progress the bourgeoisie effects by "dragging individuals and peoples through blood and dirt, through misery and degradation." Karl Marx, "The Future Results of British Rule in India (London, July 22, 1853)," in *The Marx–Engels Reader*, 2d ed., ed. Robert C. Tucker (New York: Norton, 1978), 662.

21. Although under certain circumstances, she argues, it is the landed aristocracy rather than the bourgeoisie that is actively nationalist.

22. Luxemburg here shows a fondness for the plurality and fluidity of peoples in the old dynastic empires over their separation and fortification in nation-states—a fondness that is echoed today in the nostalgia of certain political thinkers for the mingling of peoples under imperial rule. See, for example, Edward Said's poignant comment, in "Ignorant Armies Clash by Night," *The Nation* (11 February 1991): 162. "I do not want to suggest that the past [in the Arab world, under colonial empire] was better; it wasn't. But it was more healthily interlinked. . . . People actually lived with each other, rather than denying each other from across fortified frontiers. In schools you could encounter Arabs from everywhere, Muslims and Christians, plus Armenians, Jews, Greeks, Italians, Indians and Iranians all mixed up, all under one or another colonial regime, interacting as if it were natural to do so."

23. Luxemburg, *The National Question*, 125.

24. For Luxemburg, movements for national self-determination always are poseurs from the beginning, pretending to be interested in freedom but all along being interested in mastery.

25. Rosa Luxemburg, *The Russian Revolution* and *Leninism or Marxism* (Ann Arbor: University of Michigan Press, 1961), 48.

26. And "[w]ithout exception, all of today's 'nation-states' . . . [are] annexing neighbors or colonies, and completely oppressing the conquered nationalities." Luxemburg, *The National Question*, 162–63.

27. Ibid., 134.

28. Thus Nairn errs in insisting on as large a divide as he does between Luxemburg and himself, when he discusses Luxemburg in *The Break-Up of Britain*.

29. Luxemburg, *The National Question*, 124. Luxemburg describes the Caucasus as that "ancient historical trail of the great migrations of peoples between Asia and Europe, strewn with fragments and splinters of those peoples" (ibid., 274).

30. We would have to stress other factors leading to the intermingling of peoples as well, among them two world wars, colonization and its aftermath, global labor migrations, the breakdown of multinational empires, and the rise of ethnonationalism itself, with its production of new refugees, exiles, and stateless persons.

31. Marxism can avoid the authoritarian logic of its own ideal of the self-determination of the proletariat only by representing the proletariat as a universal class.

32. As for Luxemburg—although she rejects the idea of freedom as national self-determination, she does not reject the idea of freedom as self-determination per se. Indeed, her greatest grudge against both capitalism and Bolshevism is that they deny self-determination to most people inside the nation and, in the case of capitalism, outside.

33. Hannah Arendt, *The Origins of Totalitarianism*, 2d ed. (New York: Harcourt Brace Jovanovich, 1951, 1973); hereafter cited as *OT*; see esp. chap. 8 "Continental Imperialism: The Pan-Movements," 222–66.

34. Arendt nastily adds: "as though language by itself were already an achievement" (*OT* 232).

35. She even congratulates the United States for coming closer than other states to making that phrase into fact.

36. It is the preoccupation not just with gender, sexual, racial, and cultural identity, but also with question of identity per se, that has occluded material class distinction in our age.

37. In the early 1960s, even Arendt succumbs to the temptation to dismiss the twentieth-century significance of nationalism (but also of capitalism and communism), claiming that revolution rather than nationalism and internationalism, capitalism and imperialism, or socialism and communism is central to the age. Arendt, *On Revolution*, 1.

38. Ironically, the other suitable kind is the Gandhian response of passive disobedience.

# 10

## Heart of Darkness: Africa and African Americans in the Writings of Hannah Arendt

### Anne Norton

In 1958 Arendt wrote a controversial essay entitled "Reflections on Little Rock" in which she opposed federally enforced desegregation of the public schools. Arendt prefaces that essay with a passage in which she affirms her support for the civil rights movement.

> Finally, I should like to remind the reader that I am writing as an outsider. I have never lived in the South and have even avoided occasional trips to Southern states because they would have brought me into a situation that I personally would find unbearable. Like most people of European origin I have difficulty in understanding, let alone sharing, the common prejudices of Americans in this area. Since what I wrote may shock good

> people and be misused by bad ones, I should like to make it clear that as a Jew I take my sympathy for the cause of the Negroes as for all oppressed or underprivileged peoples for granted and should appreciate it if the reader did likewise.[1]

In her request that her sympathies be "taken for granted" Arendt acknowledges that she herself has put them in question. In claiming that she, as author, can declare where her sympathies lie, she reveals that the texts she has already authored do not accomplish this end. Arendt's writings on race are not, as she claims, exceptional; they are exemplary. Her constructions of Africans and African Americans, her forgetfulness of Asians, and her efforts to sequester racism in the South do not subvert or depart from what she called "the common prejudices of Americans in this area." The uneasy fit between her writings on race and her disavowal of complicity in an unjust racial order shows the danger of taking one's sympathies for granted.

 I am concerned not with Arendt's private ethics, but with the racial politics expressed in a body of canonical writings, and the strategies of denial that haunt the politics of race in America. Yet this essay may call Arendt's private ethics into question. I regret that, but I find the reasons for writing outweigh the reasons for silence.

Arendt's statements on Africans and African Americans are the statements not of her youth, but of her maturity. They are to be found in her most renowned works. They are extensive. She did not attempt to conceal, to modify, or to withdraw them. Arendt's easy dismissal of African history, African literatures, African languages; her readiness to ascribe academic inferiority to black students, and squalor, crime, and ignorance to the black community, are innocent of evidence. They evince an uncharacteristic, and profound, indifference to the historical record and to the literature available on these subjects in her time. They represent so dramatic a departure from the scholarly and civil character of her work as a whole that one might read them as an aberration, and pass over them in silence.[2]

That course might do justice to Arendt as a private woman, but it would continue the unjust effects of her public writings. What do we do when we place Arendt's writings on race before our students and our readers, without question or remark, in an attitude of respect and veneration? I wonder how many students have read those words and waited for the questions that should follow them. I wonder how many African Americans have heard approbation in that silence.

# In Black and White

I first confronted Arendt's views on race in *On Violence.*[3] In that work, Arendt contrasts "the disinterested and usually highly moral claims of the white rebels" with "Negro demands," which were "clearly silly and outrageous." White students are altruistic. "Nothing, indeed, about the movement is more striking than its disinterestedness." They are compassionate. They are "almost exclusively inspired by moral considerations" (*OV* 19, 23, 65, 28).

White students are "characterized by sheer courage, and astounding will to action" (*OV* 15–16). They "at once joined" the antiwar movement "in contrast to the Negroes, whose leaders were very slow in making up their minds" (*CR* 226). They were responsible too, for the "quite extraordinary success" of the civil rights movement. The "first to join it were students from Harvard, who then attracted students from other famous eastern universities." They "organized brilliantly."[4]

White students come from "good middle class homes." An "almost exclusively black *Lumpenproletariat*" has broken down the public school system in the cities. Blacks run down neighborhoods. "Now if a section of the city becomes black as a result of the policy of integration, then the streets run to seed, the schools are neglected, the children run wild—in short the neighborhood very quickly becomes a slum" (*CR* 225–26). In the phrase "becomes black as a result of the policy of integration" Arendt erases the role of white flight in the changing racial balance of neighborhoods. Her description of decay erases the role of discriminatory distribution of public services and private capital in neighborhood deterioration. These concealed erasures make integration the cause of blackness and blackness the cause of decay.

White students are peaceful. Black students are violent. "Serious violence entered the scene only with the appearance of the Black Power movement on the campuses." "Violence with them was not a matter of theory and rhetoric" (*OV* 18). Theory and rhetoric are the province of the white student movement. Arendt's is a segregated academy. White students are placed within intellectual traditions. The ends, methods, and ideologies of the white student movement are identified with intellectuals, and associated with canonical thinkers: Marx, Engels, Bergson, Hegel, Proudhon. Black thought, in Arendt's discussion, begins and ends with Fanon. Yet works by Wole Soyinka, Léopold Senghor,

Kwame Nkrumah, Patrice Lumumba, Amilcar Cabral, and C. L. R. James were widely read in this period. The writings of Frederick Douglass and W. E. B. DuBois had already acquired canonical status in the United States.

White students are ascribed a world-historical importance. Their ends and strategies are compared with those of previous generations. The movement in the United States is linked to student movements in Europe. Black students are without world-historical significance. The Third World is merely "an ideology," and "an illusion" that serves the interest "of those who stand on the lowest step—Negroes in Africa" (CR 209, 210).

Arendt made this statement in 1970, fifteen years after the Bandung Conference. Jawaharlal Nehru, Gamal Abdel Nasser, Mohandas Gandhi, Mao Tse-tung, Fidel Castro, and Ho Chi Minh were figures of world-historical importance in her time. In order to present the Third World as an illusion in the interest of Africa, Arendt must elide both the nationalism and the historical efficacy of these architects of the Third World. She must forget Asia and the Asians.

The Black Power movement's "commitment to the nonexistent 'Unity of the Third World'" is "of course, mere escapism—escape into a dream world in which Negroes would constitute an overwhelming majority of the world's population" (CR 210; OV 21–22 n. 37). The world is white, Arendt insists, and if not wholly white, a world in which any form of black power must be seen as an illusion, and no form of Asian power can be seen at all. Here too, Arendt can be seen to share the "common prejudices of Americans in this area."[5]

Black students in America, like Africans in the world, are said to be "those who stand on the lowest step." They are, Arendt asserts, slow, self-serving, in need of "remedial training."[6] White students are selfless, high-minded, well educated. "Negro students, the majority of them admitted without academic qualification, regarded and organized themselves as an interest group, the representatives of the black community. Their interest was to lower academic standards."[7]

Why African American students should have an interest in lowering standards is by no means obvious, and Arendt furnishes no clarification. Perhaps Arendt merely wishes to contend that, once admitted, unqualified African Americans (who would otherwise fail quietly) would endeavor to maintain themselves in the universities by lowering the standards used for assessing their progress. I suspect, however, that

Arendt is also concerned with standards of admission, that this assertion should be understood in light of her insistence that black students represented their community (a single community, in Arendt's view), and that she saw their "interest in lowering standards" as a consequence of their solidarity with that community. In this reading, African American students would wish to lower standards because they were committed to the admission of greater numbers of African Americans.

Rather than praising their solidarity, Arendt uses the support of the black community to deprecate the status of the black students as an intellectual movement. That role is reserved for whites. Black students represent interest, not intellect. They are moved by material rather than ideal concerns, bound not to an abstract conception of justice, but to the interests of a particular community. They are moved by need, and so, according to Arendt's strict dichotomies, they operate in the realm of necessity, not in the realm of freedom and will.

Arendt conceives reason as impersonal, unimpassioned, "disinterested." Passion follows from personal interest, in Arendt's account, and so belongs to the realm of nature and necessity. The needs, the interests, and the passions that unite black students with their community render them violent and alien to reason. Arendt contends that, while white students meet immediate popular opposition when they use violence, "there stands a large minority of the Negro community behind the verbal or actual violence of the black students" (OV 19). In support of this contention, she quotes what she calls a "half-illiterate fantasy" of James Forman in which he calls upon whites to accede to black leadership, and upon blacks "to use whatever means necessary . . . to bring down the coloniser." Arendt observes "that the Negro community moodily indulges today in such fantasies is no secret."[8] Her analysis gives black solidarity and black violence a common cause in passionate desire and material interest. "Black violence," she writes, "can indeed be understood in analogy to the labor violence in America a generation ago."[9] Interest, passion, violence, and solidarity are opposed to reason, in a condemnation uniting the black community and an earlier generation of the American working class.

Arendt sees the irrationality she ascribes here to the interested in arguments for changes in the curriculum. Arendt dismisses "Negro demands" as "clearly silly and outrageous" (OV 19). They have learned that "'violence pays,' but the trouble is it pays indiscriminately, for 'soul courses' and instruction in Swahili as well as real reforms" (*OV* 80). The idea of an education in "African literature, and other nonexistent subjects" is, in Arendt's view self-evidently absurd (*OV* 96). She displays particular contempt for Swahili, "a nineteenth century kind of no language spoken by the Arab ivory and slave caravans, a hybrid mixture of a Bantu dialect with an enormous vocabulary of Arab borrowings" (*OV* 96). By this standard, English cannot escape censure, and Arendt's regard for Yiddish and modern Hebrew becomes almost inexplicable.[10]

In naming Swahili a "no language," Arendt uses this language not as the antithesis of English, or some other ostensibly pure language, but as the antithesis of language altogether. Africans and, as we shall see, African Americans, are outside language. For Arendt, as for Gadamer, "we are in language." In placing Africans outside language, Arendt places them outside politics, outside reason, in the "dark background of mere givenness."[11]

## The Dark Continent

Hegel wrote in the introduction to the *Philosophy of History*: "At this point we leave Africa, not to mention it again. For it is no historical part of the World. . . . What we properly understand by Africa, is the Unhistorical, Undeveloped Spirit, still involved in the conditions of mere nature."[12]

This is Arendt's Africa, "the silent wilderness of an overpopulated continent where the presence of human beings only underlined utter solitude" (*OT* 191). In Africa, Europeans confronted "tribes of which they have no historical record and which do not know any history of their own": "What made them different from other human beings was not at all the color of their skin but the fact that they behaved like a part of nature, that they treated nature as their undisputed master, that they had not created a human world" (*OT* 192). This was the "Dark Continent where the savages were numerous enough to constitute a world of their own, a world of folly" (*OT* 191). When Europeans entered Africa, they entered a world of violence and slavery. Condemning slavery, and European policies of massacres and extermination, Arendt writes, "The senseless massacre of native tribes on the Dark Continent was quite in keeping with the traditions of these tribes themselves."[13] Africa was the continent of violence, not politics. Shaka's unification of the Zulus is presented not as an instance of political acumen, but as the very antithesis of politics. Shaka "established neither a people nor a nation": "Since discipline and military organization by themselves cannot establish a political body, the destruction remained an unrecorded episode in an unreal, incomprehensible process which cannot be accepted by man and therefore is not remembered by human history" (OT 192–93).

Africa is without history. The great events of the African past are "unrecorded," "not remembered." They are "incomprehensible," foreign not only to Europe, but to reason. They "cannot be accepted by man." They are "unreal." Africa is marked here as territory alien to human politics, "they had not created a human world." Africans are outside the realm of freedom and consent. Africans are without a literature. The African language black students wish to learn is a "no language." Africa is the realm of folly and mere nature, foreign to the reasoned discourse of public life.

Arendt's defenders have argued that she speaks, in *The Origins of Totalitarianism*, not in her own voice, but in the voice of the Boers. Her condemnations of Africa and the Africans are, these defenders claim, not a vice but a virtue, the mark of a spirit too generous to condemn even the most unremitting racists without a hearing.[14] This reading bears witness to the generosity of Arendt's readers, and the loyalty of her friends, but one would be hard put to reconcile this reading with the text. The passages I have quoted come from Arendt's discussion of Africa as it existed prior to European colonization. It is in her own voice that Arendt says of the Africans "they had not created a human world." It is in her own voice that Arendt denies history and politics to the Africans. Yet if Arendt had written these words in another voice, marking them as foreign to her own sentiments, one would still have reason to question her views of racial difference and their significance for her political theory. Arendt put herself in the minds and circumstances of the Boer. She did not attempt to enter the minds and circumstances of the African. Arendt gave a voice to the Boer. She left the African silent.

Arendt's denial of language to the African should give pause to those who have placed their faith—as Arendt herself did—in language as the servant of reason in politics. Arendt presented the politics of speech and writing, of discourse and debate as the liberal alternative to a politics of force and coercion. Yet in Arendt's own writing we see that this privileging of language can also serve the interests of an unreasonable—and unreasoning—exclusion. The establishment of language as the privileged medium of politics does not preclude the exercise of arbitrary power.

African Americans, insofar as they are African Americans, are also without history, without language, beyond the reasoned discourse of public life. They too have no history. They had a physical presence in the American past, but they do not share in the history of the "Europe-determined world of the United States" (OT 191). Arendt's denial of an African American presence in history entails the denial of an American past in Africa. American history, as Arendt reads and writes it, is merely a continuation of Europe's. Only the denial of historical presence to people present in the flesh can reduce the United States to a "Europe-determined world." Only a determined sequestering of historical events, a studied indifference to cultural provenance, can conceal the African origins of American practices and the American people. For Arendt, African Americans are present in America as Africans. As Africans they are "not remembered by human history." As African Americans they are denied a presence in America's European past. They entered American territory, but they did not enter the American nation.

Africans and African Americans lack a presence in the histories and literatures of Arendt's Europe-determined world. Arendt reads the omissions in American and European texts not as errors that might be remedied, not as silences that speak of ignorance or exclusion, not as erasures that inscribe an unacknowledged presence, but as a void. One might read this as faith in authority in the simplest sense: an acceptance of the conventional view that African Americans had had no role in the constitution of the American nation. I think, however, that Arendt's faith in authority is more profound. Arendt's account of African American slavery, of discrimination, of the debate over colonization acknowledges African American historical presence. That presence, however, finds no literary expression, and Arendt's analysis gives priority to the literary nation. More important, Arendt turns to "the intention of the author" to establish the meaning of the literary nation. This is particularly conspicuous in her reading of the Constitution.

African Americans, Arendt writes, "had never been included in the original *consensus universalis* of the American republic." Only an "explicit constitutional amendment, addressed specifically to the Negro people of America" might (but only might) have served to invite them into the nation ("Civil Disobedience," in CR 90–91). Recognizing the pervasive hostility toward African Americans among the abolitionists as well as their opponents, Arendt rejects the commonplace view that the Constitutional amendments of Reconstruction affirmed the inclusion of African Americans in the United States of America. She sees instead a pervasive and unchallenged opposition to an African presence in America. Arendt quotes, approvingly, Tocqueville's judgment that the threat to the American nation arose not from slavery, but "from the presence of a black population upon its territory" (CR 89–90). She recalls the preference for segregation and deportation among the abolitionists. She forgets those abolitionists—and certain opponents of abolition—who argued for integration. Arendt recalls Lincoln's efforts to persuade African Americans to accept colonization. She is indifferent to the African American insistence on remaining. These, and other events and practices that might suggest that African Americans claimed America, that they had made that territory, that history, that complex of ideas their own through labor and will, are elided. Historical agency, cultural work, and constitutional will are denied to African Americans. Arendt's readers are to remember African Americans only as slaves.

Arendt's insistent conflation of "African" and "slave" conceals both African American agency and the subordination of other Americans. Arendt's readers are to remember that African Americans were subject to discrimination. They are to forget that this was visited on Asians, on Mexicans, on the Irish, on Jews. They are to forget that women remained outside the "universal consensus." Arendt explicitly opposes the case of women to that of African Americans, arguing that the "failure of Congress" to propose the amendment she finds lacking "is striking in the light of the overwhelming vote for a constitutional amendment to cure the infinitely milder discriminatory practices against women (CR 91–92).

There are many troubling aspects to this argument. Arendt's forgetfulness of discriminatory practices against Jews and women affirms her own unquestioned inclusion in the universal consensus as she denies it to others. The idea that granting the vote to women "cured" discrimination against women constructs gender inequality as a problem already solved, and therefore not to be addressed. Arendt argues that the failure of a similar enfranchisement to "cure" African American inequality has produced African Americans who cannot—and will not—be included.

This argument is credible only if it is taken in isolation: isolation from an imperfect, unequal, but nevertheless constitutional inclusion in the American polity, and isolation from the experiences of others subordinated within the American nation.

Perhaps most troubling is Arendt's indifference to history. Only by setting history aside can she argue that women were (for clearly, even in her reading, they were not) included in the original consensus. Only by setting history aside can she argue that African American exclusion in the present proceeds effectively unaltered from an original exclusion in the past. Only by setting history aside can she argue that African Americans are "the only ones" for whom the promise of America "was not true," "the one great crime" in American history, the sole failure of the American regime (CR 91; "Reflections on Little Rock" 46). Arendt's seeming indictment of the American regime thus serves to absolve it from responsibility for a more extensive complex of inequalities.

This strategy shields the American republic from uncomfortable questions by confining inequality within spatial, temporal, and narrative limits.[15] Inequality is limited to African Americans, to the American South (or, for the European Arendt, to America), to the American past. The spatial, temporal, and narrative sequestration of inequality enables Arendt—as it has enabled generations of American scholars and citizens—to grant America an absolution.

Arendt's indifference to history follows from her regard for the authority of the word. The exclusion of African Americans from the Constitution (in Arendt's reading) erases their role in the constitution of the nation. Arendt's reading is, however, dependent on the history it rejects. The exclusion of blacks in practice is read back into the words of the Constitution. The failure of the Reconstruction amendments to secure black equality is read back into those amendments. Yet Arendt does not read the African American role in the constitution of American politics and culture into the Constitutional text. Ironically, Arendt, with her high regard for the American founding, is obliged to read racial hierarchies into the Constitutional text.

## "The Dark Background of Mere Givenness"

Arendt thought that in looking into race, into Africa and African Americans, she looked into the heart of darkness, that she looked into

nature. The preservation of politics depended for Arendt on an affirmation of nature's irrefragable authority in the body, and attendant denials
of the presence of the body in politics, or the presence of politics in the
body. Only that which is uttered, that which escapes the body, enters
the political world. One is not born into politics, in Arendt's account;
one is born into the body. One enters politics by leaving the body, in
the utterance of thoughts and the work of the will in labor. The body,
for Arendt, was the site of nature's constitutional authority, beyond the
reach of politics. The body was "the dark background of mere givenness,"
"the dark background of difference" (OT 301, 302).

Arendt's assumption that nature exercised a perfect authority over the
body provided a rationale for leaving certain inequalities, certain relations of domination and subjection, untouched. African Americans are
present in America only in the body. Therefore, according to Arendt,
they are not present in the polity at all. They remain in the realm of
nature, outside politics.[16]

The work that would make visible the political constitution of the
body was already under way in Arendt's time, though most, like her,
continued to regard the body as territory prior to politics. The dissemina-
tion of Freud, the work of Foucault and Althusser, feminism and race
theory have made it easier for us to recognize that we inhabit bodies
whose meaning is constituted long before we enter them, before, indeed,
those particular bodies exist in the flesh. In reading race, we know that
we read texts written on the body. We know that these inscriptions are
the work of politics, not of nature.

In Arendt's work, race remains the work of nature. Racial differences
are not the work of politics in language. They are instead "natural,
organic facts—a white or black skin—which to persuasion or power
could change" (OV 76). Politics cannot reach this constitution in the
flesh. "The principle of equality, even in its American form, is not
omnipotent; it cannot equalize natural physical characteristics" ("Reflections on Little Rock" 48).

Perhaps it was for this reason that Arendt argued, in "Reflections on
Little Rock" that African-Americans should devote themselves not to
equality in education but to the repeal of laws against miscegenation.
Those who argue that Arendt's hostility to the desegregation of public
schools was necessitated by a principled insistence on the separation of
social concerns from political ones find an insurmountable obstacle in
this passage. In this passage, Arendt once again identifies African

Americans as properly concerned with affairs of the body, whites as properly concerned with education. Here Arendt assigns African Americans the project she considers appropriate to their condition. That project is social.

Young-Bruehl noted that Arendt's regard for intermarriage might well have proceeded from her own experience of marriage with a gentile. This interpretation accords well with the dominant theme of Young-Bruehl's reading of "Reflections on Little Rock." In that essay, Young-Bruehl contends, Arendt was moved by the questions "What would I do if I were a Negro mother?" "What would I do if I were a white mother in the South?"[17]

This is exemplary of the thought exercises for which Young-Bruehl and others have praised Arendt. This method testifies to a faith in pristine interiority, in the primacy of the I, and the propriety of the separation of the public and private, as intense as that of the liberals she nominally disdained. These exercises rest on the assumption that race, gender, and other constitutional attributes, leave the mind untouched; that minds, like selves, have a pristine interiority, untouched by the public world; and that one can move in thought from one body, and one history, to another.

There is, however, a persistent asymmetry in Arendt's moral questioning. Arendt asks "What would I do if I were a Negro mother?" She does not ask "What would I write if I were a Negro scholar?" or "What would the Negro mother write if she held this pen?" The strategy of moral metempsychosis is used to question the actions of the Negro mother. The writings of the white intellectual remain closed to the questions of the Negro mother. Arendt inserts herself into the mind of the Negro mother, but she does not invite that woman into hers. The asymmetry mirrors that found in *The Origins of Totalitarianism*, where Arendt admits the Boer to an empathy she does not extend to the African.

In asking "What would I do if I were a Negro mother?" Arendt ignores the constitutional power not only of material circumstances, but of cultural constructions of race. She takes the body as a site, a vessel, a set of circumstances, into which she can inject a mind that will be unaltered by this moral metempsychosis. Because she regards the body as natural, and thus beyond the reach of politics, she fails to consider how the political construction of race can reach in to touch the mind.

The question "What would I do if I were a Negro mother?" makes a public question a private one. This device removes the issue of desegregation from the public to the private realm. Questions of civil rights, justice, and the constitution of the polity are quietly elided. Arendt confronts us not with a public, but with a private, quandary. Racism is removed from the realm of the properly political to the realm of the social. The response to racism becomes a question of private virtue rather than public duty.

I would like, in closing, to call attention to the litany of exemptions with which Arendt affirms her innocence. Prejudice is American; she is European. Prejudice is Southern; she has never set foot in the South. Prejudice moves from those within to those without. She writes "as an outsider." Arendt's absolution turns on a romantic assumption of the givenness of solidarity; on the notion that one cannot be at once oppressor and oppressed. Jews are oppressed. "As a Jew," Arendt is necessarily allied with "all oppressed and underprivileged people."

Arendt refuses the questions that would reveal the fissures in her identity. As white, is she still in sympathy with the Negroes? As European, is she still the ally of "all oppressed and underprivileged people?" Is she, as a Jew, constituted in the dark background of the given? Is she, so constituted, still capable of constituting herself? Arendt defends a self possessed of agency, authority, and integrity. The form of her exculpatory litany betrays the multiplicity and the contradictions Arendt would conceal.

In "Reflections on Little Rock" Arendt's strategy of moral metempsychosis transforms desegregation from a question of political right to a question of private virtue. The preface to the essay transforms her political sentiments into essential sympathies. In each case, a set of political questions is sequestered. In the first case, the reader is directed away from the judgment of public policy and political right to a consideration of private virtue. In the second, a critical reading of Arendt's writings on race is transformed from a political inquiry into an ethical inquisition. In each case, the categories of "the social" and "the natural" enable Arendt to deflect critiques of an unjust racial order and the practices that preserve it. The distinction that lies at the heart of Arendt's work, the distinction she thought essential to the preservation of political liberty, shows itself here as an obstacle not only to liberty, but to understanding.

## Notes

1. Hannah Arendt, "Reflections on Little Rock," *Dissent* 6 (Winter 1959): 45–56.
2. This has been the course recommended to me (rather vigorously) by a number of

Arendt's admirers, who follow it in their own work. As Jeffrey Tulis observed, the silence they preserve is particularly striking when one recalls the case of Paul de Man. De Man's anti-Semitic writings were separate in time and genre from the work for which he was later to be praised. De Man's efforts to conceal those early writings indicate a degree of shame. Yet the discovery of de Man's anti-Semitism brought not only his private virtue but the merits of his later work into question.

3. Hannah Arendt, *On Violence* (New York: Harcourt Brace Jovanovich, 1969); hereafter cited as *OV*. This essay also appears in *Crises of the Republic* (New York: Harcourt Brace Jovanovich, 1972); hereafter cited as *CR*. In that volume, it is followed by "Thoughts on Politics and Revolution," an essay based on an interview in which she discussed aspects of "On Violence." I have used her comments there to clarify "On Violence."

4. *CR* 202. Arendt's statements on the civil rights movement are remarkable for their disregard for the historical record, and for their insistent denial of African American agency. Robert Moses; Fanny Lou Hamer, Stokely Carmichael, the lunch-counter sit-ins and the Student Non-violent Co-ordinating Committee take second place to "students from Harvard" and "other famous Eastern universities."

5. The appearance and disappearance of Asians in postwar American racial discourse—popular and scholarly—is one of the most interesting and least studied dimensions of American racial politics. Arendt's treatment of Asians is characteristic of American racial discourse. Race is seen as a question of black and white. Where Asians are noted, they are constructed as exceptional. Thus Arendt writes that the Chinese "are everywhere especially favored as neighbors" (*CR* 225) a statement very much at variance with the racism encountered by the Chinese not only in housing but in employment, education, and subjection to particularly stringent restrictions on immigration.

6. Arendt, *OV* 18, 95. Arendt supplies no evidence for this assertion. She does, however, appear to be somewhat uneasy about it, for she supplements it with a long (edited) quotation from Bayard Rustin, expressing similar sentiments. The veil furnished by Bayard Rustin's borrowed skin is not sufficient to conceal her whiteness. Her use of the Rustin quote acknowledges in practice what Arendt was reluctant to acknowledge explicitly: that speech is underwritten by the body of the speaker.

7. *OV* 18. Arendt gives no evidence to support her assertion that African Americans were admitted without qualification.

8. *OV*, appendix vi, 94–95; appendix ix, 96. I should note that appendix vi identifies moody fantasies of violence with "the Negro community." Appendix ix asserts that the community "of course stands by no means behind him." The body of the text identifies those supporting violence as a "large minority of the Negro community."

9. *OV* 19. The criticism Arendt directs to solidarity in the African American community, and in this passage to the militant labor movements of an earlier generation, is not consistent with the regard she demonstrates for solidarity elsewhere.

10. I am indebted to Bonnie Honig for telling me of Arendt's study of Yiddish. Elisabeth Young-Bruehl writes of Arendt's interest in Yiddish and modern Hebrew in *Hannah Arendt: For Love of the World* (New Haven: Yale University Press, 1982), 118–19.

11. Hannah Arendt, *The Origins of Totalitarianism* (New York: Harcourt Brace Jovanovich, 1979), 301; hereafter cited as *OT*.

12. G. W. F. Hegel, *The Philosophy of History*, trans. J. Sibree (New York: Dover, 1956), 99.

13. Ibid., 192. "Senseless massacres" have, of course, marked the internecine warfare of the European tribes as well. The distinctive character of the colonial wars in Africa may lie not in their violence, but in the contempt of those colonizers who believed, like Arendt, that the Africans "had not created a human world."

14. This is the interpretation favored by George Kateb in his *Hannah Arendt: Politics,*

*Conscience, Evil* and expressed by Lisa Disch and Seyla Benhabib in their comments on an earlier version of this work, made at the American Political Science Association 1993 meeting. Kateb's work is particularly noteworthy because it provides one of the rare published attempts to come to terms with Arendt's treatment of racism in Africa. George Kateb, *Hannah Arendt: Politics, Conscience, Evil* (Totowa, N.J.: Rowman and Allanheld, 1984).

15. I have written more on this strategy in "Engendering a New American Identity," in *The Rhetorical Republic*, ed. Frederick Dolan and Thomas Dumm (Amherst: University of Massachusetts Press, 1993), 125–42. Though I concentrate there on Louis Hartz, I do not regard Hartz as the primary author of this history. (I do think he may be its most discerning reader and clearest exponent.) Rather, I take this history—with its strategic sequestering of American inequalities—to be an American history, whose broad outlines are widely accepted. In her contribution to its persistence, Arendt reveals once again that "the common prejudices of Americans in this area," their hopes, their temptations, their defenses, and their doubts, are by no means alien to her.

16. Linda Zerilli discusses the distorting effects of African American exclusion on Arendt's reading of the American Revolution in her essay "The Arendtian Body" (Chapter 7, this volume). As Zerilli argues, Arendt's insistent treatment of the body as "a transhistorical biological referent," silences debate over, and precludes inquiry into both the political construction of the body and the political construction of particular bodies, notably those of women and African Americans.

17. Young-Bruehl, *Hannah Arendt: For Love of the World*, 309.

# 11

## Political Children

### Jean Bethke Elshtain

A didactic yet nonetheless powerful film, A World Apart (1988), set in
South Africa in "June, 1963," portrays a mother-militant named Diana
Roth (Barbara Hershey), an activist whose children take second place,
although what she is doing is for "their future," too. The film opens
with Father kissing Mother. Then he leaves. He explains nothing to the
oldest daughter, Molly (Jodhi May), but simply tells her, "I love you
very much. Be cheerful for Mommy." Mommy is someone who will not
"deal" with the authorities, even when she is repeatedly reimprisoned
under the insidious 90-day detention laws. One senses the militant-
mom's fiery determination. She chastises a male comrade who wants to
spend more time with his wife and children. She must renege on
promises to her children, too.

264 Feminist Interpretations of Hannah Arendt

The two youngest children are simply there, ciphers in the tale. The real conflict is between the preteen daughter, Molly, and her mother. Fortunately, the children are well loved and tended by a grandmother and a faithful black housekeeper, Elsie. Mother, alternately distracted and secretive (trying to protect her children from knowing anything specific about her illegal activities), can't be bothered with the everyday. Molly asks questions. Mom stonewalls. We notice a contrast between Molly and her militant-mom and Molly's best friend's mother, a cheerful socialite who is apolitical but "there" for her children.

In a constant state of simmering anxiety, Molly grows more and more fraught. The film suggests that the problem isn't simply one of coveting more time with her mother in more "normal" ways but lies in the fact that Mother will not let her daughter in on anything of her secret, dangerous life. The daughter wants to know more. Mom tells her nothing and forbids Molly entry to her study and to her desk drawers. Molly suffers in school, begs her mother not to leave so much, and loses her best friend as a direct result of her mother's notorious political reputation. Losing a best friend at age eleven or twelve is a devastating event. The world, surely, will end, the child moans. Molly starts to suck her thumb in unaware moments. Mother, arrested and off to detention, is tempted by the sordid deal: "Answer our questions; make a statement and in no time you'll be back with your children." But this is not a deal Mom (a fictionalized character based on the life of a "real" militant named Ruth First) will make.

She is promised a chance to see her children and they, her. But officials transfer her to another prison even as the children and Grand-mother come to the site of her first incarceration, anticipating a visit for they have not been told of the transfer. Grandmother falls ill and has to go away "to rest." One halfway decent South African official, a police interrogator, tells Mother: "Your family is suffering as a result of your delusions. All this hand wringing, playing Joan of Arc is nothing, it will do nothing. It is nothing but an excuse for being a terrible mother. . . . You've wasted your life. You could have done so much." Mother starts to crack up. She loses weight; looks wretched. Finally, Grandmother and the children are permitted to see her, in the presence of prison officials. Molly tells her mother how she's lost all her friends. "It's horrible. I hate the school." She starts to cry. Her mother tells her to stop, "Not here. Not in front of them."

At the end of her tether after release and immediate re-arrest, Mother decides to kill herself with an overdose of medication she has stockpiled. She writes a farewell note: "I haven't given in. I love you all very much." Saved at the last moment, she is sent home and recuperates slowly. Molly, relieved but angry at her mother, invades the sanctum sanctorum of her mother's study, that space forbidden her. She rummages through things and finds her mother's suicide note inside a book. She confronts her mother about trying to kill herself. "I told you not to go into the drawer," Mother shouts. "Stop talking about that stupid drawer. You tried to kill yourself. You tried to leave us. You should never have had us," Molly reproaches her mother. Mother responds: "Listen, I was breaking apart. What good would I do to you in pieces." She adds that she was so weak she might have put her "friends" in jeopardy under interrogation. Molly: "Your friends. Your work. That's all you care about." Mother: "We have to think about the country." Molly: "What about *me*?"

Molly's *cri de coeur* momentarily stays Mother's hand as Molly's plaint continues: "You treat me like a child. You never tell me anything. I don't even know where Daddy is. It isn't fair." Mother softens. "Yes, it isn't fair. Not fair at all. And I'm so sorry. You deserve to have a mother. Well, you do have one, just not the way you want her. Molly, I love you," Mother tries to explain. Then, and really for the first time, she decides to involve Molly in her militant life. The funeral of Elsie's brother, an activist killed by the police, is the next day. Mother will go, defying a police ban. Molly begs to go, too. Mother agrees. The film shows the fists of both mother and daughter raised in defiance along with those of the black mourner-protestors at the burial site, Mother's arm encircling her daughter's thin but defiantly straight shoulders. The film ends with a freeze frame of young men throwing stones as police cars approach. Then the shocking words pop onto the screen as the film's final message: "Ruth First (Diana Roth) was assassinated August 17, 1982." There is no word on the fate of her children.

What would Hannah Arendt think of this story, of this mother, and of her decision to relent on secrecy and stealth and to draw her daughter—no longer a really young child but a child, nonetheless—into a world of activism, danger, and relentless commitment, taking her away from school, friends, the shelter of the private? Molly, of course, hasn't led much of a sheltered life prior to the moment her mother permits her to "go public." The politics of South African apartheid permeates the four walls. But it does so, in part, because of Mother's politicized identity. Molly's best friend is sheltered from it all. But the film represents that as a corrupt and corrupting reality. Children, it suggests, are never spared, not in a political world as fractured and violent as the South African reality.

In order to explore this matter with Hannah Arendt I turn, first, to Arendt's incisive strictures against the politicization of childhood. Second, I display examples of political children of the sort Arendt would either oppose outright or call into question. Finally, given the undeniable reality of political children, past and present, I revisit Arendt's argument and offer a provisional assessment of her case (and cause) in light of the many and various examples of children cajoled, compelled, or persuaded politically. By this I do not mean the near universal experience encountered by those who study or observe such matters of children "liking Ike" because Mommy and Daddy do; rather, I have in mind children marching, chanting, courting arrest, even killing and dying under a political banner or in line with a political imprimatur.

## Private Children: Arendt's Case Against Political Children

The often nasty controversy surrounding Arendt's occasional piece, "Reflections on Little Rock," in which she resoundingly thumped the school desegregationists for putting children on the front line of a political battle, had its beginnings in her 1958 *The Human Condition*. All students of Arendt are familiar with her designation of three "fundamental human activities: labor, work, and action" as the defining features of those "basic conditions under which life on earth has been given to man."[1] Childhood enters the story with her assessment of the public and private realms, for the private sphere is the *only* space that can shelter and shield children from premature, hence devastating, entry into the public worlds, and burdens, of life. The explicit political mobilization of the young erodes natality, the birth of the new, and the possibility of a later newness that it bears. Those who indoctrinate the young politically produce controlled robots or rabid zealots, not free agents. Protection of the first natality in order to make possible the second—in the form of authentic thought and action—is a private, hidden activity: it takes place in a world not open to public scrutiny and control.

The distinction between private and public is one between the things that should be hidden and those that should be shown. Without signing on to, or challenging, Arendt's categories and conclusions in their full instantiation, most important for my purpose here is Arendt's insistence that the family, or household, is there to maintain life, to contain the initial life-world of natality, as it were. A private, hidden sphere is necessary in order that children and the labor that brings children into being and nourishes them be exempt from publicity. The private is the world made necessary, in part, by shame. Shame and its felt experience as it surrounds our body's functions, passions, and desires requires symbolic forms, veils of civility that conceal some activities and aspects of ourselves even as we boldly and routinely display and reveal other sides of ourselves when we take part in public activities in the light of day for all to see. This is not to embrace duplicity and disguise; rather, it means holding on to the concealment necessary to a rich personal life and to primary human dignity in order that one might come to know and thus work to attain that which is self-revelatory and public. There are certain goods that can flourish only under privacy's veil: most important, natality, love, and intimacy. This, at least, is my gloss on what Arendt is up to with her insistence on keeping hidden childhood and, beyond childhood, certain adult human activities.

Her insistence on a complex and many-sided public/private distinction, compounded with her lament that the category of "the social" was gobbling up much that was rightly either private or public, lies behind her much-debated entries into the American fray with "Reflections on Little Rock" and the related "Crisis in Education." Although "Crisis" appeared in print first—in *Partisan Review*, 1958—it was, in fact, a response to the criticisms of her much-delayed piece, "Reflections on Little Rock," a polemic that finally saw the light of day in *Dissent*, 1959. The "Little Rock" essay had been batted around for a year before it was published. Commissioned initially by *Commentary*, whose editors were "perplexed and hostile," according to Arendt's biographer, Elisabeth Young-Bruehl, Arendt's piece was to have been paired with a reply from Sidney Hook. After many days, Arendt yanked the essay, in anger, deciding not to publish it. But the school-desegregation crisis did not abate, so Arendt accepted publication in *Dissent*.[2] She may have rued the day although, given her combativeness, she probably relished the furor, too.

Arendt's opposition to political children comes through resoundingly in "Little Rock," and is elaborated and nestled explicitly inside her framework of distinct human activities established in *The Human Condition*. I begin with "Little Rock" and the hornet's nest Arendt stirred up by challenging the liberal consensus that had emerged around *Brown v. Board of Education* and the move to desegregate the schools—meaning, primarily, Southern schools. Arendt is stunned that the federal government decided to start integration in "of all places, the public schools. It certainly did not require too much imagination to see that this was to burden children, black and white, with the working out of a problem which adults for generations have confessed themselves unable to solve."[3] Arendt goes on to remind her readers of the photographs featuring a "Negro girl, accompanied by a white friend of her father, walking away from school, persecuted and followed into bodily proximity by a jeering and grimacing mob of youngsters" (50). This young girl was "asked to be a hero." The whole thing, to Arendt, smacked of a "fantastic caricature of progressive education which, by abolishing the authority of adults implicitly denies their responsibility for the world into which they have borne their children and refuses the duty of guiding them into it. Have we now come to the point where it is the children who are being asked to change or improve the world? And do we intend to have our political battles fought out in the school yards?" (50). Clearly, Arendt's concerns revolve not only around what children are being put through but about what this says concerning the adults in their immediate surround—their parents and teachers and neighbors. She hints at a mutually constitutive relationship between adult abdication of authority and premature or forced politicization of children.

Arendt moves on to a rather terse defense of social *discrimination* by contrast to political *equality*. Only in the political realm are we equals. In every other sphere we discriminate based on a variety of distinctions. In the social sphere "like attracts like." Indeed, without this sort of freedom *for* discrimination freedom *of* association could not exist. The problem, therefore, is not to abolish discrimination but to contain it to the social sphere "where it is legitimate, and prevent its trespassing on the political and the personal space, where it is destructive" (51). Needless to say, Arendt's sharply cast conclusions perplexed and angered her readers, many of whom disdained altogether her distinctions. Arendt took as a given the right of parents to "bring up their children as they see fit," saying that this is a "right of privacy, belonging to home and family." To be sure, government does have a stake in preparing children "to fulfill their future duties as citizens," but that does not extend to compelling parents and children—unwitting pawns of social engineering—to attend integrated schools against their will. This deprives "them of rights which clearly belong to them in all free societies—the private right over their children and the social right to free association." Forced integration creates terrible conflicts between home and school of the sort "children cannot be expected to handle" and "therefore [children] should not be exposed to them" (55). If parents collapse, or are stripped of their authority in relation to children, the result will be more conformism of children with their peer group, or age cohort, and a growing homogenization of society will result. Those capable of resisting will likely be few and under tremendous pressure to succumb to the wider surround.

Denounced and excoriated, Arendt was clearly somewhat perplexed at the misreading (on her view) of her essay. The horizon of Arendt's discussion was framed by her sympathy with victims of persecution and her experience of the brutal quashing of independent parental authority in totalitarian societies. She had memories of the Hitlerjugend and the obliteration of the private sphere in the interest of an overarching (and brutal) public purpose. She had memories of the Jewish parvenu who seeks to make her way in the world of the goyim, going, or forced to go by others, where she is not wanted and assaulting her own dignity in the process because of the many compromises and denials she is forced to make in order to gain acceptance. These memories did not hold her in good stead as she gazed at the school-desegregation aspects of America's racial battles. Arendt eventually conceded, in an exchange with Ralph Ellison, that black children were not an American version of the Jewish children of Arendt's own youth who got pushed into groups where they were unwelcome. Parvenu did not apply. Perhaps Ellison's insistence on the "Negro experience" and the Christian "ideal of sacrifice" was more apt. For Ellison, getting hurt is part of the racial situation in which blacks find themselves.[4] Arendt conceded this but no more. She defiantly clung to the view that education should not be put at the service of ideologies for social and political change. This destroys parental and teacherly authority; it prematurely politicizes children; it threatens to erode associational diversity.

Paradoxically or, perhaps, only apparently paradoxically, the explicit political mobilization of the young eviscerates authentic politics, or the possibility of such. To preserve any possibility for profound, surprising, even revolutionary change, education must be conservative. How can this be? Arendt made the case in "Crisis in Education." Her argument, rather severely condensed, goes like this: in politics we always have to deal with those who are already educated. Education, for example, plays a tremendously important role in America as a vehicle for helping to forge commonalities from a vastly diverse society. But this is different from forcing children to expose themselves to a public existence. It is a betrayal of children thus to expose them. Examples of this betrayal abound. Europe has seen many such instances of dictatorial intervention, including "the belief that one must begin with children if one wishes to produce new conditions." This latter notion "has remained principally the monopoly of revolutionary movements of tyrannical cast which, when they came to power, took the children away from their parents and simply indoctrinated them."[5] This is a horror.

Whoever wants to educate genuinely must protect children from these forms of coercion as well as that abdication of parental and teacherly authority in the benighted examples of "progressive education" Arendt so detested, schools in which children are enjoined to create their own environment for learning free from adult authority. But the whole point of education is to prepare children to enter a world that is already there, a world in and through which, for better or for worse, they must get their bearings. Children cannot, by definition, *create* an environment. The result of such attempts is the tyranny "of their own group, against which, because of its numerical superiority, they cannot rebel, with which, because they are children, they cannot reason, and out of which they cannot flee to any other world" (*BPF* 181). Education must *conserve*; it must introduce children into a preexisting world even as it shields them against the full force of publicity. To turn young people out as little platoons for this cause or that eviscerates privacy; the light of public existence destroys those not yet able or prepared to perform in its steady glare. The newness of the child must be preserved so that it may become the platform of a second newness later. Childhood is not a political condition from which children must be (misguidedly) liberated. It is a necessary form or container for human being in its most fragile stage, a time of concealment and preparation. We abandon and betray children if we deprive them of this protection.

Arendt ties together the "loss of authority in public and political life and in the private pre-political realms of the family and the school. The more radical the distrust of authority becomes in the public sphere, the greater the probability naturally becomes that the private sphere will not remain inviolate" (BPF 190). This is the situation we—we late moderns—find ourselves in and it is quite literally world-destroying. When adults abdicate, children are cut adrift. That much of this evacuation of authority strikes "revolutionary poses" makes it more difficult to recognize the situation for what it is, hence to understand that conservatism as "conservation" is not only the "essence" of education but part of the overall task of cherishing and protecting "the child against the world" (BPF 192).

And this is done precisely *for* "the sake of what is new and revolutionary in every child." Education must "preserve this newness and introduce it as a new thing into the world. . . . We must decisively divorce the realm of education . . . most of all from the realm of public, political life." As well, there should be a line between children and adults but not a wall "separating children from the adult community as though they were not living in the same world and as though childhood were an autonomous human state, capable of living by its own laws" (BPF 193, 195). Where this line is drawn will vary. But that it *must* be drawn is beyond question. Do we love the world enough to accept this complex and ambiguous responsibility? On this eponymous note Arendt concludes. If we are to perdure we must endure, even embrace, the need to distinguish and to define different spheres and imperatives of our complex human condition. Thus, Arendt unhesitatingly condemns politicization of childhood and education even as she embraces making children a part of the world into which they are born.

## Politicizing Childhood: Past and Present

There is no end to the tales of terror. Terror against children in the name of politics; terror perpetrated by children in the name of politics. China's Maoist Cultural Revolution was the work of brutal, ardent ideologues whose childhoods had been spent waving Mao's "Little Red Book" in the air and chanting slogans in a Maoist version of the Nazi *Sprechor*. The Khmer Rouge enforcers—those on the ground who carried out the work of mass murder—were young, many of them teenagers, similarly inflamed. In today's Libya, young boys are put through rites of initiation that involve chanting and memorizing Colonel Qaddafi's Green Book, marching and practicing military maneuvers (of sorts) that include kicking, stomping, or beating a live animal to death. Those who really want to be bloodied bite the heads off live chickens.

This is pretty far removed from, say, pledging allegiance to the flag at an assembly in a typical American school in which the kids are giggling, jostling, and smirking at the teacher or principal when she isn't looking. Arendt recoils at revolutionary and statist mobilization and indoctrination of youth, which stand in contrast to those practices that inculcate children into a shared *civic* culture, like the pledge of allegiance in a far less fearful and coercive situation than that in place in "revolutionary" or "totalitarian" societies. She would, however, repudiate and alert us to the dangers lurking in a good bit of the "drug war" rhetoric of recent years that encourages children to turn parents in to the state for real or imagined infractions, or the zeal of some forms of mandated "sex education" in the public schools that aims knowingly to displace familial and religious moral scruples and concerns. Arendt's own memories, as I have already indicated, were of German young people engrafted onto the Nazi state through massive mobilization efforts that had as their *explicit* aim eviscerating independent parental authority and private life.

Ten million children between the ages of ten and eighteen at the beginning of World War II belonged to the Hitlerjugend. A historian of this movement, Gerhard Rempel, remarks that "Hitler was obsessed with youth as a political force in history."[6] The "youngsters" were the raw material with which he proposed to make a new world, the old being corrupt, soft, and rotten. Nazi mobilization efforts were so successful that his "uniformed army of teenagers" actually dragged "parents, teachers, and adults in general" into the Hitler cult and legend. And the Hitlerjugend were faithful unto death. About 5,000 children took part in the "twilight of the Gods," the last-ditch effort in Berlin. Of that 5,000 only 500 survived. Eyewitnesses describe children doing what they "believed to be their duty until they were literally ready to drop," that duty being killing and dying.[7] Rempel sees this story as one of misguided idealism and abuse of loyalty. Hitler's children, he concludes, were "exploited . . . misled . . . betrayed, deserted, and sacrificed by a party and a regime that had used them to attain power."[8] But it isn't just that, remember: it is also children intimidating, shaming, humiliating, betraying, and exposing adults—their own parents and teachers—for insufficient ideological ardor. It is this latter possibility that Arendt also aims to forestall with her strictures against political children.

Thus far the examples I have proffered seem rather clear-cut in their power to repel; hence, they too readily concede the point to Arendt. Consider, then, more complex examples of politicization of the young under the auspices of protest politics, or in the name of a particular faith or identity, rather than mobilization by, or for, revolutionary terror with or without state sponsorship. The reader should think along with me about what makes the following exempla more ambiguous and difficult to sort out, whether in light of Arendt's categories or as a way of putting pressure on those categories. There are ancient stories, of course: the mass suicide of Jewish families at Masada; Christians going to martyrdom with their children; children plunging off en masse on pilgrimage or crusade. But I will concentrate on more recent tales of childhood activism.

Children were a central part of union activity in nineteenth-century America; families were either union or non-union. There are many vivid examples of children as victims of the wage-labor system and as strikers and protestors. For example, Mother Jones, the legendary orator and all-purpose rabble-rouser, led a "Children's Crusade" of child textile workers to protest the children's working conditions and starvation wages. In July 1903, Mother Jones marched her band (three to five hundred strong) from Philadelphia to President Theodore Roosevelt's summer home at Oyster Bay, Long Island, a 125-mile trek, to win Roosevelt's support for abolition of child labor. After the protest, she led her children to Coney Island for ice cream and mounted a bandstand to take the children's cause to beachgoers and revelers. This first children's crusade drew so much publicity Mother Jones decided to organize a second, also composed of striking juvenile textile workers. Tagging herself "commander-in-chief," Mother Jones spoke about her project to a reporter in this way: "The employment of children is doing more to fill prisons, insane asylums, almshouses, reformatories, slums, and gin shops than all the efforts of reformers are doing to improve society. . . . The sight of little children at work in mills when they ought to be at school or at play always rouses me. . . . I shall endeavor to arouse sleeping Christians to a sense of duty towards the poor little ones."[9]

There is an irony here we should not miss: children are politicized, drawn into protests, strikes, marches and potential danger *in order that* they may return to schools, neighborhoods, and playgrounds where they belong. The fact that children have already been forced into "publicity" is made manifest in Mother Jones's strategy in a way that calls attention to this very fact and says, in effect, "Isn't this terrible? These children should be going to the beach and to school and to the playground, too. Instead their lives are diminished and stunted. They walk around with fingers severed by dangerous machines; bodies permanently twisted by harsh labor. You think taking children on protests is shameful? No, it is shame that drives them to protest." Note that children launching their own form of union protest—with a good bit of help from the redoubtable Mother Jones—were not merely children but also workers.

Consider a second example, this from World War II, drawn from stories Robert Coles retells as evidence of "the inner resources of children." Throughout Nazi-occupied Europe, Coles reports, children shared in the underground and "the term 'children's front' was used by many to describe their participation." A Rotterdam newspaper from June 1941, reports: "Children between the ages of seven and thirteen are committing offenses against the occupying forces which must be called crimes." These included booby-trapping, spying, even bombing and sniping. Coles continues of children: "They boycotted Quisling's teachers in Norway; they sang songs of protest in Danish schools; they helped derail German trains in Holland; and even murdered Gestapo agents in France."[10] The children in these stories are children *and* fighters: child-patriots prepared to sacrifice and to kill in the name of their common motherland. Coles suggests that we all "oppose mobs, and children facing them, but if children must face them, let us find out why, and what will happen to them if they don't."[11] This is an interesting move by Coles, for he intimates that *not* going public when the world is in turmoil may be much harder on children than for them to take up their share of the burden. Coles uses the story of children fighting German occupation as a way to frame his support for those children who were on the front lines of the desegregation struggle in the American South.

Coles tells a very different story from Hannah Arendt's. In Coles's tale, the involvement of children in picketing or facing "hoses, dogs, truncheons, electric prodding poles, trials, jails, criminal records" does not "necessarily cause psychological collapse" of any sort. What Coles finds remarkable is the clear-sighted political courage of some children in some circumstances and, it must be said, the fearful and ferocious zealotry of other children in other circumstances. Perhaps what we must look at, he avers, is not the *fact* of politicization in order that we might share fully queasiness of the sort Arendt underwrites but, rather, the banner under which this "going public" takes place. In whose name? Under whose auspices? In what cause? To what ends?

Noting that children "have marched by their parents' side in racial demonstrations, both in the North and the South," Coles goes on to criticize press criticism of this activity with its ostensible "cynical use" of children by adults who are more powerful, hence giving children no "choice" in the matter. Because the obsession with who has power is ubiquitous in contemporary political discourse, this matter bears scrutiny. Coles handles it by reminding readers of context, purpose, and the inherent ambiguity of the word "child" itself. To be a demonstrator is hard. But "responsible, nonviolent protest" is always hard; moreover, Negro children were acting "in a region that considers them not merely children but (as Negroes) the children of children."[12] Dignity in sacrifice and danger was part and parcel of the black struggle for self-respect, itself a necessary ingredient (not merely a "by-product") of social protest.

The most dramatic, dangerous, and ethically ambiguous example of children's desegregation protest came as part of the 1963 Birmingham Campaign launched by the Southern Christian Leadership Conference. During the first of many youth marches, thirty-eight elementary school children refused to disband on the orders of a police captain. The children "all said they knew what they were doing. Asked her age as she climbed into a paddy wagon, a tiny girl called out that she was six." At the end of "D-Day" seventy-five students "were crammed into cells built for eight." The campaign gained momentum. Soon 958 children had signed up indicating their willingness for jail and some 600 were in custody. Protest speakers extolled the courage of children. More children took to the streets and parks. Scenes of children being hit by projectiles of water from firehoses and lunged at by police dogs helped to galvanize the American conscience.

Birmingham's white leaders denounced Martin Luther King's use of children. Children, claimed the mayor, were "tools" of the movement and were being misused. The "respectable people of Birmingham," white and black, "cannot condone . . . the use of children to these ends." Attorney General Robert Kennedy, by contrast, denounced the situation that drove children into the streets, but he added that "School children participating in street demonstrations is a dangerous business." In the meantime, however, the fact that "a thousand Negro children had marched to jail in two days" and faced down water hoses and dogs, was hailed by King's forces. King told mothers and fathers not to worry about their children: "They are suffering for what they believe and they are suffering to make this a better nation." Jail is a "spiritual experience" to be welcomed. Indeed, King and his cohorts plotted a strategy to put even more young people in jail.

King faced down critics by arguing that children were "going to jail for what they believed." The "children's miracle," as it got tagged in movement circles, was a tremendous success. There can be no doubt that children were knowingly placed in situations of danger and squalor. There can be no doubt that children by the hundreds, then thousands, made themselves available for this purpose.[13] It was this, Arendt professed in her exchange with Ralph Ellison, that she had not understood. How much of a dent this makes in her overall framework I shall take up below but, first, consider a fracas of the present moment in the matter of political children that recalls the desegregation crisis and the political children to which it gave dramatic rebirth.

I refer to young anti-abortion protestors. I was drawn to this example in large part because of my memories of the Birmingham "children's miracle." Listening to harsh criticisms by pro-choice spokeswomen of pro-life activists for protesting with their children, hearing language similar to that proffered by pro-segregation officials in the 1960s, I grew vexed. By implication, the leaders of the National Organization for Women and the National Abortion Rights Action League who have pronounced on this matter *must* retroactively condemn the strategy of the SCLC and the powerful example of black children placing themselves in harm's way in behalf of a cause. I wonder if they are prepared to do that, to repudiate political children *tout court*. I am not thus prepared. There is, of course, far less of a moral consensus surrounding abortion than school desegregation where majority opinion rallied around the cause of integration as time went on. There is no such rallying for pro-lifers, but they, too, are routinely presented in the press as "outside agitators" and pests, labels of the sort segregationists pinned on civil rights protestors. Most interestingly, the particular stories told by child protestors are similar: a ten-year-old child is arrested, handcuffed, hauled off and booked. A press report describes "a growing number of children putting their bodies on the line in the abortion battle."[14] One of these, when queried, says: "I think I'm doing a good thing because I'm saving precious babies' lives" (this from Sarah Trewhella, age ten). In the

Wichita, Kansas, campaign alone (summer 1991), 183 children under age seventeen were arrested.

The response by critics? "It's a form of child abuse. It's sad to be manipulating the minds of young people. Children don't have any concept of what they're doing. Everyone who is pro-choice is disgusted [by this]," claims Susan Carone of Metropolitan Medical Services, an abortion clinic, in words that echo those of Birmingham's mayor in 1963. As well, under pressure from pro-choice forces, parents of anti-abortion children have themselves been "charged with contributing to the delinquency of a minor," if one of their children is arrested during a protest.[15] The young protestors, of course, make rejoinders to their critics—just as the young in Birmingham did or, presumably, the members of Mother Jones's "children's crusade," or underground activists in occupied Europe would have done. One thirteen-year-old, "who participated in her first protest when she was 7," said: "When the media is saying that our parents forced us into this, it's not true. Many of my friends got our parents into this." (Note, if you will, the reversal of the anticipated lines of influence and persuasion, something contemporary analysts who cling to rigid notions of who has power over whom can never appreciate.)

This thirteen-year-old girl's brother, age nine, added: "I feel if the grown-ups aren't going to do it, it's up to all the kids to do it," an uncanny echo of Arendt's plaint concerning abdication of adult responsibility. How do parents respond? The mother of these two political children says she's very concerned about the danger and it is hard for her to let her children protest in this way but "we can't stand between their hearts and their beliefs." An abortion rights activist parries: "Using children in this way is hypocritical for groups that espouse saving children," a comment that one presumes leaves the door open for pro-choice protestors to take their children on marches, for they make no similar espousal, pro-choice rhetoric and justification being cast in terms of adult rights and choices.[16] The mistake pro-choice critics of pro-life child protestors make in all of this is their politically repressive embrace of the language of "child abuse" and their representation of these children as manipulated automatons with "no concept of what they're doing," charges and language of the sort used against children civil rights protestors. Let us now return to Arendt's strictures and see what we make of them in light of political children, past and present.

## Political Children, Sic et Non

Many questions are on the table. How are we to evaluate political children? Do we draw the lines where we do because what is at stake is creating a free-fire zone around childhood in order that children be spared the depradations, the organized conformism and manipulation of powerful political forces, and in order that parental authority be preserved? Or, alternatively, do we evaluate the politicization of children depending upon what, or whose, politics is involved? We blanch when we see children giving a Nazi salute. We are moved when we see children singing hymns and marching off to jail in a desegregation protest. Are we bereft of ways to adjudicate these and other cases of political children? Does it come down to whether we are pro-Nazi or anti-segregation?

It must be said, first, that children are never *spared* politics. Every child must take his or her bearings in a particular time and place. Images of a homeland are near universal. Every culture distinguishes "us" from "them" in some manner. Robert Coles observes a "political ego" in every child, for part of a "child's awareness . . . incorporates into both the intellect and the emotions a range of nationalist values, sentiments, ideals" and uses these to "shape a life: its commitments, its purposes, its practices, and not least, its espousals."[17] A nation's or homeland's life is entangled with the personal lives of children everywhere. This I, with Coles, take as a given that can no more be wished away than the sun's rising in the east and setting in the west. It is a phenomenon that, in and of itself, neither buttresses nor undercuts Arendt's categories. She recognizes and accepts the need for a child to be inducted into his or her culture.

The problem, remember, lies elsewhere: in children facing, or being forced into, the full glare of publicity; in the abdication of adult authority; in confusing social discrimination with political inequality; in conflating violence and politics. What needs protection is the private sphere itself (hence the child) precisely in order that the child, as adult and citizen, might take his or her rightful place in the ranks of the politically equal. Political equality is the opposite of social homogenization. Premature politicization promotes, not difference, but conformity. It is the primary task of parents to induct their children into the world, not the job of the state. This guarantees that children enter the public world from many diverse sites—familial being the most diverse of all and this natal diversity, in turn, protects and nurtures that plurality essential to civic freedom. As Margaret O'Brien Steinfels notes:

> The values embodied in any family may come from religion, race, ethnicity, class, special intellectual, artistic, or manual skills, characterological or temperamental qualities, geographic setting, and occupational preferences. The unique combination of these and other factors in a family draws on and constitutes the family's history, culture, and present social organization. A given generation may embrace those values and the rules that flow from them, adapt them to the larger social and economic conditions, or come to deplore them and rebel against them. Accepted or rejected, these values are central to the story of the family, and to the identity of its members; and they form the boundaries within which children will develop, mature, and themselves come to reshape the values and rules their parents pass on to them. Family autonomy is integral to that process.[18]

Where does this leave Arendt's analysis? First, it must be said that in misunderstanding the sacrificial dignity of the civil rights struggle, Arendt undermined her own categories perhaps more than she knew. She yearned for "the gulf that the ancients had to cross daily to transcend the narrow realm of the household," but that gulf is altogether eclipsed in modernity (*HC* 33). "Little Rock" is written with a gulf or, perhaps, a chasm, in mind. A very American devotion to a broad notion of equality together with the Christian beliefs that drove protestors, blurs distinctions between *the social* and *the political*. Too many issues blend, merge, fuse, and enmesh for things to be tidied up in the way Arendt seeks. When children *do* politics *with* their parents, or urge their parents into politics (as nearly every parent of my generation can attest in the matter of environmental concerns, it was the children that compelled recycling, energy-saving, nonsmoking), we are in a world that puts pressure on Arendt's categories.

But her *concerns* are nonetheless vital. In the matter of political children, I would lift up these concerns even as the burden of this essay has been to soften or to resituate Arendt's categorical distinctions between private and public, politics and everything else. Childhood does not exist, and never has existed, in a *cordon sanitaire*. There are, however, "good" and "bad" ways for children to engage in politics. In politics, as in everyday life, by their fruits ye shall know them. That is why we repudiate Nazi state-dominated mobilization of the young. That and more. For it is not only the violent and repugnant ideology under which children were politicized but the fact that the method—the *necessary* method—was one of destroying any dignity and privacy, any familial authority. Children were mobilized in the name of saving a fatherland from external and internal enemies; in order to do so, however, they were first yanked out of their families, churches, and youth associations as all the autonomous arenas of social life were destroyed. The same pertains in the Maoist Cultural Revolution, the Khmer Rouge terror, or under Stalinism when children were enjoined to report their parents to the KGB.

By contrast, child labor protestors, desegregation children and, yes, anti-abortion children, open up a space for politics that powerful opponents would foreclose. Nazi children were instruments of a policy aimed at destroying the independence of all associations. By "doing their duty," Nazi children aided and abetted the violent antipolitical impositions of the regime. This is a different phenomenon from Mother Jones's brigade, desegregation children, and anti-abortion children who fight with and for particular, plural communities of belief and memory—familial, religious, local, associational—beliefs held with their union, their church, their families. In so doing they strengthen rather than evacuate associational possibilities of a plural nature. But this is not without irony. In two of these cases—desegregation and pro-life—the power of the state is called upon to implement passionately held convictions that segregation and abortion are wrong, undermining the moral community.[19]

If we up the ante to anti-Nazi underground children in occupied Europe there, too, a community in the form of a homeland and its people is at stake. In two of these oppositional activities, children are responding to a military or an ethical invasion of a cherished realm and its present or future inhabitants—the country, the home—with the hope, in their eyes, of rebuilding the walls that shelter these human associations. Desegregation, more complicatedly, opposes a culturally and historically sanctioned order that itself embodies a violation of a fundamental principle of human dignity; it is, therefore, necessary to disrupt the schools and families of others temporarily in order to achieve and sustain over time a more just order of things, public and private, for all, not just for some.

There is, as well, a second irony, namely, that protests often aim at restoring or creating a zone of "protected" childhood where the primary urgency of the young would be to play, to learn, to be sustained in ways the full glare of publicity is bound to displace. The child must, for a time, be a militant labor protestor, or resistance fighter, or street marcher, or arrested placard waver in order that childhood itself be sustained. The theme of "the child" as an innocent is most knowingly struck in prolife protest but it echoes, it is *bound* to echo, in all stories of political children. We—we adults in late modernity—have such a stake in locating innocence somewhere, in some site or condition of being, we often assign children the task of creating or embodying such for us. It is neither an easy nor an innocent burden to bear. Stories of political children draw us away from innocence into something far more complicated and morally ambiguous. Perhaps, thinking with Arendt, we can find ways to sustain childhood, not as a time of innocence, but as a time of apprenticeship that occupies a border *in between* private and public in a sphere or zone that adults bear the heaviest responsibility for sheltering and sustaining, not to protect children *from* politics but to prepare them *for* politics, for all the responsibilities of adult life.

The film with which this essay begins suggests that the worst damage being sustained by Diana Roth's children, or, at least, her oldest daughter, was her stealthy determination to shield them, to keep them in total ignorance of her activities and, thereby, at a distance from herself. She did not want to put her children at risk. But her daughter was "old enough" to understand and to share the risk. Anna Freud tells powerful tales of British children during the blitz. Thousands of children were evacuated from London, sent to the countryside, or to Australia, or to the United States to "protect them" from the war. Shunted about in foster homes, severed from parents and siblings, many of these youngsters fell ill emotionally. Those war conditions that break up family life "deprive children of the natural background for their emotional and mental development," writes Miss Freud.[20]

What Miss Freud and her co-workers at the Hampstead Nursery, where children were sustained and cared for in the most "home-like" environment possible and where parents were always welcome, found was that children who sustained severe and prolonged assault on their need for "personal attachment, for emotional stability, and for permanency of educational influence," were those who emerged from the war most traumatized, despondent, and lost. (The long-range effects in depression, suicide, inability to sustain relationships and work are im-

pressive evidence of the war's devastation to the integrity of being.)
Most fascinating, evacuated children fared *worse* overall on every scale
of well-being (all other things being equal) than did children who
remained at the site of maximum danger *with* their families.[21] In
fact, most children reacted quite well to the war. They had a clear
enemy—Hitler—and they worked his "badness" into their understanding
of "goodness." They learned to distinguish types of sounds—rockets,
brands of airplanes, how far away or near were what sorts of explosions.
They relished the close quarters and human warmth of bomb shelters in
the tube stations.

Those children who missed both the war and their families incurred
less danger but more lasting damage to the integrity of being. This war
story simultaneously confirms and puts pressure upon Arendt's narrative.
It confirms the vitality of the private and the need to shelter necessity.
But it challenges her insistence that "social," "political," "private," and
"public" are, or must be kept, altogether distinct. Children as workers,
patriots, and protestors are powerful evidence of the ways in which these
categories, and the realities toward which they gesture, bleed into one
another, the most important of these being the child as apprentice
citizen. Because Hannah Arendt would have us cherish and nurture this
time of preparation, she might go along with the argument here presented, for it tries to be faithful to that worldliness she so cherished.

## Notes

1. Hannah Arendt, *The Human Condition* (Chicago: University of Chicago Press, 1958),
7; hereafter cited as *HC*.

2. For the full story of the controversy see Elisabeth Young-Bruehl's biography, *Hannah
Arendt: For Love of the World* (New Haven: Yale University Press, 1982), 308–18.

3. Hannah Arendt, "Reflections on Little Rock," *Dissent* 6 (Winter 1959), 45–55.

4. Young-Bruehl, *For Love of the World*, 316.

5. Hannah Arendt, "The Crisis in Education," in *Between Past and Future* (Baltimore:
Penguin Books, 1968), 177; hereafter cited as *BPF*.

6. Gerhard Rempel, *Hitler's Children* (Chapel Hill: University of North Carolina Press,
1989), 1.

7. Ibid., 241.

8. Ibid., 262.

9. Philip S. Foner, ed., *Mother Jones Speaks: Collected Writings and Speeches* (New York:
Monad, 1983), 487–88.

10. Robert Coles, *Children of Crisis* (Boston: Little Brown, 1967), 1:325.

11. Ibid., 1:326.

12. Ibid., 1:319.

13. I draw here on chapter 20 of Taylor Branch's *Parting the Waters. America in the King Years, 1954–63* (New York: Simon and Schuster, 1988), 756–802.

14. Arlene Becker and Mimi Hall, "It's up to all the kids to do it," *USA Today* (23 June 1992), 3A. This widespread phenomenon has received remarkably little coverage. I mention this to apologize to the reader for my source but it is the only one I have found that cites actual figures on numbers of children arrested and imprisoned.

15. In this matter, one wishes the pro-choice forces might consider the old adage, "What goes around comes around." Why do they think building in repressive use of the police powers against political protest might not one day be turned against them or their supporters in a different climate from the one that currently prevails?

16. Becker and Hall, "It's up to all the kids."

17. Robert Coles, *The Political Life of Children* (Boston: Atlantic Monthly Press, 1986), 65.

18. Margaret O'Brien Steinfels, "Children's Rights, Parental Rights, Family Privacy, and Family Autonomy," in *Who Speaks for the Child?* ed. Willard Gaylin and Ruth Macklin (New York: Plenum, 1982), 254.

19. Let me add that I have no objection to children going on pro-choice marches with their parents; several of my friends have done precisely this with their children. Being far more ambivalent about this matter, were I still the mother of young children I would not engage with them actively in "protest politics" on either side.

20. Anna Freud and Dorothy T. Burlingham, *War and Children* (New York: Ernst Willard, 1943), 11.

21. There is another factor, of course, and that is the parents'—especially the mother's— steadiness. With many men off to fight the war or work in war industry, mothers tended the homefront. Those mothers who cracked under the strain imposed a double burden on their young—a broken-down mother as a presage to evacuation. The child bore the burden of the mother's breakdown as well as the trauma of separation from her.

# 12

# On Friendship in "Dark Times"

## Lisa J. Disch

In this connection I cannot gloss over the fact that for many years I considered the only adequate reply to the question, Who are you? to be: A Jew. That answer alone took into account the reality of persecution. . . . Unfortunately, the basically simple principle in question here is one that is particularly hard to

This essay was first presented at the 1994 Meeting of the Western Political Science Association, in Albuquerque, New Mexico. I have benefited greatly from exchanges with Bonnie Honig, and readings by Susan Bickford, Jennifer Pierce, and Dennis Fischman. Thanks also to Tom Atchison, Kathleen Fluegel, Susan Heineman, Jeremy Iggers, Rhona Leibel, Ron Salzberger, and Leslie Vaughan for the conversations from which it first developed, and to Steven Gerencser for those in which it was worked out.

> understand in times of defamation and persecution: *the principle*
> *that one can resist only in terms of the identity that is under attack.*[1]

Fifteen years ago, after Hanna Pitkin boldly and ironically declared that
Hannah Arendt's citizens "resemble posturing little boys clamoring for
attention,"[2] and Adrienne Rich somewhat more earnestly assessed *The*
*Human Condition* as embodying "the tragedy of a female mind nourished
on male ideologies,"[3] it seemed obvious that Arendt's work could have
nothing to say to the question of feminist subjectivity.[4] Recently,
scholars of Arendt's work have begun rewriting her position in relation
to that question, a move made possible by its rewriting within feminism
itself.[5] The address that Arendt delivered on receiving the Lessing Prize
is a resource for this project. Presented in 1959, the very same year that
she was enraged by the "witless student" who identified her as potentially
the "first woman" full professor at Princeton University, the address
seems to reverse the principle of her response to that offer.[6] By contrast
to her refusal *as a scholar* to be identified as a "first woman," Arendt
meets the Lessing Prize by questioning, *as a Jew*, a public honor that
identified her as a humanist. By the "simple principle" that "one can
resist only in terms of the identity that is under attack," Arendt calls
attention to the way that identity figures into oppression: it is a
constitutive feature of oppressive regimes to represent specific differences
as essential properties of putatively deviant groups. Once articulated,
such differences became political facts that are undeniable but not
irrefutable within the terms of that regime. The Lessing Address is a
performance that dramatizes how to acknowledge an identity as a
"political fact" and, at the same time, to refute it.

   Arendt's "simple principle" suggests a way of thinking about identity
that speaks to the debate in contemporary feminism regarding the
conditions of its own possibility—intellectual and political—without
claiming "women's experience" as its ground or individual liberation as
its aspiration. Almost simultaneously with its resurgence as Women's
Liberation in the late sixties and early seventies, the movement was
taken to task for its liberal and cultural feminist political projects,
together with the feminist empiricism and standpoint theory that were
their epistemological counterparts.[7] Those critiques came from feminists
working within different theoretical frameworks and from different social
locations. There were "radical women of color"[8] and "Black feminists"
who, positioning themselves as outsiders to both academic and main-

stream feminism, observed that only a movement of privileged women could make "gender" the central category of feminist analysis, and called for "the development of integrated analysis and practice based upon the fact that the major systems of oppression are interlocking."[9]

Within academia it was perhaps more the stability of the category "gender" than its centrality that was at stake, as radical social construc- tivists called into question the purportedly liberatory distinctions be- tween sex and gender. Initially, feminist constructivists forged this distinction to facilitate the emancipatory claim that gender is not a biological mandate but a socially imposed role. Radical social construc- tivists put sex and gender back together—but critically, claiming that gender *produces* the very biological differences that feminists took it to represent (or, in sexist societies, *mis*represent), and that sex, in turn, produces gender as an oppositional binary. It turns out, as Judith Butler puts it, that sex was "gender all along."[10] The critiques by radical constructivists and women of color leave feminists to negotiate what Donna Haraway calls the "slippery ambiguities" of arguing a radically constructivist line on sexual difference, while claiming at the same time that the fact of our sexed bodies is some aspect of oppression, and feminism a preferred framework for analyzing that oppression and trans- forming it.[11] This prompts a shift from a movement conceived in terms of a presupposed unity among women to one conceived in terms of an articulated solidarity among feminists who are divided among themselves by a system of social inequalities that are both multiple and inter- locking.[12]

The radical constructivist critique of identity does not deny the possibility of a feminist movement; it makes visible a discontinuity that standpoint theories deny. This is the gap between what it is theoretically justifiable to claim about "identity"—it is simply not the unitary ground that is so often posited—and what it means to be positioned as a subject in any given situation. Although discursively contestable, subject positions remain predictable in their effects.[13] Thus, identity is not the standpoint or ultimate ground it is so often posited to be; when it comes "under attack" it becomes a political fact, undeniable in a specific historical situation but also refutable in terms of that situation. As such, it may be a positive site of both resistance and collective agency.

When allegiances cease to be taken for granted as either rationally or intuitively necessary, the task of political organizing changes. Rather than defining *what* we believe in or declaring *who* we are, we now need to assess *how* we are implicated in a worldly event. This is the task of articulating solidarity: constructing the "facts" of a contingent situation in a way that makes possible a coordinated response by a plurality of actors who—apart from that contingency—may have more differences than affinities.

Arendt's term for articulated solidarity is "inter-est," which lies between people and therefore can relate and bind them together."[14] This inter-est—literally "between them" or, as Arendt puts it, "in-between"—denotes a web of commitments forged by speech and action that "varies with each group of people" (*HC* 182). She explains that it "can be a common ground and it can be a common purpose; it always fulfills the double function of binding men together *and* separating them in an articulate way."[15] Where constructivist models of politics explicitly raise the problem of building connections among differentiated actors in the absence of a common identity and common frame of reference, standpoint models (whether liberal or communitarian) displace the political task of bridge-building onto the faculties of reason or empathy, respectively.[16] Acknowledging this task suggests that a further move needs to accompany the constructivist shift from unity to solidarity: replacing a politics premised on either reason or empathy with a practice of what Arendt calls "humanity in dark times" (*MDT*).

The viability of "humanity in dark times" is the unspoken question of the Lessing Address, posed by Arendt only in the title of the published essay, "On Humanity in Dark Times: Thoughts about Lessing." The "dark times" metaphor, which Arendt borrows from Bertolt Brecht, describes the occlusion of the public realm by a kind of rhetorical eclipse that makes it impossible to take a principled stand without its being distorted by a dense filter of ideological propaganda. The difficulty of dark times is to make oneself heard in public in a time of political crisis: when the "light [of the public realm] is extinguished by 'credibility gaps' and 'invisible government' by speech that does not disclose what is but sweeps it under the carpet, by exhortations, moral and otherwise, that, under the pretext of upholding old truths, degrade all truth to meaningless triviality" (*MDT* viii). This difficulty confronts Arendt quite concretely on the occasion of being summoned to Hamburg, where she must answer a conciliatory gesture that seeks to recognize her as a German humanist. Invoked unproblematically, "humanism" operates here as a term of closure rather than disclosure, invoking a presupposed common frame of reference between the German intelligentsia and an exiled German Jew. Not only does this gesture effectively sweep "under the carpet" the period of the Nazi regime during which Arendt was recognized as neither a German nor a humanist but only as a Jew, it also degrades humanism to "meaningless triviality" by sidestepping the question of what such "old truths" can possibly mean after the great Nazi crime against humanity. It is this question that Arendt poses in the title to the published version of the Lessing Address.

That Arendt describes "dark times" in terms of oppositions between dark and light, concealment and disclosure might suggest that the proper task of "humanity" in such times is to restore some standard of truth by which to resecure the distinctions between action and violence, principled speech and manipulative rhetoric. And yet, such an answer would resurrect *traditional* humanist foundationalism as if it were a perfectly adequate response to "dark times"; it would confirm the position to which the award summons her. The delicious irony of this address is that Arendt takes up her position as heir to Lessing's legacy but turns that legacy to her own purposes, taking the occasion to question the very tradition the prize attempts to resurrect.

She does this by remembering Lessing for his resistance against both religious and secular foundationalism, writing: "he never felt compelled by truth, be it imposed by others' or by his own reasoning processes" (*MDT* 26). Truth, whether revealed by divine will or achieved by solitary ratiocination, is the agent, not the antithesis, of manipulation. For Lessing, Arendt writes, truth can have no bearing on politics unless it is "humanized by discourse," by contestatory debate in "an arena in which there are many voices and where the announcement of what each 'deems truth' *both links and separates men,* establishing in fact those distances between men which together comprise the world" (*MDT* 30–31; my emphasis). Arendt learns from Lessing to construe the problem of dark times not principally as a loss of light, but as a closure of the "interspaces between men" through which light passes into the public arena (*MDT* 31). Thus, the task of humanity in dark times is not to restore light by reconstructing a common moral framework (whether secured by reason or by faith), but to practice "vigilant partisanship," which involves "taking sides for the world's sake, understanding and judging everything *in terms of its position in the world at any given time*" (*MDT* 7–8; my emphasis). Complementing her "simple principle" of resistance, vigilant partisanship is Arendt's answer to the problem of constructing an inter-est that is calibrated not to common truths nor to a shared identity but to political facts.

Arendt uses the occasion of the Lessing Prize both to defend the practice of "vigilant partisanship" and to perform it. The award aspires to realign Germany with Enlightenment humanism by repatriating Arendt and positioning her as heir to Lessing. Arendt meets this gesture by attempting to confound her audience with the incongruity of the position from which they have invited her to speak: as a German Jewish woman critic of humanist universalism honored in the name of a German polemicist. By resisting in terms of the identity conferred upon her, Arendt manages to refute the award without refusing it. Her purpose is to move her audience to assess how differently she and they are implicated in the worldly event of German reconstruction, and, in turn, to transfigure their nostalgic wish to reaffirm "old truths'"—a self-congratulatory interest she cannot share—into an inter-est: their shared responsibility to permit light into the public sphere by posing the question of "humanity in dark times."

If a prize named after a person makes that person an exemplar of the spirit of an age, then the recipient of such a prize is not simply identified with that figure, but is charged with the task of reincarnating the spirit of that past age in the present. Gotthold Ephraim Lessing (1729–1801), the son of a Lutheran pastor, is considered by some to be "the paradigmatic German enlightener."[17] The German equivalent of a *philosophe*, he was renowned not as a systematic thinker, but as a playwright, essayist, and art critic who used these literary media to create a public space outside the academy in which to examine questions of theology and philosophy. Lessing wrote during an "age of crisis" for both religious and secular humanism, and managed—with what some take to be proto-Kantian intellectual genius—to reaffirm faith in divine justice together with belief in the perfection of the human species by the progress of its reason.[18] Renowned above all for advocating religious pluralism, Lessing is said to have exemplified, in his work and in his life, the possibility of mutual respect and understanding between Jews and Christians.

It was no simple gesture for a West German city to pay such a tribute to a German-Jewish scholar. And, as Arendt told her audience, it was not "altogether easy . . . to come to terms" with accepting it. Though it would be neither her first trip back to Germany since the war, nor her first public lecture there, it was the first honor she had received from her country of origin. The award summoned Arendt to take up a position as heir to the intellectual tradition of German humanism. Simply to accept that summons would be, in one way, to deny the political fact of her identity. It would be as if by returning home and taking up her place in that milieu, she could be restored—as an individual—to the status that Nazi Germany had forcibly denied her as a Jew. Such a move would also testify falsely to the continuity of the German humanist tradition, and contradict the principal thesis of her critique of modernity, which was that totalitarianism was an unprecedented evil precisely because it "exposed and exploded" the foundational truths of humanism.[19] And more, it would contravene her claim that this evil was not antithetical to the Enlightenment tradition, but a "subterranean stream of Western history [that] has finally come to the surface and usurped the dignity of our tradition."[20]

This critique of modernity is one of the most remarkable and least understood aspects of Arendt's analysis of totalitarianism.[21] At its center is her claim that totalitarianism exposed the groundlessness of the Enlightenment world order premised in abstract rights of man, and brought to light the astonishing vulnerability of the emancipated individual. She argues that the ideal of an individual whose human dignity is *in principle* guaranteed "without reference to some larger encompassing order" necessarily fails, because it can be *politically* secured only by citizenship in a particular nation which means "disappear[ing] again into a member of a people" (*OT* 291). Totalitarianism revealed the self-defeating aspect of human rights that are institutionalized by way of the territorial claims of particular peoples by demonstrating how easy it is to negate those rights by abrogating the political rights of minority peoples. That the "rights of man" turn out not to be grounded in transcendental principles but rather assigned by historically contingent nations means that the modern world order is, in Arendt's words, characterized by "homelessness on an unprecedented scale, rootlessness to an unprecedented depth" (*OT* vi). In effect, the modern individual is at once both citizen and refugee whose legal and moral independence is not secured by an inherent property like integrity, but produced by displacing the shame of this refugee status onto legally constituted minority peoples.

To welcome Arendt back to Germany and install her in the genealogy of Enlightenment humanism with a Lessing Prize replays this opposition between citizen and refugee. Conferring this honor on Arendt puts her in possession of her lost heritage, as if she were the refugee and her hosts the guardians of that tradition and its arbiters. As such, it suggests that totalitarianism displaced from the ground of humanism *only* those whom it literally expelled from Europe, as if the rupture to that tradition could be repaired by a gesture of welcome and act of forgiveness. Thus the award works simultaneously to deny the political fact of her identity by recognizing her as a German humanist, and to confirm that identity by implicitly atoning for her exile as a Jew. Arendt's difficulty is that if she cannot accept the prize as a humanist, she cannot simply refuse it as a Jew; as she tells them, to speak as a Jew in the changed political circumstances of 1959 "would seem like a pose" that succumbs to "the spirit of Hitlerism" in its own way (MDT 18).

Arendt attempts to answer the Lessing Prize without committing herself to the position of either German humanist or Jewish refugee, but by trying to show her audience that to be one of these is also to be the other. She initiates this by reminding them of "the generation and the group to which I belong," observing that "if concord with the world, which is part and parcel of receiving honors, has never been an easy matter in our times and in the circumstances of our world, it is even less so for us. Certainly honors were no part of our birthright, and it would not be surprising if we were no longer capable of the openness and truthfulness that are needed simply to accept gratefully what the world offers us in good faith" (MDT 17). This is not a self-revelation, and Arendt does not mean by it to make a plea for sympathy as one of Hitler's "victims." Instead, she attempts to confront her audience with the contradiction between the abstract universal position conferred on her by this honor, and what she terms the "political fact" of her "membership in the group of Jews expelled from Germany at a relatively early age." Her purpose is not to reproach them with that fact, but "to anticipate certain misunderstandings which can arise only too easily when one speaks of humanity" (MDT 17–18). What misunderstandings can she mean? The very misunderstanding implicit in something like a Lessing Prize: that it is by a recovery of a lost tradition of humanism that Western civilization can reinstate the moral community that was destroyed by totalitarianism.

By the way in which she defines her Jewish identity for this audience, Arendt attempts to offer them a humanism adequate to the challenge of "dark times," when the emancipatory truth of equality is not self-evident, and the moral principle of mutual respect seems to be of no consequence in the course of human events. This will be a humanism in which resistance is premised not on an appeal to the rights of abstract individuals but on taking up and refuting the "identity that is under attack." As she explains, by identifying as a Jew during the years of Hitler's rise to power and for a time after the war, "I was only acknowledging a *political fact* through which my being a member of this group outweighed all other questions of personal identity or rather *had decided them* in favor of anonymity, of namelessness" (*MDT* 18; my emphasis). The fact that political persecution "had decided" her identification with that group suggests that the identity "under attack" is a position that can be neither simply refused nor voluntarily taken up. Instead, it is given by things like explicit legal minority status, by internment as a "suspect," or by the abrogation of citizenship altogether. But while given, such an identity is not irrefutable. As no regime is ever a perfect instantiation of a monolithic force, no position within it is ever absolutely determined; rather, it is a contingent product of multiple "elements" that *might* be unified and *might* be played out as discontinuous. Although Arendt describes the process whereby the political fact of persecution imposed closure on that multiplicity, it was a negative closure, one that did not affirm her Jewishness but decided "all other questions of personal identity . . . in favor of namelessness."[22] Thus, Arendt describes her own confirmation as a Jew but affirms neither the specific authenticity nor the abstract universal validity of this particular identity. Persecution does not resolve questions of identity; it merely suspends them temporarily.

The principle of resisting in terms of the identity under attack, together with Arendt's account of what it meant to her to put that principle into practice, offers an unusual conception of political subjectivity that turns on identifying herself and her audience as if from a third-person vantage point, by the groups to which they belong. This is not the abstract third-person vantage point of the Archimedean position, a purely hypothetical construct that claims to be detached from partisan interest and innocent with respect to power. To the contrary, third-person identification links up with the disputational practice of "vigilant partisanship"—a concept Arendt borrows from Lessing—and conceives of identity as a "political fact" that is the contingent effect of specific contests. The vigilant partisan regards such facts as no more nor less than conditions without which one cannot appear in a public space.[23] I do not have to assent to the terms of those conditions, but, in accord with Arendt's "simple principle," I cannot refute them if I deny them. To name these terms from a third-person vantage point is to refuse both romantic and rationalist humanism, eschewing the first-person authenticity of the former and the abstract third-person impartiality of the latter. This refusal opens the possibility of taking up an identity without affirming it as an absolute standpoint or definitive truth about oneself. In sum, to identify oneself from a third-person vantage point is to map the positions in a specific contest in the hope of intervening in a way that reconfigures party lines.

On its face, the occasion of receiving a Lessing Prize does not look much like a partisan contest. But to Hannah Arendt, it was quite blatantly an attempt to initiate a reconciliation between Germans and German Jews by reaffirming the *Aufklärung* as their shared history. She responds by identifying herself to her audience as a Jew and identifying her audience to themselves as refugees, effectively taking up the humanism that is offered her as the unquestioned ground of the occasion and turning it back on her hosts as the question of "humanity in dark times." Arendt uses the award to pose this question in both word and deed: the address, itself a performance of "vigilant partisanship," attempts to reconfigure the opposition of citizen and refugee by defining the latter as constitutive of the former.

The transformation that Arendt works to effect in Hamburg with respect to "humanism" anticipates that which some contemporary feminists work to effect with respect to "gender." Both take up an unquestioned ground of identity and turn it back as a contestable fact. In contemporary feminism, this means refuting gender as a common standpoint, redeploying it to pose the question of how women are differently implicated in oppressive social relations, and rejecting women's experience as the shared ground of the movement. As Donna Haraway puts it, feminist solidarity is reconceived as marking "out a self-consciously constructed space that cannot affirm the capacity to act on the basis of natural identification, but only on the basis of conscious coalition, of affinity, of political kinship."[24] Framed as such, gender is no longer a ground of closure for women who center their political identities around the supposed facts of sexuality and sexual inequality. Rather, it is a space of disclosure, where differences conditioned by the facts of racial, ethnic,

class, and sexual oppression can appear, and of contestation, where the
contiguities among these differences are not assumed but articulated.

I have argued that Arendt attempts to open such a space in Hamburg
by appropriating a move she attributes to Gotthold Lessing: eschewing
the transcendental frameworks of reason and religion for the disputational practice of "vigilant partisanship." On this model, solidarity is
not based in understandings given prior to politics, but constructed by
*understanding and judging* everything in terms of its position in the
world" at a specific moment (*MDT* 7–8; my emphasis). For Haraway,
too, the practice of disputational politics brings with it a reconceptualization of knowledge: "How may a community *name* things to be stable and
to be like each other? In postmodernism, this query translates into a
question of the politics of redrawing boundaries in order to have noninnocent conversations and connections."[25] In Haraway's terms, the
Lessing Address is Arendt's attempt to strike up a noninnocent conversation with her German hosts, to both redraw the boundaries between
citizen and refugee, and dispute the implicit premise that she and her
audience share a common ground in German humanism.

It is both a strength and weakness of this address that Arendt
politicizes the question of drawing boundaries and making connections
by practicing "vigilant partisanship." The strength is that Arendt's
speaking to this audience from a partisan position greatly complicates
her usual insistence on a strict separation of public and social. Where a
commitment to that separation would dispose her either to deny her
identity as a Jew or be silent about it, in Hamburg she refuses simply to
accept an award that recognizes her as a humanist *precisely because* it
occludes her identity as a Jew. But because this is a performance, Arendt
neither theorizes this strategy nor calls attention to it. She does not
interrupt herself to explain how it is possible to deploy a "social" identity
toward the "public" end of resistance. The notion of "third-person
identification" is my tentative answer to that question. I shall briefly
explore María Lugones's "world"-travel to elucidate this phrase, and to
explain how it might account for a practice of resisting in terms of an
identity that is under attack.

"World"-travel is identification in the third person. It is a partisan
seeing that involves learning how you look from the vantage points of
the various third persons with whom you inhabit a specific world.
Lugones writes that by traveling to another's " 'world' we can understand
what it is to be them *and what it is to be ourselves in their eyes*."[26] Like

"vigilant partisanship," this travel is not oriented simply or primarily toward an intimate closure of perspectives, but instead toward disclosing the differences on which articulated solidarity depends.

Distinguishing it from both a worldview and a utopia, Lugones argues that a "world" is not a fantasy but must be "inhabited at present by some flesh and blood people." At the same time, however, "worlds" are not real in any strictly empirical sense. Rather, they are particular constructions of a society, or of one or more of the cultures, communities, or neighborhoods that constitute any society. Thus, "there may be 'worlds' that construct me in ways that I do not even understand. Or it may be that I understand the construction, but do not hold it of myself. I may not accept it as an account of myself, a construction of myself. And yet, I may be *animating* such a construction" ("Playfulness" 169). Like Arendt's public realm, a "physical, worldly in-between [which] along with its interests is overlaid and, as it were, overgrown with an altogether different in-between which consists of deeds and words and owes its origin exclusively to men's acting and speaking directly *to* one another" (*HC* 183), Lugones's "world" is neither visionary nor literal but discursive. "Worlds" and "publics" are both real, in the sense that both are systems of relationships that cannot be willed away. But while one cannot simply choose one's position in a world, neither is that position simply given. Relations in the third person, while impervious to first-person interventions, are still relations; as such, their material force depends on human investment. In Lugones's terms, they must be "animated" to be real.

"World"-travel offers a way to resist one's position in a world even as one animates it. Like W. E. B. Du Bois,[27] Lugones attributes critical understanding to "outsiders," who develop a capacity—called "second sight" by Du Bois—to picture themselves variously by the terms of the relations given in different "worlds." But Lugones sets aside Du Bois's metaphor of sight for one of travel, describing what he took to be a privileged *standpoint* as a *practice* of "acquired flexibility" to shift among "worlds" where one is "more or less 'at home' " ("Playfulness" 150). For Lugones's "world"-traveler, this entails "being a different person in different 'worlds' and yet" remembering "oneself as different *without quite having the sense of there being any underlying 'I' ' '* (170; my emphasis). This multiplicity and discontinuity means that there is no abstract vantage point from which her identity could be rendered consistent with itself, and no imaginable utopia where she could be fully at home.[28] In the absence of an "underlying 'I,'" resistance cannot mean simply "will[ing] not to animate" a construct; instead, it involves "imbu[ing] [one]self with ambiguity," setting a multiplicity of selves into play.[29] Lugones's "world"-travel complements Arendt's search for a "humanity" adequate to "dark times," by offering a conception of agency that does not reproduce the self-consistent subject of humanism.

The beauty of Lugones's travel metaphor is that it puts all social beings on equal footing as travelers, while at the same time mapping their asymmetrical social relations. Because any society is constituted by multiple worlds, no social being can avoid traveling. Travel, then, is not a "consolation prize" for the oppressed, but a general practice.[30] And yet, because travel admits of gradation by class, not all travelers are "world"-travelers. Some get to go first class, which means traveling with the comforts of home.

The distinction between "world"-travel and traveling first class might be explained in terms of a difference in the fit between one's identities in the first and third person. Where first-person identity is the vision I entertain of myself when I am most at home, third-person identity is the "I" who is defined in the categorical terms of political facts such as race, class, gender, and sexuality. "World"-travel is travel in and through regions where any one of these facts is taken as cause for suspicion, as when an African-American walks or drives the streets of a predominantly white suburb, or when young middle-class couples buy and rehabilitate property in working-class neighborhoods. "World"-travel is travel as a "suspect" class; it positions you in critical engagement with the discontinuity between the "I" at home and the "I" in the world. By contrast, "first-class" travel affords reassurance of the continuity between these two; it is travel with the illusion of a universal passport, a nonpartisan or general third-person identity that can be at home anywhere. It is not that the first-class traveler is welcome wherever she goes, but that her political, economic, and psychic resources mitigate the discontinuities and discomforts of travel, enabling her to smooth the crossings between worlds and to avoid "rough" neighborhoods.[31]

Patricia Williams tells a story of taking a walking tour of Harlem on Easter Sunday with a group of "young white urban-professional real-estate speculators" who cannot imagine that they would be identified as "suspect." During the course of the tour, the guide suggests that they venture into some of the churches to watch blacks celebrate Easter. Over Williams's objections, the group welcomes the plan, justifying themselves "with comments like 'We just want to look,' 'No one will mind,' and 'There's no harm intended.'"[32] Though she does not use the term, Williams constructs their response as a failure of "world"-travel, observing:

> As well-intentioned as they were, I was left with the impression that no one existed for them who could not be governed by their intentions. While acknowledging the lack of apparent malice in this behavior, I can't help thinking that it is a liability as much as a luxury to live without interaction. To live so completely impervious to one's own impact on others is a fragile privilege, which over time relies *not simply on the willingness but on the inability* of others—in that case blacks—to make their displeasure heard (*Alchemy* 72; my emphasis)

Williams's companions perceive no discontinuity between the first- and third-person identities. As Williams makes clear, however, their first-class travel is not an independent economic prerogative but a relational privilege: these people can be oblivious to suspicion only because they have the social position to exact of third persons a deference that erases it.

What would happen if third persons resisted this governance, abandoning their deference to engage these first-class tourists in the practice of "world"-travel? Lugones imagines the resistance that such a gesture would encounter:

> You block identification with [the self you are in the eyes of some women of color] because it is not quite consistent with your image of yourself. . . . You block identification because remembering that self fractures you into more than one person. You know a self that is decent and good and knowing yourself in our mirror frightens you with losing your center, your integrity, your oneness.[33]

"World"-travel confronts the first-class passenger not only with the facts of her privilege and power, but also with a multiple, discontinuous self. Here the need to protect both privilege and the fiction of integrity obstructs the first-class passenger's capacity for third-person identification and the critical engagement it enables.

The Lessing Prize attempts to put Hannah Arendt in the position that Lugones refuses in the above passage. She is summoned to be the mirror that confirms her hosts' humanity and enlightened tolerance. Arendt resists this summons on its own terms. She agrees to be the mirror of their humanity but then speaks to them without deference, positioning herself *not* as an honored guest, but as a vigilant partisan. She performs the Lessing Address as an instance of "world"-traveling.

Overwhelmed by her status as a celebrity after the publication of *The Human Condition,* the Princeton offer, and the announcement of the Lessing Prize, Arendt wrote Karl Jaspers to complain of her sudden visibility, asking: "[W]hat can I do? I don't really feel quite up to all this. It makes me a bit dizzy, and so I just don't think about it" (*Correspondence* 361). Arendt carried this dizziness with her into the address she delivered in Hamburg. It is a diffuse lecture, made up of self-interruptions and an abrupt tacking back and forth between the abstract juxtaposition of Lessing against Kant, and the "painful example" of the recent history of Germans and German Jews (*MDT* 20). But the digressive movement of Arendt's lecture is not a failure of argument; indeed, it marks the successful performance of her "world"-travel.

Arendt makes the literal trip to Hamburg both to accept an award and to exhort her audience to do some figurative traveling of their own. Offering them a third-person vantage point on the occasion, she suggests to them that they have invited her there in hopes of "mastering" the past (*MDT* 20). By granting her possession of her lost heritage, Arendt's benefactors restore themselves to a past they want to claim as more authentic than that of the Nazis. She responds by telling them that no past can be mastered, and "certainly not . . . the past of Hitler Germany. The best that can be achieved is to *know precisely what it was,* and to endure this knowledge, and then to wait and see what comes of knowing and enduring" (*MDT* 20). The vehicle of this knowing, she asserts, is "ever-recurrent narration," retelling the past in such a way as to detach it from the storylines that permit us to travel through history as if in first class, insulating ourselves from the ruptures in our so-called traditions as we would from the breaks in a journey (*MDT* 21).

Arendt's first retelling is to offer them a Lessing of her own design, taking their hero of the Enlightenment and making him out to be its "bad boy." Since Lessing's time, she asserts,

> little has changed for the better. The "pillars of the best-known
> truths" [Lessing's metaphor for reason and faith], which at that
> time were shaken, today lie shattered; we need neither criticism
> nor wise men to shake them any more. We need only look
> around to see that we are standing in the midst of a veritable
> rubble help of such pillars. (MDT 10)

This woman who last confronted the German state as "an individual
without rights and duties," repatriates herself by means of the "persona"
of Lessing, taking up his words as a mask by which to "replace [her] own
face and countenance, but in a way that would make it possible for [her]
voice to sound through."[34] His identity quite literally becomes the mask
that affords her standing to refute the position to which the award
assigns her in his name. Though it seems the difficulty of the award is
hers in having to accept it, she uses the metaphor of the pillars to point
out to them the possibility of *making* such an award. While it would
seem at best ungrateful and at worst confrontational and presumptuous
to do this in her own persona, Arendt does it gracefully through Lessing,
taking up the opportunity the award extends her to reincarnate him—but
with the playful twist of positioning *him* as a pariah.

   According to Arendt, she and Lessing are alike in being exiles from
German humanism. If she was literally a refugee, Lessing was a refugee
in spirit, a man who "never felt at home in the world as it then existed
and probably never wanted to, and still after his own fashion he always
remained committed to it."[35] Just what was it that put Lessing so at odds
with his age? Arendt answers that it was Lessing's "partisanship for the
world," a passionate polemicism that she characterizes as "a curious kind
of partiality which clung to concrete details with an exaggerated, almost
pedantic carefulness, and gave rise to many misunderstandings" (MDT
8, 5). Partisanship for the world, the product of "vigilant partisanship,"
involves seeing from the determinate plurality of vantage points to which
a specific conflict gives rise. As such, it is not "for the world" in the
sense of a civic virtue that steps beyond partial interest to a higher moral
plane, but in the sense that the "reality" of the public realm depends on
seeing and speaking from each of a plurality of vantage points. Playing
up the contrast to Kantian humanism, Arendt asserts that Lessing's
refusal to detach himself from the concrete "did not help his credit in
Germany, where the true nature of criticism is less well understood
than elsewhere."[36]

Many scholars cast Lessing as a thinker who, in anticipation of both Kant and Hegel, resolved the philosophical and theological crises of theodicy by systematically defending a transcendental position from which to reconcile the antinomies of both reason and religion with justice.[37] By contrast, Arendt argues that Lessing tried not to resolve these debates but to provoke them: "when everyone else was contending over the 'truth' of Christianity, [Lessing] was chiefly defending its position in the world, now anxious that it might again enforce its claim to dominance, now fearing that it might vanish utterly" (MDT 7). Arendt also agrees that Lessing resisted systematic thinking as a form of self-mastery: he had little regard for "the axiom of noncontradiction, the claim to self-consistency, which we assume is mandatory to all who write and speak" (MDT 8). Lessing was committed, in other words, to the many-sidedness of opinions in the world and to multiplicity in the self.[38] Praising him, Arendt writes that "above all he never coerced himself, and instead of fixing his identity in history with a perfectly consistent system, he scattered into the world, as he himself knew, 'nothing but *fermenta cognitionis.*'"[39] Arendt celebrates Lessing for his contentiousness, because this is what made him so effective as a *public* intellectual in "dark times."

But Lessing was more committed both to faith in divine providence and to the possibility of human perfection through reason than Arendt admits. He shared the conviction of his age that history would be a narrative of human progress.[40] Thus, the connection that Arendt forges by her appropriation of his metaphor of the pillars is really quite remarkable. Lessing knew that the "pillars" of reason and faith had been shaken, but he believed that they could be shored up by polemics, art criticism, and playwriting. By shattering Lessing's pillars, Arendt makes it quite clear that there can be no faith in progress for those who live in the "dark times" after totalitarianism has destroyed "our categories of thought and standards of judgment."[41] Though she speaks through Lessing, Arendt poses the problem of "humanity in dark times" more radically than he ever would have dared to.

Again through Lessing, Arendt launches a daring attack against Kant and his Enlightenment bequest. Crediting Lessing with having explored an "antinomy" that is invisible to both religious and secular humanism— "the possible antagonism between truth and humanity" (MDT 28)— Arendt argues that no such antinomy is conceivable within the framework of Kantian humanism, in which truth is quite plainly not the antagonist of humanity but its ground. Contentiously, Arendt asserts that the "inhumanity of Kant's moral philosophy is undeniable." For Kant, there can be no conflict between abstract duty and particular friendship because it is an imperative of the former to detach oneself from the latter, "the categorical imperative is postulated as absolute and in its absoluteness introduces into the interhuman realm—which by its nature consists of relationships—something that runs counter to its fundamental relativity" (*MDT* 27). In contrast to Kantian detachment, "criticism, in Lessing's sense, is always taking sides for the world's sake, understanding and judging everything in terms of its position in the world at any given time" (*MDT* 7–8). In sum, the juxtaposition between these two thinkers turns on a contrast between the partisan seeing of third-person identification and the abstract third-person standpoint of Archimedean impartiality.

By juxtaposing the "inhumanity" of Kantian moral philosophy against the "astonishing lack of 'objectivity' in Lessing's polemicism," Arendt's critique of Kantian humanism attacks at the root the notion that the failure to resist Hitler can be attributed to a breakdown of critical humanism. On the contrary, Arendt suggests that it was the consequence of the practice of a humanism so misconceived that it seemed a duty to betray friendship *in the name of humanity*.

Arendt goes on to explain precisely how "objectivity in the ordinary sense" mitigates against resistance to an authoritarian regime. People who believe themselves to be in the possession of an abstract imperative are reluctant to deviate from it to accommodate the ambiguous demands of friendship. They believe "that to do so would be to violate a higher duty, the duty of 'objectivity'; so that even if they make such a sacrifice they do not feel they are acting out of conscience but are even ashamed of their humanity and often feel distinctly guilty about it" (*MDT* 28). She goes on to imply that the rhetoric of duty to an abstract imperative provided German religious leaders and intellectuals with a convenient rationalization for their failure to resist Hitler's regime in its early years.[42] Though Arendt knows of course that the race laws of the Third Reich could not be farther from the spirit of Kantian critical theory, she asserts nonetheless that both disable critique and resistance by confronting the political subject with an imperative.[43]

Arendt brings the broad issues of her address back to a more accessible plane by telling two stories whose purpose is twofold. First, she wants to show her audience that they have posed the problem of genocide to themselves as a betrayal of the *Aufklärung* and a crisis for German pride. Then, she wants to move them to reframe that problem, not to see it as a violation of duties owed to humanity, but as a breach of friendship between Germans and German Jews.

The first story takes up Lessing's play *Nathan the Wise*, rewriting its story of friendship among a Jew, a Sultan, and a Crusader in two significant ways. First, Arendt pulls the play into the context of a time during which—although she does not mention it—it was banned from the stage, inviting her audience to imagine "the case of a friendship between a German and a Jew under the condition of the Third Reich" (*MDT* 23). Would such a friendship count as a "sign of humanness"? Not, Arendt says, if the friends defended their friendship by asking: "Are we not both human beings?" (*MDT* 23). In that time, to have rendered their relationship in these nonpartisan terms would be to deny the political facts of their situation and to evade the political challenge of refuting them. Recasting this Archimedean flight from "the world common to both at that time" in terms of her "simple" principle of resistance, Arendt writes: "in keeping with a humanness that had not lost the solid ground of reality, a humanness in the midst of the reality of persecution, they would have had to say to each other: a German and a Jew, and friends" (*MDT* 23). This first story tutors her audience in the practice of "vigilant partisanship." It dramatizes Arendt's conviction that it is only by acknowledging the fact that—as third persons—each (Jew and German) is a criminal to the other, that they can proceed—as first persons—to refute the terms of that relationship.[44]

The second story is a somewhat macabre thought-experiment in which Arendt sets her audience this task: pose a question that would compel a Nazi interlocutor to affirm that genocide is an intolerable crime against humanity *without recourse to* the pillars of legal, moral, or religious humanism. She complicates this task at the outset, asking them to assume that Nazi "racial theories could have been convincingly proved," and that Jews are, in fact, biologically inferior (*MDT* 29). Given that "the practical political conclusions the Nazis drew from these stories were perfectly logical," if the theories themselves "could have been convincingly proved," there would have been no rational opposition against genocide except on moral grounds (*MDT* 29). Obviously, Arendt does not think these theories were valid; she means to situate her audience in the situation of Nazi Germany so that they must debate the justification of genocide as if they lived under a totalitarian regime where theories cannot be held to the test of factual validity because "fact depends entirely on the power of man who can fabricate it" (*OT* 350). By closing off the possibility of empirically refuting genocide, she teaches them one of the claims of *Origins:* that one could not resist Nazi domination by speaking truth to power.[45]

She complicates this task still further, by forbidding them to ask whether the proven biological inferiority of a race would "justify its extermination." She tells them that this is "too easy" because it elicits a response in terms of the pillar of Western religious and secular morality: Thou shalt not kill. With this restriction, Arendt has positioned her audience with her on the rubble pile, and she invites them to proceed "in terms of a way of thinking governed by neither legal nor moral nor religious strictures." She meets this challenge by invoking Lessing, whom she says would have "posed [it] thus: *Would any such doctrine, however convincingly proved, be worth the sacrifice of so much as a single friendship between two men?* (*MDT*; emphasis in original).

Just what does Arendt mean by friendship in this context? She does not mean to recommend a relationship based in the humanist ideal of respect for man in the abstract.[46] But neither does she mean to recommend a communitarian vision of brotherhood. Both would deny plurality, the first by grounding itself in an abstract universalist sameness, and the second by depending upon a compassion that destroys the space that is the very condition of plurality (*MDT* 13). Instead, Arendt moves to the inter-est, or "between them," to sustain the kind of friendship she has in mind. The inter-est is not a common moral framework or common ground, but a space that exists where people engage in disputation about the meaning of worldly events. Such disputation establishes "those distances between men which together comprise the world" (*MDT* 31), and secures the third-person perspective and the openness to it upon which the inter-est ultimately depends. Paradoxically, then, the "between" that sustains Arendt's conception of friendship is not a common moral framework of identity, but distance.

This notion of a politics based in a differentiated and discursively contested "interspace" is one model for humanity in dark times. Distinct from both humanist friendship (which is premised on seeing beyond factual particularity to "man" in the abstract), and romantic friendship (which is premised on a special insight into the authentic self that lies behind the mask of political fact), Arendt's friendship takes into account the differences among various actors' locations in relation to an event.

But it does so without pride or pity, maintaining what Arendt describes as a relationship "without false guilt complexes on the one side and false complexes of superiority or inferiority on the other" (*MDT* 23). Arendt calls it friendship, but it is in the service of partisanship for the world, in a world lacking trust, common moral convictions, or shared cultural identity, but shaped by the "political facts" of the past and the aspirations of the future.

Arendt's refusal to acknowledge the public relevance of her womanhood is no model for feminist subjectivity. In the wake of more than two decades of feminist analysis of how constructions of gender play into social relations of domination, such a refusal is nothing less than an affirmation of the class, ethnic, and heterosexual privileges with which gender is complicit. By contrast, Arendt's "vigilant partisanship" toward the "political fact" of her Jewish identity in the Lessing Address suggests a strategy for negotiating the "slippery ambiguities" of confirming one's identity as a woman, without also claiming either an authentic or abstract universal standpoint on womanhood. This strategy, which I have termed identification in the third person, is a requisite to "noninnocent" conversations in which the faith in gender as shared ground can give way to a questioning that discloses the asymmetries and exclusions of that ground. The viability of such a strategy depends on remembering that speaking as a feminist is distinct both from speaking in the first person, as a woman concerned with finding sympathy for her experiences; and from speaking in the abstract third person, as a citizen concerned with promoting an impartial public good. To speak as a feminist is to contest with "vigilant partisanship" the meanings of gender as a political fact. On this model, it is not an identity but an inter-est, articulated in the practice of "world"-travel, that animates and sustains feminist political action.

There remains one final question to pose of the Lessing Address: Just how successful was Arendt's effort to exhort her German audience to give up their first-class privileges and join her in a relationship of partisanship? Five months after she delivered the address, Arendt received a letter from Karl Jaspers reporting that a "long quotation" from her speech was read at a "session of the Bundestag (Feb 18 [1960]) devoted to anti-Semitic acts," and that her remarks were commended as the "very profound insight" of a "Jewish emigrant" (*Correspondence* 389).

To call Arendt an "emigrant" is consistent with the gesture of the Lessing Prize: both imply that Arendt left the country voluntarily, with her German identity intact. The manifest denial in this construction seems to confirm that Arendt's audience listened to her address in first class, smoothing out the discontinuities she had tried so hard to bring to the fore by asserting her specific identity as a Jew who fled Nazi Germany under duress.

Jaspers himself responds quite differently to the address and to Arendt's disposition at the time she delivered it. If her mainstream audience erased the discontinuity in her German Jewish identity (by calling her an "emigrant"), Jaspers heard Arendt speak exclusively as a Jew, and perceived her to break with her German heritage. In a letter to Arendt's husband Heinrich Blücher, composed during the visit Arendt paid to Jaspers after the ceremony, Jaspers expresses his concern over this break:

> From Germany—which in her conversation she likes to confuse with the people visible in the Federal Republic today—she has pulled away even more, is more indifferent toward it. That pains me somewhat. I feel she is mistaken about herself, even though she truly has, together with you, achieved a state in which she exists with her feet on the ground, *even though deprived of the ground of her origins.* (*Correspondence* 383–84)

Jaspers interprets Arendt's assertion of the "political fact" of her Jewish identity as a renunciation of her German "origins" on behalf of the accident of her Jewishness.[47]

This perception of a "pulling away" is interesting enough, in light of Arendt's remarks to her audience about refusing to help them "master" the past. But it is still more interesting to take note of the way he positions Arendt by making these remarks. Jaspers's confession to Blücher that he "feel[s Arendt] is mistaken about herself," and his observation that she "truly has, together with you achieved a state in which she exists with her feet on the ground," belies his relationship to the couple. Given that Jaspers has never met this man, has barely corresponded with him, and knows him only as the husband of Arendt—one of the rare people with whom he enjoys a relationship that spans the war—this confidence is something of a betrayal of his friendship with Arendt. It presumes a kinship with Blücher that is premised on the same originary ground from which he accuses Arendt of pulling away. Superseding, at least momentarily, the understanding he and Arendt have cultivated by their correspondence and her visits to Europe in the fourteen years since the war's end, the givenness of this kinship positions her as a third party to his and Blücher's company.

It is still more interesting to know that Hannah Arendt herself put these words to paper, writing about herself in the third person from a German vantage point. Though Jaspers composed this passage, Arendt wrote it down to spare Blücher the task of reading Jaspers's nearly illegible hand. By this act, Arendt quite literally signs on to Jaspers's depiction of her as a woman who is prevented access to her original self, and only tenuously reunited to its "ground" by her marriage. She authorizes Jaspers to feel a kinship to her husband as another German who is married to a Jewish wife, and as one who takes pride in the intellectual heritage of that country, not its politics. There is an obvious parallel between the position to which Jaspers assigns her and that to which she was assigned by the Lessing Prize. Both Jaspers and the prize committee urge Hannah Arendt to see herself as the inheritor of an intellectual tradition that transcends the brutal realities of German nationalism. To situate her in this tradition is the ultimate affirmation of its continuity: how better to proclaim the rebirth of German liberalism than by an honorary gesture that symbolically marries a German Jew to the tradition of the *Aufklärung*?

What can it mean for Arendt to transcribe these words, especially this curious phrase, "*deprived* of the ground of her origins"? As she makes clear in the Lessing Address, that ground—not literally the German nation from which she was "expelled" but the foundationalist tradition of German humanism—is something that she *refuses* to take up, not something of which she has been deprived and to which she yearns to be restored. In transcribing Jaspers's words, is she reflecting back to him what can only be *his* deprivation and *his* longing? Arendt does not need her connection to Blücher and Jaspers to return her to her German "origins," any more than she needs the Lessing Prize to do so; rather, Jaspers needs her to reunite him with the "Germany in its old glory" that is his past (*Correspondence* 19). Arendt's writing of Jaspers's letter is, then, not an act of "world"-travel but one of friendship, in the service not of partisanship, but of reconciliation. Arendt gives to this friend the reassurance (and deference) she withholds from the audience in Hamburg, and thereby respects a distinction that feminists continue to affirm and contest, that between public appearances and private life.

# Notes

1. Hannah Arendt, *Men in Dark Times* (New York: Harcourt Brace Jovanovich, 1968), 18; hereafter cited as *MDT*; my emphasis.

2. Hanna Pitkin, "Justice: On Relating Private and Public," *Political Theory* 9 (1981): 338.

3. Adrienne Rich, "Conditions for Work: The Common World of Women," in *On Lies, Secrets, and Silence* (New York: Norton, 1979), 212.

4. An exception from this time period is Nancy Hartsock, *Money, Sex, and Power* (Boston: Northeastern University Press, 1985).

5. Bonnie Honig, "Toward an Agonistic Feminism: Hannah Arendt and the Politics of Identity," in *Feminists Theorize the Political*, ed. Judith Butler and Joan W. Scott (New York: Routledge, 1992).

6. *Hannah Arendt–Karl Jaspers, Correspondence, 1926–1969*, ed. Lotte Kohler and Hans Saner, trans. Robert and Rita Kimber (New York: Harcourt Brace Jovanovich, 1992), 357; hereafter cited as *Correspondence*.

7. Sandra Harding, *The Science Question in Feminism* (Ithaca: Cornell University Press, 1986).

8. Cherríe Moraga and Gloria Anzaldúa, eds., *This Bridge Called My Back* (Latham, N.Y.: Kitchen Table, Women of Color Press, 1983).

9. Combahee River Collective, "The Combahee River Collective Statement," in *Home Girls: A Black Feminist Anthology*, ed. Barbara Smith (New York: Kitchen Table Press, 1983), 272.

10. Judith Butler, *Gender Trouble: Feminism and the Subversion of Identity* (New York: Routledge, 1990), 8.

11. Donna Haraway, "Situated Knowledges: The Science Question in Feminism and the Privilege of Partial Perspective," *Feminist Studies* 14 (1988): 580.

12. Norma Alarcón, "The Theoretical Subject(s) of *This Bridge Called My Back* and Anglo-American Feminism," in *Making Face, Making Soul/Haciendo Caras*, ed. Gloria Anzaldúa (San Francisco: Aunt Lute Foundation, 1990); Kirstie McClure, "On the Subject of Rights: Pluralism, Plurality and Political Identity," in *Dimensions of Radical Democracy*, ed. Chantal Mouffe (New York: Verso, 1992).

13. Judith Butler, *Bodies That Matter: On the Discursive Limits of "Sex"* (New York: Routledge, 1993).

14. Hannah Arendt, *The Human Condition* (Chicago: University of Chicago Press, 1958), 182; hereafter cited as *HC*.

15. Hannah Arendt, "A Reply [To Eric Voegelin's review of *Origins of Totalitarianism*]," *Review of Politics* 15 (1953): 81. Clearly, Arendt's interests are not the bargaining chips of liberal pluralism, in that they are defined not in terms of juridical language that can be recognized by the state, but with reference to a specific democratic public.

16. While liberal thinkers by no means rule out the task of coalition-building, the scope of its conception of inter-est is constrained by what Benjamin R. Barber calls its "minimalist disposition." *Strong Democracy: Participatory Politics for a New Age* (Berkeley and Los Angeles: University of California Press, 1984). For a discussion of the way that some feminists used empathy to carry inter-est to an opposite extreme, see Terry Winant, "The Feminist Standpoint: A Matter of Language," *Hypatia* 2, no. 1 (1987): 123–48.

17. Sander Gilman, *Jewish Self-Hatred* (Baltimore: Johns Hopkins University Press, 1986), 82.

18. Leonard Wessel, G. E. Lessing's Theology, A Reinterpretation: A Study in the Problematic Nature of the Enlightenment* (The Hague: Mouton, 1977), 80.

19. Hannah Arendt, "Social Science Techniques and the Study of Concentration Camps," *Jewish Social Studies* 12, no. 1 (1950): 49.

20. Hannah Arendt, *The Origins of Totalitarianism*, new ed. (New York: Harcourt Brace Jovanovich, 1975), ix; hereafter cited as OT.

21. Canovan offers a thorough textual explication of this difficult argument. *Hannah Arendt: A Reinterpretation of Her Political Thought* (New York: Cambridge University Press, 1992), chap. 2.

22. Honig discerns Arendt making a similar move in response to an attempt by Gershom Scholem to privilege Arendt's Jewish identity. Honig writes that in answer to Scholem, Arendt does not deny that identity but rather "never *says* what she *is*, she never identifies herself, affirmatively." "Toward an Agonistic Feminism," 229.

23. To invoke a very different vocabulary, Arendt's distinction between a voluntarist conception of identity and identity as a "political fact" parallels Michel Foucault's distinction between a linguistic system and a "positivity" or discursive regime. *The Archaeology of Knowledge*, trans. A. M. Sheridan Smith (New York: Pantheon, 1972), I, 1 and III, 5. Where he defines the former as a finite body of rules that may be infinitely manipulated for the purpose of self-expression, the latter is a historically specific field of contest among various positions that are delimited by institutionalized relations of exclusion and inclusion.

24. Donna Haraway, "A Manifesto for Cyborgs: Science, Technology, and Socialist Feminism in the 1980s," *Socialist Review* 80 (1985): 73.

25. Haraway, "Situated Knowledges," 597 n. 5, second emphasis added. In presenting Haraway's account of solidarity, I have joined her "Manifesto" with a later work in which she refines aspects of the earlier essay. Although I treat them here as if they were consistent with each other, the two essays actually give different answers to the problem of constructing political space. In "Manifesto," Haraway uses the language of "fusion" (93) which, as she acknowledges in the later essay, is more consistent with the ontological solidarity she purports to criticize than it is with the articulated solidarity she wants to recommend (585). It is in the later work that her answer to the problem of political space parallels that which Arendt makes in the Lessing Address.

26. María Lugones, "Playfulness, 'World'-Travel, and Loving Perception," in *Lesbian Philosophies and Cultures*, ed. Jeffner Allen (Albany: State University of New York Press, 1990), 178; my emphasis.

27. W. E. B. Du Bois, *The Souls of Black Folk* (New York: New American Library, 1982), 54.

28. It is curious that the concluding pages of Lugones's essay recommend "world"-travel as a means to an empathic understanding that makes us "fully subjects to each other" (178). Given Lugones's insistence on an interior plurality for which there is no underlying 'I,' it would seem that this self is never "fully" present to itself, let alone to another. No doubt it is an act of textual poaching to appropriate one part of this essay and not the other; as I read it, however, the break between them is as much Lugones's as it is mine.

29. María Lugones, "On the Logic of Pluralist Feminism," in *Feminist Ethics*, ed. Claudia Card (Lawrence: University Press of Kansas, 1991), 43.

30. Winant, "The Feminist Standpoint," 129.

31. Cherríe Moraga's essay "I Transfer and Go Underground" maps social asymmetry in terms of this contrast between discontinuous " 'world'-travel" and the privilege of journeying uninterrupted. In *This Bridge Called My Back*, xiii–xix.

32. Patricia Williams, *The Alchemy of Race and Rights* (Cambridge: Harvard University Press, 1991), 71.

33. Lugones, "On the Logic of Pluralist Feminism," 42.

34. Arendt, *On Revolution* (New York: Penguin, 1984), 106. For a more detailed discussion of the role of the mask in theater and in politics, see *On Revolution*, 106–7.

35. Arendt, *MDT* 5. This phrase, "after his own fashion," suggests the possibility of commitment simultaneous with critical distancing, which is precisely what Jaspers cannot appreciate in Arendt's posture toward the Lessing Prize. See below.

36. *MDT* 5. This is something of a contentious remark, given that Germany can claim as its "son" the author of the *Critique* that Ernst Cassirer has claimed "overshadows the Enlightenment even while it represents its final glorification." *The Philosophy of the Enlightenment,* trans. Fritz C. A. Koellin and James P. Pettegrove (Princeton: Princeton University Press, 1951), 274. But it seems that this is precisely Arendt's point: the legacy that makes it so difficult for "the Germans" to understand criticism is Kantian moral philosophy, which makes it hard for them "to grasp that justice has little to do with objectivity in the ordinary sense." Arendt, *MDT* 5.

37. Allison offers a proto-Kantian reading of Lessing's work, arguing that his distinctive contribution to theology consists in separating the truth of a religion from either the rational consistency of its doctrines or the basis in fact of its stories, and premising it instead on the extent to which it promotes tolerance and autonomy. Henry Allison, *Lessing and the Enlightenment* (Ann Arbor: University of Michigan Press, 1966). Cassirer reads Lessing as a proto-Hegelian, claiming that in his work "the historical is no longer opposed to the rational; it is rather the way to the realization of the rational and the real, indeed the only possible place of its fulfillment." Cassirer, *Philosophy of the Enlightenment,* 194. See Wessel for a critique of Cassirer's reading (G. E. *Lessing's Theology,* 80, 92–94).

38. Arendt's portrait of Lessing as a man who put disputation ahead of reason is not unlike that of his friend and contemporary Moses Mendelssohn, who once wrote that "Mental Gymnastic [is for Lessing] more important than the pure truth"; Wessel, G. E. *Lessing's Theology,* 101, citing Moses Mendelssohn, *Gesammelte Schriften,* 5:698. Of course, Mendelssohn suggests that Lessing belongs in a different—and perhaps lesser—category of great thinkers, because he responded to the problems of philosophy and theology not as a scholar but as a polemicist.

39. Arendt, *MDT* 8. This is an idiom that would probably correspond most closely to the expression "food for thought," but is more expressive if construed more literally as "yeasts" of inquiry or disputation.

40. Wessel, G. E. *Lessing's Theology,* 143.

41. Hannah Arendt, "Understanding and Politics," *Partisan Review* 20 (1953): 382.

42. In a 1964 television interview, Arendt explained that the "shock" of Nazism to her and other German Jews in 1933 was not "Hitler's seizing power," but the fact that religious and secular intellectuals cooperated with him without being coerced to do so. In Elisabeth Young-Bruehl, *Hannah Arendt: For Love of the World* (New Haven: Yale University Press, 1982), 108.

43. Arendt is not entirely serious when she accuses Kant of dogmatism and inhumanity. She argues elsewhere that Kant's moral philosophy is not fundamentally wrong, but simply contradictory due to a "self-misunderstanding in Kant" that prompted him to formulate the principle of autonomy as an "imperative, instead of defining it as a proposition." ("Some Questions of Moral Philosophy," lecture notes for a seminar at the New School, Library of Congress, container 45.) For further discussion of Arendt's critique of the imperative to self-mastery in Kant, see Bonnie Honig, "Arendt, Identity, and Difference," *Political Theory* 16, no. 1 (1988): 77–98.

44. The scene in the film *Schindler's List* where the German Schindler and his Jewish bookkeeper Stern share their first drink together might also demonstrate this "simple" principle. Though the scene could be read as a gesture of gratitude by Stern toward his benefactor, I suggest instead that it is simultaneously a recognition of shared complicity and undeniable difference. Stern has refused the drink with Schindler up to that point because

the German has tried to claim a commonality with the Polish Jew as a fellow businessman; in this scene, however, Schindler has finally acknowledged his participation with Stern in systematic criminal resistance against the Nazi regime. He has also recognized that he will survive the war and Stern almost assuredly will not. Regardless of its accuracy in fact, the scene dramatizes the truth of Arendt's claim. The Jew can accept the German as an ally only when the German will both recognize the Jew as an enemy of the Reich, and acknowledge the ambiguity of his own position as a criminal—not only in the eyes of the Reich but also in those of the Jew.

45. Although it may seem that her story of the German and the Jew proclaims the efficacy of asserting truth (friendship) in the face of power (Nazi racism), the key to the story is that the hypothetical friends position themselves in terms of political fact. Further, the rhetorical force of this example does not depend on its truth—on Arendt's knowing of friends who asked themselves her question about humanity—but on its enabling her audience to travel.

46. I disagree on this point with Margaret Canovan who, in her very insightful essay about the Lessing Address, characterizes Arendt's conception of political friendship as "a cool, reflective, impartial concern for 'the dignity of man.'" Canovan, "Friendship, Truth, and Politics: Hannah Arendt and Toleration," in *Justifying Toleration: Conceptual and Historical Perspectives*, ed. Susan Mendes (Cambridge: Cambridge University Press, 1988), 193.

47. For a discussion of an instance of a similar dynamic between these two thinkers with respect to the priority of German to Jewish identity in Arendt's biography of Rahel Varnhagen, see Dagmar Barnouw, *Visible Spaces: Hannah Arendt and the German-Jewish Experience* (Baltimore: Johns Hopkins University Press, 1990), chap. 2.

# 13

## In the Presence of Others: Arendt and Anzaldúa on the Paradox of Public Appearance

### Susan Bickford

"Identity" has played a central role in contemporary feminist thought, one best known by the credo "the personal is political." In this feminist account, identity acts as a conceptual link between the public and the personal; it is the lens that reconfigures both by showing how public power permeates intimate relations and our sense of self. Redescribing and revaluing a particular sense of self (in the words of Michelle Cliff, "claiming an identity they taught me to despise") has been an emancipatory exercise for feminists. Such a claim is "an act of resistance," as bell hooks has said, against "processes of domination."[1]

More recently, hooks and others have begun to question the role of identity in politics, or rather the extent to which (they argue) concerns with identity have overshadowed expressly political activities.[2] Shane

Phelan, for example, explores the antipolitical implications of a focus on identity by tracing the development of lesbian feminist political consciousness. In the context of lesbian feminism, the stress on identity was of political value because it provided a means to articulate new conceptions of oppression and power. But the insights possible through recognizing the political significance of personal identity were soon distorted, Phelan argues, as lesbian feminists blurred any distinction between the personal and the political, between self and politics. One's political opinions were taken to be defined by one's identity, which was in turn defined by desire. Speaking was not the practice of deliberation, but rather an act of "empowered truth" by an authentic, essential lesbian self. The kind of political community based on this understanding of self has no room for differences; differences of opinion cannot even be conceptualized.[3]

An alternative approach, Phelan suggests, is not to ignore identity but to relate it to politics in a somehow different way: "Identity politics does mean building our public action on who we are and how that identity fits into and does not fit into our society. . . . Politics that ignores our identities, that makes them 'private,' is useless, but non-negotiable identities will enslave us whether they are imposed from within or without."[4] hooks comes to a similar conclusion in her critique of identity politics. The danger is not in focusing on identity per se, but in regarding it as static, and neglecting to link it explicitly to political action.[5]  We cannot collapse politics and identity and thereby avoid examining and discussing as political questions their relation to one another. But hooks's and Phelan's reconceptualization of identity raises the question of the character of the link: What does a politics that neither ignores nor imposes identity look like?

This is a question, I think, about the meaning of identity as a public phenomenon. There are two issues central to such a consideration. The first has to do with the dual-edged role that identity plays in feminist political thinking. "Identity" is part of a debate about difference, about the meaning and consequences of differences among women as members of social groups delineated not only by gender, but by race, sexuality, class, and ethnicity as well. But this very focus on difference makes it necessary to wrestle with the issue of sameness as well—what precisely it means to belong to a particular social group, what shared characteristics identify one as a member of that group, and what the political significance of those characteristics are. These issues of identity/difference/

sameness create specifically political problems regarding who we are, who we can join with as political actors—and how.

The second issue involved in thinking about identity as a public phenomenon has to do with figuring out what is behind that "how." The connection between who I am and how I can be with others hinges on *responsiveness*, on the attention we give to one another. Feminists have analyzed the ways in which attention is systematically distorted in an inegalitarian society. But we have thought less (or less clearly) about the more difficult question of what emancipatory relations of expression and attention involve. Yet these relations are central to politics; even the liberating action of "claiming an identity" is always an interaction. The very expression of my identity inevitably relies on the receptive presence of others from whom I may differ, and whose attention I cannot strictly govern.

In order to examine the complex and attentive links between politics and identity, I bring together an unlikely set of interlocutors: Hannah Arendt, and contemporary feminist theorists of race, class, gender, and sexuality. Both identity and the attention of others play a central role in Arendt's political thought. Her analysis of the characteristics and conditions of political identity lead her to an understanding of politics in which subjectivity and intersubjectivity—our sense of self and the presence and responsiveness of others—are profoundly yet paradoxically enmeshed with one another. Feminist analysis gives a different cast to this understanding, by redescribing the conditions of politics. Gloria Anzaldúa and the other feminist writers I draw upon argue that both "self" and "others" are socially grounded and grouped in ways that have consequences for public identities. Yet their analysis of these consequences overlaps significantly with Arendt's understanding of identity, for they share an understanding of identity as always active—and interactive.[6] By reading Arendt and these feminists together, and probing the tensions and overlaps between them, we can come to recognize the implications for feminist politics of what I will call "the paradox of public appearance": our urge to appear in public as particular and mobile identities and the fact that such appearance depends upon the attention of others who will judge for themselves.

Let me begin by noting that the juxtaposition of difference and sameness that characterizes feminist discussion of "identity" also characterizes Arendt's conception of plurality. Plurality links politics and identity, and suggests that both are intertwined with attention.

Arendtian plurality has two characteristics: equality and distinctiveness. It is our distinctiveness that impels us into politics, Arendt says,
not our desire to escape a state of nature, say, or to satisfy certain shared
needs. Humans come to politics as more than merely needful creatures,
and cannot be reduced to these common needs, for each of us is distinct
"from any other who is, was, or will be."[7] Here Arendt is not referring
to sheer bodily existence; rather, plurality means that who we are is
unique. If humans did not have this quality of uniqueness, we would not
need speech nor a space in which to speak to one another: "signs and
sounds to communicate immediate, identical needs would be enough"
(HC 175–76).

Here is where equality, the second characteristic of plurality, comes
in. The paradox of plurality lies in the fact that each human being is a
unique "who," yet every human being shares equally this quality of
uniqueness. The tension here is not between "levels of existence";
Arendt is not pointing to the fact that we are all the same on some
material or physiological level, and yet on another level we are all
different. Rather, human plurality means that we are both undeniably
distinctive, and inescapably more-than-one. In Arendt's words, "we are
all the same, that is, human, in such a way that nobody is ever the same
as anyone else who ever lived, lives, or will live."[8]

Plurality is not an essential equality for Arendt, but an existential
one: it comes from the fact that we exist in the world in the presence of
others. It is a central condition of human existence, but it is also fragile;
it can disappear under conditions of tyranny, mass society, or any time
the public realm is supplanted or destroyed (HC 40–41, 58).

What kind of uniqueness, what kind of identity is it that is so crucial
yet so circumstantial? What is the content and meaning of the plural,
unique "whos" that we reveal in action and speech? The "who" that is
our unique self cannot be described, Arendt cautions: "the moment we
want to say who somebody is, our very vocabulary leads us astray into
saying what he is; we get entangled in a description of qualities he
necessarily shares with others like him . . . with the result that his
specific uniqueness escapes us" (HC 181; emphasis in original). My
"who-ness"—my identity—is not captured by the qualities I possess, the
interests I have, or the sociological categories I belong to. These are all
characteristic of others, too, and so they do not help locate or point to
the unique identity that is "me." My unique self is not something like

personality, or inner self, either.[9] The "who" is a public identity, not an intimate one, and only appears by speaking and acting in public.[10]

To try to get a fix on this "who"—to try to figure out what political identity is for Arendt—let us look at what Arendt thinks we are doing when we speak in public. *Opinions* are the content of speech in the public realm; my opinions—how "it seems to me"—are a central part of my unique identity. Unlike interests or personality traits, opinions belong "exclusively to individuals," and "there are few things by which men are so profoundly distinguished from each other as by these" (*OR* 227; *BPF* 247). Opinions are "inspired by different interests and passions" and grounded in fact, yet opinions about the same facts can "differ widely" (*BPF* 238). Differing opinions or judgments about the world are always characteristic of "men in the plural," as unanimity of opinion is characteristic of mass society and tyranny.[11]

But it is not just a string of disconnected opinions that can be said to be "me." Rather, this speech-as-action, or any other action, discloses me insofar as they are part of my "unique life story." It is precisely stories, "the result of action and speech" that "reveal an agent" (*HC* 184). This emphasis on the story that derives from speech and action seems to indicate that my identity arises not simply from what I say or do, but also from the circumstances in which I do it, and the history of what I have done. That I act, and say particular things in specific situations in response to particular issues, shows me to be a certain who, a certain public self—or rather becomes part of the story through which my identity takes shape.

Implicit in this account of identity, with its stress on appearance, is the need for a particular kind of attention on the part of others. Arendt does not say that by listing "what" someone is, we simply have not addressed the question of "who" he is. Rather, focusing on the "what," the qualities shared with others, "entangles" us and "leads us astray." So it is not merely that who-ness cannot be put into "unequivocal verbal expression," but that such attempts misdirect our attention, actively distract us from who-ness. It is for this reason that Arendt sees positive possibilities for public identity in the device of "the mask." She invokes the Latin *persona*, which originally "signified the mask ancient actors used to wear in a play . . . it had to hide, or rather to replace, the actor's own face and countenance, but in a way that would make it possible for the voice to sound through." The public persona of legal equality both conceals politically irrelevant qualities, and enables our voices to be publicly heard (OR 106–7). The mask does not itself constitute our public identity; it is rather a device that permits the appearance of a "who" whose interlocutors are not misled by "what."

Some feminist writers have used the metaphor of "the mask" not to solve this problem of public appearance but to describe it. The problem again is not the characteristics themselves, but the kind of attention paid to them. Feminists have examined the way in which social forces like racism, sexism, class discrimination, and heterosexism influence who gets paid attention to, what gets heard, and how. What we say is often filtered through the screen of our visible self; as speakers we are also white women, black women and men, well-dressed professionals, persons with disabilities, etc. And the way we look and sound may animate socially constructed stereotypes. Assumptions are made, based on how I look or speak, about who I am and what I have to say, about my opinions, concerns, interests, character.[12]

What prevents the appearance of some as citizens in the public realm is not their literal absence from the scene, but rather the imposed "masks" that present a false face and prevent what the mask covers from being visible and audible.[13] The effect of these masks (unlike the Arendtian one) is to blur and muffle individuality, rather than let it sound through. Stereotypes, by focusing on qualities of "what-ness," avoid another's personhood, "denying them their variousness and complexity," their equality and individuality.[14] If my membership in a group is the only lens through which I am perceived, then I cannot appear as a person with a unique story and singular opinions. Human plurality is blocked by assumptions that I am simply a representation of others who look and sound like me.[15]

Politically speaking, then, it matters quite a lot how others regard us, despite the tendency of some writers to treat such concerns as somehow whiny, exhibiting *ressentiment* or a compulsion toward "group self-assertion."[16] Appearance is the only ground of human reality, for Arendt; to be deprived of the possibility of appearance before others is "to be deprived of reality, which humanly and politically speaking, is the same as appearance. To men the reality of the world is guaranteed by the presence of others, by its appearing to all."[17] We depend upon the perceptions of others for the only quality of realness the world has. (This is evident in our ordinary language, as we ask one another "Do you see that?" or "Did you hear that noise, too?" or "Did you think she seemed more subdued than usual?") To make my presence as a distinctive individual felt in the world requires not the mere existence of others, but their active attention.

Many feminists would agree with Arendt here: how we are perceived affects how we can appear in public, and being perceived simply as a member of a social group obscures our distinctiveness, obscures who (in a richer sense than that captured by sociological categories) we are. At first it might seem that the type of attention that would overcome the problem of stereotyping is one that perceives others as simply, equally human and individual in a way that disregards group identity. This is the Arendtian answer (since group identity is a characteristic we share with others, part of what rather than who we are). The Arendtian mask of the public persona is supposed to obscure this group identity by creating a persona that we all share, yet that allows our own voice to sound through. The mask operates as a neutralizing device, perceptually dispersing certain kinds of sameness and equalizing certain kinds of difference.

From a feminist perspective, however, we might point out that such a mask is inevitably constructed in particular ways, by particular hands, and with particular faces, voices, and bodies in mind. Its earpieces might amplify certain kinds of voices, its eyeholes might be composed of materials that filter perception in non-neutral ways. To accept the mask as equalizing sidesteps the question of whether it is possible to have a "universal" conception of citizen identity, whether there is some discernable quality that we all share as citizens for which the mask could be a metaphor. Feminists have argued that men are in fact the implicit norm of conceptions of the abstract individual; men's viewpoint and experience have been considered "universal," while women are clearly marked as a group that does not meet universal criteria.[18] Similarly, as feminists of color and their allies point out, many white feminists have regarded their experience as "women's experience," rather than specifically white women's experience.[19] In an inegalitarian society where race, class, gender, and sexuality are relevant categories, not being seen—or not seeing oneself—as a member of a group is a marker of power and privilege. Just as part of oppression is only being able to appear as a stereotype of one's group identity, part of privilege is being able to ignore that identity. This "privilege" is not simply a matter of a socially influenced perceptual style; rather, as Martha Minow has so effectively shown, it comes from the fact that the world is built up with particular unstated norms in mind that make specific structures and arrangements seem "natural."[20]

Arendt does not tell us much about how her mask works, and feminists might wonder whether one designed to cover up our qualities of what-ness would actually serve equalizing purposes. *What* we are would still affect *who* we are because the mask that facilitates political appearance is inevitably constructed with only certain "whats" in mind—and in a way that makes it possible for them to ignore their particularity. But it is not just the impossibility of a genuinely equalizing mask that leads feminists to be suspicious of universal citizen identities, ones built on ignoring "what." To argue that who we are and how we attend to each other as citizens should somehow disregard social identities is to overlook that the connection between what we are and who we are can be an empowering one. Our group identities may subject us to stereotyped attention, but they are often also where we "draw our strength to live and our reasons for acting."[21] Our color, ethnicity, gender, class, or religion may be a constitutive part of our public identity because they are the contexts in which we learned to speak and think the languages that shape us and enable us to give voice to our unique selves. And it is within particular social groups that we first are paid attention to, and learn to attend to others—the very capacities necessary for an Arendtian politics.

Perhaps surprisingly, this point can be underscored by a closer analysis of Arendt's conception of identity. For her, the very thing that is central to our individuality—our opinions—itself requires the presence of oth-ers. Opinions are not simply gut preferences; they are judgments arrived at by a particular thinking process. "No one is capable of forming his own opinion without the benefit of a multitude of opinions held by others" for "opinions are formed and tested in a process of exchange of opinion against opinion" (OR 225 and 227, also 247). Our opinions are affected by the others and by their "possible judgments": "the thinking process which is active in judging something . . . finds itself always and primarily, even if I am quite alone in making up my mind, in an anticipated communication with others with whom I know I must finally come to some agreement" (BPF 220). Publicity, or communicability, are the conditions for opinion-formation; Arendt refers to this as thinking "with an enlarged mentality" or representative thinking.[22]

Such thinking is not, Arendt insists, a question "of empathy, as though I tried to be or to feel like somebody else." Plurality makes such empathy impossible, or at least presumptuous. Human uniqueness prevents me from being or feeling just like someone else, or knowing by myself exactly how they think. Rather, forming opinions through representative thinking is a matter of "being and thinking in my own identity where actually I am not" (*BPF* 241). But what can it mean to "be and think *in my own identity* where actually *I* am not"? This "exertion of imagination" requires "liberation from one's own private interests."[23] When I put myself into another's place, it is actually some modified version of myself, for I leave my worldly interests behind. The "I" that is left behind must be something like "me-in-terms-of-my-interests." But Arendt clearly does not believe that representative thinking requires selflessness, or a total stilling of one's own concerns, for such thinking is not empathy or taking on another's feelings: "my own identity" is still central. What's left about myself—"my own identity"—that I bring along to another's place must be the "me" that is not determined by my interests, me insofar as I am a unique and opinionated human. It is important to notice that both terms—both "me's"—are preserved in representative thinking. So although my traveling self may be "liberated" from private interests, those interests are still present as a sort of comparative self; in other words, there is still a connection, or perhaps a communication, between the "I" left behind and "my own identity" that goes traveling.

The model we have for understanding this comes from Arendt's understanding of the duality of the thinking ego (*LM* 181–91). For Arendt, the thinking consciousness is always "two-in-one"; thinking is a "dialogue . . . between me and myself." It is precisely "this *duality* of myself with myself that makes thinking a true activity, in which I am both the one who asks and the one who answers" (*LM* 185; emphasis in original). The recognition that as a thinking self we are more than one makes it possible for us to be divided in thought without erasing ourselves and others through attempted empathy. In representative thinking, just one of the partners in the dialogue assumes the standpoints of others. We do not exactly leave ourselves behind; rather, we position ourselves differently in order to do justice to the presence of others, not in a way that assumes identity, but in a way that gives voice to difference. We mimic, through the activity of thinking as a dialogue, the conditions of communication among plural beings, which is to say that we think as individuals in something like a public space.

As I travel to different "locations" in the world, then, it is still always *me* that is traveling. I am imagining that I have someone else's place in the world, which does not tell me how they think or feel, but "how I would feel and think if I were in their place."[24] There is no automatic answer that comes from this process; the tension between thinking in my own place and thinking with an enlarged mentality is never simply or neatly resolved. At the end of my travels, I still have to judge. And in judging, as Arendt so strikingly puts it, one "tells one's *choices* and one chooses one's company."[25] In making those judgments, the story of who I am unfolds. But this is not to say that the "I" of judging and the "who" of action are the same. Through my imaginative travels, I make the choices that momentarily bring the two-in-one together; I say who I think I am by making those judgments. But I express them in a context of plurality: my public appearance ("who" I am) depends on the attention paid by those differently located others with whom I share public space.

Acknowledging the presence of differently located others is essential for making the judgments and forming the opinions that shape and disclose my unique individuality. Human plurality conditions us in the sense that our very individuality only takes shape through our recognition that we share the world with others (otherwise there would be no impetus to travel, and no need). Notice here that Arendt's metaphor changes, from "the mask" to traveling and location. These specifically spatial metaphors are more generally characteristic of her writing; the mask metaphor is most prominent in *On Revolution,* and even there Arendt moves from criticizing the French revolutionaries' understanding of "the mask" to celebrating the American concern with constituting a public "space." She shifts from a device for individuals to a place that is constituted by more-than-one. If we take seriously the spatial metaphor, though, then we also have to consider the role of *distance* in making judgments. Some locations will be closer, and we may be more familiar with what things look like from there; other locations may be farther away, or somehow involve greater effort of imagination. Some places we may not know the way to. In other words, where we come from has an effect on how we see our destination, and on what we think when we get there. It is not simply the human condition of plurality that conditions "who" we are, but also the diverse social conditions— locations—in which we live.

Feminist analysts of race, class, gender, and sexuality point out that the way in which "location" conditions us is neither simple nor predictable. They contend that once our public self is understood to include our location in particular social conditions, what immediately complicates the question of identity is not simply individual distinctiveness but the fact of multiple locations. Thus they question a link between identity and politics that relies on either the singularity of identity or the unity of political community, for such conceptions cannot do justice to the complex selves that we are. As Anzaldúa writes:

> "Your allegiance is to La Raza, the Chicano movement," say the members of my race. "Your allegiance is to the Third World," say my Black and Asian friends. "Your allegiance is to your gender, to women," say the feminists. Then there's my allegiance to the Gay movement, to the socialist revolution, to the New Age, to magic and the occult. . . . They would chop me up into little fragments and tag each piece with a label.[26]

Anzaldúa's response to this fragmenting competition is not to accept the implied contradictions, but rather to assert the connections: "only your labels split me." Moraga agrees: "what is my responsibility to my roots—both white and brown, Spanish-speaking and English? I am a woman with a foot in both worlds; and I refuse the split." And Lugones insists, "we want to be seen unbroken, we want to break cracked mirrors that show us in many separate *unconnected* fragments."[27]

The challenge that multiple identities present is not answered by a proliferation of ever more narrowly defined locations, and there is more going on here than the embrace of "fractured identities," as Harding would have it.[28] These writers in fact "refuse the split": they insist that political identity is not captured simply by a comprehensive listing of "what" we are, *and* they maintain that "what" we are is central to our political identity. In so doing, they articulate a new understanding of the relationship between identity and politics. This insistence on the multiplicity of identity, with its concomitant refusal of fragmentation, provides an important alternative for thinking about the distinctive self-as-citizen, one that challenges neat "categories of marginality," and that takes into account the fact that our itineraries are constructed (to quote Arendt against herself) "not on the moon, but in the midst of human society."[29]

This alternative first begins to take shape in the recognition that the political importance of a multiple-voiced consciousness, a plural self, is that it allows perception from a variety of perspectives.[30] For example, Anzaldúa's *la mestiza* occupies opposing locations; her multiple identities do not peacefully coexist: "*la mestiza* undergoes a struggle of flesh, a struggle of borders, an inner war. Like all people, we perceive the version of reality that our culture communicates. Like others having or living in more than one culture, we get multiple, often opposing messages. The coming together of two self-consistent but habitually incompatible frames of reference causes *un choque,* a cultural collision."[31] Existing as a plural self is not necessarily a matter of "celebrating" differences; it is a struggle among competing perspectives within oneself (as well as among groups competing for one's loyalties). One result of this struggle can be what Anzaldúa calls a "counterstance," simple mirror-image defiance of "the dominant culture's views and beliefs." Although a counterstance can be liberating, it is limited; it is constrained by and "dependent on what it is reacting against." Moving beyond that step means deciding "to act and not to react." Action creates an "assembly," but not one

> where separated pieces merely come together. Nor is it a balancing of opposing powers. In attempting to work out a synthesis, the self has added a third element which is greater than the sum of its severed parts. That third element is a new consciousness—a mestiza consciousness—and though it is a source of intense pain, its energy comes from continual creative motion that keeps breaking down the unitary aspect of each new paradigm.[32]

*La mestiza* is a creative agent; the necessity of "switching modes" is transformed into an emancipatory capacity to shift perspectives. As in Arendt's representative thinking, the result is not a blending of views, nor a taking on of any particular view, but the creation of a new view. "Refusing the split" means creating from one's multiple loyalties a (nonfragmented but not complacent) public self with a new consciousness, a new view, a new opinion. The emphasis on struggle and work indicates that this kind of self is always active. Such activity requires courage: courage to be open to the possibilities of contradiction and conflict within oneself, to hear different voices and see from different vantage points, and to move beyond shared vantage points to make a judgment. This "moving beyond" does not make social identities irrelevant, any more than settling on an Arendtian judgment makes the presence of others irrelevant. Our social identities point us toward the possibility of traveling, provide the fuel for the creative motion, and cause us to think about the materials and activities, the desires and demands, out of which identity is created.[33]

Like Arendt's representative thinking, this shifting of perspectives seems mostly about internal opinion-formation; but it is accompanied by a political need to listen to those whose vantage points we do not share. There is an implicit move in Anzaldúa's work, from subjective to intersubjective creative action. She switches from a personification—*la mestiza*—to an activity: making faces. In this later work, identity is something created, constructed in the presence of others, and largely through words (speech and writing).

"Making faces" is Anzaldúa's "metaphor for constructing one's identity." These faces are different from the masks "others have imposed on us," for such masks keep us fragmented: "After years of wearing masks we may become just a series of roles, the constellated self limping along with its broken limbs." Breaking through these masks is not, for Anzaldúa, a matter of revealing one's true inner nature, an essential self; rather we "*remake* anew both inner and outer faces."[34] Identity is then a matter of active re-creation, which happens through speech and action: "According to the ancient *nahuas*, one was put on earth to create one's 'face' (body) and 'heart' (soul). To them, the soul was a speaker of words and the body a doer of deeds. Soul and body, words and actions are embodied in Moyocoyani, one of the names of the Creator in the Aztec framework."[35] Speech and action here are entwined with embodiedness and embeddedness, not simply as constraints or necessary conditions, but as the materials with which we create, and out of which we are created. Anzaldúa stresses the conscious making of identity, but such consciousness is not separate from the physical and social realities of our lives. We have the capacity to create a public identity that is more than just a string of labels, without ignoring the relevance to our lives of the groups those labels name.

This depiction of identity is suggestive not simply because of its stress on active construction, but also because of what it constructs. A face is an outward appearance ("the world knows us by our faces").[36] We cannot see our own face, except in a mirror. A face is oriented toward others. Thus, identity is not merely an internal affair. "Face" stresses intersubjectivity. The "face" metaphor admits of a conscious expressiveness (I can to some extent compose my face to reflect or conceal what I want) but also an inescapable concreteness (my face is physically my

326 Feminist Interpretations of Hannah Arendt

face, its color, shape, its moles and markings and features undeniably mine.)[37] It brings together—rather than regarding as contradictory—our embeddedness in the socially constructed givens of our existence and our capacity to present ourselves self-consciously in a way that engages but does not simply reflect those givens.

This conception of identity—as actively created through being present in public—takes seriously the political significance of the connection between "what" and "who" we are; it obscures neither our distinctiveness, nor our location in the world. As a political actor, I do not require a mask that conceals these givens; I require from others an attentiveness to what I do with them, a listening and a looking flexible enough to perceive my activity.

It was precisely when such attentiveness was not forthcoming that Arendt herself was willing to pay attention to social identities; indeed, under certain conditions she insisted upon it. Such attention can be justified on Arendtian grounds by noting that the forces that create and give particular meaning to different social groups have real worldly effects. Treating group identities as politically relevant is necessary to confront those effects, yet such treatment does not necessarily obscure human distinctiveness. Arendt herself felt the reality of her Jewishness: "for many years I considered the only adequate reply to the question, Who are you? to be: a Jew." If attacked as a Jew, Arendt argued, one must respond in that identity, as a Jew; not to do so would be "nothing but a grotesque and dangerous evasion of reality" (MDT 17–18; see also JaP 121). By "a Jew" she did not mean "a special kind of human being" but was rather indicating a "political fact" (MDT 17–23). And responding "in terms of the identity that is under attack" means challenging interpretations of that fact, not denying its worldly reality.[38]

Although she defended a conception of the world in which there were firm distinctions between what should be private and what public, Arendt recognized that worldly conditions may require actions that are perverse in those terms; the political importance of social identities may vary with the conditions under which one lives. Speaking as "a Jew" was a necessity brought about by the existence of totalitarian regimes who used social identities to determine not only who could be citizens, but who could live as humans on the earth. Under such conditions, Arendt could only resist "in terms of the identity under attack." Not surprisingly, she could only regard the necessity of such resistance with something like regret.

It is at this point of Arendtian regret that feminists resolutely forge ahead. If public identity is a response to worldly conditions and worldly necessities, then there is no transhistorical attitude toward identity and politics that is appropriate or emancipating at all times. Feminist writers contend that what counts and has counted as "public" is itself not neutral, and that no constructions of the public and the private are natural or given. What is emancipating in terms of these particular worldly conditions and political problems is part of what we as feminist political actors have to argue about. In our world, social identity is a political fact even if often a hidden one; one way to "resist in terms of the identity that is under attack" is by insisting on its publicness, and using that publicness to redefine the terms of identity: to make faces.

That resistance, however, can also carry with it a certain kind of regret. Part of these feminists' project is to point to the oppressive worldly effects of the kind of perception distorted by racism and other forms of "arrogance," and to articulate the possibility of an emancipatory appearance in the world.[39] And in the work of Anzaldúa, Lugones, Jordan, and others, there is the recognition that we rely on others' perceptions in order to appear at all. In Lugones's words, "I am incomplete and unreal without other women . . . we are fully dependent on each other for the possibility of being understood without which we are not intelligible, we do not make sense, we are not solid, visible, integrated; we are lacking."[40] Knowing that I need a certain kind of regard from you to appear in the world influences my own actions; the need to be listened to leads us to think about how to speak, and which "voice" to choose.[41] The continual need to make such choices can prompt impatience or reluctance. As a feminist actor, it is tempting for me to see the struggle against being erased or distorted as a struggle to appear in some unmediated sense, a struggle to appear politically as who I think I am, to be heard as who I want to be.

It is not surprising to sense this in feminist thought; we have a pressing political need to appear in ways that are not stereotypical, that allow us to speak as political subjects in diverse ways and from diverse locations. This need to challenge unjust ways of seeing can lead to a kind of frustration with the opacity and distance that are not necessarily results of oppression but rather the inevitable accompaniments of plurality. Even if through conscious effort we try to overcome the effect of structures that distort some voices and subordinate some ways of speaking, it is not simply a matter of providing a polite silence in which everyone's voice can sound without generating any response.[42] Political actors have to engage with each other, challenge, question, argue. The responsiveness of others is central to public appearance and political action, but those others are creative distinctive selves as well. The "who" that is formed by the story of my public actions and judgments is not necessarily the heroine of the story I would write, precisely because others' reactions to me are themselves *actions*, unpredictable and novel (*HC* 190). This is the paradox of public appearance: our very appearance as an active unique who relies on the attention of active others whose perceptions we do not control. We cannot simply demand to be a particular public "who," to be heard in a particular way. Arendt's crucial reminder is that communicating with each other in the realm of citizenship is still struggle, is still action; as such it is as unpredictable and uncontrollable as the other citizens with whom we necessarily engage.

There is a difference between being stereotyped or being otherwise not-heard (a kind of attention that is antipolitical) and being heard differently than we want to be. *The latter is an inevitable political possibility.* But there are no neat ways to mark the difference or to identify what lies between distortion on one hand and an impossible empathic transparency on the other. And this is why political interaction can be so difficult, so frustrating, so demanding—particularly in a context of inequality. The feminists I discuss here address the issue of stereotyping by exploring an active, creative understanding of public identity, but they do not address the inevitable uncertainty of political communication. We as feminist thinkers have yet to consider what this uncertainty means for egalitarian political interaction, and what active, flexible political attention involves.

The Arendtian language of plurality may be more helpful in thinking this through than the language of identity; plurality reminds us that both subjectivity (my sense of myself as uniquely opinionated and diversely located) and intersubjectivity (how we interact and take action together) are crucial in politics. The paradox of plurality points precisely to the tension between the two. Some democrats (e.g., Benjamin Barber) resolve the tension by shifting the political terms wholly to the intersubjective, arguing that democratic identity is not about who I am and what I think, but about who we are and what we do.[43] But for Arendt, politics requires that we maintain the tension between subjectivity and intersubjectivity; plurality disappears when it is wholly resolved either in favor of the "I" (a lack of public imagination, a sort of solipsism that does not take others into account or is overly concerned with merely private ends) or the "we" (as in a "mass society" that unthinkingly shares a unanimous opinion). To be fair, a mass society is certainly not the kind of "we" Barber has in mind. But neither does he confront the problems inherent in a democratic practice where the larger community morally trumps individual or subgroup concerns—problems with which feminists are quite concerned.[44]

Although the concern with oppression has led us to focus on subjectivity, feminists have begun to confront the necessary political tension between subjectivity and intersubjectivity. Groups based on identity have in recent decades been building up a place in the world by creating bookstores, presses, coffeehouses, record labels, cultural centers, shelters, newspapers, and cooperative businesses and residences. These places, and the political groups that are rooted in them, can act as political "homes," to use Bernice Johnson Reagon's terminology. They can provide important and empowering contexts where we feel we can appear as most ourselves. However, as Reagon points out, the hominess of such groups often turns out to be based on exclusion, or a false sense of sameness. Our multiplicity and distinctiveness as individuals means there are differences even within groups that are seen (from within or without) as homogeneous.[45]

This recognition of multiplicity within groups as well as within individuals has pointed feminists to the need for a second model of togetherness. Established social groups do not exhaust the possibilities of human togetherness; it is not simply individual identities that are created, rather than given, but those of political groups as well. If our group membership does not automatically produce a particular political opinion, then our politics need not be defined by lines that we had no hand in drawing. Moraga says "I would grow despairing if I believed . . . we were unilaterally defined by color and class." Anzaldúa agrees: we cannot let "color class and gender separate us from those who would be kindred spirits."[46] Political collectivities are created, and created in ways that do not necessarily accord with existing groups, or with fully shared experiences. This insight has led to critiques of "sisterhood" as a model for feminist solidarity, and an increasing emphasis in feminist theory and practice on alliances and coalitions.[47] These specifically political groups are created through a conscious decision to ally with others with whom we share political commitments or interests or simply through the recognition that we share a world.

This reasoning recalls Arendt's understanding of the generativity of action. Here, however, it is not only individual identities that are created through political action, but new group identities as well. The creation of alliances contests established lines of difference and sameness, allowing us both to claim and transfigure given identities: to resist in terms of the identity that is under attack and to challenge those terms by creating new political confederations. Coalitions might be the model for a particular kind of political togetherness, one that is not based on established group identity but not dismissive of it either. But what sort of responsiveness to one another might make the creation of such alliances possible and emancipatory, in the face of the paradox of public appearance?

Perhaps Arendt, with her emphasis on plurality and spatiality, can provide some useful theoretical resources here. Let me conclude by discussing one example. The possibility of alliances is often a source of exuberance and hope in feminist writing, yet all who stress its importance attest to the difficulty and pain involved. As Reagon points out, a coalition is not necessarily safe, comfortable, or nurturing; it can be threatening to our sense of self and community. Molina talks of *el miedo*, the constant fear "of exploring, of exposing ourselves, of daring to be vulnerable and risk looking at each other."[48]

Some feminist writers suggest that the motivation for overcoming this fear must come from love for one another.[49] But, as Lorde asks: "What about interracial cooperation between feminists who don't love each other?"[50] We may share political commitments, interests, or opinions without loving one another or feeling a deep sense of community. As does Arendt, Lorde recognizes that in this context, being ourselves and being with others—subjectivity and intersubjectivity—are both contradictory and crucial: we both fear and need "the visibility without which we cannot truly live."[51] And like Arendt, Lorde argues that this tension is not resolved by love, but addressed by courage: "we can learn to work and speak when we are afraid in the same way we have learned to work and speak when we are tired."[52] We cannot wait for "the final luxury of fearlessness":

> You do not have to be me in order for us to fight alongside each other. I do not have to be you to recognize that our wars are the same. What we must do is commit ourselves to some future that can include each other and to work toward that future with the

particular strengths of our individual identities. . . . Only within that interdependency of different strengths, acknowledged and equal, can the power to seek new ways of being in the world generate, as well as the courage and sustenance to act where there are no charters.[53]

This kind of joint action need not spring from substantive common interests. Even conflicting interests, in Arendt's words, "constitute, in the word's most literal significance, something which *inter-est*, which lies between people and therefore can relate and bind them together" (*HC* 182). The fact that our interests relate us does not necessarily mean that we have common interests—a thing may relate us precisely because we are fighting over it—but that we communicate about them.

Arendt tells us something about what kinds of attention this communication requires and it involves neither love nor devotion. In the private realm, it is love that enables us to perceive another's unique "who-ness" (*HC* 241–43). But love is unworldly; it erases the distance between us that is an existential condition of human public life. Love's counterpart in the public realm is respect: "what love is in its own, narrowly circumscribed sphere, respect is in the larger domain of human affairs. Respect, not unlike the Aristotelian *philia politike*, is a kind of 'friendship' without intimacy and without closeness."[54] Respect, like love, enables us to see not simply *what* people are, but *who* they are. With respect, we can pay attention from "across the distance the world puts between us," acknowledging others as different in some ways from us, yet, like us, a unique and active who. The value of Arendtian respect is that it comes not out of liking or "esteem" for others' particular personal qualities or group memberships, nor because they personally resemble us. It comes from and expresses what Arendt calls the principle of solidarity: viewing another as (like us) capable of action.[55] Respect does not solve the paradox of political appearance (our urge to appear in the world as a particular and mobile who, and the fact that such appearance requires the attention of peers who will judge for themselves). But might not this notion of respect, which is different from admiration or mere politeness, provide a kind of conceptual guide for us as listeners?

Even with such a guide, politics remains an inevitably messy and unpredictable practice—which is in part why it calls for courage. For Arendt, the courage and respect that make politics possible do not spring from our feelings for each other so much as from a kind of care for the world. It is the world that we share, that relates and separates us, the human artifice that is built up on earth and populated by us humans: the houses, the office buildings, the vacant lots, the parks; the hospitals, factories, restaurants; the schools, the shelters, the streets. We share this world together, and we cannot evade that togetherness if we want to preserve a world with space for the exercise of distinctively human capacities, and the perhaps distant possibility of a just politics. Sharing a commitment to living in the world together may sound like a pretty minimal basis for political interaction; it does not involve love, compassion, or even civic friendship. But it is of great significance in a world where there continue to be so many attempts to determine by violence who will live on this earth and who will not.

This difficult togetherness requires individuals who feel the need and responsibility to speak and act from their unique perspective (BPF 229). Yet it also requires accepting that my perspective cannot prevail or my self remain unaltered in the presence of others, for no individual can control the responses of a body of unique individuals (except through violence). Politics will always be a messy and uncertain practice, because it takes place in the "already existing web of human relationships with its innumerable, conflicting wills and intentions" (HC 184). Respect and courage cannot change that. But they can help us think about the exigencies of political action among those with disparate, multiple social identities. Thus they point to a politics that seeks to do justice to the differences among us, not to erase those differences in the name of citizenship or in the name of love.

## Notes

1. bell hooks, *Talking Back* (Boston: South End Press, 1989), 109.

2. The critique of "identity" also gets framed as a critique of the focus on subjectivity or the psychological. See, for some very different examples, hooks, *Talking Back*, 105–11; Shane Phelan, *Identity Politics* (Philadelphia: Temple University Press, 1989); Todd Gitlin, "The Rise of 'Identity Politics': An Examination and Critique," *Dissent* 40, no. 2 (1993): 172–77; Wendy Brown, "Wounded Attachments," *Political Theory* 21, no. 3 (1993): 390–410; Wendy Brown, "Feminist Hesitations, Postmodern Exposures," *differences* 3, no. 1 (1991): 63–84; B. Honig, "Toward An Agonistic Feminism: Hannah Arendt and the Politics of Identity," in *Feminists Theorize the Political*, ed. Judith Butler and Joan W. Scott (New York: Routledge, 1992); and Hester Eisenstein, *Contemporary Feminist Thought* (Boston: G. K. Hall, 1983).

3. Not surprisingly, the presumed homogeneity of the lesbian community was challenged first through an argument about different *desires*, when lesbians engaged in sadomasochistic practices began to articulate different conceptions of lesbian desires and identity. Ironically,

other lesbian feminists, whose politicization had involved resisting enforced definitions of lesbian identity, denied that such persons and practices could be part of lesbianism (Phelan, *Identity Politics*, chaps. 4–6, 8).

4. Phelan, *Identity Politics*, 170.

5. hooks, *Talking Back*, 106–10.

6. Feminist writers like Gloria Anzaldúa are often read simply as critics of racism and class discrimination in feminism movements. Such readings ignore the fact that these writers are theorists in their own right, engaged in an endeavor to analyze what identity means for feminist political action *as* interaction. See Norma Alarcón, "The Theoretical Subject(s) of *This Bridge Called My Back* and Anglo-American Feminism," in *Making Face, Making Soul/ Haciendo Caras*, ed. Gloria Anzaldúa (San Francisco: Aunt Lute Foundation, 1990).

7. Hannah Arendt, *The Human Condition* (Chicago: University of Chicago Press, 1958), 175, 8; hereafter cited as HC.

8. HC 8; also see Arendt, *On Revolution* (New York: Penguin Books, 1965), 175; hereafter cited as OR.

9. It is precisely the sameness of our "inner psychic ground" that makes possible a science of psychology. Arendt contrasts such inner sameness to the "enormous variety and richness of overt human conduct" in *The Life of the Mind*, one-volume ed. (New York: Harcourt Brace Jovanovich, 1973), 29, 34–35; hereafter cited as LM.

10. Arendt, HC 178–79; see also Arendt, *Between Past And Future*, enl. ed. (New York: Penguin Books, 1968), 263; hereafter cited as BPF.

11. Arendt, BPF 235; OR 225–26; and *The Jew As Pariah*, ed. Ron H. Feldman (New York: Grove, 1978), 182; hereafter cited as JaP.

12. E.g., June Jordan, *On Call* (Boston: South End Press, 1985), 117.

13. For a discussion explicitly in terms of "masks," see Gloria Anzaldúa, "Haciendo Caras, una entrada/an Introduction," in *Making Face, Making Soul/Haciendo Caras*.

14. Barbara Christian, "The Race for Theory," in *Making Face, Making Soul/Haciendo Caras*, 341. For more on the problem of stereotyped visibility, see Patricia Hill Collins, *Black Feminist Thought* (New York: Routledge, 1991), 67, 69–70; Audre Lorde, *Sister Outsider: Essays and Speeches* (New York: Crossing Press, 1984), 42; Michelle Cliff, "Object into Subject: Some Thoughts on the Work of Black Women Artists"; and María Lugones, "Playfulness, 'World'-Travelling, and Loving Perception," in *Making Face, Making Soul/ Haciendo Caras*, 274 and 396–96; Mitsuye Yamada, "Invisibility is an Unnatural Disaster: Reflections of an Asian American Woman," in *This Bridge Called My Back*, ed. Cherríe Moraga and Gloria Anzaldúa (New York: Kitchen Table: Women of Color Press, 1983), 36; Iris Marion Young, *Justice and the Politics of Difference* (Princeton: Princeton University Press, 1990), 59–60.

15. A similar version of this mask is put into place through tokenism, which works through the expectation that a person with a particular identity (as a member of a group) is a proxy for all other members of that group. See Lynet Uttal, "Inclusion without Influence: The Continuing Tokenism of Women of Color," in *Making Face, Making Soul/Haciendo Caras*, 43–44.

16. E.g., Brown, "Wounded Attachments" and "Feminist Hesitations"; Gitlin, "The Rise of 'Identity Politics'."

17. Arendt, HC 199; see also HC 50, and *The Origins of Totalitarianism*, new ed. (New York: Harcourt Brace Jovanovich, 1973), 475–76.

18. Susan Moller Okin, *Women in Western Political Thought* (Princeton: Princeton University Press, 1979); Okin, *Justice, Gender, and the Family* (New York: Basic Books, 1989); Genevieve Lloyd, *The Man of Reason* (Minneapolis: University of Minnesota Press, 1984); Young, *Justice and The Politics of Difference*.

19. E.g., bell hooks, *Feminist Theory: From Margin to Center* (Boston: South End Press, 1984), chap. 1; see also Elizabeth V. Spelman, *Inessential Woman* (Boston: Beacon, 1988), 52–54 and chap. 5.

20. Martha Minow, "Justice Engendered," *Harvard Law Review* 101 (1987): 10–95; see esp. 14, 38–45, 57.

21. Lorde, *Sister Outsider*, 113, quoting Simone de Beauvoir.

22. BPF 241; *Lectures on Kant's Political Philosophy*, ed. Ronald Beiner (Chicago: University of Chicago Press, 1982), 43.

23. Arendt, BPF 242; see also *Lectures on Kant's Political Philosophy*, 43.

24. Arendt, BPF 241; also *Lectures on Kant's Political Philosophy*, 41–44.

25. Arendt, *Lectures on Kant's Political Philosophy*, 74, emphasis in original; see also BPF 224–26; and *Men in Dark Times* (New York: Harcourt Brace and World, 1968), 7–8; hereafter cited as *MDT*.

26. Gloria Anzaldúa, "La Prieta," in *This Bridge Called My Back*, 205.

27. Anzaldúa, "La Prieta," 205; Cherríe Moraga, preface to *This Bridge Called My Back*, 34, Lugones, "Hablando cara a cara," 47, emphasis in original.

28. Sandra Harding, *The Science Question in Feminism* (Ithaca: Cornell University Press, 1986), 163–64.

29. The phrase "categories of marginality" is Anzaldúa's, in "Haciendo Caras, una entrada," xvi. The remark of Arendt's comes from her reply to Voegelin's criticisms of *Origins of Totalitarianism*. Arendt, "A Reply," *Review of Politics* 15 (1953): 76–84). I owe the latter citation to Lisa J. Disch, "More Truth than Fact: Storytelling as Critical Understanding in the Writings of Hannah Arendt," *Political Theory* 21, no. 4 (1993): 665–94.

30. Anzaldúa, "Haciendo Caras, una entrada," xxvii, and *Borderlands/La Frontera* (San Francisco: Spinsters/Aunt Lute Press, 1987), 79–80.

31. Anzaldúa, *Borderlands/La Frontera*, 78.

32. Ibid., 78–80.

33. An alternative "standpoint" style reading (based on Anzaldúa's claim that the mestiza is the "officiating priestess at the crossroads" [*Borderlands/La Frontera*, 80]) might argue that the significance of the mestiza is her particular position of marginality, and not the more general capacity to shift perspectives. However, elsewhere it seems that Anzaldúa thinks of mestiza consciousness as a more generally applicable kind of political thinking that we can all learn, for it highlights a creative capacity present in all (*Borderlands/La Frontera*, 83–86).

34. Anzaldúa, "Haciendo Caras, una entrada," xv–xvi; my emphasis.

35. Ibid., xvi.

36. Ibid., xv.

37. Unless I undergo plastic surgery, of course. See Lucy Grealy, "Mirrorings: To Gaze Upon My Reconstructed Face," *Harper's* 286 (February 1993), 66–74.

38. Arendt, MDT 23. There are, as Arendt herself would note, "important differences in degree" in worldly conditions (*JaP* 249); she herself made a different argument about her Jewishness later, in a different context. See her exchange with Scholem over *Eichmann in Jerusalem* (*JaP* 240–50).

39. The notion of "arrogant perception" is Marilyn Frye's, and is developed further in Lugones, "Playfulness, 'World'-Travelling, and Loving Perception."

40. Lugones, "Playfulness, 'World'-Travelling, and Loving Perception," 394.

41. Anzaldúa, "Haciendo Caras, una entrada," xxiii.

42. Lynet Uttal examines the adverse consequences of unresponsive politeness in "Nods That Silence," in *Making Face, Making Soul/Haciendo Caras*.

43. Benjamin Barber, *Strong Democracy* (Berkeley and Los Angeles: University of California Press, 1984).

44. See, for example, Young, *Justice and the Politics of Difference;* Jane J. Mansbridge, *Beyond Adversary Democracy* (Chicago: University of Chicago Press, 1983).

45. Bernice Johnson Reagon, "Coalition Politics: Turning the Century," in *Home Girls,* ed. Barbara Smith (New York: Kitchen Table: Women of Color Press, 1983), 357–60; see also Gloria Anzaldúa, "En Rapport, In Opposition: Cobrando cuentas a las nuestras," in *Making Face, Making Soul/Haciendo Caras;* Anzaldúa, "Bridge, Drawbridge, Sandbar, or Island: Lesbians-of-Color Hacienda Alianzas," in *Bridges of Power,* ed. Lisa Albrecht and Rose M. Brewer (Philadelphia: New Society Publishers, 1990).

46. Moraga, Preface to *This Bridge Called My Back,* xiv; Anzaldúa, "La Prieta," 205–6.

47. For the critique of "sisterhood," see Bonnie Thornton Dill, "Race, Class, and Gender: Prospects for an All-Inclusive Sisterhood," *Feminist Studies* 9, no. 1 (1983): 131–50; hooks, *Feminist Theory,* chap. 4; and Martha A. Ackelsberg, "Sisters or Comrades? The Politics of Friends and Families," in *Families, Politics, and Public Policy,* ed. Irene Diamond (London: Longman, 1983). On coalition/alliances, see Reagon, "Coalition Politics," and the following collections: Albrecht and Brewer, *Bridges of Power;* Moraga and Anzaldúa, *This Bridge Called My Back;* and Anzaldúa, *Making Face, Making Soul/Haciendo Caras.*

48. Papusa Molina, "Recognizing, Accepting and Celebrating Our Differences," in *Making Face, Making Soul/Haciendo Caras,* 328.

49. Lugones, "Playfulness, 'World'-Travelling, and Loving Perception," 401; Molina, "Recognizing, Accepting and Celebrating Our Differences," 329; Anzaldúa, "En Rapport, In Opposition," 228–29. I do not draw on Lugones's conception of "world"-traveling, despite its suggestiveness (and some commonalities with Arendt), precisely because such activity relies on a kind of lovingness that enables us to see with another's eyes (Lugones, "Playfulness, 'World'-Travelling, and Loving Perception," 394). Elsewhere, Lugones suggests that the effort of mutual recognition discussed above may require "the devotion of friendship" (Lugones, "Hablando cara a cara," 47). As the following discussion indicates, I do not agree. For an insightful exploration of the significance of the commonalities between Arendt and Lugones, see Lisa Disch's essay in this volume (Chapter 12).

50. Lorde, *Sister Outsider,* 113.

51. Ibid., 42.

52. Ibid., 44; Arendt, HC 186–87.

53. Lorde, *Sister Outsider,* 142 and 111. Like Arendt, Lorde tends to use the language of war and warriors, but precisely when she is indicating the possibility of politics and not war, power and not simply violence.

54. Arendt, 243. Arendt here and elsewhere uses the language of friendship, which she also calls a kind of "gladness to talk to one another." However, in conflictual political settings, this kind of gladness may be conspicuously absent, and yet communication still necessary in order to address conflict politically. I discuss these and other reasons for rejecting "friendship" as the bond underlying political communication in "Listening, Conflict, and Citizenship," Ph.D. diss., University of Minnesota, 1993.

55. Arendt, HC 243; OR 86. Arendt does not herself draw this connection between respect and solidarity.

# 14

# Forgiving Trespasses, Promising Futures

## *Melissa A. Orlie*

During the summer of 1990, I participated in two feminist activities with other members of a New York City political association. The first included ad hoc efforts to offer simultaneously antiracist and antimisogynist perspectives on the "Central Park jogger" attack and trial.[1] Media coverage and public response to the assault and trial often were subtly or

This essay extends arguments developed in "Thoughtless Assertion and Political Deliberation," *American Political Science Review* (September 1994). Conversations at the University of Maryland, College Park, and Midwestern Political Science Association Annual Meetings (Chicago, April 1994) were instructive in its formulation. Thanks to Natasha Levinson, Jacq. Madden, Cris Mayo, and especially Nick Burbules and Bonnie Honig for helpful comments on an earlier draft and to my political friends at the Center for Anti-Violence Education. I dedicate this essay to my grandmother who died as I was finishing it.

deeply racist,[2] passively or aggressively misogynist,[3] or both simultaneously.[4] We questioned and challenged prevalent ideas and images
surrounding the rape and trial through public discussions and demonstrations. In the second, we helped organize a march to publicize
"bias-related" attacks against lesbians. A physical attack against a
biracial couple in a Park Slope diner that spring prompted the march.
We were involved in the earliest stages of planning the march, but many
members of the association eventually ceased to support it and joined
with others to organize a counterdemonstration (informational leafleting
to march participants). In this case, a multiracial group of Brooklyn
women hoped to accomplish what leading march organizers would not
attempt for fear of diluting *their* message—to encourage participants to
consider (we proposed no definitive answer) how "race" and "class"
intertwined with "gender" and "sexuality" to infuse "hate violence" and
responses to it.[5] We reluctantly adopted this counterstrategy after the
defeat of numerous efforts to address both racism and the diversity of the
lesbian and gay communities.

Some participants and observers thought these actions absurd. How
could so-called feminists like myself refuse to approve a march contesting
violence against lesbians while supposedly lending support (because we
interrogated public discourse about the rape and trial) to young African
American and Latino men charged with brutally beating a white woman?
But were our actions absurd? From what perspective, if any at all, could
they be judged politically sensible and successful? All participants in
these activities were committed to political action. For us, political
action required that we question our own and others' "identities." For
others, however, such questioning was not integral to political action.
What is at stake in this difference?

The concerns and questions inspiring my participation in the events
of that summer remain. Then and now, I regard my own and others'
activities against a backdrop of historical harm and wrongdoing, of
inherited or institutionalized advantages and disadvantages. How can we
conduct ourselves ethically when we are conditioned by history and the
governing powers we carry as much as others are influenced or harmed
by our effects? How might we recognize and respond to the past and
present, collective and individual, harms and wounds that suffuse our
relations with one another? If harm and injustices are an inevitable, and
to some degree (which cannot be predetermined) ineluctable effect of
human living, how should we acknowledge these grievances? What does

it mean to live responsibly and freely in such contexts? This is one of the principal challenges facing contemporary feminist practice.

Unfortunately, resentment is a prevalent response to this challenge. But Hannah Arendt's writings are a propitious resource for engaging it in alternative ways. For those who share my questions, Arendt is appealing because she suggests why and how resentment at our own and others' injuries might be overcome while political action assumes its place. In my interpretation of Arendt, we live responsibly and freely when we put our identities in question and refuse merely and passively to reinscribe what I call social rule. Social rule represents the effective rule of the social, the predictable ordering of self as subject, what Arendt calls *what* we are. To live responsibly and freely—to act extraordinarily and to reveal *who* we are—requires that we disrupt and unsettle social rule because when we do not, we reinforce and expand the "necessities" that not only harm others, but also constrict the power of our own action. But disrupting social rule and seeking forgiveness for the harm we bring to others is not sufficient to break hopeless cycles of resentment. We must also make promises, for promises institute and sustain the political spaces where we answer to one another. In my Arendtian account, responsibility implies incalculability and unpredictability, and freedom requires that we be *responsive* to the harms that invariably accompany the good we would do. To live ethically we must, in Judith Butler's illustrative formulation, "begin, without ending, without mastery, to own—and yet never fully to own—the exclusions by which we proceed."[6]

## The Rule of the Social

In Arendt's writings, the correlative to Butler's "exclusions by which we proceed" are the *trespasses* that arise as we position ourselves in the world.[7] According to Arendt, trespasses inevitably inhere in all human activities through their establishment of new relationships (HC 190–91, 240–41). Our activities engage us in a weblike world; our words and deeds may (re)make that world, reinforce it, or initiate something new within it (HC 8–9, 188). But nothing we do is free of harmful effects. We cannot undo those effects ourselves, nor can we prevent them: They occur under circumstances where we did not or could not have known what we were doing (HC 239–40). Trespasses are unavoidable because they flow, not from our intentions per se, but from our identities as they are conditioned and constituted by social rule. The thoughtless, indirect and (usually) inadvertent character of trespasses, mirror and even fortify the apparent necessities of social life. When our identities reiterate social norms, we *extend* the rule of necessity, as well as the violations and exclusions it abets.[8]

Why this preoccupation with violations and exclusions? In Arendt's view, necessity and compulsion persist wherever human life is sustained. Harm and grievances are an ineluctable effect of human living. Not only our historically constituted identities, but also the world of human artifice condition (though, Arendt emphasizes, do not determine) our words and deeds and the web of human relationships created by them (HC 9–11, 182–83, 204). The world of human artifice is fabricated. Such *making* (as principally a matter of *poiesis*) seeks to master necessity by means of force, coercion, and even violence, toward nature and other human beings (HC 31, 129–30, 140). Because making a world and forging locations masters our selves and others, an element of violation—and potential violence—inheres in all fabrication. In our time, fabrication's conditioning effects are manifest in the force of the social and its normalizing imperatives. The modern project of mastering "natural" necessity produces formidable *social* necessities of its own. In modernity, necessity is increasingly hidden precisely because it is so pervasive (HC 121, 125, 130, 135). Throughout her writings, Arendt surveys the expansion of human artifice and accumulation of capital incessantly extending the rule of the social.[9] In *The Origins of Totalitarianism*, she emphasizes the "imperialist political philosophy" that rationalizes the boundless economic forces which destroy political bodies (OT 138, 135–47). In *The Human Condition*, she emphasizes social rule's homogenizing effect on the ways we envision and make the world (HC 38–47). Boundless social rule engenders conformity because it destroys the political spaces where different perspectives might emerge to challenge dominant social codes, identities, and relations.[10] The process is circular and self-perpetuating. The force of social rule and the weight of human artifice increase and press for our conformity, even necessitate it. We become incrementally disinclined to act or we become incapable of acting spontaneously. We lose the will to create political spaces where a plurality of perspectives might appear to challenge social imperatives. In *Origins*, Arendt explicitly links the failure or incapacity to act spontaneously with irresponsibility. Flowing with (but not also against) social norms leaves us without any sense of our effects upon others (OT 139–47). We are rendered, and proceed as if we are, thoughtless. Arendt's *Eichmann in Jerusalem* explores the dire consequences of this development.[11]

According to Arendt, social rule normalizes. Behavioral codes embrace and control all members of a community equally and with equal strength (HC 40–41). By contrast, Michel Foucault accents the processes whereby social norms differentiate and exclude individuals in the interest of administering and homogenizing a population.[12] Here I follow Foucault. A body politic's prevailing views and practices reflect and reinforce congealed patterns of social rule. Governing powers—exhibited in the norms, practices, and efficacy we bring to bear upon our own and others' conduct—institute often invisible social patterns. These powers are not wielded exclusively by government, but are borne and extended by subject-citizens forging their locations in the world. We do not possess these powers, however; we carry and exercise them. For example, race secures protection by and from the police in my case, but renders African American and Latino men and (some) women subject to them. Likewise, I inadvertently contribute (others do so explicitly) to the demand for more policing by renting an apartment in a gentrifying neighborhood. Even shared goals that bind us to others (as in the political activities I sketched at the outset) reveal and mobilize our differential effects partly fashioned by disparate histories. Our locations, identities, and pursuits resonate with, extend, resist, and are stifled by force fields traversing the body politic. Subject-citizens continually display conflicting, asymmetrical effects begot by our differential relation to norms, the varied social efficacy that accrues with those norms, and the diverse psychological and material consequences issuing from our locations. For example, residents of my neighborhood predisposed to organize against violence were reluctant to march under the "militant" banner "Queers Bash Back." We were dismayed by our fellow organizers' imperviousness to our different degrees of vulnerability to violence (whether from "fellow citizens" or the police) rooted in dynamic interactions of race, gender, and class. When we are indifferent to our conduct's continuation and expansion of social rule, we not only exclude others; we also intensify the social necessities that circumscribe our own action. Our irresponsibility and calculability govern not only others, but also our selves.

Trespasses arise as we live our locations; they are effects of our body's ways of being in the world.[13] Sometimes we retrace old wounds, at other times we trespass anew. Each individual is a multiplicity born of convention and artifice, and we have a heightened sense of this in a body politic constituted by multicultural urban centers. Social rule's relational and pervasive, yet shifting, character is confirmed as I move through the streets of a city where my race bestows protection, my gender is perceived as vulnerability, and my sexuality is viewed as provocation. At any given moment, my location changes through its relation to others' locations. By actuating spaces for our selves, we contest other locations, remold or destroy them altogether. As a result, and with our aid, the world is made pliant to some persons and projects, recalcitrant toward others. Minnie Bruce Pratt traces the urban crossings that enact trespasses:

> [W]hen I walk out in my neighborhood, each speaking to another person has become fraught, for me, with the history of race and sex and class; as I walk I have a constant interior discussion with myself, questioning how I acknowledge the presence of another, what I know or don't know about them, and what it means how they acknowledge me. . . .
>
> In the space of three blocks one evening, I can debate whether the young Black woman didn't speak because she was tired, urban-raised, or hates white women; and ask myself why I wouldn't speak to the young professional white woman on her way to work in the morning, but I do at night: and she doesn't speak at all: is it about who I think I may need for physical safety?
>
> And I make myself speak to a young Black man: If I don't, it will be the old racial-sexual fear. Damn the past anyway. When I speak directly, I usually get a respectful answer: is that the response violently extorted by history, the taboo on white women?[14]

Sedimented social patterns condition our locations and the identities they foster. We are not responsible for, nor can we substantially change, *what* we are: how and what we have been made to be by history, institutions, and patterns of social rule preceding us for which no one person alone is responsible. In my view, Arendt's writings suggest, however, that we may become responsible for *who* we are: how we carry and pass on the social effects configuring what we appear to be. What we are represents all that appears to be given or beyond the reach of our agency while who we are is revealed through our words and deeds. In the end, what we are cannot be known, so the relationship between it and who we are is contingent, changing, and finally, simply an analytic distinction.[15] For example, race and gender are usually regarded as aspects of what we are, but their meaning and significance changes depending on who we are, that is to say, depending on how we convey the social effects they generate. By transfiguring who we are, we may overcome (though not transcend) the trespasses embedded in our locations and the resentments they rouse.

## Resentment and a "Crisis of the Subject"

The increasing weight of what we are precipitates a "crisis of the subject." First, often we find that we can neither recognize nor conceive of how to alleviate the harm brought to others by our imbrication in social rules and their governing ways of imaging and making the world. How can and should we respond to the collective trespasses our locations impart? This is a problem of responsibility. Second, freedom becomes a problem as our own and others' locations and actions are thwarted by constrictive social patterns and threatened by unthinking social behavior. As Arendt first suggests in *Origins*, these problems are intimately related (*OT* 139–46). To her mind, we are both irresponsible and unfree when we behave predictably. Our unthinking behavior reproduces patterns of social rule and magnifies the reign of necessity. This not only thoughtlessly harms others, it also limits our freedom to act.

Increasingly, many people experience their individual lives as fated.[16] As Arendt puts it, fate "is something dark and mysterious, something which a man receives but does not create and which he can therefore observe but never fathom."[17] Fate is a way of naming the weight of what we appear to be. Our fate emerges in the convergence and combination of the past and present makings of the world; that fabricated world conditions what and who we are. Often we passively receive our identity as if we cannot affect it or, as in Arendt's reading of Kafka, as if it comes from "above" ("JaP" 118). A tragic perspective appeals to a growing awareness of our progressively circumscribed ability to affect the conditions of our lives thoughtfully. Arendt attributes this reduction of action's power to the boundless expansion of human artifice and limitless drive to accumulate capital. Our efficacy is diminished even as we respond to heightened demands for order and discipline that aim to control the increased global interdependence and contingency that boundless economic pursuits unleash. As Wendy Brown aptly states: "Starkly accountable, yet dramatically impotent, the late modern liberal subject quite literally seethes with *ressentiment.*"[18] In my view, Brown (and others) rightly identify resentment as a predominant reaction of late modern subjects to the weight of the past and the apparent foreclosing of futures, to the diminishment of action's power in the present and the prevalent strategies of responsibility designed to master our selves and world.[19]

Resentment takes a variety of forms, however, and it engenders a variety of responses to our plight. First, we may feel and claim that the weight of what we are so severely governs us that speaking of our responsibility toward others is no longer useful, may even be harmful. Second and alternatively, facing the fatefulness of our lives, we may reassert our self-fashioning potential and the plasticity of fate, whether through heroic self-assertion or willful ignorance. Because these orientations—irresponsibility in the first case and willful self-creation in the second case—take a passive or unthinking bearing toward the human condition, Arendt would regard them both, for all their obvious differences, as reactive and resentful (HC 5, 240–41). But they are more than that. They play a role in a cycle of resentment that is exceedingly difficult to interrupt.

The first view that responsibility is no longer a useful category, may evoke the resentful counterassertion that surely others must be held responsible (and blameworthy) even as (that much more so as) we acknowledge the degree to which we are unfree, at least from the perspective of a sovereign subject.[20] In response to the second view, reassertion of willful self-creation, our resentment is evident in our apparently ceaseless (and ultimately passive) iteration of the ways our ascribed social positions deny us the freedom of agency others celebrate. Immobilizing guilt or reverse resentment are common responses to these countercharges that only further cycles of resentment.

In a political culture steeped in resentment, some of us feel guilt or rancor at being accused for what we are (for instance, white or male), namely, something we did not "choose," while others of us conceive our identity in terms of the wounds we imagine to have been inflicted upon us by what we take those others to be. (Of course, many of us may assume both these positions depending upon our location at any particular moment.) In both instances, we may seek enemies to blame for our suffering and see others only for what and not who they are. In neither case are we likely to prove particularly adept at asking the question of how to live both responsibly and freely nor at provisionally enacting answers to that question. Our failure to do that is symptomatic of the modern subject's ethical crisis. In Arendt's view, our resentful rage at what we are, or at the demands made upon us by virtue of what we appear to be, forecloses promising futures (HC 240–41). Contestants locked in a battle of escalating recriminations, far from releasing or redeeming the past, repeat and increase its weight. A problematic orientation toward fate or our locations, identities, and how we live them is one source of this hopeless, cyclical movement of resentment. Recognizing the harm and wounds that permeate our relations with one another means we must rethink the dispositions that incite resentment toward what we appear to be.

All of the above responses (irresponsibility, self-creation, blame, passivity, guilt) exhibit one of two equally problematic orientations toward fate. Arendt sometimes calls them specific human types (OT 66, 56–58, 79–88). First, the *social pariah* embraces what-ness as given and unalterable. She gains her orientation by means of this certainty and is suspicious of the demand to transfigure who she is, seeing it as an assimilationist demand, predicated upon dissimulation, denial of her self and her pain ("JaP" 110; OT 65). For example, she might regard others' efforts to include racism in "our" political agenda as diversionary because it dissipates the centrality of her claims. Second, the *parvenu* dismisses the relevance of what she is, either ignoring it or treating it as so plastic as to be susceptible to willful transcendence. For example, a parvenu may be confounded by others' insistence on difference(s) and determined to emphasize "our" common concerns. When the parvenu's will to be treated as a "human being in general" is frustrated, however, as it inevitably will be, she grows resentful like the social pariah (OT 79–88). In neither case can we imagine exodus from our wounded existence. Both perspectives finally regard what we are as immutable, but while the social pariah is subjectified by it, the parvenu seeks, if always unsuccessfully, to flee it. Trespasses define who the social pariah is while the parvenu flees what she is by ignoring her own and others' trespasses.

Arendt (following Bernard Lazare) regards the *conscious pariah* as the best alternative to these *self*-defeating perspectives.[21] The conscious pariah politicizes what she appears to be and thereby creates and enters a space of freedom where she can reveal who she is. She accepts at least partial responsibility for what she has been made to be ("JaP" 109). She endeavors to transmute her self because she discerns its conventional and artificial character; she decries the social rule that registers the meaning and significance of what she appears to be. By acting with and *against* the social rules that would determine her, she engenders a self. The conscious pariah's political bearing toward what she appears to be distinguishes her perspective from a resentful sensibility. She freely renounces the passivity of the social pariah, and continually and responsively chastens the unthinking social effects ignored by the parvenu. Guiding the effects of the apparent necessities of her life, she responsibly seeks and discloses her freedom.

The distinctions between "necessity" and "freedom," "making" and "action," are crucial to Arendt's understanding of politics. The distinctions turn on the degree of articulation in the latter term of each pair. Freedom and political action define relations where we "answer," "talk back," and "measure up to" what has happened, what we are or have done, the effects of our location in the world (HC 26). Arendt says that political action "is like a second birth in which we confirm and take upon ourselves the naked fact of our original physical appearance" (HC 176–77). She means, as I interpret her, that we act politically when we become responsive to those injurious effects of social rule that condition our identities and are continued by our locations. Necessity and making define nonpolitical relations—leveling, forceful, and unresponsive relations. When necessity and making reign, as they typically do in the daily forging of our locations, we simply have effects upon others and receive their effects upon us. Neither we, nor they, are called to answer for our trespasses. To whom or to what ought I to be responsible when a few short years after renting an apartment I find my neighborhood transformed, gentrified? Thoughtless social behavior always fosters combative not cooperative relations and, as a result, foments resentment.[22]

By contrast, we enact political relations when we reckon the social necessities that reign outside politics and often intrude into it.[23] In my Arendtian account, a space becomes political whenever and wherever we try to fathom our fate, acknowledge our trespasses, and open each to creative and spontaneous action (HC 198–201). In the spaces of politics, we encounter others who call to our attention our social effects, and we, in turn, may do likewise.[24] We constitute ethical political relations when we think together about the ruling and violence that dwell in all locations, whether they become manifest in individual acts, social behavior, or governance. If we do not attend to the pervasiveness of ruling and violence, spaces of collaborative action will be undermined and then destroyed by thoughtlessness. Indeed, we may soon find that those we assumed were "with us" have departed. Ethical political relations afford us the opportunity to discern and answer for our trespasses and, at least potentially, to employ the political power we generate when we act in concert to metamorphose the patterns of social rule that amplify those trespasses.

## Overcoming Resentment: Forgiving and Promising

Forgiving and promising are ethical and political practices of overcoming. They are the practices that enable us to live responsibly and freely amidst inevitable and ubiquitous trespass; when we forgive and promise, we recognize and respond to trespasses by interrupting, not repeating, cycles of resentment. Creating and sustaining political relations and spaces requires forgiving and releasing trespasses, and promising to (re)direct how our effects bear upon the future. Arendt writes: "without the faculty to undo what we have done and to control at least partially the processes we have let loose, we would be the victims of an automatic necessity bearing all the marks of inexorable laws" (HC 246). Forgiving and promising leaven the weight of human artifice and social rules that always threaten to routinize human relations and render us predictable creatures of necessity, capable not of action, but only of acting out parts that are always already scripted for us.

The possibility of political action, Arendt maintains, depends upon our continually considering and releasing one another from what we have done unknowingly or thoughtlessly (HC 237, 241). Without forgiveness, or the possibility of being forgiven, our capacity to act would be consumed by our first act or, more likely, by all the activities that precede and condition us. Trespasses go unrecognized and unanswered for when what we appear to have been made to be is allowed to consume who we are. The result is an apparently irrevocable logic of identity and social law: my resentment at what you appear to be and your resentment of what I accuse you of being seem irredeemable because the "origin" of resentment appears determined. Without forgiveness, it would not only be difficult to remedy our own violations and those of our forebears (it's rare enough), but impossible. Without forgiveness, we are doomed to carry on the trespasses of those who came before us and perhaps as inevitably we would be subject to the resentment and vengeance those acts provoke (*HC* 237, 241). Political action and relations would be foreclosed, and with them, the principal way of learning who we are as opposed to what we appear to be. It would not be possible to live freely and responsibly.[25]

Forgiveness requires that we become responsible for who we are, for how we display the effects of what we appear to be.[26] We cannot altogether change what we are, nor the fact that in the course of living we trespass against others. But we can change the meaning and significance of what we are when we transmute its effects by challenging the patterns of social rule that multiply our trespasses. If we are to challenge social rule, we must not live our locations thoughtlessly; we also must resist believing that our fate may be exchanged by simply and individually willing it so. Rather, we must interrupt the social effects that accrue with our location in the world.[27] First, we must recognize how we become what we are and examine the views and habits that our locations encourage. When we combine this genealogical project with a facility for imagining and incorporating the diverse perspectives animated by and in political spaces, we may begin to distinguish who we are from what we have been made to be. Our efforts to conceive another view and to answer it may prevent us from living out identities and locations in quite the way expected by social rules. Thinking from the vantage of others, responding to the perspective born of their locations and measuring up to the relation of our locations to it, may change who we are. When we become responsive to others' claims about our effects and when we show a willingness to transpose them, we may disrupt what we are predicted to be and redirect the social necessities that flow from our inherited subject positions. Such free yet deliberate and responsible action may evoke political forgiveness.

Is political forgiveness offered or expressed with a simple "I forgive you"? The formulation is inadequate because it presupposes an "I" and a "you" fully present and self-made. It denies the extent to which you and I are, and remain, pieces of fatefulness. A "you" alone did not make the harm and wounds permeating our relations, anymore than an "I," any

"I," has the authority or power to release them. Political forgiveness is a more provisional, reciprocal release but, like any political action, it may have boundless, unexpected, even miraculous, effects (HC 246–47, 7–11). By breaking cycles of reactive resentment and beginning something new, Arendtian forgiveness opens futures and, if only momentarily, frees from the consequences of previous activities both the one who forgives and the one forgiven (HC 241). Recognition of trespasses and then a desire to reveal who (as distinct from what) you are initiates such release. This revelation of who we are, as opposed to what we might have been expected to be, may engender mutual respect, trust, and political friendship (HC 241, 243), all three of which are conditions of collaborative action.

Forgiving and promising are political actions that upset what in their absence seem to be "inexorable laws." Once I seek forgiveness, my co-actors may grant it when the desire to answer for my unthinking social effects follows in the wake of my recognition of them. For Arendt, promising to live together in the mode of political speech and deed anchors forgiveness by binding us to political spaces where we answer to one another (HC 244–45). Founding promises embodied in documents like the Declaration of Independence or the U.S. Constitution are important, but just as important are the everyday promises that brace political spaces; they are the springboard for refashioning founding promises.[28] Like the revolutionary spirit Arendt sought to recover in On Revolution, responsibility and freedom demand that we not only begin anew and disrupt social expectations, but also establish political spaces and act so as to sustain them. Political action is preservative as well as rebellious, conservative as well as radical (OR 222–24). This is the case, Arendt argues, because freedom as a tangible reality is always spatially limited and dependent upon the establishment of political bodies (OR 275; OT ix, 126, 137–38; HC 50–58, 199–204). Thus, she challenges those of us who (like Butler) would "own the exclusions by which we proceed" to establish political theoretical links to locatable (feminist) practices. Everyday promises embody the willingness and commitment that support political spaces; such spaces hold out the only hope of releasing and refashioning our trespasses—the violations and exclusions that have made our personal and collective histories.

We cannot will a different past, but we can change its meaning for us. We can achieve that change neither by recognizing the intrinsic worth of the past nor by simply desiring or deciding not to be burdened by it.

We renew the past's meaning not by abstracting from our own and others' interests in past actions nor by somehow forgetting, before "healing," our wounds. The former always threatens to become wishful thinking blithely ignorant of the social effects at stake in the past and its present incarnations. The latter call to forget our wounds, absent political action and spaces, similarly ignores the weight (both material and psychological) of what we have been made to be. These responses promise a return of the repressed, a repetition of the past, not its metamorphosis.[29]

Meaningful changes in perspective require political action; they require us to make alterations in our ways of life, in who we are, in our locations and how we live them. By forgiving trespasses, and by making promises that rechannel social rule, we transpose the past's significance, transmute the way we live in the present and face the future. When we open a way to an acceptable future, we "redeem" the past that can now be seen to have made promising futures possible. But since refiguring the past is a never-ending process of reinterpretation and action, the practice strains the meaning of redemption.

Recognizing trespasses and transfiguring their effects may yield promising futures. By this I do not mean fixed futures. That would be to close the future not open it, to specify what we will be at the expense of who we might become. But that who will always carry traces of the social rule that it interrupted. What we are can never be left completely behind. This means that forgiveness is the twin of promising for a very good reason: not only to protect Arendtian actors from the contingencies that lead to broken promises or to their misfires, but also to protect Arendtian actors from the ill-effects of promises kept. Promising is a way to forge a location in the world with others. Since no location-forging can be free of trespasses, promising must always be an occasion for forgiveness, as well as for gratitude and wonder. If we are to avoid sacrificing our capacity for spontaneous action to predictable behavior (and all the dangers it forebodes), we must gauge, as best we can, how effects coming from the past, and pressing upon the present, bear upon the future. This is my provisional answer to the question of what it means to live freely and responsibly today. To be free is to act unpredictably, that is, to upset expectations based on what you appear to be in order to reveal who you are becoming. To be so incalculable is to act responsibly because we thereby abate the deadening weight of harm and wounds; we arrest rather than replicate unjust pasts. Facing the future in such moments, it may indeed appear promising and forgiving.

## Returning to Feminist Political Practice

Political spaces and the political friendships that vivify them may redress individual and collective trespasses. The antiracist, feminist, antiviolence association to which I belonged in New York City exemplifies such a political space. My participation in the association was multivalent given my own locations. On the one hand, acting together we pursued our shared goals of empowering vulnerable people to defend themselves against violence (through self-defense training) and changing the social conditions that make people vulnerable to violence to varying degrees (through an array of political activities). On the other hand, since a plurality of women of diverse locations were collaboratively pursuing those goals, we had to recognize and find ways of dissipating our differential effects because they threatened to undermine our definition and pursuit of shared goals. Our common understanding, amid our differences, included the belief that persons' locations entangled them in harm experienced by others outside the political space in ways that affected relations within it. For example, for much of its history of now twenty years, the association had been predominantly white and, though it was changing, this history and the associational culture it promoted rendered some people (namely, white and college-educated women) more efficacious within the political space. Conditions "outside" of the association colluded to perpetuate these circumstances by affording certain persons greater resources and leisure to participate and more assuredness in doing so. The history of the association and the public personae it fostered also worked to perpetuate these conditions within it, discouraging many from entering the political space and claiming it as their own. A narrowing of political vision and compromise of political effect were the result. Over time, however, these circumstances changed; they are still changing. The condition of this transformation (by no means always actualized) is the desire to respond to others' claims about our effects, to alleviate them when necessary, and to alter them when possible. Participants thereby endeavor to *amend* (OR 196–214) the association's direction, its public image, internal life, external effects, and history.[30]

Both political activities I described at the outset were efforts to overcome resentment by responding actively and creatively to the harm and wounds that suffuse our relations with one another. Each illustrates the political possibilities and more promising futures afforded when we seek political forgiveness and transfigure trespasses in the hope of (re)directing their future effects. When spontaneous, incalculable action interrupts what we are and disorders patterns of social rule, forgiving and promising are possible.

For months I observed with dismay media coverage of the Central Park jogger rape and trial. I felt called to action one morning, however, when I opened my *New York Times* to the image of prominent white feminists publicizing the attack seemingly incognizant of the effects of their pronouncements on an already racially divided city. They appeared to speak for all feminists and did so, in my view, in a way that recapitulated the entire sordid, often unjust history of "white woman-hood" charging the "black rapist," effectively supporting the social rules that conditioned that history. Their promise-based action in concert had harmful effects to which they were unresponsive. As feminist, antiviolence activists, we contested their opposition between the claims of "white women" and "black men," between feminism and antiracism. By questioning the confluence of feminist claims and racist history, we changed not only the external effects of the association, but also relations within it. Political friendships, particularly among African American and white women, were strengthened and our collaborative power enhanced as we (white women) took upon ourselves what had been conventionally regarded as "their" issue. Predictably, the same actions strained relations among some white women.

These women made promises to feminism that had harmful effects. Should they be forgiven? What would forgiveness entail in this case? If we recognize our trespasses, and act on the desire to answer for and redress them, we may evoke forgiveness. But forgiveness will not follow from just any interruption of social rules. Interruption must be joined to the aspiration to live ethically. The passivity and thoughtlessness that characterize the social pariah and parvenu must give way to the conscious pariah's mindfulness of inevitable trespass and continual effort to live responsibly and freely. To be forgiven, these feminist actors would have to move to overcome their thoughtless social effects. Forgiveness is evinced by a commitment to act together. It signals that valuable willingness of those who have reason to resent our trespasses to engage us nonetheless as political friends.

In the second case of organizing and then countering the march publicizing hate violence against lesbians, we questioned our and others' identities. Did our political action defy social necessities or recite them? The majority of white activists regarded racism as a diversion from "our" (their) central concerns, even in the face of African American, Latina and some white women's alternative perspectives (particularly ironic given that the attack prompting the march was against a biracial couple). At stake in this political argument were not only the representation of lesbian and gay communities, but also the social processes of gentrification. Only from within gentrified enclaves in the heart of Brooklyn (and in a city where white people are a numerical minority) could lesbian and gay communities be represented in "racially neutral" images, that is to say, as white. Though it cannot be established here, I suspect that white activists, by behaving so predictably in accordance with their social rules, intensified the necessities and resentments infusing hate violence. Their calculability and irresponsibility not only excluded others, it proved self-defeating.

Were the association's actions successful? We certainly could not claim in either case that we transformed patterns of social rule nor did we once and for all release specific trespasses. Yet if we allow Arendt's criteria for evaluating political action to steer our judgment, then we might conclude that our actions were worthwhile. They actualized our capacity to do the unexpected and to live responsibly and freely. They generated a site for dissent from, resistance to, and amendment of social rule. Under pressure to conform, whether under a totalitarian regime or the relatively benign requirements of social rule, Arendt believes that most people will comply. But not everyone will. Herein lies the meaning and significance of political action. Each political action memorializes our human capacity to act incalculably, to interrupt social rules, to resist wrong and harmdoing, and to assuage their effects. In Arendt's view, and in the face of our fate, such hopeful stories of action keep our planet fit for human habitation.[31]

## Notes

1. I refer to the attack and trial that were often lead stories in the *New York Times* from 22 April 1989 to December 1990.

2. For example, prominent white feminists deploying imagery and slogans unmindful of the legacy of rape and lynching in the United States or images of African American and Latino youths "savagely wilding." I briefly return to this event in the essay's conclusion.

3. For example, African American media and activists trivializing the attack or denying the rape.

4. The standard wares of what Angela Davis has called the "myth of the black male rapist" in *Women, Race, and Class* (New York: Vintage Books, 1983), 172–201, coupled with suspicions about the sexual past and cavalier behavior of the contemporary, unmarried, urban woman.

5. In my view, this can be said of whoever is the target of such attacks. I attribute no intrinsic substance or meaning to race, gender, sexuality, etc. for reasons specified below. I briefly return to this event in the essay's conclusion.

6. Judith Butler, *Bodies That Matter* (New York: Routledge, 1993), 53. Butler's framework is more psychoanalytic than my own. I believe, however, that this essay affirms the spirit of her suggestion (if not her theory of agency).

7. As Arendt elaborates the concept, to trespass is to miss, fail, or go astray, rather than to sin; Hannah Arendt, *The Human Condition* (Chicago: University of Chicago Press, 1958), 240; hereafter cited as *HC*. It does not apply to the extremity of crime and willed evil (239).

8. I use identity to refer to a constrictive image of what we are as conditioned by social rule. This usage departs from the letter but not the spirit of Arendt's conception. Following Augustine (*Confessions*, x), Arendt introduces a distinction between what and who one is (*HC* 10–11), upon which I elaborate. She defines who we are as representing our "unique personal identity" (179). But in contemporary political discourse, identity has assumed resonances antithetical to Arendt's meaning: political identity often denotes membership in a social category not unique individuality; it is a sign of what we have been made to be not of who we might become. I argue that revealing who we are requires questioning and interrupting the social rules that would prescribe our identities.

9. *HC* 38–47, 58–61, 68–73, 105, 112, 126–35, 159–67; Hannah Arendt, *The Origins of Totalitarianism* (New York: Harcourt Brace Jovanovich, 1973), 124–57; hereafter cited as *OT*.

10. *HC* 39; Hannah Arendt, *On Revolution* (New York: Penguin Books, 1977), 166, 171, 174–75, 225–28; hereafter cited as *OR*.

11. Hannah Arendt, *Eichmann in Jerusalem: A Report on the Banality of Evil* (New York: Viking Press, 1964), 26, 47–49, 114, 126–27, 150.

12. Michel Foucault, *Discipline and Punish*, trans. Alan Sheridan (New York: Vintage Books, 1979), 182–84, 192–94; "Afterword: The Subject and Power," in *Michel Foucault: Beyond Structuralism and Hermeneutics*, ed. Hubert L. Dreyfus and Paul Rabinow (Chicago: University of Chicago Press, 1983), 212–26. Arendt's conception of normalization emphasizes social equality (where Foucault highlights differentiation and asymmetry) because she presupposes "biological sameness" (*HC* 30, 36, 45–47). I follow Foucault (and Nietzsche) in regarding the body's appearance as an undifferentiated mass, and the conformism Arendt identifies in mass society, as "instituted by an act of violence . . . and carried to conclusion by nothing but acts of violence" (for a fuller argument, see "Thoughtless Assertion and Political Deliberation," *American Political Science Review* 88, no. 3 [September 1994]: 684–95). At the same time, Arendt suggests that she might have agreed with Foucault that the distinction between domination and power is often merely a verbal one (*The Foucault Reader* [New York: Pantheon, 1984], 378). She notes that power, violence, strength, and force are rarely entirely distinct and often slip into one another; see her *Crises of the Republic* (New York: Harcourt Brace Jovanovich, 1969), 145, 143–46. Thus, the importance, whether Arendt recognized it or not, of political action addressing and challenging social imperatives.

13. I introduce the notion of *location* to refer to the continually changing space in which our "body" appears and thus seek to keep in play the body's nonconscious and material, individual, social, and political significance.

14. Minnie Bruce Pratt, "Identity: Skin Blood Heart," in *Yours in Struggle: Three Feminist Perspectives on Anti-Semitism and Racism*, ed. Elly Bulkin et al. (New York: Long Haul Press, 1984), 12–13; Biddy Martin and Chandra Talpade Mohanty, "Feminist Politics: What's Home Got To Do With It?" in *Feminist Studies/Critical Studies*, ed. Teresa de Lauretis (Bloomington: Indiana University Press, 1987).

15. For the precariousness of the distinction between what and who we appear to be, see e.g., *HC* 179–81; also Nietzsche, *On the Genealogy of Morals* (New York: Vintage Books, 1967), 45. Arendt herself sometimes speaks as if we can know what (though not who) someone is (*HC* 179); this is a common interpretation of her view of the relationship between what and who we are. But the question *What is man?* Arendt says, is a question that can be settled only within the framework of a divinely revealed answer; that is, it is humanly unknowable (10–11). Arendt notes the all too human tendency to believe that we know what someone is, particularly when faced with the difficulty of saying who someone is (179, 186). Thus, the related tendency for "unique personal identities" to be subsumed under identities constituted by social rules.

16. Thus the resurgence of interest in tragedy where a few decades ago George Steiner wrote of its death, even as he hoped for its reincarnation. In my view, awareness of the inevitability and ubiquity of trespass calls for a tragic rather than a utopian political outlook, for mindfulness of the complexities and ambiguities of our condition rather than visions of a final "redemptive" solution. Among the recent treatments of tragedy noteworthy from a political theoretical perspective are Martha Nussbaum, *The Fragility of Goodness* (Cambridge: Cambridge University Press, 1986); J. Peter Euben, *The Tragedy of Political Theory* (Princeton: Princeton University Press, 1990); and C. Fred Alford, *The Psychoanalytic Theory of Greek Tragedy* (New Haven: Yale University Press, 1992).

17. Hannah Arendt, "The Jew as Pariah," *Jewish Social Studies* 6 (April 1944): 118–19; hereafter cited as "JaP." On the hostility evoked by differences appearing as given, "dark and mysterious" within cultures that conceive of equality as social (rather than political) and are committed to mastery, see *OT* 300–301, 54–55. Arendt's antipathy toward "naturalizing" social characteristics, and her astute sense of the dangers of doing so, are especially pronounced in *Antisemitism* (*OT* 2:79–88).

18. Wendy Brown, "Wounded Attachments," *Political Theory* 21 (August 1993); 402, passim; see also William Connolly, *Political Theory and Modernity* (New York: Basil Blackwell, 1987), 1–15, 137–75.

19. E.g., Bonnie Honig, *Political Theory and the Displacement of Politics* (Ithaca: Cornell University Press, 1993), 42–75; William Connolly, *Identity\Difference* (Ithaca: Cornell University Press, 1991), 16–35, 95–122, 158–97.

20. See Arendt, *HC* 234, on the problematic equation of freedom and sovereignty.

21. Arendt, "JaP," 107–10. Bernard Lazare, *Job's Dungheap* (New York: Schocken Books, 1948).

22. The practice and posture of politicization I recommend also may foster combat rather than cooperation, especially among the resentful or those who would prefer to remain unaware. But, unlike unthinking social behavior, politicization does not necessarily foment resentment. Indeed, I argue, if Arendt is right that trespasses are ineluctable, then forgiveness—forgiving and being forgiven—is the only possible response to this situation that avoids resentment or a simply reactive meeting of one trespass with another. Relatedly, promising is the only basis for relations that, if they cannot avoid trespass, maintain mutuality in awareness of trespass.

23. Arendt *might* deny the latter point given her most explicit views about the relationship between our bodies and political action, the "private" and "public" (see "Thoughtless Assertion and Political Deliberation"). At the same time, Arendt consistently claims that the political precludes the *merely* necessary (e.g., HC 25, 39). The point is that political relations need not exclude "social questions," only certain methods of normalizing and governing political action.

24. I emphasize the ethical quality of relationship as definitive of Arendtian politics. Thus, a vast array of intermediate associations can be political spaces while the practices and places we typically regard as political are often vehicles of governance and resentment.

25. For Arendt, assuming responsibility for the conditions that condition us and others is fundamental to ethical political relations: "For insofar as man is more than a mere creature of nature, more than a mere product of Divine creativity, insofar will he be called to account for the things which men do to men in the world which they themselves condition" ("JaP" 109).

26. Arendt appears to deny that what we are has any effect upon who we are. But her understanding of the world of human artifice's conditioning effect upon the web of human relationships (our words and deeds) problematizes this radical distinction (HC 9–11, 182–83, 204). Her own writings suggest that who we are revealed to be through political action can never altogether leave behind what we are. Additionally, reflection upon the force of social imperatives suggests that ignoring what we have been made to be does not protect but imperils who we might become.

27. To say that we should interrupt social rules is not to say that we should never decide to affirm them. Affirmation can be a form of interruption so long as it departs from thoughtless repetition.

28. Arendt, OR 215–81. On the former see Honig's excellent discussion in *Political Theory and the Displacement of Politics*, 76–125.

29. For an example of the former see David Ingram, "The Postmodern Kantianism of Arendt and Lyotard," *Review of Metaphysics* 42 (September 1988): 67–77; and of the latter, Wendy Brown, "Wounded Attachments," 400–408. Brown's emphasis on the politics of desire and will-to-freedom is welcome, but to my mind she moves too quickly (or does not sufficiently elaborate an alternative) to "getting over" our wounds. After all, even Zarathustra was tempted and instructed by resentment to the end; *The Portable Nietzsche* (New York: Viking, 1954), 250–53, 309–10, 438–39.

30. In Arendt's view, a particular association, or a polity as a whole, delimits the arbitrariness that marks every spontaneous, incalculable deed by binding us back to its (the association's) beginning. The purposes that initially brought us together, and the promises that subsequently keep us together, conduct and circumscribe political action. (They also help us decide which trespasses warrant our attention since the pervasiveness of trespass precludes answering for them all.) I might be asked what principles determine whether forgiveness should be granted and promises made. This question is just. But my view of the mutual promises founding this association, or the American polity generally, would require another, quite different, essay. Suffice it to say, deliberating about the promises "we hold" (to be sure, with varying degrees of explicitness) is central to what transpires in political spaces. For Arendt's discussion of these issues, see HC 244–45; OR 179–214, esp. 188–99, 192–94, 198–206, 211–14.

31. After recounting one of the few stories we have of a German (Sergeant Anton Schmidt) who risked his life and ultimately died to save the lives of his (once) fellow citizens, Arendt writes: "For the lessons of such stories is simple and within everyone's grasp. Politically speaking, it is that under conditions of terror most people will comply *but some people will not.* . . . Humanly speaking, no more is required, and no more can reasonably be asked, for this planet to remain a place fit for human habitation" (*Eichmann in Jerusalem,* 233).

# Annotated Bibliography on Hannah Arendt and Feminism

## Patchen P. Markell

The following bibliography lists works on Hannah Arendt written from feminist perspectives or addressing issues of concern to feminists. It includes works written in English, German, French, and Italian, although only the English and German works are annotated. The bibliography is limited to those works that are centrally concerned with feminist issues and that include sustained engagements with Arendt's thought. Works of feminist theory that mention Arendt only briefly, as well as works of Arendt scholarship that note feminist concerns only in passing, have been omitted.

The annotations are meant to describe the works in their own terms as far as possible. Nevertheless, because many of these works were not written *exclusively* as feminist interventions in Arendt's thought, I have occasionally deemphasized some aspects of an author's project in order to highlight the engagement with Arendt and make the annotations as useful as possible for the readers of this volume.

## English

Benhabib, Seyla. "Feminist Theory and Hannah Arendt's Concept of Public Space." *History of the Human Sciences* 6, no. 2 (1993): 97–114. While criticizing the masculinity of Arendt's agonistic public sphere and the inflexibility of her exclusion of social issues from politics, Benhabib argues that feminism can benefit from Arendt's view of the private realm as a site of preparation for the political, and that Arendt's model of public space allows feminists to distinguish between "democratic empowerment" and "bureaucratic administration" as responses to women's problems.

Brown, Wendy. *Manhood and Politics: A Feminist Reading in Political Theory.* Totowa, N.J.: Rowman and Littlefield, 1988. Brown locates Arendt, along with Aristotle, Machiavelli, and Weber, in a tradition for which freedom means freedom from the body, life, and necessity. The quest for freedom so construed is self-undermining because it estranges people from their embodiedness and sanctions the subjection of women; this self-defeating tendency is evident in the "anxiety" and "panic" with which Arendt defends the purity of the political.

Cornell, Drucilla. "Gender Hierarchy, Equality, and the Possibility of Democracy." In her *Transformations: Recollective Imagination and Sexual Difference,* 156–69. New

York: Routledge, 1993. Drawing on Lacanian psychoanalytic theory, Cornell reads Arendt's sharp division between the realms of freedom and necessity, and her valorization of freedom, as an "unconscious reinstatement" of a gender hierarchy in which woman is constructed as essentially lacking. Cornell contrasts Arendt with Derrida, whose "feminization of the rhetoric of civic friendship" points toward a democracy that does not merely reproduce old hierarchies.

Curtis, Kimberley. "Hannah Arendt, Feminist Theorizing and the Debate Over New Reproductive Technologies." Forthcoming in *Polity* (Summer 1995). Curtis employs Arendt's analysis of the human condition to criticize existing feminist arguments over new reproductive technologies. Curtis finds that Arendt values the perspectives not only of the actor and of *homo faber* but also of *animal laborans;* Curtis argues that those new technologies that go beyond the mere control of fertility to make fertility an object of human production threaten the sensibilities of *animal laborans,* and thereby also endanger our ethical and political capacities.

Cutting-Gray, Joanne. "Hannah Arendt, Feminism, and the Politics of Alterity: What Will We Lose if We Win?" *Hypatia* 8, no. 1 (Winter 1993): 35–54. Cutting-Gray draws on Arendt's biography of Rahel Varnhagen to produce a conception of feminist subjectivity as politically constituted, plural, and contingent; this feminist politics is offered as an alternative to a politics of "sympathetic sisterhood" in which differences among women's experiences are effaced.

Dietz, Mary G. "Hannah Arendt and Feminist Politics." In *Feminist Interpretations and Political Theory,* edited by Mary Lyndon Shanley and Carole Pateman, 232–52. University Park: Pennsylvania State University Press, 1991. While acknowledging that Arendt was insufficiently attentive to the gendering of the public/private and labor/work/action distinctions, Dietz employs Arendt's criticism of the hegemony of the laboring mentality to criticize feminisms—like those of Rich, O'Brien, Hartsock, and Kristeva—that are grounded in women's reproductive roles, and to call for a specifically political feminist theory that acknowledges the importance of plurality and speech.

Disch, Lisa J. *Hannah Arendt and the Limits of Philosophy.* Ithaca: Cornell University Press, 1994. Disch presents Arendt's method of storytelling as an alternative both to feminism's "marginal critics" who attempt to give voice to authentic experiences of exclusion, and to poststructuralist feminists who challenge the idea of authenticity and favor instead the perpetual contestation of political narratives. By inviting listeners to assume a plurality of perspectives on the world, Disch claims, Arendt's method of storytelling facilitates impartiality without making a claim to the absolute impartiality of an Archimedean standpoint.

Elshtain, Jean Bethke. "War and Political Discourse: From Machiavelli to Arendt." In her *Meditations on Modern Political Thought: Masculine and Feminine Themes from Luther to Arendt,* 103–13. University Park: Pennsylvania State University Press, 1992. Elshtain argues that the Machiavellian realist tradition constructs war as a masculine activity, conducted sometimes for the sake of, but never by, women. She then employs Arendt's critical distinction between power and violence, along with the Arendtian concepts of natality, hope, and forgiveness, to argue for a politics in which both men and women participate as citizens and not as warriors.

Fowler, Pauline. "The Public and the Private in Architecture: A Feminist Critique." *Women's Studies International Forum* 7, no. 6 (1984): 449–54. Fowler criticizes the devaluation of domestic architecture in mainstream architectural theory, focusing on the work of Kenneth Frampton, who draws upon Arendt's distinctions between public and private and among labor, work, and action. Fowler turns to the work of Hanna Pitkin and Jean Elshtain to criticize these Arendtian distinctions, calls for renewed attention to domestic architecture and vernacular traditions, and suggests that architecture be used as a site of experimentation with alternative models of community.

Fraser, Nancy. *Unruly Practices: Power, Discourse, and Gender in Contemporary Social Theory.* Minneapolis: University of Minnesota Press, 1989 (see especially chapters 4, 7, and 8). Drawing on Arendt's concept of the social but refusing to accept her insistence on the insulation of politics from domestic issues, Fraser criticizes the tendency of the contemporary welfare state to treat needs, including and especially women's needs, as "givens" and therefore as mere matters of administration. Focusing instead on the discursive and constructed character of needs, Fraser outlines a "social" sphere in which needs are repoliticized and open to interpretive contestation.

Hansen, Karen V. "Feminist Conceptions of Public and Private: A Critical Analysis." *Berkeley Journal of Sociology* 32 (1987): 105–28. Using historical data about women's activities in early nineteenth-century New England, Hansen challenges simple, gendered dichotomies between public and private, and transforms Arendt's concept of the "social" into a third term representing activities that mediate between public and private life.

Hartsock, Nancy C. M. "An Alternative Tradition: Women on Power." In her *Money, Sex, and Power. Toward a Feminist Historical Materialism,* 210–30. New York: Longman, 1983. Hartsock argues that Arendt tends to deemphasize the dualisms and the fierce agonism that marked the Greek conceptions of power and community. Hartsock then associates Arendt with other women who theorize power as "potentiality" rather than domination, including Hanna Pitkin, Dorothy Emmett, and Berenice Carroll; she suggests that this distinctive approach to power is grounded in a structural difference between male and female experiences.

Hertz, Deborah. "Hannah Arendt's Rahel Varnhagen." In *German Women in the Nineteenth Century: A Social History,* edited by John C. Fout, 72–87. New York: Holmes and Meier, 1984. Hertz situates *Rahel Varnhagen* within Arendt's own life and career and evaluates the accuracy of Arendt's historical claims; she criticizes Arendt for failing to notice that the possibilities for Jewish assimilation in Rahel's Berlin were conditioned by gender. This article should be read together with Hertz's *Jewish High Society in Old Regime Berlin* (New Haven: Yale University Press, 1988), in which Hertz's own research fills in this gap in Arendt's treatment of salon society.

Jones, Kathleen B. *Compassionate Authority: Democracy and the Representation of Women.* New York: Routledge, 1993. Jones argues that much contemporary feminist political theory tacitly accepts a traditional, masculine conception of authority as sovereign control, and suggests that impasses in feminist theory may be overcome if the concept of authority itself is transformed. Jones draws on Arendt to construct an alternative view of authority as the collective construction of a meaningful community through compassionate dialogue, while criticizing Arendt's claim that compassion can have no place in politics.

Klawiter, Maren. "Using Arendt and Heidegger to Consider Feminist Thinking on Women and Reproductive/Infertility Technologies." *Hypatia* 5, no. 3 (Fall 1990): 65–89. Klawiter reads Arendt's critique of the technological impulse to transcend human embodiment and plurality against the background of Heidegger's "The

Question Concerning Technology," and redeploys Arendt and Heidegger in order
to attack the claim of reproductive and infertility technologies to liberate women.
Landes, Joan B. "Jürgen Habermas, *The Structural Transformation of the Public Sphere*: A
Feminist Inquiry." *Praxis International* 12, no. 1 (April 1992): 106–27. In the
context of a feminist critique of Habermas's theory of the public sphere, Landes
employs Arendt's account of performative action as a useful supplement to
Habermas's disembodied model of communication, yet also criticizes Arendt's
own apparent indifference to the gendering of the classical polis. Landes finds
traces of Arendtian theatricality in the more explicitly feminist historical work of
Marie-Hélène Huet and Dorinda Outram.
Lane, Ann M. "The Feminism of Hannah Arendt." *Democracy* 3, no. 3 (Summer 1983):
101–17. Lane discusses the significance for feminism of three concepts drawn
primarily from Arendt's analyses of Judaism: the perspective of the conscious
pariah, which mediates between assimilationist and radically isolationist feminism; the idea of a "hidden tradition," which for women would encompass
practices related to processes of life and death; and the example of social
experiments like the kibbutz, paralleled by groups and collectives in which
women explore new forms of community.
MacCannell, Juliet Flower. "Facing Fascism: A Feminine Politics of Jouissance." *Topoi*
12 (September 1993): 137–51. MacCannell reads Arendt's portrait of Adolf
Eichmann through the lens of Lacanian psychoanalytic theory, arguing that
Eichmann's administration of the Final Solution can be understood as a perverse
submission to the will-to-*jouissance* of the Other (i.e., of Hitler). MacCannell
then argues that the feminine relation to *jouissance* constitutes an ethical
alternative to Eichmann's genocidal perversity.
Markus, Maria. "The 'Anti-Feminism' of Hannah Arendt." In *Hannah Arendt: Thinking,
Judging, Freedom*, edited by Gisela T. Kaplan and Clive S. Kessler, 119–29.
Sydney: Allen and Unwin, 1989. Arguing against easy dismissals of Arendt as an
antifeminist, Markus considers the importance for feminism of Arendtian themes,
including the "conscious pariah," exemplified in different ways by Rahel Varnhagen and Rosa Luxemburg; the idea of "solidarity," as opposed to fraternity, as a
basis for political community; and the distinction between the social and
the political.
Minnich, Elizabeth Kamarck. "Friendship Between Women: The Act of Feminist
Biography." [Review of Carol Ascher, *Simone de Beauvoir: A Life of Freedom*;
Ruth First and Ann Scott, *Olive Schreiner: A Biography*; and Elisabeth Young-
Bruehl, *Hannah Arendt: For Love of the World*.] *Feminist Studies* 11, no. 2 (Summer
1985): 287–305. Minnich presents Arendt's book on Rahel Varnhagen as a
model for a practice of engaged and relational feminist biography, and uses this
conception of feminist biography as a standard by which to evaluate Young-
Bruehl's biography of Arendt.
Minnich, Elizabeth Kamarck. "Hannah Arendt: Thinking As We Are." In *Between
Women: Biographers, Novelists, Critics, Teachers and Artists Write about Their Work
on Women*, edited by Carol Ascher, Louise De Salvo, and Sara Ruddick, 170–85.
Boston: Beacon Press, 1984. Through a recollection of years of study and
friendship with Arendt, Minnich describes how her engagement with Arendt
and her thought, particularly her idea of the "conscious pariah" and her
conception of "thinking" as independent, critical, political, and sensitive to
plurality, led her toward her present self-identification as a feminist.
Nye, Andrea. *Philosophia: The Thought of Rosa Luxemburg, Simone Weil, and Hannah*

*Arendt.* New York: Routledge, 1994. Nye reads Luxemburg, Weil, and Arendt as members of a women's philosophical tradition that is not governed by old dichotomies between theory and practice, mind and body, and (for Arendt in particular) subjectivity and objectivity. Nye explores each author's innovative engagements with the masculine philosophical canon and draws out the implications of this alternative tradition for feminist social thought, and in particular for debates between liberal and socialist feminist theorists.

O'Brien, Mary. *The Politics of Reproduction.* Boston: Routledge and Kegan Paul, 1981 (see especially chapters 3 and 4). Employing a broadly Marxist technique of ideology-critique, O'Brien reads Arendt's appropriation of the gendered Greek distinction between public and private, as well as her related devaluation of physiological reproduction, as examples of "male-supremacist" ideology.

Phillips, Anne. *Engendering Democracy.* Cambridge: Polity Press, 1991. Phillips explores the relations between feminism, liberal democracy, and its participationist and republican critics. She reads Arendt as an exemplar of republicanism, which converges with feminism in its critique of interest-based politics but which diverges from feminist concerns in its insistence upon a sharp division between public and private.

Pitkin, Hanna Fenichel. "Justice: On Relating Private and Public." *Political Theory* 9, no. 3 (August 1981): 327–52. Pitkin notes Arendt's apparent hostility to private, social, economic, and women's issues, but argues that Arendt does not object per se to the discussion of such issues in political spaces; rather, she is concerned with the threat posed to politics by a particular attitude or spirit. Pitkin concludes that the linkage of public and private through the category of justice, neglected by Arendt, could allow for a properly political consideration of social problems and women's issues.

Rich, Adrienne. "Conditions for Work: The Common World of Women." In her *On Lies, Secrets, and Silence: Selected Prose, 1966–1978,* 203–14. New York: Norton, 1979. Drawing on Arendt's theorization of the common world as a realm free from the repetitive and transitory labors of daily life, Rich describes a feminism in which women create a world among themselves; at the same time, she criticizes Arendt for ignoring the exclusion of women from the common world of men and the gendering of the categories of labor and the private.

Ring, Jennifer. *Modern Political Theory and Contemporary Feminism: A Dialectical Analysis.* Albany: State University of New York Press, 1991. Ring's introduction contrasts Arendt's diagnosis of modern "worldlessness," or the loss of stable boundaries, both with Marx's conception of alienation as division and with feminist critiques of dichotomous thinking; against this background, Ring criticizes the work of such feminists as Irigaray who, in "shattering all conventions," threaten to produce an unstructured and unreliable world rather than a "solidly grounded" alternative.

Riot-Sarcey, Michèle, and Eleni Varikas. "Feminist Consciousness in the Nineteenth Century: A Pariah Consciousness?" *Praxis International* 5, no. 4 (January 1986): 443–65. Bringing Arendtian concepts to a study of nineteenth-century feminism in France and Greece, Riot-Sarcey and Varikas distinguish three historical modes of response to women's pariahdom: assimilation; "subversive feminism," in which consciousness of exclusion produces radical questioning of and revolt against the existing social order, and "feminism as the art of the possible," in which existing constructions of women's difference are appropriated and inverted in order to glorify and revalue women and their roles.

Rose, Gillian. "Love and the State: Varnhagen, Luxemburg and Arendt." In her *The Broken Middle: Out of Our Ancient Society*, 153–246. Oxford: Blackwell, 1992. Rose reads Varnhagen, Luxemburg, and Arendt as authors who respond to the contradictions of modernity, including the simultaneous political sovereignty and social subordination of women facilitated by the distinction between "droits de la citoyenne" and "droits de la femme," by developing "agonal authorships" that explore the problems inherent both in political universalism and in efforts to escape from the state into the "ethical immediacy of love."

Skoller, Eleanor Honig. *The In-Between of Writing: Experience and Experiment in Drabble, Duras, and Arendt*. Ann Arbor: University of Michigan Press, 1993. Skoller contrasts certain feminist appeals to the authority of unmediated female experience with the postmodern move away from the pursuit of authentic "experience" and toward open-ended experimentation with language. Drawing in particular on *Rahel Varnhagen*, Skoller reads Arendt (along with Drabble and Duras) as among the neglected women writers who have written in the postmodern mode, seeking not merely to represent women's experience in language but to constitute that experience through experiments in storytelling.

Winant, Terry. "The Feminist Standpoint: A Matter of Language." *Hypatia* 2, no. 1 (Winter 1987): 123–48. Characterizing the "mother tongue" in Arendtian terms as the language spoken in private and among friends, Winant argues that women have no such "common idiom," but that one might be created. Winant argues that Hartsock's critique of masculine ideology and Fraser's Arendtian critique of the juridical-administrative-therapeutic state are examples of emancipatory standpoints that nevertheless are grounded in a shared feminist philosophical stance.

Yaeger, Patricia. *Honey-Mad Women: Emancipatory Strategies in Women's Writing*. New York: Columbia University Press, 1988 (see especially chapters 3 and 8). Bringing Arendt into conversation with Derrida, and offering examples drawn from the writing of Mary Oliver, Adrienne Rich, Malcolm X, Lewis Carroll, and Herman Melville, Yaeger uses Arendt's concept of natality to discuss the potential of women's writing for unexpected, emancipatory transformation, even from within male language, by virtue of the lapse between word and signification, or the "animality of the letter." Relying on Arendt's conception of power as acting in concert, Yaeger also suggests that such writing serves as the locus of women's empowerment by facilitating the construction of "a community of speaking women."

# German

Blättler, Sidonia. "Hannah Arendt: Geschichte und die Weltlichkeit der Welt." *Die Philosophin* 4, no. 7 (April 1993): 48–62. Tracing the development of Arendt's view of the telling of history as political speech through which a world can be created, Blättler suggests that women's experience has been marked by the absence of their own public stories; Blättler also finds in Arendt a model of publicity and the political that is important for feminism because it does not exclude any substantive themes from public speech, but instead leaves the question of the content of the public sphere open for contestation.

Brander, Stephanie. "Hannah Arendt, Simone de Beauvoir—eine fiktive Begegnung." *Die Philosophin* 1, no. 1 (March 1990): 57–73. Brander constructs an imaginary conversation between Arendt and de Beauvoir on various philosophical and political subjects, including the transgression of the boundary between the public and the private through the writing of personal memoirs, the idea of an "exceptional woman" and the pariah/parvenu distinction; and the relative importance of personal and economic issues to the broader question of women's emancipation.

Kubes-Hofmann, Ursula, ed. *Sagen, was ist. Zur Aktualität Hannah Arendts.* Vienna: Verlag für Gesellschaftskritik, 1994. This collection of mostly previously unpublished essays includes feminist contributions from Kubes-Hofmann, on the relevance of Arendt's concept of plurality to debates over difference and identity politics; Ina Paul-Horn, whose essay expands her discussion of Arendt annotated below; and Eva Kreisky, on the public-private and power-violence distinctions as resources for feminist theory.

Ludz, Ursula. "Hannah Arendt: Unabhängig weiblich." *Du. Die Zeitschrift für Kultur,* no. 11 (November 1993): 48–52. Ludz surveys the reception of Arendt by feminist scholars and reviews the history of Arendt's engagement with women's issues, making extensive use of previously unpublished correspondence. Ludz suggests that although Arendt maintained a distance from the feminist movement, she was more self-conscious of her status as a woman and more sensitive to the particularity of "feminine" modes of thinking and philosophizing than has often been acknowledged.

Meyer, Eva. "Die Autobiographie der Schrift: Selbstthematisierung und Anti-Repräsentation." *Materialienband,* no. 6 (undated, probably 1989): 67–79. Meyer contrasts the classical and typically masculine genre of autobiography, which serves to confirm the unity of the subject whose life it depicts, with the typically feminine practice of letter-writing, which refuses to fashion a single history out of a plurality of perspectives. Meyer reads Arendt's biography of Rahel Varnhagen, in which Arendt positioned herself as the reader and recipient of Rahel's letters, as an example of an alternative sort of *auto*biography that resists narrative closure by passing its contradictions on to a new recipient. For an overlapping but slightly more detailed reading of Arendt, see Eva Meyer, "Was heißt biographisches Denken?" in her *Die Autobiographie der Schrift* (Basel: Stroemfeld/Roter Stern, 1989): 41–64.

Nordmann, Ingeborg. "Nachdenken an der Schwelle von Literatur und Theorie: Essayistinnen im 20. Jahrhundert." In *Deutsche Literatur von Frauen,* Vol 2, *19. und 20. Jahrhundert,* edited by Gisela Brinker-Gabler, 364–79. Munich: C. H. Beck, 1988. Nordmann compares the experiences of alienation and exile that motivated the writing of three German women: Arendt, Margaret Susman, and Alice Rühle-Gerstel. This essay is of particular interest because Arendt's review of Rühle-Gerstel's book, *Das Frauenproblem der Gegenwart,* is one of Arendt's only published discussions of feminism or the women's movement. Arendt's review was published in *Die Gesellschaft* 10, no. 2 (February 1933): 177–79. An English translation of the review appears in Hannah Arendt, *Essays in Understanding,* edited by Jerome Kohn (New York: Harcourt, Brace, 1993).

———. "Über das Gewalttätige am Opferdiskurs." *Materialienband,* no. 13 (undated, probably 1993): 63–78. Nordmann deploys Arendt's analysis of totalitarianism to criticize the use of the "discourse of the victim" in analyses of women's conditions—including under National Socialism and in Bosnia. To understand women in these circumstances as victims is misleading, Nordmann claims, because it falsely homogenizes women's experiences and because it perpetuates the illusion that traditional concepts of guilt and victimhood are still meaningful under, and after, totalitarianism; Arendt's analysis helps us to understand the severity of the break with our traditional concepts introduced by the experience of totalitarianism.

Paul-Horn, Ina. *Faszination Nationalsozialismus? Zu einer politischen Theorie des Geschlechterverhältnisses.* Pfaffenweiler: Centaurus, 1993. Mixing philosophical reflection with oral history, Paul-Horn employs Arendt's distinction between power and violence and her analysis of the destruction of authentic public and private realms under totalitarianism to help understand the experiences and assess the actions of Austrian women who participated in various ways in National Socialism.

# French

Collin, Françoise. "Agir et donné." In *Hannah Arendt et la Modernité,* edited by Anne-Marie Roviello and Maurice Weyembergh, 27–46. Annales de l'Institut de Philosophie et de Sciences Morales. Paris: Librarie Philosophique J. Vrin, 1992.

———. "Du privé et du public." In *Hannah Arendt.* Les Cahiers du Grif, no. 33: 47–68. Expanded edition. Paris: Tierce, 1986.

———. "Un héritage sans testament." In *Les jeunes, la transmission.* Les Cahiers du Grif, no. 34: 81–92. Paris: Tierce, 1986.

———. "Histoire et mémoire ou la marque et la trace." *Recherches féministes* 6, no. 1 (1993): 13–23.

———. "Praxis de la différence; Notes sur le tragique du sujet." In *Provenances de la pensée: Femmes/Philosophie.* Les Cahiers du Grif, no. 46: 125–41. Paris: Tierce, 1992.

———. "Le temps natal." In *Nouvelle Pauvreté, Nouvelle Société. Les Cahiers du Grif,* no. 30 (Paris: Tierce, 1985). Republished in Italian as "Tempo natale." *DWF,* no. 4 (1993): 33–48.

Duval, Michelle. "La mobilisation politique des mères-travailleuses en vue de changer l'organisation du travail." In *Mères et travailleuses: De l'exception à la règle,* edited by Renée B.-Dandurand and Francine Descarries, 163–86. Quebec: Institut Québécois de Recherche sur la Culture, 1992.

Leibovici, Martine. "Action politique et pouvoir chez Rosa Luxembourg et Hannah Arendt." In *Femmes, Pouvoirs,* edited by Michèle Riot-Sarcey, 83–107. Paris: Editions Kimé, 1993.

Riot-Sarcey, Michèle, and Eleni Varikas. "Réflexions sur la notion d'exceptionnalité." In *Le genre de l'histoire.* Les Cahiers du Grif, nos. 37–38: 77–90. Paris: Tierce, 1988.

# Italian

Boccia, Maria Luisa. "Autocoscienza." In *L'io in rivolta: Vissuto e pensiero di Carla Lonzi,* 191–221. Milan: La Tartaruga edizioni, 1990.

———. "Singolarità, pluralità e genere nel femminismo." *Reti,* nos. 3–4 (May–August 1989): 143–56.

Boella, Laura. "Figure rubate alla filosofia." *Reti,* no. 6 (November–December 1990): 27–29. [A review of Adriana Cavarero's *Nonostante Platone.*]

————. "Pensare liberamente pensare il mondo." In *Diotima: Mettere al mondo il mondo. Oggetto e oggettività alla luce della differenza sessuale*, 173–88. Milan: La Tartaruga edizioni, 1990.

Cavarero, Adriana. "Dire la nascita." In *Diotima: Mettere al mondo il mondo. Oggetto e oggettività alla luce della differenza sessuale*, 93–121. Milan: La Tartaruga edizioni, 1990.

————. *Nonostante Platone: Figure femminili nella filosofia antica*. Rome: Editori Riuniti, 1991.

Collin, Françoise. "Pensare/raccontare. Hannah Arendt." *DWF*, no. 3 (1986): 36–44.

*Iride*, no. 10 (1992–93). This issue's special section on sexual difference includes contributions addressing Arendt's work by Laura Boella, Giovanna Borrello, Luisa Muraro, and Wanda Tommasi.

Rossolini, Roberta. "Nascere ed apparire: Le categorie del pensiero politico di Hannah Arendt e la filosofia della differenza sessuale." *DWF*, nos. 2–3 (1993): 69–84.

## Other Bibliographies

While I know of no other bibliography of specifically feminist work on Arendt, there are a number of excellent general bibliographies about Arendt; I mention them here both to acknowledge my debt to them and to recommend them to others:

Joan Nordquist's *Hannah Arendt: A Bibliography* (Santa Cruz, Calif.: Reference and Research Services, 1989) includes a comprehensive listing of secondary works, although readers should be aware that a large volume of material on Arendt has been published in the few years since Nordquist's volume appeared.

Especially useful as points of access into the non-English Arendt literature are the bibliographies by Wolfgang Heuer, in *Hannah Arendt* (Reinbeck bei Hamburg: Rowohlt Taschenbuch, 1987); Simona Forti, in *La Pluralità Irrappresentabile: Il Pensiero politico di Hannah Arendt*, ed. Roberto Esposito (Urbino: Quattro Venti, 1987): and Geneviève Even-Granboulan, in *Une femme de pensée: Hannah Arendt* (Paris: Anthropos, 1990)—though these, too, have inevitably become somewhat outdated.

The bibliography in Elisabeth Young-Bruehl's *Hannah Arendt: For Love of the World* (New Haven: Yale University Press, 1982) remains the best and most convenient listing of Arendt's own published works.

# Contributors

SEYLA BENHABIB is professor of government at Harvard University. She is the author of *Critique, Norm, and Utopia* (Columbia University Press, 1986) and *Situating the Self* (Routledge, 1992). She is the editor (with Fred Dallmayr) of *The Communicative Ethics Controversy* (MIT Press, 1990) and (with Drucilla Cornell) of *Feminism as Critique* (University of Minnesota Press, 1987). She and Andrew Arato edit *Constellations: An International Journal of Critical and Democratic Theory,* and she is currently completing *The Reluctant Modernism of Hannah Arendt* (Sage Publications).

SUSAN BICKFORD is assistant professor of political science at the University of North Carolina at Chapel Hill. She is currently completing a book on listening, conflict, and citizenship.

JOAN COCKS is associate professor of politics and chair of the Program in Critical Social Thought at Mount Holyoke College. She is author of *The Oppositional Imagination: Feminism, Critique, and Political Theory* (Routledge, 1989) as well as articles on Marxism, feminism, and body politics. She is currently writing a book tentatively titled *Political Philosophy in the Light of the National Question.*

MARY G. DIETZ is associate professor of political science at the University of Minnesota. She is the author of *Between the Human and the Divine: The Political Thought of Simone Weil* (Rowman and Littlefield, 1988) and editor of *Thomas Hobbes and Political Theory* (University of Kansas Press, 1990). She has also written on Machiavelli, Arendt, Beauvoir, and feminist theory and politics.

LISA J. DISCH is assistant professor of political science at the University of Minnesota. She is the author of *Hannah Arendt and the Limits of Philosophy* (Cornell University Press, 1994) and has published articles in *Political Theory* and *Hypatia.*

JEAN BETHKE ELSHTAIN is the Laura Spelman Rockefeller Professor of Social and Political Ethics at the University of Chicago. She is the author of many books including *Public Man, Private Woman: Women in Social and Political Thought; Power Trips and Other Journeys; Women and War; Democracy on Trial.* She is the editor of *The Family and Political Thought;* co-editor of *Women, War and Feminism;* and co-author of *But Was It Just? Reflections on the Morality of the Persian Gulf War.* Elshtain is the author of some two hundred articles and essays in scholarly journals and journals of civic opinion.

BONNIE HONIG is associate professor of government at Harvard University. She is the author of *Political Theory and the Displacement of Politics* (Cornell University Press, 1993) and of articles in political and feminist theory published in *American Political Science Review, Political Theory, Social Research,* and elsewhere. She is now writing a book, tentatively titled *There's No Place Like Home,* on the effects of home-yearning in ethics and politics.

MORRIS B. KAPLAN, assistant professor of philosophy at Purchase College of the State University of New York, was the inaugural Rockefeller Foundation Fellow in Legal Humanities at the Stanford Humanities Center in 1993–94. He returned to college teaching in 1987 after almost fifteen years practicing law, primarily as a trial attorney with the Legal Aid Society of New York. His articles have appeared in *Praxis International, Philosophical Forum, Virginia Law Review, Metaphilosophy,* and *GLQ: A Quarterly Journal of Lesbian and Gay Studies.* His book *Sexual Justice* will be published by Routledge in 1995.

JOAN B. LANDES is professor of politics and women's studies at Hampshire College, Amherst, Massachusetts. Her publications have focused on questions of gender and family relations in Western political and critical theory, the contours of public and private life, and the relationship of feminism to democratic theory and institutions. She is the author of *Women and the Public Sphere in the Age of Revolution* (Cornell University Press, 1988) and coeditor of the exhibition catalogue, *Representing Revolution: French and British Images, 1789–1804.* She is currently completing a study of eighteenth-century French political culture in which she examines the co-presence of sexual and political body metaphors, and representations of feminine virtue in visual and political discourse; and is also working on a series of essays on theories of freedom and the democratic public sphere.

PATCHEN P. MARKELL is a graduate student in political theory in the Department of Government at Harvard University. He is currently writing a dissertation on the relation of political identity to ethnicity, language, and national culture in modern German political thought.

ANNE NORTON is the author of *Republic of Signs, Reflections on Political Identity,* and *Alternative Americas.* She is professor of political science at the University of Pennsylvania.

MELISSA A. ORLIE is assistant professor of political science and of the Unit for Criticism and Interpretive Theory at the University of Illinois, Urbana-Champaign. She received her B.A. degree from the University of California, Santa Cruz, and her M.A. and Ph.D. degrees from Princeton University. She is at work on a book tentatively titled *Living Ethically: Power and Responsibility in Late Modernity.*

HANNA FENICHEL PITKIN is Professor Emerita of Political Science at the University of California, Berkeley. She is the author of *The Concept of Representation* (1967), *Wittgenstein and Justice* (1972), and *Fortune is a Woman: Gender and Politics in the Thought of Niccolò Machiavelli* (1984). She is currently working on a book about Arendt's concept of the social, tentatively entitled *The Attack of the Blob.*

LINDA M. G. ZERILLI is associate professor of political science and associate director of the Walt Whitman Center for the Culture and Politics of Democracy at Rutgers

University. She is the author of *Signifying Woman: Culture and Chaos in Rousseau, Burke, and Mill* (Cornell University Press, 1994). Zerilli is currently working on a project entitled "A Tower of Babel: Feminism, Democracy, and the Dream of a Common Language."

# Index